9/23/05

To Evelyn...

Remembering those lovely years we enjoyed with you. and Seymour. Our fondest good wishes to you... alway...

Hope you enjoy this romp through my colorful life..

Van (Harris)

Thanks for the Warning

A Memoir

by

Van Harris

Euclid Books
Upland, CA

Published by
Euclid Books
1320 N. Euclid Ave.
Upland, CA 91786

International Standard Book Number (ISBN)
0-9770385-0-5

Printed in the United States of America

2nd Printing

1 Wilbur

*Memory is a nursery where old children play with
broken toys...*
-Claude Houghton

They sat around at Dubrow's Cafeteria on Eastern
Parkway, at any hour of the day or night, some of the wittiest
and most-colorful characters, none of them famous, but each
one an individual gem. They were guys from assorted walks of
life, all capable of creating uproarious laughter, of verbally
slaying you with a totally unexpected bon mot, what a group
this was. They're all gone now, dead a long time, most of them
anyway, except us "younger ones" just a few years behind,
well on our way to wherever they are. How lucky we all were
to be touched by their greatness. They were the unpaid
teachers. None of them were rich, except in humanity. None
of them were successful. None of them were particularly what
we'd call "glamorous," but what a bunch they were. At that
very special table they occupied, they reigned supreme. They
brought joy to our hearts, twinkles to our eyes. Nothing was
that serious in life that it couldn't be overcome by laughter.
How lucky we were to be privy to their gatherings. I owe so
much to their having existed, and I miss them to this very
day. I loved you all, fellas. Thank you, thank you for instilling
in me the value of laughter, and thank you for showing me
how to convey it to others so that life can truly have its bright
side.

Hence the title. If anyone would get up to leave n' say,
"See ya later," any one of them would retort, "Thanks for the
warning." This has been my trademark ever since those
memorable days. It never fails to arrest, and always brings a
smile to one's face. I've passed it on to my children, and they
to their children, and hopefully into perpetuity. Why even my
theatrical agent tries to beat me to the punch whenever either
of us uses that common goodbye, "See ya later," by quickly
retorting, "Thanks for the warning."

Another unforgettable expression, gleaned from among the
many, was the retort to, "Oh, I've gotta go home n' take a
shave," and that would be the cue for the whole chorus to

chime in, "Ya shouldn't shave 'cause hair looks good on a schmuck!" And if they'd see you sitting all alone somewhere they would remark, "I see you're sitting with all your friends." What a bunch of grown-up cut-ups ... never mean, never malicious, just flat out funny ... and with such a delightful touch of charm.

The "Elder" was Davey Sperling. Davey, the sign painter had a fleck of reddish hair and matching bloodshot eyes. For a man in his forties, he seemed wizened beyond his years, and very likely he was. As a teenager, I looked upon him as though he was an old man. He was of medium height and medium weight. He carried a halfway burned out cigar between his thumb, forefinger, and middle finger, (a la Groucho Marx) and he was never at a loss for words, and combined with his mischievous smile, every word emerged as a humorous gem. He would get at the end of the line in the bank in those years before ballpoint pens were invented. Fountain pens were all the rage, and banks would give away free souvenirs with their names on them. He'd finally manage to get to the teller's window, unarm her by widening his piercing blue eyes with the red streaks running through them, and innocently inquire, "Have you got any free blotters today?" That was Davey's daily ritual 'cause he knew that the boys were watching, and howling with laughter at the sight of this Runyonesque character wending his way to the head of the line, only to (in his own sheepish way) attempt to panhandle a free blotter.

The "boys" were all like Davey, in early middle age (more than twice my age), surprisingly single. They were guys who worked at their leisure, at their own sweet pace, never asking for any governmental financial aid, and each one with a different and nondescript profession. They dressed as they pleased, never shabbily, and oddly, though they seemed to be together all the time, never alike.

There was "One Ball Barney," slim and dapper, who wore his brown hair parted in the middle and pasted down the sides. His face bore marks of a past childhood illness, perhaps rubella, that left tiny craters in its wake. Barney's eyes were twins to Davey's, and whereas Davey preferred to go coatless in all seasons, Barney was notorious for his pegged pants, pointy shoes, a long chain hanging from his belt, running down to below his knees and back up into his pocket, and loud sports jackets. He also preferred to wear a wide-brimmed felt hat. He worked part time as an exterminator's assistant. In fact, when people would inquire about his pointy shoes, he would explain, "That's to kill the cockroaches in the corners." I had heard that the "One Ball" label came as a result of his having lost a testicle from developing a hydrocele due to an earlier sports injury. He also had a hernia which he insisted upon controlling by wearing a truss, and took delight in telling everyone how its hardness would impress his lady partners when he would squeeze very close to them while dancing in those "Dime-A-Dance Halls." He had a great, biting sense of humor, was both brilliant and quick with "put-downs," and he was also a nimble, self-taught tap dancer, much to the envy of us all.

The only guy in the crowd who could give Barney a run for his money in the dance department was baby face Mendel Berman. Mendel had a complexion like a ripening peach. He had a calm and lovable disposition, and he hardly ever raised his voice in anger. He was good natured and accommodating to everyone and anyone, and he was a superb repairman. In fact he made his living by restoring porcelain appliances that were scratched or dented in delivery, to their original, unblemished status. He laughed readily, which served as a necessary repository for those outrageous lines that the others threw around so deftly. Mendel had a rubber face that he used animatedly, and so expertly, that he could make a statue smile. When the boys would break into a singing chorus of "Valentina" and insert his name instead of the name "Valentina," he would go into a convulsive rubber-legged dance with expressions that would make you laugh until you cried.

These were the ringleaders of that whole bunch of Runyonesque characters that hung around at Dubrow's. However, they were what was known in show biz as "party guys." Each and every one was capable of making you scream with delight, but if they ever set foot on a professional stage they would freeze, and fall into a catatonic state. Throughout the whole world there are such people, and many, like the "Dubrow Gang" have unquestioned taste and superb native intelligence when it comes to dispensing humor, but they lack the one underlying ingredient that's required in order to become a professional, and that's the guts that it takes to get out onstage and face a paying audience. Luckily for me, these lovable, laughable, incredible mentors of mine felt that they had detected that missing link in me, and thereafter they spent a good deal of their time instructing me, directly, subtly, and subliminally. They were willing to bet the farm that I was going to "make it," as an extension of themselves, and then be content to sit back and accept all the laughter and applause vicariously.

Yes, I'm a professional comedian! I've done this practically all of my adult life, earning my first salary for "telling jokes" while still in my late teens. No, I was not some kind of "wise ass" kid. I never embarrassed anyone or picked on anyone deliberately. I have always considered myself a gentleman, expecting the same from others, and I've learned (like everyone does, invariably) that this sort of expectation is a myth, but if I were a betting man, which I'm not, I'd bet that in this savage world, there are so many, many more good people than bad, and there always will be. Let me digress here for a moment, and tell you a true story ... see ya later ... Did I just hear "Thanks for the warning?"

It was a damp, dreary spring evening in the intelligent city of Boston. I had flown into Logan several hours earlier, taken the convenient subway from the airport, and was now in the general area of the auditorium in which I was scheduled to perform a few hours hence. I was looking around for a place in which to grab a quick bite, and then go on to a "talk over" rehearsal and then the show. I was delighted that I was in one of those cities in which the airlines still offered late, "redeye" flights back to New York. If there's anything a performer hates, it's "layin' over." Nothin' like the luxury of sleepin' in one's own bed, especially for a grizzled veteran who has spent so many years on the road. There was a time that my colleagues referred to me as the "King of the One-nighters," a title I enjoyed and felt that I had rightfully earned. Another thing that a performer hates is dining alone (an occupational hazard) and tonight was another instance of such anticipated loneliness.

I studiously try to avoid the commercial fast food restaurants, finding them to be mostly honky tonk, and oft-

4

times noisy, and at this particular instance there didn't even appear to be any of those around. Luckily for me, I spotted this rather immense building complex nearby that turned out to be the famed Boston Children's Hospital, and my quick mind told me that they've got to have a restaurant on the premises. I headed in that direction, and, sure enough, I was pleased to discover a clean, busy eatery that also boasted a good-sized circular counter, in addition to the assembled tables and chairs. I sat myself down at that counter, removed my damp trench coat, which I folded neatly on my lap, and proceeded to order some tasty tidbits from a friendly and courteous waitress. I hadn't sat more than maybe five or ten minutes, and was already savoring a superb grilled cheese and tomato combination, when I felt a hot stare, with accompanying similar breath over my shoulder. I placed the cheese n' tomato down on my plate and turned to find a wide-eyed, thin, young Black boy of maybe twelve or thirteen, with huge brown eyes, looking directly into my eyes, and very innocently inquiring, "Mister, can I have a bite outta your sandwich?" Before I could reply, the waitress was on him with a gesture like one uses to brush off a fly, and said, "Wilbur, go 'way! Don't bother the man!" As the disappointed lad started to move away, the waitress was quick to point out to me that Wilbur was one of the retarded children at the hospital. Since they were harmless, the authorities thought it a lot healthier for them if they were allowed to roam about the hospital and mix with the people. I agreed wholeheartedly, and while Wilbur was still within earshot I invited him to sit next to me, and instructed the good-natured waitress to give him whatever he'd like, and put it on my bill.

As we sat, munching upon our respective sandwiches, I lifted my glass of Coca-Cola to my lips and Wilbur quickly exclaimed, "Mister, can I have a sip of your coke?" I said, "Waitress, please give Wilbur a coke." Now the two of us sat like old friends, dining together. When Wilbur seemed to gain more confidence, and he suddenly volunteered, "You're a nice man mister," then a pause, "Are you a doctor?" I chuckled, and said, "No, I'm not." He stared at me awhile longer and bravely asked, "What are you?" I replied, "I'm a comedian." He tried to look like he understood, and finally inquired, "What's a comedian?" His naiveté brought a great big smile to my face and I hastened to explain that I tell jokes to people. Looking apparently puzzled, he stared straight at me with those saucer eyes, and after mulling over what I had just told him, he asked, "And people pay you for that?"

Yes, I'm a COMEDIAN! I say that in capital letters! It's a profession to be proud of. I'm not a cockamamie "comic," or "funny man," or "clown," or "stand up." Not individually am I any one of those lightly tossed descriptions. I am, proudly, all of the aforementioned in one! I perform an extremely vital public service for which I am fairly well paid, in which I invest a great deal of energy and preparation and serious forethought. With all its obstacles, and sometimes horrible human "impediments" in the forms of businessmen, plus some desperate, unscrupulous competitors, I wouldn't trade my blessed profession for anything. I am eternally grateful for having had the good fortune to have been honed into a genuine, professional, CIVILIZED comedian, both respected and admired by many, with a necessary modicum of dissenters. To do something for humankind, while at the same time, being able to make a living and support a marvelous family, what more can any human being ask out of life? Though not world-famous, I have arrived, for which I am eternally grateful. The Chinese have a saying: "Pick something that you love and you'll never have to work a day in your life."

2 Williamsburg

Williamsburg — a congested part of the famous old New York borough of Brooklyn. Manhattan's Lower East Side was already woefully overcrowded, so the newer arrivals from the ghettos in Europe (especially those from its eastern end, along with the others from places like its southern boot, and the unhappy green sod that abutted the great colonial empire on its western flank, plus a few minorities from assorted parts of the pernicious Old World) came pouring over the recently built Williamsburg Bridge to settle, however they could, in whatever they could, with fervent hopes and prayers for a better life. This was the place I called home, the only place that I and all those many other kids, ever knew. We were born there. We were a lot luckier than our grieving parents, and grandparents, who, somewhere, sometime, had at least seen better places, and, although they weren't privy to them, at least, knew they existed, and came to the new world imagining that such beauty was theirs for the asking. Small wonder that they grew old and ill before their time. Arranged marriages and desperate couplings were common. They were decidedly affected by loneliness and hopelessness, and they searched for diversion, for distractions, for a way out (no matter how fleeting) from their misery, and somehow, miraculously, the longed-for osmosis materialized in a variety of unanticipated forms. However they did it, they survived, and we, the innocent adored children, were their windows to a better, happier world.

Summertime ... early 1930's ... hot ... steaming hot ... so damn hot ... no place to hide from the punishing sun. Even the long shadows cast by row upon row of five, and six, and sometimes even eight story walk-up houses, could not offer any respite from the crippling heat. These "tenements" had as many as four (sometimes more) families, each one occupying its own apartment, called a "flat," on each level of the tenement, with three or more communal toilets on that level. And the mood was somber. Early that morning the terrifying news that the bad kid on the street had been playing with a broken piece of a phonograph record early last evening, and in a moment of insanity, had jabbed a jagged edge into poor little Shiye's eye, virtually removing it from its socket. Shiye was, of course, now being attended to at Kings County, the free, city hospital. The piercing animal screams of this poor, savagely wounded little boy were still ringing in our ears, as the retelling of this horrible crime (inflicted by an obviously troubled child whose frantic parents had already become the neighborhood pariahs as a result of their uncontrollable child's actions) added a total aura of gloom to what was rapidly becoming the most unbearably hot day of this never ending summer.

How old could I have been when all this was occurring? Five? Six? They say that the so-called "formative years" are up until around the age of seven. On that nightmarish day, so indelibly inscribed in my memory, I was to discover the therapeutic value of humorous distraction. It was a day that I came close to drowning, in a most ignominious and embarrassing manner. Now, so many years later, the sequence of events remains as vivid as when it occurred.

There were no public playgrounds with swimming facilities anywhere nearby in our poverty stricken enclave. The only place to go to was far off Coney Island or its adjacent Brighton Beach, or Rockaway, which was even further away. Canarsie was closer, but even less accessible by public transportation, and Canarsie also presented a danger called quicksand. Whether this was a frightening rumor, or not, somehow there was always someone around who had "personally witnessed somebody disappear in the quicksand at Canarsie." No one had the ten cents for the subway fares to any of those beach areas, and from Williamsburg, the trip required a trolley car to the subway. Free transfers were issued, I think, but the trip seemed interminable. Besides, nobody from our area went during the week. If we were able to scrounge up the money, better to wait for Sunday, when Pop was generally home (if he was lucky enough to get Sundays off) so that the whole family could go on an outing together.

So what'd we do to escape the oppressive heat? We'd cover the gratings over the corner sewer with cardboard, newspapers, rags, wood, just about anything, then surreptitiously approach the nearby fire hydrant, look around very carefully to make sure that there were no cops around, and then, whoever secretly owned that priceless wrench that

Van Harris (1926)

fit the plug, would quickly unscrew it while we clasped our hands over our mouths to muffle the joy at the sight of that wonderful, refreshing, cold water gushing out with a fury. We grow up being taught that the cops are our friends, and that we must always obey the law. It's against the law to open a fire hydrant, and everyone knew it, but desperate situations oft times require desperate measures, and New York neighborhoods abounded in that particular "crime" in those years, and some still do. Cops and power go hand in hand. There were always those gentlemen (in those years I don't recall any lady cops) who were a tribute to their profession (also one of the few steady jobs, with a pension yet, in those depression years), and there were, and still are, in a very small minority those hooligans who were the neighborhood bullies while they were growing up, and who never lost their sadistic tendencies, and, with the power bestowed upon them by the "badge," took delight in flexing their muscles. It's still not beneath some of them to enjoy terrorizing so-called "lawbreakers," and when I was a little kid, with a strong conscience, aided by honest, law-abiding parents and grandparents, I still got the occasional "whack on the ass" from the grinning, sadistic cop, who, somehow, amused himself that way, and then forgot all about the pain and embarrassment he had earlier inflicted when he came home, kissed his wife, hugged his kids, and cried when he heard that the dog was clipped by a car.

How did we escape the heat in Williamsburg? We waded in the street-long gutters, splashing ourselves, and everyone around us with dirty water, cooling ourselves off, while inadvertently, or perhaps, even willingly, flirting with the dread disease called "infantile paralysis," better known, later on, as "polio," which both crippled, and annihilated several generations of us.

I had gleefully splashed my way all the way down the line to where the big puddle was, the part over the grating. I did not know that someone had removed half of the grating, and, although the sewer was backed up from the trash that had fallen in, it was still deep (way over my head) and I had never learned to swim. I went down once, came up gasping for air, clutching for whatever I could grab to prevent my going down again. My eyes were bulging, my ears were ringing, I couldn't breathe, and I was sure I was going to die, when my foot stepped on the half of the grating that was still there and I jammed it against the iron mesh, trying to leap up at the same time. Others, who had seen what was happening, dragged me out of the water onto the sidewalk, just as I was turning blue and red all at once. I lay on my back, facing the torrid sun, thankful that the air was coming back into my lungs.

In a moment the scene changed as a crowd of concerned, frightened little kids formed a circle around this trembling little body, lying prostrate on the ground whimpering, coughing, embarrassed by the attention being given him. Inwardly I was praying that Momma wouldn't be among the adults that were descending out of the doorways or craning their necks through open windows in an effort to see what had happened. (Then there would be hell to pay, and all the attempts at explaining would not make things better.)

Suddenly, I heard squeals of laughter, growing louder by the moment. All heads were turning as the volume kept increasing. All the attention was rapidly diverted to another direction. I was left all alone, and, fortunately, I had just about regained my strength and composure. I arose slowly in an effort to peer over the assorted crowd to see what all the hysteria was about, and there I saw it, and I joined the cacophony of giggles and outright belly laughs. Mrs. Schultz, one of the few Germans residing in our melting pot, a rather wide, young, blonde, fastidious lady, who always dressed in cool, summery white dresses, was strolling by with the twins, two tow-headed little preschool age brothers, also dressed so neatly in their little white shorts, and, once again, "the show" was going on. They were the neatest, cleanest family in the entire region, and white was always their summer color of choice. The two little blonde haired boys were miniature clones of their mother. The little guys were forever having problems controlling their bowel movements (We often wondered what the dear lady fed those "Katzenjammer Kids"), and whenever they passed by, all heads would turn to see the backs of the neat white short pants with the mustard seeping through, practically in congruity, while the kids wailed out loud from discomfort. This constant occurrence could not have happened at a better time, and now, so many, many years later (who knows, they may have grown up to become successful, important men), thanks to those ubiquitous twins, stained pants and all, I treasure the memory of their presence, which taught me the value of "comedy relief."

Ignorance is bliss. I knew only the world that was immediately around me, and I loved it. All the adults, except the schoolteachers, spoke with an accent. We knew who "the others" were 'cause their accents were not like ours. We American born kids spoke English for the most part, though Yiddish was really the earliest language we spoke, and our English had a singsong quality about it that came about as a result of giving both those languages equal time. Only in school, guided by those wonderful, dedicated ladies (as I recall, so many of Irish descent) did we strive to perfect the proper use and pronunciation of our adopted, beautiful English language whose mysteries were unfolding constantly, much to my everlasting delight. I never gave much thought to whatever ethnic groups my friends sprang from. I was told that my very best friend was Ukrainian, something that mattered very little to me or my elders. They loved him as much as I did. I was introduced to the fascinating world of recreational reading by a great Jewish kid, who had such inspiring parents, and who lived up the street from us in another dingy tenement. By the time I was ten, I had read just about every book in the children's section of the Bushwick Ave. Public Library, and was awarded special dispensation by that library to take books out of the adult section. Through the minds of the many talented authors, I was beginning to discover the world and so many other cultures, and each day became an adventure for me. How lucky I was. Little did I ever anticipate that, many years later, thanks to show biz, and the part where I performed on all the famous cruise ships I would be privileged to visit, world wide, first class, and in person, most of these places that I had read about. I would have the added reward of being able to have Shirley, the greatest love of my life, always along (no, she's not a cocker spaniel),

Gourmet meals? Yes, on the cruise ships and the resorts. In Williamsburg? Who knew the difference? Our main meal consisted of potatoes, potatoes, and more potatoes. Throw in a sour pickle, and God's gift to the earth, a raw onion, and we all felt like royalty. Luxury living? You bet! When it was below zero degrees out, and we didn't have enough firewood or coal to heat up that old, wood burning, pot-bellied stove that reigned in the middle of the kitchen (proudly attempting to bring warmth to every distant corner of our four room flat on those frigid wintry days), we were all comforted by the knowledge that we had two large, downy quilts that were called perenes, guaranteed to keep all who slept under them comfortable beyond belief. And, as for the other extreme, those excruciatingly torrid summer days and nights, there were those good old reliable fire escapes to both, sit around on while waving a paper fan, and, later, sleep on, in either event, with a bare minimum of clothes on, just enough to be considered legal.

Pop loved us n' sang Russian songs to us on those rare moments when he wasn't off to work, and Mom would take us all on the trolley ("all" meaning my brother Joe, fifteen months younger than I, and myself ... that's all there was), to the great big meadows of Prospect Park, and on those rare occasions when generous Uncle Fyvel would show up with his Buick, then we'd really get adventurous and go as far away as the very beautiful Forest Park which was located way out in Queens. All my life I've cherished the memory of sitting on those great lawns while Mom amazed us all by creating magnificent crowns out of the colorful assortment of flowers that grew wildly and abundantly there. She'd place them on our heads as we squealed with delight. Amid all the misery and frustration, never knowing if Pop would be able to provide us with enough to pay our ever-lagging bills, those beautiful days in the park were the only times that Mom seemed to be completely relaxed, and her momentary happiness was contagious.

We little ones were happy as long as we had things to do and friends to play with, and our parents found joy in their camaraderie with their friends, neighbors, and assorted relations, but, I soon discovered that the rare times that we were totally blissful as a family unit were when we had the good fortune to be enjoyably distracted by entertainment. It was in those very early years of my life that I made the amazing discovery, ... the therapeutic value of good entertainment, and, in looking back now, I sense that it was way back then that I developed a burning desire to become a practitioner of entertainment and make the whole world happy.

Our vaudeville theater was practically around the corner, on Graham Ave., and it was called Fox's Folly, and as I sit here and recall those days, I can still picture its majestic lobby, with its stunning theatrical appointments and sparkling, polished atmosphere, and I can still smell that wonderful smell of floor wax, cleaning fluids, and all the other ingredients that go into keeping a first rate theater constantly looking like new. And those magnificent people onstage with clean, colorful, dazzling, expensive looking clothing. The way they carried themselves. The artistry in every type of performance, from those stupefying magicians in their top hats and tails, to those gifted singers, and dancers, and jugglers, and breathtaking acrobats, and all those many and varied heroes and heroines of my life that I adored more and more each time I was fortunate enough to see them perform. My beautiful "escape world." Whenever I was there nothing else mattered. That was the home I longed for. And, how eagerly I waited, while the talented orchestra provided such ingenious and unique backgrounds for each individual performance, and for the announcement card to come up "Comedian." The collective audience would hold its breath in anticipation, so eager to laugh ... and laugh we did ... till our sides hurt. Oh those comedians. Those wonderful comedians. That unbelievable world of laughter. I loved it. I genuinely, and truly loved it!

Then there were those precious moments when we all attended the Yiddish theater, which was performed entirely in Yiddish, with some English thrown in for effect. We spoke Yiddish fluently, and totally understood that most-descriptive, and colorful language. And talk about comedians. They were not only great ... they were sensational! They had to be, in order to overcome the sheer tragedy that tore at everybody's heart in each and every Yiddish show. NY's lower east side was booming with Yiddish theater, a glorious, thriving industry saturated with some of the most talented actors and actresses that the world had ever seen. (A few even made it to worldwide stardom in Hollywood.) And, there were "regional" theaters in the other boroughs of NY and in a number of the big American and Canadian cities that contained enough of a Jewish population to support such theater. Our local Yiddish theater was called the Lyric and no less a star than Jennie Goldstein (one of the most highly regarded of them all) oft times graced our stage. Mom was so enamored of that stage that she actually applied for non-paying "walk-on" roles, and, being a slim, beautiful red headed woman, she had no problems in obtaining such work. Of course, being able to get us all into the theater free as a result, was no small reward in anyone's eyes. Let it freeze like hell outside, or let the heat swelter our aggots out there, who knew or even cared? We were all being marvelously distracted by theater ... the great escape.

3 Heartbreak

Life is not a matter of escape however, and early on I began to encounter its grim reminder that the human condition is also subject to many vagaries. Joe, or "Yussel" as those more steeped in Yiddish used to refer to my little brother, suddenly started to limp noticeably. Being barely able to scrape together enough money to consult a doctor, Mom pulled off a miracle by getting together enough for one visit, and it was then that she was advised that he needed additional tests and care which could only be provided, in our circumstances, at the (free) Kings County Hospital. The hospital was far enough away that it required a trolley car ride to a faraway point, and then a transfer to a bus to a further away point, and then the long, time-consuming reverse trip coming home. How lucky I was to be preoccupied by school (which I loved dearly), and even Pop, with his long, long, days on the truck, delivering beer had the advantage of being distracted from this newly developing crisis. (Pop worked as a "helper." He used to be the driver, but his "Jacksonian Epilepsy" once caught up to him at a rather inappropriate time, causing him to lose his license to drive.)

Yussel was diagnosed, at the age of four, or thereabouts, as having Leggs Perthes Disease, which is a failure of the ball in the hip joint to fully develop, thereby causing great discomfort and an inability to walk normally. The doctors at this free institution (not wishing to go through the long and costly procedure of trying to undo this rare condition) suggested to my mother that she allow them to fuse the hip bone and prohibit the condition from worsening. "It won't take as long as the attempted cure, and he'll be left with a limp that he could learn to live with."

I must digress here for a moment or two to tell you that, a few times in our youth my mother displayed a fierce protectiveness of her children that any kid would be proud of, and should earnestly expect, and this was another one of those times. Once, when Yussel and I took the walls apart in an abandoned factory building nearby, and brought loads of wood lathe home for firewood, two burly Irish detectives came to our home to "arrest" us. My mother displayed a menacing fist at both of them and threw them out of the house saying, "How dare you come after two little honest boys who brought home wood from an old, broken down building? If you wanted to keep kids out, you shouldda put a sign up, or posted a guard! Now get the hell out of my house, and don't you dare refer to my kids as criminals." ... and they never came back. Some years later, when we were residing in the notorious Brooklyn section called Brownsville, some kid displayed a handful of money and asked us to accompany him to Davega's to buy a football, which we, with our expertise, gladly consented to do. Turned out the kid had stolen the money at school, and, once again, two burly Irishmen with badges confronted me n' Yussel in the principal's office, and the principal implied that we had been a party to the theft. Based on past performance I knew what "the ol' redhead," as we affectionately referred to her, was gonna do, and she did! She grabbed the principal by the collar, tightening his tie around his neck, and, as he was turning color and gasping for air, growled at him, "Take that back, you sonavabitch (she very rarely used expletives, but when she really got mad, watch out!), my boys have been raised to be honest. They are not crooks." ... and, once more ... case closed!

Well, upon hearing what the doctors had recommended, there came that expletive again ... "Yes, that's what I called you! A limp he can learn to live with? You think I'm gonna let my little boy become a cripple? Okay, let's go the long, hard way, and cure him." ... Long and hard it was ... The procedure entailed putting him into a full body cast and keeping him home for however long she could, coming into the hospital clinic about every two weeks to check on his progress, and the whole thing ran like that for over two years. Picture that poor lady carrying that "dead weight" on her shoulders, first walking to a trolley car, then getting on a bus, then walking to the hospital, ... and returning the same way, and that part went on for a year, in all kinds of weather, until she could do it no longer. Then they put him away into a pediatric (Wave Crest) convalescent home somewhere in Far Rockaway, which was so distant that we couldn't afford the fares for all of us to visit him together, so I didn't see him for well over a year. He came home cured, small, and as thin as a reed, and, from the moment he was released from that cast, he desired to stretch,

Joe and Van (1928)

and stretch, and stretch, and develop his body (in gym, a hundred pushups were like nothing to him) and he eventually grew up to be one of the finest athletes in the neighborhood. In fact, when he went into the army he was assigned to an infantry division, but once they saw him play baseball, he was immediately reassigned as an M.P. and he spent the remainder of his army career representing his division as a baseball player.

And so, after little Yussel was home again from the convalescent home, things seemed to go back to normal, but only very temporarily. Pop was still breakin' his back with very long hours and very little compensation. I was doing sensationally in school, in every way. I appeared in school plays; I had perfect scholastic averages; I had numerous good friends, especially the Ukrainian kid whose single mother worked as a domestic somewhere, so he spent a great deal of time at our house and was like another brother; and I was on my way to becoming the Captain Of The Guards, which was the most prestigious student position in the entire elementary school. Then my euphoric world suddenly started to unravel.

I don't exactly remember what time of the year it was. Seasons had no truly significant bearing on a nine-year-old boy who loved every waking moment of his young life. School was great. The time after school was great. Except for the extremely cold days in the winter and the very hot ones in the summer, every day, rain or shine, was beautiful, and through the process of conversation (whether just casual with my assorted friends, or those colorful, wondrous stories of the old world, as told to us by my parents, their friends, and our surprising collection of relatives), I reveled in the new adventures that each moment brought. And, when I was all alone ... those books ... those magical carpet rides to other people's worlds. We could barely afford to pay our electric bills, so when Mom or Pop said, "Lights out!" ... it was lights out. I would then proceed to stretch out towards the window, and continue to read by the light of the outside street lamp until the strain would exhaust me into sleep, a habit that would eventually have an adverse effect upon my vision.

School had just ended for the day, and as I exuberantly rounded the corner and approached our tenement, I was shocked to see an ambulance, with those ominous lights flashing, standing in front of the building. The attendants were bearing a stretcher that they were about to place into its interior. I hastily squeezed myself into the gathering crowd to try to catch a glimpse of who the unfortunate person was that was on the litter, and the unexpected shock of seeing my beloved mother lying there, pale and trembling, hit me like a ton of bricks. Before I could say or do anything, the doors were shut, the sirens began to wail, and they were on their way. For the first time in my life I felt alone and helpless, and, as I stood there in shock, with the tears rapidly welling up in my eyes, several of our neighbors put their arms around me to comfort and console me. Pop was, as usual, away at work, and Yussel was out somewhere, and, although I was surrounded by sympathetic people, I did not hear them, nor see them. I was all alone and devastated. Since none of us had any telephones, there was nothing to do but wait at home till Yussel at first, and then, much later, Pop got there. It was at that moment that I became an adult.

Mom came back home in several weeks and was confined to her bed to recover from what those free doctors at Kings County diagnosed as a heart attack. I quickly learned to clean, wash clothes, cook simple things, look after my recuperating mother and my little brother, and still manage time for school and recreation. Mom eventually recovered and we all celebrated by going to see a new show at the Yiddish theater, which did us all a world of good.

This was the first of many instances of such "heart attacks," that Mom would suffer throughout the seventy-six years that she lived. Through the intervention of her cousin, a widely respected physician who practiced medicine in the imposing Lower East Side building that the popular newspaper, The Jewish Daily Forward, was housed in, we discovered that what the charity doctors had offhandedly diagnosed as heart attacks were actually severe nervous reactions to all the emotional buffeting she had taken in her life (i.e. a childhood in war torn, cholera infested Poland; a haphazard marriage here in America; the demoralizingly embarrassing effects of trying to raise a family in abject poverty, tortured by hopelessness, and reliance upon hand-me-downs and Public Assistance), that had resulted in the kinds of breakdowns that had all the outward appearances of

Mom (Pauline) by Junior High School 210, Brooklyn - 1943

Pop (Morris) - 1943

heart disease. Actually, realistically speaking, it was a "disease of the heart," it's called "heartbreak."

Pop was to be pitied too. Lord knows, he worked hard, long hours in a supreme effort to support his wife and his devoted little boys, who both gave and received love and affection from all and who accepted the (oft-times heated) domestic arguments as a way of life. He loved Mom more than she loved him ... a situation not unique in countless immigrant marriages where they stayed together "for the sake of the children" ... hah? What else could they do? Pop died at seventy-nine. He went before Mom did. They stayed married to the end and he loved her to the end, and his devotion to her throughout her bouts with physical adversity, especially in their latter years just plain wore him out. When she was about seventy, Mom had to have her leg amputated as a result of arteriosclerosis. Up until the very end, I must point out, Pop continued to maintain his quiet easy style. I never saw him get excited (except when he watched the tap dancers at Fox's Follies, and in the movies, and later on TV. There was something about tap dancing that stirred his innermost feelings. I think he would have given his eye teeth if Yussel or I would have become tap dancers). His serene nature, at times, seemed to make him almost invisible. There were times he would react to injustice quite vocally, and he was always outspoken about politics, where he steadfastly defended anyone who was in favor of the working man, but for the most part he had a penchant for anonymity and laissez faire. I used to do a little routine about my pop's desire not to bother anyone: My mom sent him to the grocery for some pot cheese, which was served right out of a big vat in those years. The grocer, holding a small dairy shovel full of loose pot cheese in his hand, asked, "Do you want it in a bag or a container?" and Pop replied, while opening his side pants pocket "Don't bother, ... put it in here." Pop once got mugged in the middle of the night (something that unfortunately, happened to him several times). He didn't wanna wake anyone up, so he whispered for help.

Typically, Pop expired quietly at Kingsbrook Hospital in Brooklyn, as a result of congestive heart failure, while in the care of my dear friend and a very devoted physician, Dr. Gershbaum. I always had the feeling that even his death was way premature and partially attributable to his not wanting to "make waves." To this very day I have a great deal of compassion for people who are poor and are forced to rely on charity, something, except for some brief intervals, my parents had to endure most of their lives. Pop and Mom had been Medicaid members of one of those very early HMO's, frequented largely by older people. The harried doctors in that system were far from attentive, and, by the time that they recognized that his complaints were genuine, it was already too late. All the royal care that my friend Dr. Gershbaum bestowed upon him, failed to save him. Pop was of medium height and slender for most of his life, except for his muscular upper torso, which got that way from heavy lifting. He had an interesting habit of furrowing his brow while raising only one eyebrow, and his hair hadn't receded too much, and was still, for the most part, brown. As he lay in his coffin, dressed in his best suit, with a new shirt n' tie, the two dedicated, grief stricken Black ladies who had been caring for Mom and Pop (courtesy of The Human Resources Administration) over the last several years, peered down at him, with tears falling from their eyes, and exclaimed, "You sure are a good lookin' stud."

Mom was never again that beautiful, indestructible redhead after that fateful day in Williamsburg when the ambulance had taken her to the hospital. Though she appeared to have regained her strength, she now tired more easily, and it seemed that she was not as resilient as she had always been. The coldwater flat, the pot-bellied stove that tried to warm the whole place, the two or three flights of stairs that we had to climb ... all was not as easy to live with anymore. It was time to look for more comfortable lodgings, and Mom and Pop got all excited when they found a real steam-heated three room flat, on the ground floor yet, in another part of Brooklyn called Brownsville. This turned into the single, unhappiest, most devastating change in my entire youth. Although I'm a strong believer in fate, and I owe my entire, rewarding, fruitful life to its chain of events, I shall never forget, for as long as I live, the absolute pain that this "move for the better" inflicted upon me at that time.

I had had everything in the world that represented security, fulfillment, and happiness, and then came that move ... that awful, destructive move. I should have known that things were going to go downhill when soon after we were told that we were going to relocate, and about a month before we actually moved, something happened to me to shatter my youthful innocence, ... something that could happen to just about anyone ... and it served as one of my early introductions, a rather brutal one, to the vagaries of life.

Education was the byword in our humble household in Williamsburg, as it appeared to be in the homes of everyone we ever knew then. In addition to the public school that we attended, all the Jewish kids had to also attend Hebrew schools or Yiddish schools. There is a difference, with the former emphasizing religious education, and the latter more concerned with Yiddish reading, writing, and Jewish history. I attended the Yiddish school, which the conservatives in our society frowned upon as "left-leaning," but then again, there were so many unhappy people, and still are, that assume that, if you're a Jew, ... you're automatically a Communist! To this innocent child it was another area of knowledge, superbly taught by some very gifted teachers, and I took to it with alacrity. I loved those after school, and sometimes evening, classes. I shall never forget that balmy, late spring evening when, filled with the usual enthusiasm, I headed into the darkened hallway, ready to bound up that one flight of wooden stairs to the classroom, when a bunch of hands reached out and pulled me behind the pitch black stairwell. Yelling savage obscenities peppered with references to "Jews" and "Communists," they proceeded to beat me with sticks and curtain rods. I sensed the warm feeling of blood running down my face, my back, and into my shoes, until I passed out.

Shocking incidents such as these never quite leave you, and the pity is that such mindless and cowardly bestiality often goes unpunished. For a very, very long time afterwards, the victim keeps asking himself, over and over again, "Why?" Who knows why? When I awoke I staggered up the stairs into the classroom, and I can still picture the profound shock that registered on the faces of my classmates. My teacher, Mr. Halperin (funny that so many years later, I still remember his name, and can still picture his kindly face), sized up the situation and attended to me without a moment's hesitation.

No need to go into the details of my mother's hysterical reaction when I was brought home, and my father's silent, frustrated anger, not to mention little Yussel's disbelief that such a thing could have happened. My face became one big scab from my hairline to my chin (scarred from a long ago accident). After a number of weeks I recovered and except for the nightmarish memory of the atrocity, I was one happy kid again, though somewhat less secure (that is, until that traumatic move to Brownsville, where things worsened).

I once heard some Holocaust survivors being interviewed on our radio. (It was a luxury we never owned until Mom brought home a Philco, with a big face with the front speaker shielded by cloth and a carved wooden grill. She purchased it "on time" at Mullins, and it took the next five years to pay it off.) The host asked the survivors a valid question, "When they loaded you onto the trains, why did you go so willingly?" and the reply was, "We were told that we were being relocated, and we had that natural curiosity to see where we were going." For a child to be told that we were moving to a new neighborhood and an apartment located on the ground floor (with no flights of stairs to walk up and steam heat yet) sounded very exciting. No more pot bellied stove. No more firewood or coal. Heat in every room. Naturally, we were ever so eager, forgetting for the moment all those wonderful things that we loved so, that we were leaving behind.

4 Brownsville

Reality struck on the very first day that we lived on St. Marks Ave. (conveniently located directly across the street from the elementary school), when I walked out of my apartment door to acquaint myself with our new surroundings. I saw a tall, blonde, stocky kid, whom I gauged to be a couple of years older than I, and before I could say, "Hello," he growled at me, "You're the new kid, eh? My father is the landlord here. I own this building and don't you ever forget it, and this is to remind you who's boss around here," and he proceeded to give me a lusty wallop on top of the head that almost knocked me senseless. From that day forward, I had to develop all my resources to avoid this psychopathic bully, and as crafty as I became, I caught many a beating at his hands.

There was the all important business of registering in a new school, where I quickly learned that I was the new kid, a nobody. I longed for that important existence that I had had in Williamsburg, which I realized was no longer there. I had many new things to learn: A new system in a new school; how to play at various sports, which I hardly, if ever, did in the confines of my old neighborhood; how to make new friends; how to find out where the library is and wonder if they will be as accommodating to me as they were on Bushwick Ave., etc., etc., ... and I was very lucky that the new school had wonderful, dedicated teachers who showed their concern. I still remember the handsome, sinewy, lithe Mr. Conklin, the gym teacher, who displayed such patience with the new, awkward kid who had never played softball or basketball before, and he actually turned me into a pretty fair player. I am eternally grateful to all those good souls, like Mr. Conklin, in the public school system, whose genuine interest in developing growing children is a divine gift.

I soon discovered that the new neighborhood, with our steamed heat, and no stairs to climb, and the convenience of a school right across the street, was no bed of roses. There was a breed of adult people out there unlike what I had known in Williamsburg. The feeling of competitiveness was everywhere. There was a huge marketplace around the corner with all sorts of stores next to each other and pushcarts crammed side by side on the streets and even into the roads. You could purchase almost anything on that big street, and I quickly learned that the customer should never settle for the asking price, an art that takes time to develop. I had said that my father rarely showed anger. Well, there was this one time that my mother sent me around the corner with a dollar bill to buy some vegetables (something I was rather adept at.) Pop had not come home from work yet, and it was getting quite late, and I remember it was raining. Pop worked very long hours for the meager compensation of three dollars a week. I brought the vegetables home and Mom put the change on the table and proceeded to prepare supper. Pop walked in and asked his usual question, "What's for supper?" and, as long as the answer wasn't "Fish!" he'd step further into the house (call it a "flat," an "apartment," ... whatever ... it was still our "house"). Mom was an extremely capable cook, given the limited menus she could prepare on Pop's meager earnings, and her Russian borscht, flavored with raisins, was the talk of the family, but fish was her downfall. Like all the other poverty stricken immigrants, she would, occasionally (fortunately for all of us) buy a rather inexpensive, but popular fish called, "buffle," and she knew only how to boil it, head n' all. Believe me, it wasn't her forte, and when she had the temerity to prepare that "treasure" we would all threaten to run away from home. She, like all the other mothers in the neighborhood, insisted that fish was "brain food," and that we all must have it once in awhile, and Pop thought out loud, "I'd rather be dumb." It had reached the stage where, if she had prepared that "delicacy," and he had enough time to be forewarned, which required only an instant, he would say something like, "Excuse me, I forgot something at work. Eat without me. I'll grab a quick bite there," and he'd disappear into one of the local diners.

This time it was safe to come in and he was already starting to remove his clothes. (Pop always took a hasty bath before he would sit down for supper. It served two purposes. He would clean up, ... and it would relieve the aches and pains of the hard day's work.) He spotted the half dollar lying among the change in the ashtray. He reached over, picked up the coin, examined it closely, and let it drop onto the table, and listened closely as it made a rather dull thud. He repeated this action several times, and we all watched as his eyes started to darken, and the wrinkles in his brow deepened, and, suddenly he became filled with rage. "Where did you get this thing? It's lead! It's a phony!" My heart sank. My legs got weak. "Who gave this to you," he bellowed, "where did you get it?" I stammered that it was part of the change I got when I bought the vegetables. Mom and Yussel stood there trembling. (It wasn't hard to figure out that this constituted one-sixth of his hard earned salary.) Pop took me by the hand, and out we went into the rain to find "the sleazy S.O.B., the scum who would stoop so low as to slip a little kid a lead half dollar.

The rain became more intense and we were getting soaked to the bone, as we wove through the maze of pushcarts that all seemed to look alike. Vendors huddled under their awnings, wide-eyed, watching an angry father, grimy and unshaven, pulling a hysterical little boy by the arm, approach each vendor, pointing a finger directly into his face, and asking the weeping child, "Was it him?" If nothing else, I take great pride in my memory to this very day, and, after going from stand to stand, I came upon the evil bastard that had cheated me, and pointed him out and cried, "It was him!" My father demanded that he give him a true half dollar for the phony, and even threatened him, but the seasoned petty thief adamantly denied that he was the culprit. He even dared Pop to hit him while threatening to "call a cop." It was so painful and embarrassing, and the shouting was attracting a crowd. In the end we had to give up and go back home, thwarted, ... defeated, ... and a whole fifty cents poorer ... victims of a scurrilous, small time, insensitive gangster, disguised as a "businessman," who, no doubt, went to his house of worship when that time of the year came around, to cleanse himself of his sins. When we got back home Mom was weeping softly. Pop was too distraught to eat, we kids went right to bed, and nothing more was ever said. It took me a long, long time to get over that incident, but, as my dear old friend Barney (one of the stars of that pack that hung out at Dubrow's) had always said, "Time is a great healer ... but a lousy beautician!"

To us kids it was a painful learning experience that put us on our guard forever, and we'd both be rich men if we each had a dollar for every time we were cheated, in one way or another. My father was too busy trying to survive all his life, but like all decent, thinking people with feelings, he would occasionally deliver a philosophical remark. I sometimes, in using my father's memory in my comedy routines, embellish his sayings. This is one I use whenever applicable: "My father taught me ... don't trust anybody over thirty, ... under thirty ... or thirty!" By the way, many years later, when Shirley and I had our first home, in Island Park on L.I., our parents came to visit one Sunday afternoon. We had befriended a lovely young couple in the mountains, at a resort hotel we had worked at the summer before. They had a little boy who was our eldest son's age, and the tots got along famously. We invited them to come and visit that same day. While they were there and we all were having a lovely time, the couple's parents, who were the little boy's loving grandparents, were visiting somewhere nearby, and they dropped in for a moment and were very gracious. The moment the "grandpa" walked into our house I recognized him. I said nothing. It was that underhanded vendor that had slipped me that lead half-dollar all those many years ago. All those many years later, I felt a pang in my heart. I pictured this blubbering little kid, standing in the rain with the mucous running down onto my chin, and Pop looking as though he was going to have a fit. I swallowed hard and walked away.

I've always tried to live by William Shakespeare's "To thine own self be true, and it shall follow as night follows day... Thou cans't not then be false to any one." One's conscience can be enough to keep anyone in line, with no need for "outside interference." Of course a little rationalization goes a long way, but keep it within bounds, y'hear? I've developed a rather healthy mistrust of the (fallible) "wearers of the badge" who are empowered to uphold the law, and I have a good deal of respect for those people who drive around with those bumper stickers on their cars that say, "Question Authority." Some of the abuses heaped upon us by omnipotent policemen, backed up by ersatz magistrates, are totally unacceptable, and I don't believe in turning the other cheek if you can help it. Granted, among them are some of the bravest and most upstanding, dedicated human beings, but, as Henry Kissinger pointed out in referring to his own line of work.

"Ninety percent of our politicians make it bad for the other ten percent."

Ever notice how some of the worst kids in the neighborhood when you were growing up, somehow became attracted to the field of law enforcement. Those of us who don't suffer at the hands of some unscrupulous "policeman" are very fortunate. Spending as much time as I do on the road makes me more vulnerable. Sometimes some damn fool will pull me over in the dead of night, hassle me 'cause he's bored (but he has the license to play games), n' because I did nothing to break the law, would "allow" me to go on my way. After some such incidents, one tries to minimize its dismaying effects, and, after awhile, I try to get that sort of legal hooliganism out of my system, but if it happens to any of my children (and it has) then I go into a rage, and try my darndest to help and advise them, and, if they let me, even intercede on their behalf, but when it comes to contesting these petty bureaucrats who are in a position of authority, it's like "pissin' against the wind."

Several years ago, while driving home after a job, with my wife at my side, somewhere near the antiquated Taconic Parkway, about 60 miles above New York City, I stopped at a full stop sign, lingered a moment to make certain what direction I was to go in, and then continued on a dark, poorly marked road. Out of the corner of my eye I spotted a car making a U-turn, and, in my rear view mirror, watched it follow me. I remarked to my wife that we were being followed and I began to feel somewhat apprehensive when, after about a half mile or so, flashing lights began to twirl above the car that had been pursuing me. I quite correctly pulled over on the shoulder of the road, and awaited the next move. I was approached by a short, wide-bottomed blonde in a trooper's uniform who immediately began to shout orders at me as though I was an escaped convict. Shirley was incredulous, and so was I. I asked why she stopped me, and she snarled, "Ya passed a full stop sign!" I realized right then and there that this was a case of extortion, and protested, but to no avail. She went back to her vehicle, where, I saw in the dark, another person was seated, and, as she handed me the citation I said, "I'll see you in court." She snarled and snorted some more, and drove on.

I had my moment in some dinky little courtroom presided over by a soft-spoken "judge" who tried hard to give the appearance that he was interested, and, with Shirley testifying as my witness, we both soon discovered that the trip to the courtroom, the plea, all the correspondence, was a total waste of time and energy. In the courtroom, the trooper continued her smug, officious demeanor. The cost of being found "Guilty," for something that never happened, was $55, and I just refused to take this highway robbery lying down. I immediately got off a letter to the Supt. of NY State Police, describing her ugly manner as an affront to her uniform. I suggested that she should enroll in sensitivity training, and stated that, as a taxpaying citizen I resent the entire contrived affair. I followed up with a letter to the then governor of NY Mario M. Cuomo, describing the whole matter. I complained to one of the Citizens' Social Agencies in Albany, and even got hold of a Special Prosecutor who is assigned by the NY State Attorney General's office to investigate N. Y. State Police corruption. All reacted favorably to my complaint, and I received a telephone call from the witch's commanding officer, inquiring into the details of the incident and assuring me that she was being brought up on the carpet. Right after that Shirley and I departed for Singapore where I was scheduled to board a cruise ship touring the Far East and Australia for six weeks. When I returned home I called the barracks to inquire as to the result of the investigation and was told that they were not allowed to divulge any information regarding internal affairs. No, I never got my fifty-five bucks back, but I did make certain that "his honor" was made aware of my actions (unless his overly protective court clerk withheld it from him). All this led to a lifetime of disgust with official corruption. The little guy seldom, if ever, wins, but his self respect grows when he takes the time, and has the courage, to fight back.

My turbulent introduction to Brownsville continued. I made some lifelong friends, and also saw some terrible things happen. A beautiful little girl who lived a few doors down was sexually molested by a gang of feral young thugs that lived way over on the far end of the street. Another pretty child was innocently "gang-banged" in the schoolyard by a playful bunch of the so-called "better kids," initiated by a neighborhood troublemaker. Over at the junior high school, a few blocks away, a huge hand-to-hand combat scene, with baseball bats, knives, etc. took place between the Italian kids and the Black kids when it was announced that Mussolini had invaded Ethiopia. All the while, I was busy sharpening up my softball and basketball abilities (two things that I had arrived very deficient in, when the family had moved to Brownsville) in the schoolyard. Oh, one more bit of local color, a number of the grown men from the other end of Brownsville were making headlines taking daily trips to Sing Sing's electric chair.

I would never, in my wildest dreams, ever demean Brownsville though. Like so many other places on this earth, it had its abundance of negative aspects, but they were far outweighed by its greatness. I liken Brownsville to Russia. When one thinks of all the mindless brutality and all the various atrocities that Russia has been noted for throughout all the centuries, how do we explain the brilliance, the artistic sensitivity, those outstanding scientific minds, the math, the literature, the music, the unbelievable genius that emerged out of such conditions? Brownsville, despite its abundance of anti-social activity, could boast of fine, hard working, honest, decent people, who were kind to their fellow human beings, and well above average in intelligence. So many of the inhabitants, my own family included, had their roots in Eastern Europe, from which they, and their ancestors were fortunate enough to escape. Brownsville, in Brooklyn, can hold its head up high, and take long, sweeping bows for all the fantastic people that emerged from there ... true champions in just about every field of endeavor, except maybe fox-hunting.

Thomas Jefferson High School, its most famous institution of learning, has an endless list of illustrious graduates whose many, and varied abilities, in all walks of life, have helped make America great. Why even its famous principal, Elias Lieberman (besides being a renowned educator) was a highly respected poet. The surrounding high schools, like Samuel J. Tilden, Franklin K. Lane, and Alexander Hamilton, can all be justifiably proud of what they turned out.

A number of years ago, I was booked to perform aboard the final world cruise of the S.S. France, sailing on the Indian Ocean (Bombay to Capetown) with stops throughout exotic places like Sri Lanka (then known as Ceylon), the Seychelles, Kenya, etc., etc., etc. Their so-called "Cruise Director" was a dastardly, ultrachauvinistic French junior naval officer who knew nothing about show business, except that he hated all the English speaking performers and he did his best to try to make us uncomfortable in whatever manner he could (like scheduling our performances in the lesser ballrooms at off hours when fewer passengers were around; assigning us to smaller, semi-livable cabins; anything to make our lives miserable). The only compensating factors were the generous remuneration, and the fact that my wife and I, and all the other "show kids" loved those breathtaking ports we were fortunate enough to dock in. If I knew that I could throw the scoundrel overboard and get away with it, I might just have done it as a favor, not only to all of us, but all mankind in general.

It was on that cruise that I also learned how devious theatrical agents can be. The agent that had booked me on numerous cruise ships before this one, asked if I would like to take my wife on an exotic trip on the S.S. France. He offered me the same paltry weekly amount of money that he had paid me on his Caribbean cruises. The trip to very distant places sounded delightful and enticing, and I told him that I would come to his office to sign the contracts. Coincidentally, on the following day I was having lunch with my then manager, Elliott Gunty, and several of his agent friends. One of them, a dapper gentleman who managed some big, European stars, inquired if I would like to perform on that very same cruise. I asked him how much he was paying and the offering came to about four times as much as the other fellow's (and he was still adding a profit for himself). Elliott and I couldn't believe our ears. Of course I called the other booking agent back and told him I couldn't accept the date. "Why?" he asked, and I told him about the other agent's generous offer. "Oh?" was his surprised answer, "I'll call you back." About an hour later the phone rang and it was him. "Van, I would greatly appreciate it if you didn't accept the offer from the other fellow." "Why?" I asked, "d'ya wanna match his offer?" "No," he replied. "Then why shouldn't I take it?" He paused for a moment. I could sense his discomfort. "Er, let's say it would place me in a very embarrassing situation. Don't take it and I'll try to make it up to you sometime." I must have surprised the hell out of him when I said, "Okay, I won't take it."

When I reported to Shirley what I had just done, she could hardly believe her ears, for two reasons. One reason was that he had attempted such a dastardly move on a "friend," and long time client, and was caught red-handed. The other was that he had the chutzpah to ask for my cooperation. My manager was just as surprised, as was the other booker who was a very decent fellow. They didn't anticipate any difficulty in finding someone else to do the job. Naturally my "friend's" credibility suffered immensely, but not as strongly with other, seasoned agents, who had seen such shenanigans before. Several weeks later he called and offered me a great cruise to Africa and India. It seemed that someone else had "fallen out," and I was selected to be his replacement, for the higher fee that his competitor had offered me. Naturally, I accepted, but I could never trust that agent again (although I worked many subsequent jobs for him) and I'm certain that, in other ways he managed to deceive me. That's the curse of show people's relationship with smart agents. They can sense when you're most vulnerable and know just when to apply the screws. There are ways they can cheat you, feign innocence, and if the performer is "on a roll," feeling flush, he (stupidly) looks the other way, and I'm certain that this sort of thing happened several times during my continued relationship with this scurrilous "smoothie."

Among the passengers on this cruise was a famous Hollywood writer that we befriended, who, in typical Hollywood fashion was traveling with another writer's "lady." They were delightful, gregarious people, and we hit it off quite well with them, and spent quite a bit of time together until they disembarked in Kenya to join a safari at the world famous Serengeti. We got to talking, and discovered that we were from the same neighborhood in Brownsville. He was a few years older than I, and, whereas I attended Thomas Jefferson High, he was a most-gifted and prominent student at Samuel J. Tilden (a school which, just coincidentally, my wife had also attended). We got to reminiscing and I asked him if he ever played softball in the schoolyard of P.S.144, and he told me that he wasn't a very good athlete. He was shorter than the other boys, and had a tendency to stutter, and kids would often laugh at him. "But," he injected, "I once got into a game 'cause it was my ball." I inquired, "What position did you play?" and he replied, "Right field."

Now P.S.144 had a very peculiarly shaped schoolyard. It wasn't exactly square, and had no right field. Left-handed batters would invert (pigeon toe) their right (outside) foot, in an effort to, heroically, hit one over the (short) left field (black iron grated) fence. The schoolyard had too many such obstacles, and it was one of those grated fences that I ran into when I got my first really prominent scar at the side of my left eye. Once again, charity played an ugly (but minor) role in my young life. They rushed me over to Novick's drugstore, on the corner, till the ambulance from Kings County hospital arrived (it seemed to take forever), and Novick was relieved when they arrived, as I had bloodied his floor pretty good. To clean the wound, the (inexperienced?) attendant put alcohol right into the open wound before he started stitching me up, and the screaming could be heard for miles, and even got to my mother's ears. She had been cooking in the kitchen, and recognized my screams, ran into the drugstore with her apron on, took one look at her little boy, bleeding profusely around the eye, and she fainted.

I said to the passenger, "There was no right field." He agreed, "I know, they stood me against the wall." I inquired further, "Well, how did you do?" He went on, "During the game a right-handed hitter hit one over the fence just as a Burns Bros. coal truck was passing by. The ball landed in the truck and the truck just kept on going." Then, just as though this successful Hollywood celebrity was that insecure little boy again, he looked at me as though he was about to cry, and said, "Y'know, ... they took me out of the game ..."

Returning to my youthful days in Brownsville, in what seemed like an eternity, I was doing my best to dodge the brutal son of the landlord, and I studied the oaf's habits so that I could avoid him as much as possible. I'd still get an occasional rap on the head, a kick below the belt, etc. Then one day, miracle of miracles. I couldn't believe what I was witnessing. I was attracted to a crowd of kids who were cheering at the top of their lungs in front of the schoolyard as they encircled what appeared to be some heavy activity on the ground. I pushed my way to the front of the group and couldn't believe what was going on. There, lying on the hard ground, and bawling like a baby, was the landlord's son, with my little brother and a handful of other little kids, savagely pummeling the bully. It was like a scene out of "Gulliver's Travels," except that, unlike Gulliver, this giant wasn't tied down. These feisty Lilliputians, led by my brother Yussel, were getting even with the bastard for all the havoc he had wreaked, and they taught him a lesson he would never forget. He never laid a hand on anyone ever again.

I thought we were the poorest kids on the street until the day that Big Red and his brother, Filthy Miltie (whom we later learned to address as "F.M.") appeared on the scene. Much later, when he actually adopted radio repairs as his profession, he maintained that the "F.M." stood for "Frequency Modulation." One of the great advantages of living in a grossly populated neighborhood like the one we were living in, is that, with so many turnovers, people constantly moving in and out of the plethora of apartments (the running joke was "let's move before the landlord comes for the rent"), there are always new kids appearing, seemingly out of nowhere. Such was the case when these two, very colorful, brothers approached me in the schoolyard one day, and asked if "I could use another man in the game?" They were both larger than most of us, though around the same age. Big Red (later we learned that his real name was George) was quite tall, had very broad shoulders for a kid his age, and an imposing head of curly, flaming red hair. He looked like a natural ballplayer. I immediately envisioned him as our new "cleanup hitter" on our softball team. Miltie, on the other hand, was almost as big as his brother, though a lot chubbier. He had a huge mop of curly brown hair, was not at all interested in athletics, but had a winning personality (actually, both boys did) and an obvious interest in just about everything. Funny, Miltie was left handed, and, because of the many gifted lefties in professional baseball, one would automatically assume that all lefties are talented athletes. My own personal observations about lefties (in which I have a more than a passing interest, having been born left handed, and quickly converted as a small child because the immigrants brought along a superstition that left-handedness is some sort of physical and mental handicap) is that they are gifted in so many, many ways. Those that are not dexterous in athletics are unusually awkward in that area, and Miltie fell into that category. Interestingly, he played the violin left handed, and later on, as an adult, he was an absolute genius at figuring things out both mechanical and electrical. He had a very keen imagination, and an uncanny ability to fix things, with the precision of a surgeon, but as a ballplayer he was a total failure. In self-defense he would point out that the left hand is attached to the right side of the brain, and the right hand is attached to the left side of the brain, which proves that only left-handed people are in their right minds! Both boys had quite a penchant for mischief making and in no time at all became very well known in the neighborhood.

How did I immediately realize that they were poorer than we? Well, my brother and I both wore hand-me-downs that we got from my mother's sister, Yuspe, a feisty redhead like my beloved mom, who accepted no nonsense from anyone, and who made herself a nice bit of extra money by bootlegging homemade whiskey. Yuspe used to drop in on us several times a year, along with her winsome brood of children (three handsome boys and two very beautiful girls, all older than we, except for little Charlie who was a change-of-life baby), and it was always a noisy, grand occasion when they would visit. Along with their exciting visit came shopping bags filled with clothes that the boys had outgrown, toys, baseball cards, etc., ... and our eyes would pop out of our heads in anticipation of what wonderful goodies these marvelous merrymakers would pull out of their bags of tricks for us. How we welcomed their visits. And dear, darling, salty-tongued "tante" (Yiddish for "aunt") Yuspe, her bright eyes darting around like ballet dancers, always quick with a quip. For example, they'd converge upon us unannounced (we didn't own a telephone), and sometimes they'd crash in as we were running around unclothed. Naturally, at the sight of them, we'd quickly cup our hands in front of our exposed "privates," and Yuspe would remark, tauntingly, "What are ya hidin', ... your bundle with the diamonds?" And so, whatever better clothing we wore came from our beloved cousins. Our newer clothing was what we "bought" at a department store in downtown Brooklyn with vouchers that were issued by the Home Relief Bureau, so you can well imagine the quality of the stuff. At holiday time, when we showed off our new "duds" to each other (most of the kids in the neighborhood acquired their new clothes in much the same fashion), we'd, oft-times, get down on our knees to shoot marbles, and when we'd get up again there'd be fresh holes in the pants. That's when I first learned that there's really no such thing as a "bargain," and all the parents in the neighborhood soon adopted the same philosophical expression, "Ya get what ya pay for!"

The first time I laid eyes upon those two brothers in their shabby clothes, I noticed that they had no belts on their pants. They wore ropes to hold their pants up! We, at least, had belts. They were paper thin and didn't last very long, but were a helluva lot more esthetic looking than ropes. Later on, when the boys took us to their flat around the corner (located on the fifth floor of a shabby tenement on the street that the pushcarts were on) and we met their parents who they called "Maw" and "Paw," and saw how sparsely the place was furnished, we compared situations and came to the conclusion that we were a lot richer than they were. As freewheeling as "Maw' and "Paw" were (they let the boys do just about anything they wanted), we felt a lot more fortunate to be living where we were. We didn't have much, but, thanks to Mom, what little we had, was neat, and clean, and everything sparkled.

We soon became inseparable, and yes, "Big Red" became our "cleanup hitter" at which he excelled, and also our fullback on our sandlot football team, and, because of his height, the center in our pickup basketball games. "Maw" would occasionally stand around in her precious old caracal (a type of raggy-lookin' fur) coat which she wouldn't let out of her sight (after all, it was "fur") and which she wore throughout three seasons, until it just got too warm, and "Paw," a huge, muscular man who, when he felt well, would pick up an occasional job as a loader on a moving van, but who, most of the time just sat around complaining about the pains he had from a bleeding ulcer. He used to love to banter with us kids about all professional sports, about which he had a fair amount of knowledge. I still remember his favorite riddle, which he'd pose from time to time thinking we kids had forgotten the answer. "Why can't the Dodgers play pinochle in Brooklyn?' The answer? "Cause the Cards are in St. Louis."

We moved to another part of Brownsville after a few years, and Big Red and Miltie just altered their direction and hung out with us constantly in our new neighborhood, which wasn't very far from the old one. Of course we made lots of new friends, but Red n' Miltie were always included in the gang, and it wasn't hard for the grownups to observe that those two active kids, especially "the redheaded one," bear watching. And our Mom felt a little harassed knowing that the other boys were always around and needed an extra glass or two of milk, which we could barely afford, or an extra onion, or a potato, or sour pickle, but she rarely complained. It was when our one little toilet became occupied too often that she would voice her disdain, for which none of us could blame her. Then we moved to a "better" neighborhood about six long blocks away, an area I would soon learn to love, called Crown Heights. Thanks to FDR's WPA program, Pop was able to pick up extra work like shoveling snow or performing menial tasks at construction sites, and the additional compensation enabled us to "move up." Some of the greatest kids I ever knew lived in that poor, working class neighborhood, and they remained my good friends well into adulthood. And, as usual, Red n' Miltie found their way there too.

We lived directly across from John Marshall Junior High School, undoubtedly one of the most popular public schools in the borough of Brooklyn. Everything about it was great, and it boasted of having some of the most capable teachers and brightest students in the whole wide world. It also had a great big, wide schoolyard, half of which was concrete, and the other half just plain good earth, which made it ideal for football, and boys, and girls, both, used to congregate there. To us John Marshall was the center of the universe, ... and Mom, from her kitchen window, had a ringside view of all that was going on in that arena. As the seasons changed, so did the sports, and we boys participated in everything. Yussel, who, by then, had already blossomed into one of the better athletes in the neighborhood, was also considered one of the "hotheads." He would openly argue a decision by the umpire, and, if necessary, get into a long, hard fight over what he deemed as unjust. He was considered among the most vocal, along with some of the older legends in the area, not much older than he. In that environment, kids who were as little as

Van and Joe. Park Place, Brooklyn.

a year apart would not bother with each other and each age group had its own peers. Yet, in sports, gauged only by their ability on the field, the groups intermingled. There was Big Metz, tough little Julie Woolf, and the worst menace of them all, Meyer Knubowitz, who, one balmy evening, on a dare, with everyone gathered around looking on, shimmied up a lamp pole and urinated into our window. When Mom saw a noisy crowd in the schoolyard, with insults and fists flying every which way, her sole interest was to make sure that Yussel was not in the midst of the brawl. Many's the time she would breathlessly bound down that long flight of hallway stairs, and dash across the street and wade into the crowd to extract her excitable little ballplayer from the fracas.

Most of the kids in the neighborhood were good, law-abiding boys and girls guided by hard working, but interested, caring parents. I can't recall any kids that went bad except one, and he was the only one on the whole block who had a ne'er-do-well, violent father who was always in trouble with the law for striking the poor kid's working mother. Whereas just about every child there was an achiever that the parents could be proud of, this bright, popular boy became a hardened criminal at an early age.

Big Red and Miltie had so much fun in the neighborhood that they never wanted to go home. On warm nights they would even sleep out in the back yard of our tenement building, since our own three room flat was barely big enough to accommodate us. So these two purposefully homeless boys were forever in evidence, and, given their mischievous behavior, Red especially, soon became known as the scourge of the neighborhood. Whenever a problem of any sort arose, whether he was involved or not, and most of the time he was (though this big, good-natured redhead was never cruel or destructive in any way), he was invariably singled out as the culprit. Somehow that crop of flaming hair had the same effect upon people that a red flag has upon a bull. Poor Red, always in trouble, guilty or not.

Now each big tenement building, such as ours, had a janitor, and ours was the most infamous of them all. Actually he was a harmless little hard-working man with a funny little moustache, who always wore the same little gray suit and a faded gray baseball umpire's cap. He looked and walked, like

Charlie Chaplin, and appeared like he was forever muttering under his breath. It was as though he was bemoaning his lot in life; cleaning other people's garbage, washing down marble hallways and stairs, shoveling coal constantly, stoking furnaces, removing the heavy barrels of ashes, and like Tevya, in "Fiddler," he was exhorting God, "Why me?" ... It didn't take God to point out to him that he had a wife and two adult children to support, and this seemingly menial job was providing them all with food to eat and a roof over their heads. And if he blamed his Maker for his sad fate, then he should also have thanked Him for what He had presented to him as a mate.

Mrs. "Pete" (Pete wasn't his real name. It was a nickname that the kids had somehow bestowed upon him, and somehow it seemed to fit, ... like some kind of a cartoon character, "Little Pete.") was a total antithesis of her milquetoast husband. She was tall, burly, big breasted (they hung down to her navel), had large, muscular arms, wore a babushka on her head, and when she got mad she breathed flames. The poor lady, because of her physical assets, did all the heavy work that her husband had signed up for, and when angered, it appeared as though all her pent up emotions, all her frustrations, would erupt in a roar, a sound we overly-playful kids learned to fear. And fear her we did. When Pete would spot a childish "indiscretion," he would react with, "I call da missus," and that would set us all scrambling for the nearest shelter. Her weapons of choice were ashes. She was the one that rolled out the barrels from the cellar, and she had developed a fantastic technique. When she was intimidated, she was able to, with amazing ease and precision, pick a large, half-burnt ash out of a barrel, and hurl it at a fleeing culprit with such accuracy that she could "skull" a kid, on the run, as far as a block away, while, at the same time, yelling profanities at him in Russian. We were a great assortment of fun loving kids, and each and every one of us grew up in mortal fear of those four devastating words, "I call da missus."

It was a lazy mid-summer afternoon and a bunch of us were attending a session at the He-Bo-Be Penthouse, a small tent that we had put together with some tall sticks and old bed sheets, located atop the roof of our five story tenement. He-Bo-Be stood for Herbie, Bobby, and Bernie. Herbie was chubby little Herbie Goldman, a lovable kid who lived on the ground floor of the tenement next door to ours; Bobby was Bobby Christian, a very intense, muscular, continually angry little guy who lived a few blocks away but hung out with us because he was always in the schoolyard, where he seemed to engage himself in his one great big love—football—no matter what time of the year. Bernie Austin, who lived on the ground floor with his exceptionally obese, divorced mom (a generous, beautiful lady), was the president and founder of our newly-formed weight-lifting club. Bernie, whose nickname was "Skinny," looked like his mom, in facial features only, had her same, sweet disposition and kindliness, and he had earned a reputation for miles around for something that was considered a badge of honor among kids. Bernie could belch longer and louder than anyone I had ever known in my life, and he actually trained for that dubious endeavor by consuming unbelievable amounts of carbonated water, in any and all flavors. Many a bet was won by us when we matched him against any "hotshot" from any other neighborhood, ... anywhere.

It was mid-day, and the air was so thick and torrid that, although we were all wearing shorts, and stripped to the waist, we couldn't contain the sweat that consumed us. Hardly a day for lifting weights, but what else was there for us to do? We didn't have the cash to take the subway to the beach. The Dodgers were outta town, so hitching' a ride on Eastern Parkway to Ebbets Field was out of the question. Nothin' wrong with grunting and groaning in the intense heat while jawing about the likes of Whittlow Wyatt vs. Howie Polett, or if DiMaggio is a better hitter than Williams, or was Bob Feller gonna be the greatest pitcher of all time, and movies, and girls, of course, etc., etc., ... not at all a bad way to pass the day.

In addition to the aforementioned officers of the club, there were yours truly (whom Red had recently given a very fancy nickname, "Montague Theobold Van Harris", part of which I retained later on, when I went into show biz); and those ubiquitous "terror twins," Big Red and brother "F.M."

In the midst of all that was going on, Red suddenly announced, "Fellas, I gotta take a crap." "Where?" I asked. "My mother just washed the floor, and just put down the

"Forvitz" (a popular daily Yiddish newspaper that many of the immigrants read.) The paper was actually called "The Jewish Daily Forward" and the back copies were used to cover the floor linoleum (or "oilcloth" as the immigrants used to call it) after it had been washed down. Besides, you'd have to run down four flights of stairs. D'ya think you can make it?" "I doubt it," replied Red. "So whaddya gonna do?" we all chanted. "Don't worry," he answered, "I know what to do." Whereupon he dashed towards the skylight in the center of the roof, continued past it to the other end of the roof, where he found a flattened old gallon oil can (we could never figure out how it had found its way up to our roof), and hastily let down his pants, and proceeded to plant down a large, steaming hot pile right into the can. Then came happily skipping back, quite relieved, to continue with the weights.

Things were humming' along pretty good when, like a bolt out of the blue, the skylight door was suddenly flung open, and onto the roof, in his dusty gray suit, umpire's hat and all, with that unique walk that belonged only to him and Charlie Chaplin, strolled our nemesis, Pete. In typical fashion he peered around, looking desperately for trouble. We reacted indifferently, as though we had nothing in the world to fear, and continued with whatever we were doing. Seeing that he couldn't rile us, he sneered and continued to explore the entire roof. Moments later we heard an anguished cry as he raced back to us, red faced, and screaming in his native tongue, "Der Rayte hut ungekokt afn roof!" Literal translation, "The Redhead shit on the roof!" How in the hell did he know it was Red? Of course the answer was very simple. Anything that was wrong was always blamed on Red. As we stood there terrified, out of the corners of our eyes we caught the stealthy motion of Miltie sneaking behind Pete's back, picking up the "evidence," which was gleaming in the mid-day sun, emitting smoke, and giving off an odor which you didn't have to be a scientist to identify, and quickly and carefully hiding it behind the ledge that separated our roof from the one next door.

Seeing this, we all became animatedly defensive and challenged our oppressor. "Show us! Whaddya talkin' about? Show us da shit!" Pete hastily turned around and fuming, said, "Follow me! I show you." (He spoke English brokenly, but when he had to pour out a number of words in a row, as with so many others like him, he reverted to his native tongue, which was, of course, that colorful, descriptive Yiddish). We followed this funny little man, with his funny little walk, to the spot where he had discovered the "terrible turd," and could barely conceal our laughter when he looked down and discovered that there was nothing there. "Gevalt!" he yelled, "Gegonvet di drek!" "Emescher hut gegonvet di drek!" Literal translation … Gevalt! The shit has been stolen! Someone has stolen the shit! … and then he bellowed the bloodcurdling words that would strike fear into the hearts of wrongdoers everywhere, "I call da missus!" and, hastily, he disappeared down the stairs like Rumplestiltskin in a rage.

What to do? What on earth to do? He went for "da missus"! If she finds the shit we die! Should we all join hands and leap off the roof in one big mass suicide? What should we do? Keep cool. Let level heads prevail. Keep calm. We've got to get rid of the shit … and fast. "Quick, Red, … dump it!" Red picked up the flattened oil can, with the damning plop ticking like a time bomb, and, without a moment's hesitation, just heaved the shit off the can over the side of the roof down into the alley five stories below.

Now as luck would have it, at that very moment down there on street level, Little Artie Tanenbaum was casually strolling into the alley, busily engrossed in reading a copy of the New York Journal, which he had spread out in his hands. We knew that it was the New York Journal because all six sets of eyes that were peering down from atop the roof immediately recognized the red colored headlines that The Journal was famous for. As the shit hit like a bomb, not only did it knock the newspaper out of his hands, pasting it to the ground, but it showered unfortunate Little Artie from head to toe with a vaporous cover that I'm sure he would remember for the rest of his days, and, as he struggled to regain his composure, without even bothering to look up, he raised his right arm in a gesture of defiance, and righteous indignation, and proceeded to yell, at the top of his lungs, "YA RED-HEADED SONAVABITCH!"

With the steady accumulation of good friends, plus all the varied and interesting activities, with John Marshall Junior High School with its magnificent teachers and that magnetic schoolyard serving as a nucleus, for the first time since having left my beautiful Williamsburg, I truly felt at home. No one could ever suspect how I had pined for that once heavenly existence that I had known for the first ten years of my life, though I secretly suspected that my loving mom had always sensed my unhappiness but her burgeoning health problems, had to take precedence, and, by this time she was steadily in and out of hospitals. Fortunately, those times that she was away, with Pop always at work, and unable to attend to us, our devoted relatives stepped in and took us into their homes which were a couple of trolley car rides away. Pop's big brother Abe (a rangy, no-nonsense, but very kind man, with a family of his own to support) owned a house in verdant, middle class Flatbush, and I became his ward if Mom became ill while school was out. On school days we had to stay put, at our own place and fend for ourselves, and I soon became very adept at housekeeping and minor electrical repairs. The small Philco radio in our bedroom became my constant companion. In fact, I soon was able to remember the famous comedians' routines, and even able to do some pretty impressive imitations of those delightful people. I used those routines to entertain family and friends on numerous occasions, including Abe and Dora and their great kids, Rick (who was a superb athlete and, though still a teenager, almost as big as his tall father), and Evelyn (who was my age, and pretty like her mother, and a friendly, happy, animated child). They also had a big old victrola in their finished basement that you wound by hand, with a great assortment of records with which I kept myself amused for hours on end. "Cohen On The Telephone," "Gallagher And Sheen" (Al Sheen was the Marx Bros.' uncle), "Burns and Allen," Al Jolson, Sophie Tucker, etc., etc., etc. So very, very many wonderful artists all, and how I wished that I would some day be accepted into their very special fraternity. How I screamed and rolled on the floor, consumed with unending laughter when I came across a remote recording by some unknown (to any of us) English artist doing a hilarious takeoff of a flatulence competition, announced like a prize fight, which was called "The Crapitation Contest." I memorized every word, and was soon doing it for anyone who would listen, with sidesplitting effects. Throughout my life I must've made hundreds of recordings of that remarkable routine for anyone who would ask. I felt like

Arthur Brisbane. When Mr. Brisbane applied for a job with William Randolph Hearst, Mr. Hearst removed Mr. Brisbane's glasses, knowing that he could not see very far without them, and sent him up to the roof of the tall building that the NY Journal was housed in, and instructed him, "Write me a story about what you see up there." When Brisbane returned, he handed William Randolph Hearst a detailed observation on the habits of the ants that were living on the roof. So it was that if you asked me what it was like to hang out alone in Uncle Abe's cellar, with only a victrola for company most of the time, I could tell you one hell of a fascinating story about making the most out of solitude.

My little brother Joe, on the other hand, stayed with my Uncle Morris and Tante (aunt) Annie. Morris was my mother's handsomest brother, who, when he left Poland, in his youth, stopped off in England, and served a stint with the Royal British Navy before eventually coming to the U.S. ... and what a good looking sailor he must've made. He had an engaging smile, and was not at all shy, but also never flamboyant or foolish. Wherever I went with him, somehow the ladies would always seem to strike up a conversation. He was that charming. I envied Yussel for staying at his rather large apartment (also in Flatbush) because Tante Annie was the most prodigious cook and baker of all time, and their grown children (at least two were already married) showered him with affection and even lavished gifts upon him. Their daughter Lillie bought us both our first set of roller skates, and what an expensive present that was back then. Like Uncle Abe's children, though quite a bit older, Morris' four kids were very kind and very friendly, and, also very able. All four amounted to something. Lillie was a buyer for a retail pharmacy chain, Miriam (called "Mickey") had an excellent job before running off and marrying a Scotsman named Joe, and the boys, Arthur and Charlie (whom we called "Kalman") both became lawyers. Arthur, whose long distance track records when he ran for Newtown High School in Queens, still remain unbroken, later served as the Chairman of the NY State Workmen's Compensation Board under then Gov. Hugh Carey. So Yussel and I were both very fortunate to have such caring relatives, and, in retrospect, each contributed mightily to our development.

5 Murray Grossman

Radio definitely made an everlasting impression upon me, and, although, once I got into show biz I did appear on several variety and talk shows, I'd have given my eye teeth to have worked steadily on radio for the rest of my life, that's how much I loved it. Once I appeared in a comedy spot on NY's "Caravan Of Stars" on WHN, on alternate Sunday afternoons. I had had the privilege of working with some of the most talented radio performers (a number of whom went on to greater heights, both on radio, and later TV, the theater, and even the movies). I couldn't wait to do my routine and watch their amiable announcer Dick DiFritas, explode with laughter at my funny lines. Dick was an inspiration to every comedian that appeared on that show, as was the very capable producer-director, Sholem Rubinstein. That variety show ran longer than any other show of its kind. It went on Sundays at noon, and many New Yorkers still remember that versatile hour, chock full of some of the greatest radio fare ever. Of course, my dream was to appear on Orson Welles' Mercury Theater, but, by the time I became an adult that show was long gone. One of the most memorable announcers on that formidable radio station was Jim Ameche, who was Don Ameche's brother, and, like his famous sibling, he had a most mellifluous voice. When Jim was very young he was the voice of the legendary "Jack Armstrong, The All American Boy." Announcer, Bob Bradley, (out of Cleveland, where he had worked as the color announcer for the great Cleveland Browns football games, and later, when I was doing early TV, he was the announcer on the Jan Bart Show which came on after mine) once told me a most humorous story about the Jack Armstrong radio show: It seems that they hired a new, young, "hotshot" actor for that show, and, in his first appearance, he was supposed to say, "There's Jack, in his plane, and I think he's gonna crack up" ... Only it came out, "There's Jack, in his plane, and I think he's gonna crap up!" There was stony silence as the rest of the cast stood mortified. The momentarily startled director quickly regained consciousness, and gave the young actor the sign to "try it again." And once more the flustered new kid said, "There's

Jack, in his plane, and I think he's gonna crap up," whereupon the frustrated director signaled to the quartet to sing the commercial, and four voices, hardly able to control their laughter, sang, "Ha-ave y-you t-t-ried Wheat-ties ..."

To the best of my recollection, aside from the elementary school plays, plus a huge performance in Yiddish (at the world famous Madison Square Garden in NYC) when I was about six or seven, my first memorable "stand up" which intoxicated me and gave me the urge to go into the business, happened very quickly, and unexpectedly. I hadda be about ten years old at the time. Our class was taken to a Coca Cola bottling plant somewhere in Brooklyn. This was a really big school outing for us kids, especially since a lot of other classes went at that same time. After watching the whole procedure on how Coca Cola is made and bottled, we were all ushered into a large auditorium, given some free samples, and awaited the arrival of one of the company officials who was going to address us. It seemed to be taking a long time for that person to show up, and someone strolled into the front of the room and announced, "Mr. So- and- So is delayed in a meeting, and should be here soon. Is there anyone among you pupils who would be willing to come up here and entertain us until he arrives?" I was actually new, and fairly unknown in the school, and the big talent there was a girl named Alma, who was constantly performing at school, but, somehow, Alma wasn't along on the trip that day, or else she would have been the first to volunteer. Meanwhile, the gentleman's request met with stony silence. I'm not a very religious person, and I have always asked questions regarding the existence of that Supreme Being, but, agnostic or not, I could swear that, at some very critical times in my life, He, or She, has whispered in my ear, and that was the very first time I recall it having happened. Someone, or Something, whispered in my ear (and only I am able to hear it) "Get up on that stage kid," and you can imagine everyone's surprise when this quiet little pipsqueak bounded up on stage, brimming with confidence, and in a very well modulated voice, proceeded to command the attention of every individual in the place. And, the laughs started coming fast and furiously. I had the good sense to stay on just long enough, so as not to overdo it, though I must admit that they were yelling for more when I walked off.

For the love of me, I can't remember the routine I did (borrowed from all those great radio comedians that I had listened to, so attentively, all those many times), but the only joke I remember from that whole appearance, that still stands out in my mind is, (and, with no professional experience, only a damn good sixth sense, which I pride myself at having, to this very day, I actually tailored it), "I have an uncle who has tattoos on his body. On his chest he has a tattoo of a ship on the ocean, and on his Adam's apple he has a tattoo of a sailor, and every time he swallows a sip of Coca Cola, the sailor jumps into the ocean."

There were several other instances when I was the very fortunate recipient of that Supreme whisper in my ear. In my very early years as a professional comedian, I was in my first, of three summer seasons working as a "Social Director" at a small, rather exciting resort hotel, called the Dixie Lake Hotel, in NY's Catskill Mountains. Wherever I spent a summer in that highly exalted, and most important capacity, as part of my contractual arrangement, I insisted that my wife and children be part of the deal. They were to spend the entire time with me, free room and board, and be treated like guests, or else I would not take the job. Actually the management was getting the bargain. Shirley performed in all those hilarious comedy sketches, in both major and minor roles, and proved to be a boon, socially, while also putting her own spin on those popular "game nights," when we weren't doing shows, and all that extra for just room and board. We were a highly valued "team" at the Kenmore, in Kauneonga Lake, before then, and Zalkin's Birchwood Lodge, in Wooodridge after the Dixie Lake, and Lebowitz's Pine View, in Fallsburg, after the Dixie Lake's disastrous fire. In fact, Shirley became the full-fledged emcee, and Social Director at the Pine View when in-house entertainment was no longer in vogue. My arrangement was to accept no salary at all, just room and board for all of us (by then we were six, Shirley and me, plus four children, and a dog, a funny little mutt that we named "Alfie.") I had taught some tricks to Alfie, and he occasionally performed onstage with me. To make up for the lack of remuneration at the Pine View, I had carte blanche to perform at all the many other hotels (on the traveling shows circuit, where I was well paid). I did those highly entertaining old-fashioned comedy sketches and songs that I had become noted for, on those nights that I was not working elsewhere. In addition to performances onstage, I was in charge of their whole social program, conferring with their booking agent, Jack Segal, regarding the selection of incoming performers (among them some of the finest talents in the business, a number of which went on to fame and fortune, and also some of the "not so finest," who were also abundantly available in those halcyon days). I also made certain that the guests were never bored. I prepared all the programs for the entire summer, and also saw to it that the entire social and athletic staff did what they were hired to do. In fact, I hired most of them, and also, whenever necessary, which, fortunately, was not very often, did the firing. Shirley, so beautiful and charming in those glamorous gowns she wore onstage, very soon became the full fledged emcee, a job she excelled at, for the next twenty-five summers at Pine View. Originally, our "athletic director" (a would-be comedian at the time, who was hired to also perform the introductions onstage) did not live up to his "press notices." Mickey Lebowitz, the boss, watched him do his "thing" onstage on that very first show night of the season, and when I returned from my "away job," Mickey greeted me with, "Get him the ... off that stage!" ... This marked the beginning of Shirley Harris' illustrious summer career that, surprisingly, ran a quarter of a century.

Meanwhile, back in those early days at Dixie Lake where one of the advertised activities was "superb fishing on our glorious, picturesque lake," I was doing my utmost to endear myself to management. Funny, each hotel up there had the most colorful owners. I was a neophyte with a great deal of ambition, a minimum of material that I had learned to develop expediently and stretch beyond its limits. I was eager to please, and had no trepidation whatsoever about putting in long, hard hours at my work, ever cognizant of my parental duties. I managed to take many a pail of freshly washed diapers to the clothesline, even in the midst of a long, exhausting rehearsal. The owners of the Dixie Lake in Ferndale, were real "mentschen" (good people) with wonderful dispositions, easy going and cooperative. Legend had it that Buddy Hackett had to be discharged from his job as Social Director two summers before I got there. I can't imagine what he must have done to have the Herring, Chaddock, and Colton families ask him to leave. Most likely it was his inexperience at the time, as Buddy is one able comedian. Sidney Colton was the youngest partner (they were all related to each other) and I used to tell a joke: "I worked at a hotel that had sixteen partners for owners, and they were constantly having trouble with the swimming pool. In the middle of the season they had to drain the pool, and, on the bottom they found three more partners." Sidney was a mild-mannered gentleman who looked like Terry Thomas, sans moustache. He had that wide space between his two front teeth that the British actor was famous for. Unlike Robert Zalkin of the Birchwood Lodge, who was a very excitable, yet lovable tyrant, (who spent the first few hours of every morning loudly cursing in Russian at the next door neighbor's herd of cows that would have the audacity to wander onto his lawn ... a rude wakeup call for all his guests who were unlucky enough to have their windows facing that area); or tough, businesslike Dinah Schumer and her attorney husband Carl, who ran the Kenmore with Carl's jolly, but extremely parsimonious dad, "Pop" Schumer (notorious for cutting the paper napkins in half and serving them to his rather wealthy clientele); or the Lebowitzes of Pine View (a highly educated family that ran a no-nonsense operation); Sidney Colton had an amazing amount of patience and was a hard working gentle man who easily earned everyone's respect. He was a real gem.

The evenings spent in our small playhouse at Dixie Lake were fun-filled in every sense of the word. The guests looked forward to the nightly activities that we had thoughtfully prepared for them, and we made certain that they all got to know each other quite well, and, usually, by the end of a vacation period it appeared as though members of the family were going home. That's how closely knit we all became. And, for the most part, they were all nice people, well behaved, courteous to each other, truly a homogeneous group. There's something to be said about people on vacation. They're generally on their best behavior and very relaxed. The only one that's not relaxed is the Social Director, who is working diligently every moment of every day to make certain that everyone's vacation runs smoothly. That was my job, and I was dedicated to it.

There was one lady, a rather large, beyond middle age individual, who was an annual guest at Dixie Lake, and who spent several weeks there in prime time, when prices were at their highest. I believe she came there with her husband, but we rarely saw him, as the dear lady was a tremendous source of embarrassment to him. It seemed that she was going through some sort of psychological crisis that made her appear like a fool. In all outward respects, the lady was rational and intelligent, but, whenever she would come into the "casino," which was what we used to call the playhouse and hear music, even if it was playing during a show, she would lose herself completely. It was quite a spectacle to see this overweight matron prance about the entire place as though she was Pavlova herself in the middle of a ballet, totally oblivious to any and all, except that when the music ended, she would come out of her trance, and discover that she had become the laughing stock of everyone that was there. Soon all the guests were joking about the "crazy lady," and she decided that I was the instigator, a label I hardly deserved. I was trying my utmost to be compassionate. Obviously this was a person with a definite problem. Soon she made me the object of her scorn, and, while she still evoked derision from the other guests, she decided to complain to the management about this hostility that the Social Director had engineered against her. She demanded that I be relieved of my duties, "or else she will check out and never come back to Dixie Lake again." To me this was a real dilemma. I knew that I was important to the hotel, but the customer is more important, as he's the one who pays the bills. The tension started to increase, and each day she kept asking in the office, "Well, when are you gonna fire him?" while, at the same time, continuing to make a fool of herself nightly. I, being young and spirited, decided that I was not going to take it lying down, even if it meant losing my job and having to pack up my wife and two sons, and going back to our little apartment in hot Brooklyn, in the middle of the summer. The ridiculous situation was steadily becoming worse, and appeared to be headed for a dangerously unpleasant denouement. I decided that, once and for all, I was going to throw all caution to the winds, and finally tell this foolish, mean-spirited woman what I thought of her.

Very early one morning, before breakfast, I was returning from the clothesline behind one of the distant cottages, where I had just hung out the baby Andrew's diapers. As I walked down the path to the main building, with the sun just starting to appear from behind a surrounding hill, I spotted a figure in the distance briskly walking on the path directly towards me. As that person came closer I recognized that it was my nemesis, and I decided that, right then and there, I was going to get everything off my chest and tell her off. I set my jaw and clenched my fists, and psyched myself for the occasion, and that's when it happened. That guiding voice, the same one that inspired me at the Coca Cola outing years before, whispered softly into my ear, "Don't be an idiot. Be nice to the lady," .... and, instead of carrying on like an enraged juvenile, I came face to face with my adversary who appeared as though she was about to bring down the wrath of the gods upon my head. Her lips were drawn downward, there was a bitter scowl upon her face, and just as she was about to let loose her own barrage, I smiled and said, "Good morning. Don't you look so fresh and lovely this morning." In an instant she turned to putty. It was like watching a magical transformation as the startled lady's angry face gradually turned angelic, and in dulcet tones she softly replied, "Thank you." That marked the end of our misunderstanding. She did nothing but praise me from that moment on. Unbelievably, from that instant of "Divine Intervention" she became my biggest supporter, lauding me to all who were in earshot, and, once again, that mysterious Guiding Light came to my aid, bailed me out, and taught me a very valuable lesson that I would remember for the rest of my life.

One of the biggest breaks in my life came about as a result of this mysterious "intervention." It happened at a time when I was already a well-respected entity in the club date field ('club dates" are one nighters, the area of show biz that I have always felt most comfortable with, as opposed to the many horrendous nightclubs that I had to learn my trade in). I had just made a tentative arrangement with an amiable and ambitious young, (believe it or not) part-time rabbi and semi-successful comedian, named Jerry Cutler, whom I had known very casually for a number of years. I was then being managed by another individual who had promised me the moon, and with whom I had signed a three-year contract. Like the others I had dealt with before him, my manager was a good businessman, and pleasant and able enough, but never a career builder. Like the others, he was content to take orders on the telephone for his saleable clients (and I was very high on that list), and content himself with collecting his 15% commission. My contract with him had already expired, but we let things continue as they were without any further discussion, he being reticent about trying to point out, "Look at all I've done for you," and I, fully convinced by then that, the concept of "a manager who does all he can to build a talented client into a star" is nothing but a great big myth.

My manager's office was located on the third floor of one of those renovated old buildings that surround NY's famous landmark (itself renovated several times) Carnegie Hall. On that same floor were several useless cubbyhole offices that were rented out by the realty corporation quite inexpensively, to anyone who didn't have much money to spare and was desperate for an office space at a decent theatrical location. One such cubbyhole was being occupied by this tall, handsomely disheveled young Jerry Cutler. I bumped into him one fateful afternoon as I was getting out of the elevator. "Jerry," I asked, "what brings you to this part of the world?" Last time I had seen him he was catering kosher parties at some old hotel somewhere up on the west side, in the seventies. "Come into my office, if you've got a moment," he replied, and he ushered me into this closet sized space that could barely accommodate the two of us and his desk. "Buddy (meaning Buddy Hackett) staked me to the rent for this place. I'm tryin' to get on my feet as a writer, or a P.R. (Public Relations) man. Got a wife n' three daughters y'know, and I have too much talent to stay in catering. I can always fall back on my rabbinical credentials, but I think I can make it big in this." I laughed, "Jerry, first thing ya gotta do is try to make this poor excuse for an office big." He graciously chuckled at my flip retort, and went on, "I know you've got an agent, and I know that you're bogged down like all the other comics, really goin' nowhere, just being content to make your living. I've always had a great admiration for your abilities.

Would it be against your principles if I tried to do somethin' for you?" "My contract with my agent ended a couple o' months ago," I volunteered, "I'd be delighted."

And so, a relationship began that resulted in some excellent achievements, and, just to point out how stupidly fair I was to all concerned, I continued to pay my commissions to my manager for another couple of months, while, at the same time, giving Jerry Cutler commissions for whatever he added to my income. In other words, I was paying double commissions, and, of course, no one objected, until I smartened up one day and cut out the other guy n' went with Jerry. We did very well together, but that story has to wait till later, much later. What I'm about to relate is one of the incidents that is indelibly inscribed in my memory, and it all came about during that short, exciting period that I enjoyed under the tutelage of the gregarious, "ballsy" Jerry Cutler.

Jerry called me one morning n' said, "Van, Buddy's wife, Sherry, is the head of a philanthropic organization that raises heaps of money to combat a fatal disease that attacks people whose ancestors came from eastern Europe. The disease is called Tay Sachs, and the charity is named after the disease. They're sponsoring an expensive black tie dinner in the grand ballroom of the Waldorf Astoria, and they're honoring Jack Carter, and a lot of notables will be sitting at the dais, and there's room for one more. I've suggested you to Sherry, who doesn't know you, but she's promised to come see you perform somewhere where it's convenient, and, if she likes what she sees, you can fill that vacant chair, ... but we've got to find a convenient place, and very soon." Luckily, I had a club date booked at the Essex House, a famous hotel on the main street in Newark, NJ for the following Saturday night. Some of the biggest affairs in NJ were held at that popular hotel that boasted an excellent grand ballroom. At that time, Newark was still a safe, cosmopolitan city, perhaps the most popular city in all of NJ, and we used to joke about the large neon lights in front of the Essex House. The orange colored lights, contrasted against the night sky, used to blink the words "E-S-S-E-X H-O-U-S-E," on and off for all to see. Only most of the time the "E" and the "S" in the word "ESSEX" were out of commission, so it made for a very attractive, eye catching advertisement, and was much talked about for years. We picked Sherry up in Fort Lee, where she lived, and took her with us to the club date.

It was, as I recall, a foggy, damp night, in early November, and the chill went through your bones. The crowd was large and unruly, and to add to my discomfort, I was in the midst of a full-grown migraine by the time I went onstage. As I was telling my jokes, I was also experiencing a pounding headache and fighting down the bile that was trying to make its way up into my throat. I was a mess, and both Jerry and Sherry recognized it. I was surprised when, while driving Sherry back home, undoubtedly based upon pity, more than anything else, the dear lady said, "Van, I'm looking forward to having you seated at the dais at the Jack Carter dinner, ... and I want your wife, and Jerry's wife to also come along as our guests. At that moment I could have thrown my arms around her and kissed her, but I left the "thank you's" to Jerry, who was quite adept at such matters. I was doing all I could to try to stay alive long enough to take Jerry back to Manhattan and then take Sherry to Fort Lee, and then come back home again.

The big dinner was a lavish affair on a festive Sunday evening with a great deal of excitement in the air. The dais was brimming over with celebrities and I was off to one end, one of the lesser known, but obviously important speakers. The late William B. Williams was the very witty toastmaster, and among the others were: the ubiquitous Milton Berle ("Uncle Miltie" himself), Alan King, Johnny Carson (who came a little late), Bobby Darin, Frank Gifford, and a host of other stars in the field of entertainment and sports. Buddy Hackett was not there but sent greetings from the coast. Jack Carter sat next to the toastmaster, beaming from ear to ear, while I was way over on the far side, sandwiched in between avuncular Al Kelly, the renowned double talker, and the huge Texan Kyle Rote, who was then winding up his illustrious career with the NY Football Giants. To coin an old burlesque phrase that I had heard so often from my wonderful mentors in Dubrow's, "only my laundry man knew how scared I was." Meanwhile, sensing my unease, dear, kind, Mr. Kelly (whose real name was Kalish) kept patting me on the head, assuring me, in his own inimitable way, "Don't worry boobele, you're gonna do just great" (and as much as I tried to listen, he could have been doing his double talk specialty, which he actually did later in the program with uncanny success). Rote, on the other hand, approached my nervousness from a different angle entirely. He kept pouring whiskey into my glass saying, "Here kid, drink this. It'll relax you." Between the sincere help I was getting from these two good Samaritans, I had my hands full trying to do all that I could to stay alert and sober and keep an eye, and an ear, on all that was going on, so that I could endeavor to come up with a quick opening that would be an immediate attention grabber, and, at the same time, endear myself to this professional and sophisticated audience. I kept wondering if my darling Shirley and my dear pal Jerry were feeling my pain vicariously, somewhere out there in the crowd. And, also, I didn't even know the guy they were honoring, Jack Carter.

The festivities began with the great Willie B., after a resounding bit of recognition from the audience, welcoming all in attendance, and saying, "Ladies and gentlemen, I approach the task of honoring Jack Carter with the enthusiasm of a gynecologist who is about to examine Phyllis Diller," which brought down the house immediately. "Calling Jack Carter – The Man Of The Year, is like calling Belle Barth – The Nun Of The Month," and on and on it went with the laughter increasing in hilarity. Next came a beautiful stint by poor Bobby Darin, whose future looked incredible at that time, as, in addition to his recording successes, he was already acting in movies. There were a number of others who lent their unique talents to the party, and Al Kelly just mesmerized 'em as they struggled to try to figure out what on earth he was talking about. I looked up at one point and saw Tom Poston turning blue, he was laughing so hard. And all the while the turbulence in my stomach was rising to a fever pitch as the time for me to go on grew ever closer.

Now came one of the long awaited highlights of the evening ... the great Milton Berle. Uncle Miltie approached the microphone with a yellow legal pad and a pencil, in his hand, with his famous, wonderfully aromatic cigar glowing in the forefront and proceeded to read off a list of fictitious congratulatory telegrams, mugging appropriately after the reading of each one, and tearing off the page and tossing it over his shoulder. He began with "Here's one from Lyndon Johnson (who was then still finishing out his full, elected term in office, and who was widely known for his openly unashamed toilet behavior), and it says, 'Dear Jack, would love to be there with you to celebrate the momentous occasion, but I'm busy takin' a crap!'" ... then the appropriate mug, as only Berle can get away with, followed by a huge scream from the audience. He continued on ... "Here's one from Darryl Zanuck in Hollywood, 'Dear Jack, would love to have been there but would rather stay home n' watch Ed Sullivan, who's funnier than you are anyway.' ... And here's one from Laurence Harvey ... (and he used an "inside" joke here)... 'Dear Jack, would have loved to have been with you tonight, but I'm a-broad!'" ... and the roars continued. Then he got serious and there was a sudden hush over the audience, as he read, "Dear Jack, you're a real credit to your profession: The envy of every great comedian in the whole wide world. You are a true master, and a great human being, and I couldn't think of anyone more deserving of this prestigious award than you. You are my idol and the idol of all time." Then Berle studied the fictitious telegram that he had just read so seriously, and, in an inquiring tone he read the name of the sender ... "Murray Grossman???" The timing was superb. It took just a moment for the audience to realize that Berle had added a fictitious, unknown name as the "adulator," and the entire house caved in. Like the true master that he was, once again Berle did what was expected of him, and superbly.

Now came the moment I had dreaded. It is my personal opinion that many stars can be sadistic S.O.B.'s. I'm not insinuating that such was the case in this instance, but what else could it have been to throw me to the lions on the very heels of the major triumph of the evening? In a casual, almost indifferent manner, as if to imply, "Go ahead kid, it's time to die," the inimitable toastmaster announced, "And now ladies and gentlemen, here's a fairly new guy in the business (and I swear, that was about all the buildup I was given) ...Van Harris!" The drums were pounding in my ears, which, in retrospect must've been the echoes of my heart beating a-mile-a-minute. My eyes appeared to be spinning like twin cyclones as I struggled to my feet, attempting to steady my legs as I took that long walk from the other end of the dais to the "electric chair," and all the while I kept thinking to myself,

"Why the hell did I let Rote keep filling my glass?" And, in the distance I could've sworn that Al Kelly was still consoling me with, "Don't worry boobele, you're gonna do just great." I tried to appear nonchalant and composed as I struggled to the mike, when, in reality, as they say in the business when one is confronted by such a seemingly insurmountable obstacle, "I didn't know whether to shit ... or go blind!" Slowly, and deliberately, I cradled the mike in the palm of my hand. All eyes were upon me ... and then came that marvelous, mysterious whisper in my ear, with Divine instructions. I looked directly into the eye of the storm and said, "Ladies and gentlemen, ... I don't even know the guest of honor. I'm a friend of Murray Grossman!!!!" ... The pause ... the laughter broke out like a tidal wave ... and all that followed was a piece of cake.

Back to my youth in Crown Heights. It was fun growing up in that lovely kaleidoscope of mostly good, hard working people of all ages, all sharing the same joys and sorrows, with all, more or less, on the same low, but livable economic level, with hopeful parents inspiring their beloved children to go onto bigger and better things. Such a varied assortment of great kids, all instructed by their truly interested teachers, along with their loving parents, to attempt to live by the golden rule, avoid violence, and, above all, obey the law. The local candy and newspaper stores were where we kids usually hung out, and where we were tolerated by the friendly storekeepers, to a point. When we got too noisy and rambunctious, we were asked to leave, and, as much as we protested, we did as we were told, or else suffer the consequences when we got home. Everyone seemed to know everyone else's business, on the surface at least, and word of bad behavior got around very quickly. That is not to say that there weren't instances of disrespect, but, for the most part, our neighborhood, with Rochester Ave. as the epicenter, could only be described as a "damn nice neighborhood," and we were all exceedingly proud and happy to be living there.

Our own family was in that transitional stage where we were getting off Home Relief. (Oh, how I hated walking home from the Home Relief Bureau on Fulton St. before the Passover holidays, carrying those telltale shopping bags filled with matzos and brown eggs, along with the other free holiday goodies that were a dead giveaway that we were charity recipients, and I would dodge behind a fence or into a hallway, if I would see anybody that might recognize me). Any money that I could earn and contribute to our household was greatly appreciated. Since I needed time for homework, and I was actively engaged in virtually all the seasonal sports that were played in that great schoolyard, I had to find a way to squeeze in time to work.

Big George (he was getting grownup enough by then for us to address him by his true name, instead of "Red") had a deal going with Yamo, the newspaper distributor. They needed a kid to deliver the Sunday early editions to the storekeepers on Saturday nights on busy, bustling Pitkin Ave. I received all of two cents per paper as my compensation, but I was allowed to solicit people on the street, so I carried exceptionally heavy loads, and, by golly, by the end of the night, I actually wound up with some paper money. On Saturday nights, in any and all kinds of weather, Pitkin Ave. was almost the exclusive domain of yours truly, Big George, and "Stinkweed" (a kid named Harvey whom we others had sadistically given that terrible nickname because he had difficulty controlling his elimination, both solid and liquid), and who was only too delighted to become the third member of the "Saturday Night Pitkin Ave. Newspaper Deliverers Brigade."

I was always into reading about good health. In fact, I started doing calisthenics upon arising, at the age of nine, and I make it a point not to miss a morning, in sickness or in health, no matter where I'm at, to this very day. I can't say that everything I read about fitness is factual. For example, I read, a long time ago, a quote from one of the Baseball Hall Of Fame outfielders, that he keeps his eyes in excellent condition by looking directly up into the sun, without sunglasses, when he's out in the field, so I emulated him. Result? I developed cataracts at a very early age. I'm a strong believer in good diet, and I had read that carrots are very beneficial to good vision, so I decided that a raw carrot a day would be a good habit to get into, and that became a long standing routine. Result? It didn't do anything to make my eyes stronger, in fact, it gave my skin a pale orange pallor, a result of too much carotene. But, because of that carrot habit I got to know Rosie.

Rosie was Max Vinitzky's other half, the colorful owners of Vinitzky's Fruit And Vegetable Emporium, located in the heart of Rochester Ave. She was the most kind-hearted lady I had ever known. The two of them operated the busiest store of its kind in the neighborhood, working seven long days a week, and barely making a living because they virtually gave everything away. They had earned the respect of all who dealt with them because of their unquestioned honesty. Max was about as eccentric a man as you would ever want to meet. He had boyish good looks to go with his noticeable Yiddish accent, and had a naive curiosity about everything and anything. If a customer would complain about the appearance of, let's say, a tomato, by saying something like, "It looks a little soft," he would immediately lower the price. And the stuff he brought back to the store from the wholesale market was prime quality. He had an excellent eye for produce, and shopped later than all the other retailers so that he could buy cheaper, and thereby sell cheaper, but his being such a soft touch had a nullifying effect on his profits. As much as the vociferous, outspoken Rosie, his devoted and long suffering wife, would try to keep him in line, it was, as the old expression goes, "like talking to the wall." Rosie was a bit on the plump side, had a beautiful face with a very sweet nature that made her that much more lovable, but when she lost her patience with him, which was becoming more and more frequent, you could hear her bellow as far away as Coney Island, which was really far away. She too, was as big a "pushover" as he was. There were no two finer people in the whole world than those two, but you'd never know it to hear them argue. As my own dear mother, along with so many of their other customers, would point out, "no husband and wife should be working in the same business together."

Directly across the street from Vinitzky's store was Bennie's Barber Shop. It wasn't a very fancy place, but Bennie did a brisk business, and, among his assortment of male customers were the local "bookies" and their numbers runners. It was a good place for them to congregate, as from Bennie's storefront windows they had a birds eye view of the entire street. Now Max, as I mentioned earlier, stayed later than most in the wholesale market, and, whereas the normal fruits and vegetables dealers would be back from market in the very early hours of the morning, Max could always be seen casually driving down the Rochester Ave. hill (with hordes of impatient women, visibly annoyed, waiting on the curb in front of the store), in the middle of the afternoon. He would pass the store and go onto the next corner, make a u-turn, and smilingly pull up in front of the place, and not turn off the engine on his well-worn Chevrolet workhorse until he got his right rear wheel exactly into a groove in the road that was there for years due to an oversight by the road workers who had paved the street. Across the street at Bennie's, the Venetian blinds were drawn because the sunlight was streaming into the large windows that time of the day, and if you looked real hard, you could see small separations in the blinds, with eyes peering through from behind them. The bookmakers were taking bets from the other customers, guessing as to how many times the eccentric Max would go up and back until he finally got that rear right wheel into the groove. The banshees were screaming for him to stop the truck and come into the store already, and Rosie's authoritative voice was booming above all the others, sternly admonishing him for his constant tardiness.

I had made a deal with Rosie that I could pick out the biggest and best carrot in the bunch, for which, to the best of my recollection, I gave her the tidy sum of one penny, and she'd always throw in an extra one "for later." It was while I was still attending junior high school, probably my last year there before going on to my beloved Thomas Jefferson High School, which was so far away, that I stopped off at the store for my usual carrot, and, as I was reaching into my pocket for the penny, Rosie casually asked me, "How would you like to get your carrots for free ... and make some money besides?" That was her way of inviting me to work at the store, a job that I readily accepted, and continued to work at dedicatedly, with a good deal of sacrificing the leisure time I had previously enjoyed. I worked there from then on and all through high school. (In addition to my salary, on payday, which was after a long, concentrated Sunday morning, Max would fill up several poultry bags with all kinds of fruits and vegetables to take home to my family.) This marked the beginning of a relationship that was destined to last much, longer than I could, in my wildest dreams, ever anticipate.

Vinitzky store bicycle delivery. Rochester Ave. (1940)

6 Shirley

An incident that is indelibly embedded in the recesses of my memory, occurred one day, after school, in front of Rumish's candy store, down the block from the fruit store. I don't remember if it was Rumish that had the candy store at that time, or Sandick. These people were all very important to us kids, as they were the proprietors of our unofficial "clubhouse" and had to have a world of patience. It was no profession for anyone with a "short fuse." We kids were terribly trying on their nerves. The longevity of the average candy store keeper couldn't be too long, as just how much crap can you take from kids? And, as kids go, as pointed out before, we were a fairly decent lot. These stores were husband and wife operations, and they all had kids of their own, who were generally older than we, and always, mercifully for them, out of sight. They didn't have to suffer those long, grueling hours along with their hard working parents. Anyway, the Rumishes were there before the Sandicks, and both families survived for a longer than usual period of time. I don't remember which family owned the store at the time, and, quite frankly, it really doesn't matter too much, except for authenticity, yet whoever owned the store at the time had nothing to do with what I'm about to describe, which is no earthshaking happening anyway, only somehow it will live on in my mind into eternity.

I don't recall just what kind of day it was, or even what time of the year it was. All I can remember is that I rounded the corner and saw a crowd of kids gathered around as a bunch of boys, a bit younger than I, were teasing the prettiest little girl that I had ever laid my eyes on. I think they had removed her hat and were passing it around. She was such a feisty kid, didn't cry, or get flustered, just proceeded to punch her tormentors, one at a time, and even a few together, until she got her hat back, and they scattered. My brother was watching all this with me, and he was getting the same kick out of the scene that I was. I asked him, "Joe, who is that adorable girl?" and he replied, "Oh, that's Shirley Vinitzky, and she's in my class at school. Quite a girl, eh?"

That was the very first time that I had ever seen Shirley Vinitzky. I was, perhaps, all of twelve, and she was about ten. I never forgot that little girl, and, of course, as time went on I would see her in the store after I began working there. She certainly was a beautiful child, but I had much more on my mind than girls for the moment, being a lot more concerned with survival and what the future had in store. She, being younger and a lot more carefree, was doing whatever her own thing was, and she would certainly brighten the atmosphere every time she would walk in. As time went by, I learned that she played the violin, and I saw that she was not lacking for company. She had lots of friends, and I think that every boy in the neighborhood was after her. She was very bright, and obviously, very popular. She also blossomed into an excellent dancer, and as she got a little older, she, and her then "steady" soon became recognized as perhaps the best dancers in the entire neighborhood. When I graduated from Thomas Jefferson High School at age sixteen, I asked her to be my date on "class night', and we went to Coney Island with Harold Brooks and his date. We all had such a good time that we stayed out until five in the morning with nary a word of admonition from her parents. In the wildest stretches of my imagination would I ever have dreamt, at that moment, that that lovely child, Shirley Vinitzky (the charming young lady with the steady boyfriend) would someday become my wife, the greatest love of my entire being, to cherish and adore, forever and ever, and evermore. I'm still amazed at how that all came into being. Fate and circumstances play major roles in our lives and the serious business of love and marriage occurred quite a bit later on, so I will have to come back to that after I have established what further developed in the critical time of our young lives, I going one way, and Shirley another, until that magical moment.

After I had graduated from high school, I attended Brooklyn College, evenings, while I got a full time job as a law clerk for the former Commissioner of Accounts of the City of New York. The Japanese had bombed Pearl Harbor and we were involved in a war. I was only sixteen at the time, and I went to work for the richest man I'd ever met. His law firm was located on the thirty-third floor of the Woolworth Building, one of the original skyscrapers. I was replacing the

High School Graduation (1941)

clerk who was moving on. (I don't recall if he was joining another law firm, or going into the armed forces.) I still chuckle when I think of part of the instructions that he left for me, "... air mail letters are picked up every evening at five ... be on the roof by a quarter to five, ready to meet the plane." For a sixteen-year-old kid, street smart as I may have been, this was a whole new world to me, and I was anxious and willing to please. The partners in the firm were most gracious and kind, and I tried to learn as much as I could, as quickly as I could ... all for the huge sum of fifteen dollars a week, in return for five (sometimes five and a half) days of work. I gave fourteen of those dollars to my parents, keeping a dollar for myself. Mom always prepared lunch for me to take along to work. Subway fare was ten cents each way, so I broke out even. If I needed any extra money, Mom would always provide. I learned to use the monitor board, which was what we used instead of a switchboard, and actually enjoyed immersing myself into this new existence. Oh, Mom also gave me money back for my fare to my evening classes and a few extra cents for "mad money." I soon discovered that I was much too young to be attending college as everyone there was older and more sophisticated (to a degree), and I also found that I could not concentrate on doing my homework while trying to give my employers a full measure for their money, especially with the witch of an executive secretary who appeared to be perpetually unwell, and rode roughshod over the sixteen year old, inexperienced law clerk. She was a horror. That was my first brush with an extremely nasty superior whose deliberate provocations startled me. I shall never know what prompted the poor young lady to act as she did, but she certainly had a bearing upon my future. She, and the fact that I felt as though I was wasting my time in school, were sufficient reasons for me to consider going elsewhere for employment.

At Brooklyn College, a number of my professors were interesting and dedicated, but they were overshadowed by a couple of louts who, rather than teach, spent a good deal of the time posturing, and reminding us of how intelligent they were. To this very day, it never ceases to amaze me as to how many people, as qualified for their jobs as they may seem, lack that all important ingredient called "dedication," and for reasons that elude me, seem to get away with murder. And so I bid adieu to both Brooklyn College and a possible career in law. Now, so very many years later, in thinking things over and considering how well I seem to be able to handle the "tools" I have, thankfully, been blessed with, I might have made a damn good lawyer at that (and the lawyers I had worked for implored me to stay on), but I have no regrets about what I eventually chose as a career.

My eldest son, our first born, Dan, is a teacher, ... and what a teacher he is! He is the consummate teacher, ... gentle, communicative, ...and patient, ...ever so patient. He is currently a research scientist, employed by the United States Navy. He has written books on analytical chemistry, and his most recent tome is among the most popular of all college textbooks on that subject and is currently going into its fifth revised printing, and is translated into numerous languages. Before going to work for Uncle Sam, he taught at U.C. Davis. Talk about dedication, I watched him in action. Besides having a marvelous sense of humor (I dare you ... go make chemistry funny!), he took the liberty of photographing all of the two hundred and fifty students in his class, boys and girls from all over the globe, and memorized each individual's first, and last, name, and every conversation in class between the professor and the student was on a familiar one-to-one basis. Shirley and I marveled at his ability. That's what you call a teacher! A true educator.

In the early 70's, Dan was also the president of the Flying Club, while attending his graduate classes at Caltech, and had logged many, many hours of single engine flying, and had his Instrument Rating and Instructor's License. Dan was teaching a fellow student, and new club member at Caltech, how to fly, in the club's Cessna 150 in the area surrounding Riverside, CA. Dan was very thorough, and had the student at the controls doing takeoffs and landings over and over again. On their umpteenth takeoff, the small plane did not successfully climb out, and it crashed into a mountain. Miraculously, they both survived, but barely, at the time. Fortunately, a private pilot who had been flying in the vicinity saw the plane go down and called for help. The rescuers came in and rushed them both to a hospital. The student had serious head damage and his surgeon brother flew in from

Little Rock, AR. and, just like you see in the movies, operated on him, and saved his life. Dan shattered the fourth lumbar in his back and had been taken to Riverside General Hospital, paralyzed from the waist down.

We were awakened very early in the morning by a call from his wife Sally describing what happened, and updating us on Dan's condition, which was grim. Shirley and I caught our breath and nervously formulated our plan of action. Our situation at home was like this: David, our youngest son, was away at school in Oregon. Andrew, our middle son, was at school in Pittsburgh. That left ten year old Madelaine at home with us, so we could get one of our aunts, or cousins, or other family, to stay with her while we scoot out to California. One problem, I was scheduled to open on the following evening in a nightclub in Chicago. I had signed a contract. Oh hell, I could call the agent out there and inform him as to what happened, and he'd get a replacement for me. I had to wait a bit to call him 'cause Chicago was an hour behind our time, and we phoned the airlines to make the arrangements.

My call to the agent in Chicago was met by polite sympathy, and an exclamation that it would be impossible for me to cancel, "as people have already made reservations based upon my appearance, etc." Shirley and I looked at each other in amazement, and, with no time to spare, we decided that she would leave as quickly as possible for the west coast, and I would go to Chicago to fulfill my obligation, and, if necessary, depart from there for California. With very heavy hearts, and with Madelaine crying quietly in the background (we assured her that Dan was in good hands and implored her to "keep her chin up") we continued to formulate our plans.

Shirley was met at the airport by Sally, and her aunt, arrangements were made for Shirley to stay at her aunt's next door neighbor's home (a most gracious, middle aged couple), and they whisked her right over to Riverside General. As Shirley described the scene at the hospital to me, "There was Dan, lying there, pale, bandaged, and swollen, with apparatus all around him, and assorted tubes connected into various parts of his body. He managed a weak smile as a greeting to his loving mother, who was struggling so hard to maintain her composure, and, though, he was unable to move from his waist down, he did manage to respond, weakly, and as best he could, with his arms, as she bent over to kiss him.

Meanwhile, back in cold Chicago, I was met at the plane by my dear old, corpulent, trumpet-playing pal, Leroy Altosino, a great musician whose father was also a trumpet player, and he offered his sincerest sympathy. I had called ahead to tell him I was coming, and explained what had happened, and he volunteered to help me get set up in a motel, rent a car, etc. We drove to a motel near the nightclub, leaving the car rental for the following day, and, as I started to unpack my bags, with the tears rolling down my cheeks, dear old Leroy put his big, beefy arms around me, and said, "Van, I can't leave you alone like this. My mom is crippled by arthritis and can hardly attend to her housework, but it would do her a world of good if you stayed with us, and Johnny (his father) and my sister would be thrilled to have you livin' at the house with us, while you're here, provided you make 'em laugh once in awhile." I could have kissed him right then and there. His generous invitation was the most marvelous thing that could have happened, feeling as downcast as I did, and to this very day I am grateful for the existence of people like big, affable Leroy Altosino. Leroy had to be a three hundred pounder, two hundred of which must have been his big heart alone, and did he ever laugh, loudly and enthusiastically, and the rest of his family were just like he was. What a pleasure to have been in the company of such a delightful group. And, I fulfilled my contract at the club, where business was terrible, and was flabbergasted when the manager of the club said to me, as he was thanking me for a job well done, "Didn't the agent tell you that we would have preferred that you open a week, or two, later, as we're too close to the holidays and it's a very slow time?"

Meanwhile, out in Riverside, Shirley learned that Dan would be placed in a Stryker frame because his back was broken, and the pain was so severe that he was unable to have anything pressing on it. Sen. Ted Kennedy had once recovered from a similar mishap in a small plane, and was also was in a Stryker frame, which is like a soft cocoon that comforts, instead of putting pressure on the accident victim. The only previous time that I had heard of that particular apparatus was when I had read about Kennedy's plane crash.

Dan was now lying in the hospital with the doctors observing him and pondering their next move. When asked what they intended to do, they replied, "We noticed that one of his toes moved, so we must wait and see what happens next."

After returning from the hospital, that evening the family sat around at Sally's grandmother's house discussing all that was happening. Fate was playing a hand that night. Sally's grandmother was suffering from a cold, and her family doctor made a house call and joined in the conversation. Shirley asked him for advice, and he replied, "If that was my son, I'd get him out of that hospital immediately and move him into another hospital where he can be looked at by the very best orthopedist and neurosurgeon in the whole area, and he gave her instructions as to how to proceed. The very next day Shirley did as the family doctor had suggested and could barely breathe when the Chief of Staff at the hospital he was in, took it as a personal affront, pleading with her to let Dan remain where he was. As Shirley describes it, in retelling the story, "I felt as though I was going to faint when the Chief of Staff was pleading for me to change my mind, and prayed that I was doing the right thing."

Dan was examined by the aforementioned specialists, and they performed eight tense hours of surgery upon him, cautioning Sally and Shirley, beforehand, that, "He may never walk properly again; he may never eliminate properly again, and may need a bag; he may never be able to father a child, etc." It still brings tears to her eyes whenever Shirley describes the scene. Dan came out of it all much better than expected. Though it took a long time to recover his ability to walk, his determination, coupled with concentrated physical therapy, and a healthy healing process, eventually put him back on his feet, and he resumed a normal life. The only reminders of his accident now, are the braces he wears on his legs because nerve damage left him with what's known as a "dropped foot," a condition that requires a little prosthetic help, and his back has a tendency to stiffen if he skimps on the exercising that has always been a way of life with him. And, to prove to us that he was well again, as soon as he felt up to it, he came to New York, rented a small, single engine plane, and took his mother and his siblings on a sightseeing tour. And, oh yes, he is now the father of two fantastic sons.

Back to Chicago, Shirley and I had a tearful reunion when she stopped off in Chicago on her way home from California, and I told the agent what I thought of his greed and callousness, and he and I became estranged. Once again I must refer to my old pal Barney, of Dubrow's Round Table days, and his fabled observation, "Time is a great healer ...but a lousy beautician!" ... and, after many years have gone by, we've become friends again, and are still doing business. Show biz! Spit in yer face and ya think it's raining! The show must go on ... Why? 'Cause if it doesn't, ya don't get paid!

7 First Break

During my teenage years, with the war rapidly proliferating and more and more young men being called up for military service, naturally, the job market was being thrown wide open. We "depression babies" were so conditioned, that we didn't dare leave our employment without another job waiting. References were lightly taken, as the need for manpower took precedence. Then again, when an employer is interested in obtaining a young employee, what possible experience could he expect? Such was the case when my uncle Ben, who was a successful fur manufacturer, recommended me for a job to be trained as a shipping clerk for a successful Manufacturer's Representatives firm. The job started at ten dollars a week more than I had been getting as a law clerk, and the owners of the firm were very decent people and good instructors, and I was a quick and able learner. The job entailed more than just wrapping packages. It required trips into the surrounding fur market, acquainting one's self with the various manufacturers, learning about the quality of the product, and even waiting on buyers when everyone else was busy. And busy they were because more and more women were working all over the country, and, with their newly found earning power, they were rewarding themselves for their hard labor with luxury items like furs. Of course it became a field day for the sales of cheap, perishable furs, like "mink-dyed rabbit," which the fur people called "'cooney." Cooneys were selling by the millions. I learned a lot about business practices, human nature, skullduggery, lasciviousness, and lots more. That does not mean to imply that all this is the norm, but it sure opened my eyes as to what to look out for in the mercantile world. It was a helluva lot more educational than that cubbyhole at the law office where the only real excitement was the bitch yelling.

In addition to everything else, I was becoming keenly aware of what makes people laugh. Once again, when I stepped into a departing employee's shoes (Benny the clerk had been drafted into the army), I found a whole new list of instructions like: "Each morning, go out n' get a pound of steam," (which I caught onto almost immediately), and, "Get yourself a left-handed kyle turner which makes packing

79

neater and easier." I'm sure it caused a great deal of laughter at my expense when I nearly went crazy asking everyone where I could find a left-handed kyle turner. The atmosphere was busy, and with some exceptions, it was fun, and I even did a little "moonlighting" in my spare time, like helping a manufacturer of Persian lamb coats, curl his fur pieces. It was my first insight into how the unsuspecting public can be duped, and taught me the very valuable lesson that it's truly rare when one gets a bargain, and the poor get screwed the most, by the smart-ass schemers in their own ranks who profess to know it all. In the case of the curly lambskins, that fairly durable and not inexpensive fur should have a good, tight natural curl that keeps its shape under all conditions: the tighter the curl, the more valuable the fur, hence, the higher the cost. However, there are Persian lamb coats, sold much more cheaply to the bargain hunter, that are made from very inferior, hybrid skins, and the wily manufacturer will curl those flatter skins with a hot iron. When the wearer, who has already purchased the coat and knows only that she got a real bargain on a Persian lamb, goes out in the rain or snow with that stylish garment, the curls uncurl, leaving the poor lady flustered and in tears.

It was, in the time that I worked at Samilson-Romer (where both partners were gregarious, generous, and delightful men) that I learned that women in the workplace have to be constantly on their guard. We employed a few models and secretaries. There were always those salesmen, buyers, and customers, good family men, who figured, "Why not? Let me try to cop a feel, or more, between the coat racks," and there were those girls who truly resented it. (Some were married women trying to earn a living.) The smart ones were the ones that learned to put their potential molesters in their place, deftly, and diplomatically. It was a constant struggle, but nobody lost her job, and nobody was raped. Once a girl got the hang of "self defense," verbally, or physically, or both, she survived, and fairly peacefully. But, until that knack was acquired, it was truly a nerve wracking experience. Conditions like this have always existed, unfortunately, and males have their own pitfalls to avoid in the workplace everywhere, but to this seventeen year old kid, the shuffling of the feet, the soft squealing of voices, the sound of a hard slap in the face, all going on behind those coat racks, it was another lesson in growing up.

I became so proficient at my work that I soon was promoted to "assistant to the buyers," with more time out on the street, and I even had a hand in getting people to replace me in the busy shipping room. Replacements were at a premium, as more and more young men were going into the armed forces. Luckily for us though, there were still a few around who were very young and as capable as I, like Herbie, and Iggy, and, until we were called to military duty, we were all able to fill the bill. Much to my pleasant surprise, Shirley Vinitzky, who was rapidly blossoming into a slender beauty, got a job as a model, down the street, and you can imagine how delighted I was when she'd accept my offer of a malted milk at Shapiro's, every once in awhile on a lunch break. Still, she was someone else's steady, and I recognized that, and our relationship remained purely platonic and friendly.

My time for conscription was rapidly approaching. Shirley's brother Herman, older than I by a couple of years, had applied for enlistment in the Marine Corps. He'd been rejected because of color blindness (something we inherit from our mothers, I'm told), went into the Army Air Corps instead, and, after basic training, was on his way to the European Theater of Operation on a huge troop ship. On the way, the ship was intercepted by a German submarine and blown out of the water. From what I remember of the incident, he was among the survivors who clung perilously to floating debris in the water until they were rescued. It was a major tragedy. Many, many lives were lost. He was reassigned to another group and spent the rest of his army career in China under the command of the hero, Gen. Chennault, who was in charge of the China-Burma-India operation.

Funerals were becoming more frequent in our neighborhood. The Jews were paying their respects for their fallen neighbors in the churches, and the Italians were saying their last goodbyes in the synagogues to their former teammates and friends. The realities of war were really hitting home. My fellow sports team members of the Hurons, a few who were a bit older than I, were going into the service, one by one. Shirley's "steady," Bobby Spencer, enlisted in the Navy. Little by little the neighborhood was being emptied of men. My "Greetings" arrived in the mail, and I reported to Grand Central Palace in New York City. I found myself in the company of a number of people that I knew from the neighborhood and previous neighborhoods. Among them was Frayim, one of the most sardonic kids I had ever known. Even when he was a very little boy, he never smiled. He certainly was a strange one, that Frayim. It was common knowledge that he had had a very unhappy home life. Yet we accepted him into our social circle. He was openly outspoken about his poor relations with his overtly strict parents, but we all agreed that, that was his problem, and as much as we sympathized with him, it was not ours to deal with.

The procedure was that, if you were accepted into the military, after taking thorough physical and mental examinations, you were given about two weeks to clean up your affairs before reporting to a designated reception center. If you were rejected they would also inform you of that. The categories were as follows: "1A" meant you were in. "4F" meant you were out. "1AL" meant that you were, due to some deficiency, accepted for "limited service," but free to go back home until recalled at a later date "at their discretion." If you knew of any "disabilities" that you may have, then you were instructed, beforehand, to bring written (medical history) evidence of same. I had had a chronic problem with my left ankle which was injured in a fall when I was about eleven, and which presented me with no end of pain and discomfort until I graduated from high school and found the time to have it surgically corrected. The doctors told me that the foot would never, ever be entirely like new, so I came armed with that information. I also had a vision problem, correctable with glasses, and the two "handicaps" placed me into the "1AL" category. I was instructed to return home and go about my business until they would call me back, which turned out to be much later than I had ever expected, and resulted in my not being conscripted into the army until the war was over.

There was a huge bank of public telephones located in one of the marble hallways of Grand Central Palace. Naturally, as soon as the potential inductees learned what their fate was going to be, the rush to the telephones was on. Just like the scene we've seen so often in the movies when a big trial is over, and the reporters have to phone in their stories to their newspapers, so it was with all of us. We were anxious to inform our loved ones, who were waiting with baited breath and palpitating hearts, to hear what had happened. Frayim had gotten to the last available phone, and while a number of us, his erstwhile friends, clustered around awaiting our turn, we overheard Frayim, who had just been rejected, blurting out to his overwrought mother, in his usual, unemotional monotone, "Ma, say goodbye. I've been drafted and I've got only a couple of days before I leave for the army." That was it! Curt and devastating! The wailing coming from the other end was ear-splitting, and Frayim aimed the ear piece in the direction of just about everyone assembled so that they had to hear the sustained shrieking and crying. After awhile, when he felt that we had heard enough of his mother's uncontrollable sobbing, he abruptly slammed down the receiver, much to everyone's astonishment. "Frayim," I said, as he stood there calmly, "you're 4F! You've been rejected! Why the hell did you tell your mother you've been accepted?" Barely looking at me, with eyes casting down at the floor, he blurted out, "Let her suffer ... she's a sneak." I don't remember ever seeing Frayim again after that, and I'm not even going to try to dissect his peculiar behavior psychologically. From what we all knew, this was very much like him, and although shocking, not entirely unexpected. In fact, we were all so young, and in our immaturity we found it hilarious, and for years afterward, at parties and other social gatherings, someone would always break up the crowd by lowering his eyes, and, in that recognizable monotone, recite, "Let her suffer ... she's a sneak!"

The younger kids were becoming eligible for the service while I remained a civilian, awaiting my turn. I kept up a steady correspondence with all my many friends in the various branches of the service. I wrote articles for an ingenious little local newspaper, appropriately entitled "Hometown" which was the brainchild of one of the deferred, married young fathers, Murray Chernow, who devoted an enormous amount of time and effort to his project. It was sent out constantly, to everyone from the neighborhood who was in the service, and to anyone else, even strangers, who requested this wonderful touch of home. Meanwhile, my brother Joe, who is fifteen months younger than I, received his "Greetings" from the President, and he wound up in an infantry unit at Camp Blanding, Florida. Just coincidentally, by that time I was already in the early stages of a show biz career, and I appeared in a USO show for all the new conscripts (brother Joe among them) at Fort Dix, NJ. Boy, was he surprised ... and delighted.

Joe had been drafted, along with a number of his good friends, and a number of them were kept together in basic training. Joe got lucky. Some of the officers saw how well he played baseball and decided to keep him there awhile to represent his company's team in the inter camp league. Later he was transferred to a military police unit in another part of Florida, where he served out the war, playing baseball on behalf of, perhaps, the entire service command. I've always maintained that, in life, you've got to be ready for the breaks by perfecting whatever your ability is, but, without that other ingredient called "luck," you can "piss against the wind" for your entire life. Joe's original infantry unit was sent over to Europe with the war there already winding its way towards a conclusion, but, to quote that earthy philosopher, Yogi Berra, "It ain't over till it's over," and quite a few of those young replacements lost their lives in combat, including one of his close and dear friends, a good looking, slim, blond kid from up the street named Sonny D'Amico (another tragic, unbearable Rochester Ave. contribution to America's war effort).

Life goes on, and those of us who were home went about the business of trying to live it to its utmost. There were a lot of theaters thriving in New York City, and I had never lost my lust for comedy. The so-called "presentation houses," like the Loew's State, the Paramount, the Roxy, the Strand, the Capitol, and the glorious Radio City Music Hall (home of the world famous Rockettes) were all doing a landslide business. The big bands, headed by the likes of Glenn Miller, Benny Goodman, Artie Shaw, Count Basie, Woody Herman, Charlie Barnett, Duke Ellington, Stan Kenton, were having a field day all over the country. People were working. They had more money than they had ever had before. Death and destruction were in the news every day. They were gonna live it up while they could, and we in the NY area were blessed with an abundance of entertainment emporia. These theaters were what were referred to as "presentation houses" and the basic fare was: the big (well known) orchestra; a popular singer or group; an occasional great "novelty" act; and, of course, the ubiquitous comedian. The true vaudeville shows were still playing in cities throughout the entire country, but fading fast, with movies replacing the live acts, and, eventually, only the major cities still had the vaudeville houses. Little by little, vaudeville houses too were changing their policy and slimming down to three-act presentation houses. The vaudeville shows always featured eight acts and an orchestra in the pit, and the next-to-closing act was the star attraction. New York City still boasted of the greatest vaudeville theater of them all, the world famous Palace, which continued to reign supremely and challenge the presentation house fad, long after all the vaudeville theaters across the country had ceased to exist. However even the Palace, much later on, in its waning years, reverted to the presentation procedure, generally featuring a major, major star like Judy Garland or Danny Kaye. In Marian Spitzer's great book, entitled "The Palace," she brilliantly takes you through the history of that hallowed institution, starting in 1913, when it was founded, until its curtains came down for the very last time in the late sixties. (She was a member of The Palace publicity staff.) She describes how the legendary E. F. Albee, the king of the vaudeville impresarios, who occupied an office in the Palace Theater building, was ignominiously deposed by the pragmatic and insensitive new owner, the harsh businessman, Joseph P. Kennedy.

I attended these wondrous theaters regularly. There was so much to choose from. The shows changed constantly, so, to me it was "smorgasbord." The more I saw, the more passionate I became about becoming a comedian. With few exceptions, the comedians made me laugh. When there was a lull on the Broadway menu, then I'd take the bus into New Jersey and have a most-satisfying time howling at those outrageous burlesque comedians at the Hudson Theater in Union City. I memorized a great many of the jokes that I heard at all the theaters, and soon put them into routines and entertained at parties, private little clubrooms, the place where I was working, on street corners, and just about anywhere that anyone would listen to me. I soon discovered that I was good, without being pushy, overbearing, boorish, or obnoxious, and, the more I performed, the more sanguine I became.

Comedy is an art, and we all have our individual tastes. Those who appeared on Broadway may not have been major stars, but they had learned to "roll the ball down the middle" and appeal to the majority. The tremendously talented and funny people included Jerry Lester, his brother Buddy, Pat Henning, Harry Savoy, Dave Barry, Larry Storch, his brother Jay Lawrence, Billy DeWolfe, Jean Carrol, Gene Baylos, Jackie Miles, Lenny Kent, Dean Murphy (who did an excellent impression of FDR), and Joey Adams (accompanied by fighter Tony Canzoneri and tall, handsome singer Marc Plant). I recall a show at the Strand that featured the supercharged Louis Prima, and his orchestra, spotlighting his singer, Lillie Ann Carrol, and the comedian Jerry Lester. Occasionally, the fare would change in these theaters, and instead of a comedian, they'd put the emphasis on a singing sensation. Who could ever forget the time that Frank Sinatra burst onto the scene at the Paramount? At that particular time, the Four Ink Spots were among the hottest acts in the business. The bandleader usually emceed the shows (unlike in vaudeville where they had huge placards at each side of the stage, announcing the performers, and the acts would come on without a verbal introduction), and Prima was among the most animated and charismatic. That particular evening, after some very familiar and exciting orchestral selections, along with some great vocal renditions, there was a resounding roll on the drums. The famed orchestra leader stepped up to the microphone and announced, "And now, ladies and gentlemen, here comes our comedy star," and he paused ever so briefly for dramatic effect, "along with a very special surprise ... Jerry Lester ... and The Four Ink Spots!" The audience went wild. And, out bounded Jerry Lester onto the stage, wearing a white dinner jacket ... with four big blotches of ink on it! The laughter was uproarious!

All I can tell you is that audience was mesmerized by these funny people, and occasionally we were treated to Hollywood people. The first one that comes to my mind is Red Skelton, who used to destroy the audiences when he'd go into his trademark "Guzzler's Gin." Jimmy Durante was another one of those greats that guaranteed sold out houses.

Naturally, movie exposure was a tremendous attraction, and such stars would pack the theaters. It was at the appearance of one of the most important comedy stars in the business that I suffered one of my biggest disappointments, and I learned something about the industry that I still resent to this very day. The famed Roxy Theater was presenting the inimitable Jack Benny for a limited engagement and the people were flocking to see him. I usually attended shows with friends who had that same intense interest that I had: guys like "little ugly Gootch" (who, when he smiled, with his profound overbite, had an amazing resemblance to George C. Tilyou, the face on the Steeplechase sign in Coney Island); Carl Epperly, the enigmatic wisp of a kid with the sardonic wit; Black Heshie, who rarely laughed out loud, but nodded his approvals; and Filthy Miltie, who sometimes got so hysterical that we'd be asked to leave the theater, but one Saturday afternoon I sneaked off by myself because I feared that seats would be at a premium, and, as it turned out I was right.

I got there early enough to get a good orchestra seat, smack in the middle and not too far from the stage. The air of excitement was all around me. Everyone sat with great expectation. The applause was deafening when Benny strutted out onstage in his familiar manner, and laughter erupted all around me. He stood for what seemed like an eternity, with that famous pose, the right hand fondling his chin, and when he uttered his famous "We-ell," they roared, like trained seals. That's all he did! He did not say one funny thing. Just posed, and postured, and proceeded to talk about his radio show and his movies, and mention the right names, but nothing funny came out of his mouth, ... and the "sheep" all around me continued to giggle and guffaw at everything he said and did. I kept asking myself, "When does he start?" At long (boring) last, he said, "Here comes Rochester," and I figured that now things were going to pick up, remembering the lovable Eddie Anderson and his gravelly voice. Rochester was even more disappointing. Lord knows, he tried hard, but, like his boss, he was just trading on his reputation, and it just didn't work. After that came Phil Harris, then big Don Wilson, both pressing onward, but as far as I was concerned, to no avail. And much to my bewilderment, the audience laughed, and laughed, and I still couldn't figure out what they were laughing at. I came to the conclusion that these "squares" considered it a great privilege (that they paid for with their hard earned bucks) to see these famous people in person. The only breath of fresh air that afternoon was the appearance of Dennis Day, the Irish tenor on the Jack Benny Show, whose boyish charm was contagious, but, ... lightly funny, ... very lightly funny, and, ... surprise, surprise, ... the "sheep" kept right on laughing. This is what irks me to this very day because that's the format on so many of those inane, insipid TV talk shows, especially the late night "entertainment" with their "inside" conversations. The studio audience has been all psyched up beforehand to laugh at everything and anything, funny or not. They're fortunate to have gotten into the studio, and they're sitting close to "celebrities." All these guests on these shows do, generally, is talk about themselves, like Jack Benny did that afternoon at the Roxy, and that's "entertainment??" This BS has carried over into in-person appearances in nightclubs, theaters, resorts, etc. I remember seeing an old friend, comedian Corbett Monica performing on a late show at a Catskill resort hotel. He was, at that time, a "steady" on the Joey Bishop TV Show, and his whole act consisted of telling the audience about his private life, for example, "Joey and I played a practical joke on Jackie Mason when we went to so-and-so's party, etc." ... and the "sheep" kept right on laughing. That's where the great, working comedians (like those I grew up watching at those now long gone presentation houses) had it all over these so-called "personalities." They were, and those that are like them, still are, the "workers," ... the truly funny people. I would like to add that Corbett does a very entertaining comedy act, and he is booked everywhere to perform it, but the trend towards, "Hey, look at me, I'm a well known personality. Telling you about myself ought to be enough," has diluted the business of "entertaining" and the public "thinks it's raining."

The catalyst for me was the excitement engendered by the release of Danny Kaye's musical album. For the deejays on the radio this was like an infusion of oxygen. It was different than the usual big bands that dominated their programs, and the surge of versatile genius that this super talent displayed was intoxicating. It was a refreshing, original spin on comedy and delighted the world. A brilliant new star burst out on the horizon and everybody loved him. Many of us tried to emulate him or do impressions of him, and those who did record pantomimes, where they spun the records behind them while silently mouthing the words, had a field day with Danny Kaye's artistry. I took the liberty of memorizing several of the hit songs from his album, and, not being a seasoned singer, I sang these songs "a cappella" (without the benefit of musical background) before anyone who would listen. The response was exhilarating, and I started to put together little packages in my mind. These were my first routines. I did a series of jokes, followed by a Danny Kaye song, the most popular of which was "Deenah" (a Gypsy version of the old standard "Dinah"), and I was on my way to becoming a comedian. Now all I had to do was find a way to get into the business professionally, which required a bit of legerdemain and a whole lot of luck.

My friend Mannie Gaer had a very pretty and vivacious sister who lived around the corner from where I lived. Her name was Debbie, and she was quite a gregarious young lady. She was married to a handsome young man who was a flashy dresser with a most engaging personality, and who walked with a unique hop that made him appear like he was a plane about to take off. He wasn't around too often, and Mannie explained to me that his brother-in-law, Willie Wayne, was in show business and on the road a lot. He was a comedian and a very able tap dancer who had worked in vaudeville with two other men. Their act was called "The Three Century Boys." The act had broken up because the other guys had gone into the army, and Willie himself was in the process of waiting to be called. Willie had had extensive experience performing at the Catskill resorts, and as a Social Director, heading up the entire staff. (They used to do approximately four different shows per week, for four weeks so as not to repeat anything for the longer staying guests, and then start over again). That meant that he had to have in his possession lots of material. In fact, Mannie, with whom I had gone all through junior high school, had a very keen sense of humor and was highly intelligent. He found out where Willie had kept his cache of jokes and songs and sketches, and soon the two of us were rummaging through Willie's "gem-laden" suitcases quite regularly, and laughing our sides off.

Willie was both friendly and kind, and the thought occurred to me to ask him for some help. I had subsequently learned that no one can go it alone. In order to succeed we must be aided by others, and who you know has a very strong bearing upon the degree of one's success. If one is fortunate enough to gain through others, then he too should display the same generosity. I told Willie about my ambitions, explaining that I had a fairly good job with opportunity to succeed even further, but that, while I was still so young, without the encumbrances of a family (though I was contributing to my parents' household) I would like to take a stab at becoming a comedian. Since there was a need for entertainers, even in their embryonic stages, what with so many having been called away, Willie surmised that, if I could audition and display any semblance of talent, and with the busy Catskill resort summer season just around the corner, it shouldn't be too hard to get myself booked as a "fifth banana" on some social staff and really learn the ropes.

Willie gave me some blank stationary bearing letterheads from a few hotels that had either burned down or had gone bankrupt, and were no longer in business. He advised me to get someone to type in a letter of recommendation, telling "To whom it may concern" how able an entertainer I was on their social staff. He then supplied me with the detailed locations of where the theatrical agents had their offices, most of which were on and around, W. 46th St. in NYC, He added, "All it takes to start off with is a modicum of talent, and a whole lot of guts," and he wished me "Good luck!" ... or, as they say in show biz ... "break a leg!"

The first thing I did was ask my mother and father if I had their approval to quit my job and pursue my true calling. Both, having been smitten by love of theater from way back, also remembering how facile I was in that area since early childhood (no doubt remembering the pleasure they used to get out of rehearsing my lines with me, and then vicariously enjoying the finished product), immediately acquiesced. Of course they didn't anticipate that things would develop as quickly as they did, and the underlying question, "What would happen if I strike out?" was not a major concern. Pop was earning enough now, delivering beer for a local distributor, and, although things would be tighter without my income from Samilson-Romer, whatever else I was going into would have to pay something, certainly enough to help support myself. Besides, there was still a large shortage of manpower, and, if push comes to shove, finding another job, perhaps even in that same (fur) area shouldn't be too hard.

The necessary guts to go into show biz was something I wasn't certain I possessed. Like anyone else about to go into something he's never done before professionally, a little moral support, or more than that, was something to seriously look for. I discussed my plans with Gootch and Epperly, two of the funniest guys in the whole neighborhood, and their enthusiasm swelled. These were the same two guys that used to sit around with me on the empty newspaper stand on the side of Max Geyser's strategically located candy store (just about everyone's new hangout), and the three of us would draw large crowds as we sang and recited the various comedy routines that we had both written, and borrowed from those comedians we used to see in the theaters and listen to on the radio. Max, who was lucky enough to have escaped from Germany a step ahead of Hitler's murderers, bought the candy store on Sterling and Rochester, and he and his wife worked long hard hours to make his investment pay off. We three "trumbeniks," as he called us, were his nemesis, only because the crowds we drew would block the entrance to his store. However, underneath his angry facade beat the heart of a truly good man, and, as much as he'd chase after us with a wet rag in his hand, yelling, "Get away da stand!" he knew that his actions brought laughter to all that observed them. We all suspected that he secretly loved breaking up our presentations, without any real malice. As a matter of fact, we even made up parodies that we used to sing to him, ending up with rags in our hands yelling, "Get away da stand!" which he and his wife, Helen, used to howl at.

Gootch, Epperly, and I, decided that we were going to seek employment in the Catskills as a trio, and we spent weeks rehearsing what we were going to do for our auditions. When we felt that the time was ripe, armed with my "glorious," self-composed "letters of recommendation," we took the subway uptown, got off on 42nd St., and hoofed over to 46th St. to "pound the pavement," going from building to building, and office to office. Not surprisingly, we were rejected everywhere. We weren't even granted the opportunity to display our wares. When they saw how young we were, these seasoned theatrical agents, quick to recognize amateurs, and especially kids, politely informed us that there were no jobs available. We finally gave up on 46th St. and were ready to go back home defeated, when someone in the Theatrical Drug Store suggested that we try the Palace Building, which was located just around the corner on 7th Avenue. With renewed hope and new found energy, we figured, "What have we got to lose? We'll give it a try."

We had a little more success in the Palace Building, where, surprisingly, some of the offices were real tiny cubbyholes. Nevertheless, there was an abundance of agents in that building, and we actually got to do one or two auditions, with almost instantaneous rejection, but, at least, it raised our expectations. We finally got into the office of two character actors from the Yiddish theater who were moonlighting as theatrical agents. Morris Bleiman and Max Metzger, the former thin and high-strung, the latter pudgy and soft spoken, were both friendly and attentive and we did our prepared routines for them (a cappella, of course. None of us had any idea if we could sing on key.) They appeared to listen with interest, and then, very politely said, "Sorry." At that moment I got a brainstorm, and went into my version of Danny Kaye's "Deenah" delivering it as dramatically as I possibly could. Their eyes suddenly revealed some sort of signs of recognition, and when I got through singing they asked us to step out into the hall (they had only this one small office, and, like with so many other agents, the public halls were used as waiting rooms) while they confer. The three of us stood outside for several minutes wondering what was going to happen next. Finally the door opened and they pointed to me and said, "You! What did you say your name was?" I replied, hesitating for a moment, "V- -Van, - - Van Harris." That was the first time I had actually used that name professionally. I had decided, before we had gone looking, that I was going to use the waspy-sounding nickname that "Big Red" had bestowed upon me years ago, and only he had used. "Van Harris," I repeated, feeling even a little more secure, enjoying the sound of that theatrical combination (though Harris had always really been my last name).

"Wen," repeated the diminutive Morris Bleiman, who spoke with more of an accent than his partner, who actually had a Yiddish inflection, but no profound accent, "would you be good enough to come back into the office? I want to speak to you personally. Fellas do you mind waiting outside?" Good manners and theatrical agents were not a combination in those years, and I daresay that this insulting condition somehow prevails until this very day, with few (studied) exceptions. It's the nature of the beast, ... and it prevails in our emotional jungle, and if you're going to survive, you'd better get used to it. Who was it that said, "To be in show business you've got to have the heart of a lion, the brain of a fox, and the hide of a rhinoceros?" We all looked at each other, gave our shoulders a slight shrug, and I excused myself, and stepped back into the office with Bleiman and Metzger, leaving Gootch and Epperly standing there wondering what was going to happen next.

"Wen," Bleiman continued, "you've got some talent. If you can get rid of the other two guys, I can get you a job for the summer," and Mezger stood next to him, nodding his head in agreement, to assure me that this offer was for real. "The job pays twenty-five bucks a week, with room and board, less ten percent commission to us, of course, and you'll be on the staff with a Jewish actor and an actress, both from the Yiddish theater, and also an American songstress, and a great six piece orchestra. If you keep your eyes open, and listen to your bosses, you can learn a lot." I was overjoyed and frightened at the same time, and I blurted out, "I'll have to let you know. I'll have to go home and discuss it with the other guys." They replied, "We haven't got time for that. If you want the job, you'll have to let us know right here and now. Tomorrow it may be gone." My legs turned to jelly. I said, "Wait, I'll step out into the hall and talk to them." I walked outside and told the boys about the proposition that I had just gotten, and asked them, "Well, whadd'ya think?" Without a moment's hesitation they answered, in unison, "Don't be a fool, take it!" Confidentially, I think they were both relieved, as they had been as apprehensive as I was. A future in show biz is tenuous to say the least, and especially if one has had no real training except for parties and the street corner. I hugged them both and said, "Thank you!" and continued, "Give me a minute. I'll be right back." And so was launched a career that was destined to consume me for over a half-a-century, play havoc with my emotions, right up to the hilt at times, provide me with indescribable joy and maddening disappointments, and yet, if I had to do it all over again, I would jump at it with alacrity and enthusiasm. Only next time I'm sure I would do it better. And don't cry for Gootch. He wound up being a shoe importer and became a millionaire. And, as for poor little Epperly, he developed the ability to sell financial securities and did very well in that profession until he died, much too young.

8 Catskill Summers

It seemed like ages till the "hacker" got to the Brookside Hotel in Loch Sheldrake, NY. Very few people that I knew owned a car. In our neighborhood that was a real luxury, and anyone going to the mountains for a vacation would hire a large automobile from a car service, complete with driver, for a nominal fee. These services were located in all five boroughs of New York City, and in the summer they did a thriving business. The cars were referred to as "hacks," and the immigrant population somehow elongated the word to "hackers," with many even mispronouncing that word and calling them "heckers." They would pile as many customers as they could into these well-worn vans, making as many stops as they could along the way to pick up their assorted passengers and their luggage. It took ages to finally get out of the teeming city, cross the George Washington Bridge into New Jersey, and Route #4 until it linked up with Route #17, the famous old highway that ran all the way up to the pristine "paradise" that beckoned. There were large metal racks on the top of the car, and likewise, on the back, and the whole idea was to fit in as many passengers and their luggage, as they could. Vacations usually began and ended on the first day of the week, so that on any given Sunday those roads were cluttered with these "Jewish Stagecoaches," with assorted suitcases and cardboard boxes strapped and roped to every available inch of their exteriors, for as far as the eye could see. Cars and hacks, cars and hacks, one long procession, in both directions, going and returning, for miles and miles, hour after hour, and not without the inevitable accidents and breakdowns. A vacation in the mountains was truly an adventure from beginning to end, but whatever the sacrifices, when it was all over, it was worth it, and people couldn't wait to do it again. If one wishes to compare this medieval caravan to today's so-called sophisticated travel, it's practically the same, not too much different than the lineups at the airports, or on cruise ships, only on a slightly different level.

All along the four or five hour trip, the "locals" were grumbling. Never mind the prosperity they brought to the eateries and gas stations along the way, the eternal scapegoats, the Jews, were clogging up their roads, and many a taunt was made by natives who were only too quick to point out the tourists' egregiousness, while failing themselves to look into the mirror. That good old human disease called prejudice was very much in evidence, and many a local policeman along the way would make certain to add his crude and costly perniciousness to the scene, indiscriminately flaunting his authority in an effort to show these "odd-looking city folk" who's in charge. Yet, when the chips were down, and any kind of tragic mishap would occur, they would be the first to follow their human instincts, and come to the rescue.

It is indelibly inscribed in the back of my cerebellum (or is it the cerebrum where the brain stores memory?) that we went up to the mountains on a Friday (and a torrid one at that) so that we members of the social staff could quickly prepare for the big, opening Fourth of July Weekend. By the time the "hecker" (why should I be different?) got through picking everyone up, then dropping everyone off, which was truly an eternity, I arrived at my destination (like some of the others, worn, apprehensive, and bewildered) very late in the day. I was led to my "quarters" which turned out to be one small section of an abandoned car trailer that I was going to share with a couple of the older musicians for the summer, and I was advised that there was going to be some kind of orientation in about an hour. As curious and frightened as I was, I conjured up a vision of my tough, redheaded mother waggling her finger at me and instructing me, in her familiar way, to "be a man!"

Psyched, and "ready to go," armed with only a friendly smile, a yellow legal pad on which to take notes, and my big collection of twenty-five or so of my best jokes, neatly written in an old composition book, I found my way to the "casino," which was what they all called the theater in those days. I felt a wonderful surge of excitement as I gazed around at its colorful ambience, from its deep red velvet stage curtains, to its highly polished wooden rails encircling the bandstand (handsomely carpeted, and strategically placed in the right hand corner just where the stage ended) already equipped with a large, upright piano and assorted music stands. The rows and rows of wooden folding chairs were already in position eagerly awaiting an audience. The ceiling was equipped with a professional array of spotlights, all facing down on the stage, and a huge spotlight stood in the very back of the theater (which was actually the entrance), no doubt to assist in highlighting the center of attraction onstage. I couldn't believe my eyes and my good luck. This was it! A real, honest to goodness theater, and I was a part of it all. I felt like pinching myself to see if I was dreaming.

The room soon began to fill with people, and everyone clustered around a barrel-chested, curly haired, handsome gentleman, and a slightly younger, dark-complexioned, slim, attractive woman. I soon found out that they were Max Rosenblatt and Fanya Rubina, two versatile stalwarts of the Yiddish theater, and they were going to be the stars and headliners in all that transpired in that casino for the forthcoming summer. A very young, dark haired pretty girl stood off to a side, seemingly enthralled by the presence of those two, and I soon learned that she was the other neophyte on the entertainment staff. Her name was Joyce, and she was going to be what was referred to, in that era, as the "blues singer," which actually meant the one that was going to sing in English. And the imperious orchestra leader, a bald, middle aged, rather intense gentleman who was holding a violin bow in his hand was deeply involved in heated conversation with Mr. Rosenblatt and Ms. Rubina. I soon learned that he was the highly respected, no nonsense, Abe Schwartz, of Second Avenue theater fame. I walked over and introduced myself. It seemed like all eyes were upon me. My apparent innocence, coupled with my eagerness, seemed to have made an impression upon these wizened veterans, and we proceeded to the next order of business. Max was very enthusiastic. "I want you all to meet me here tomorrow after breakfast. We're gonna rehearse our big July 4th show. Van and Joyce, you'll help out in the sketches we do, and you'll each do a short spot of your own. Joyce, you'll prepare three songs, two and an encore, and Van, you'll open our show with a five minute performance and then introduce me, and I'll take over from there, so prepare a good spot. Now, all of you, you're free to roam around. Find out what time the meals are served. You know where you'll be sleeping. Enjoy the summer. Give me your best efforts. See you all at rehearsal."

Cut to the show. No need to describe how poorly I ate, how badly I slept, or how many times I pored over that composition book with its paucity of jokes. I wrote, and rewrote, and rewrote them again and again, and I was still not satisfied. It seemed like an eternity until showtime, and, at long last, when that time arrived I approached the moment of truth, (spiffed up in my only good suit) with an air of enthusiasm that was totally eclipsed by numbing apprehension. To the best of my recollection, the orchestra began with a medley of memorable Yiddish theater standards that was greeted with rousing enthusiasm by a large and lively audience that had not anticipated anything other than the fine quality that these superb musicians presented, under the skilled direction of the renowned Mr. Schwartz. The resounding cheers that greeted this gifted and elite group of seasoned klezmers would have served as a catalyst for any experienced performer that followed, to go out n' "destroy them," except that, quite understandably, my nervousness was consuming me, and, as the old burlesque expression went, "only my laundry man knew how scared I was."

No introduction. Only a brief drum roll, then a musical chaser, and out on the stage I strolled, confident and smiling, while inwardly frozen. The external polish was at odds with the inner turmoil. The strong spotlights blinded me so that I could only look out n' see perhaps the first two or three rows of people, though I knew that the house was well overflowing. What a strange feeling, to talk into a bright light and listen for group reaction. What an eerie feeling. I didn't know if, or where, the hoped for response was going to come from. How I learned to love that challenge, later on, throughout my long and varied career, but this was my very first time. How weird. What's gonna happen? My mouth felt as though I had just eaten a whole bag of cement, and my constricting throat was not allowing any sounds to emerge. Suddenly remembering why I was there in the first place, I pulled myself together, managed a big, engaging smile, and said, in a well modulated voice, "Good evening." Just like that, "Good evening." ... and I heard back from the blinding canyon that faced me, "Good evening." "They like me," I surprisingly discovered, and I continued to engage the audience in conversation. I had no idea that I could be this charming, but it didn't take long for the sanguinity to set in, and I continued on with, "Here's a good joke I heard," ... and so on, and so on, and, fortunately, the audience, comprised mostly of Jewish immigrants, was not sophisticated, and, fortunately, very good natured and empathetic, and certainly wizened enough to recognize that this was a brand new kid out there, still wet behind the ears and giving it his all, and the reaction was most pleasant. I felt as though I had been on for an eternity, glanced down at my watch (a sold gold Wittnauer that I had once bought cheap from a chronically ill patient who made a living repairing and renovating used watches while living out his years at Kings County Hospital), and I almost died when I had seen that only about two minutes had gone by, and the boss had asked for five. Years later, when I was appearing, to some degree of regularity, on Johnny Carson's "NBC Tonight" show, I was allotted, like every comedian that performed on his long running show, a total of six minutes, and it's utterly amazing how much varied material can be packed into a six minute stint. Yet, here I was, a novice, attempting to give it my best shot, and my well was running dry. I ad-libbed (an extremely gutsy move, especially for a newcomer), then threw in another (hopefully) time-consuming story, looked down at my Wittnauer again, and saw that the hands had barely moved (and all the while I was thinking, "Where the hell am I gonna get material for my next show?" As the season progressed I found out that one can build up, in those years anyway, a repertoire, by trading, and doing favors, like performing at benefits for them, with other comedians), and right then and there I decided it was time for my "piece de resistance," the piece that got me this far, Danny Kaye's "Deenah." Between the heat from the spotlights, and the reaction of my nerves, I was, by then, perspiring throughout. "Hit 'em with this big one, and you're in," I said to myself. I announced to the still friendly audience what I was going to do, and, having never had any previous experience at singing professionally, and not having bothered to rehearse (good thing that I didn't, for once my superiors, and the orchestra leader, would have heard me, they never would have allowed me to sing), I launched into the song I had been doing, a cappella, at so many parties, entertaining my friends. Mr. Schwartz, the orchestra leader, ever mindful of his responsibilities, was taken totally by surprise, and, with violin in hand, struggled every which way to conduct the orchestra, as he played along, in order to keep up with my changing tempos, and, even worse, my changing keys. I finished my turn in about the right amount of time, walked off to applause, and handed the show over to Max Rosenblatt, who introduced Joyce, who did a very commendable, professional job despite her youth. Then Max and Fanya rounded out the rest of the show in gargantuan fashion, being the great professionals that they were. When the evening was all over, after everyone but the entertainers and band had left, the esteemed, serious Abe Schwartz, hurried backstage to confront Mr. Rosenblatt, and, in a rage, making certain that I was well within earshot, screamed at him, with his Yiddish dialect very much in evidence, "If da kid ever tries to sing annuder song dis summer, I kvit!"

I did sing more that summer, only after I had apologized profusely to Mr. Schwartz, and begged for another chance, and his generous help (eventually, he even scribbled a musical lead sheet for me), but that opening night unsettled me so and shook my confidence so, that, by the following day, after a sleepless night in which I kept rehashing the events of that first show over and over in my mind, I had made up my mind that I was not meant to be in show business and was planning to pack my bags n' go home before I could cause some really serious damage. Only a strong vote of confidence, amiably delivered to me by my newly found friend, and "counterpart" on our social staff, the pretty and very talented young Joyce, while on a walk into town, on the following day, convinced me to stick around. Eventually we all became one big happy family of entertainers, so popular that we even booked ourselves out to other hotels on our nights off, and we experienced not only the joys of acceptance, but also something called "extra money."

I guess it's only human to want to "throw in the towel," and to just give up the struggle. Abort! Nuts! That's not the way to go. Do that and you'll be forever chasing rainbows. Quitters are losers. As my old pal, Howard always remarked, "God has little regard for cowards." I don't know how true that is, and I personally doubt that He would be so callous. I wanted, so desperately, to hang in there. That requires real courage and fortitude. We're all capable, but how much easier it is when there's someone right close by to inspire you. That was the vital role that my new, and thankfully interested, friend Joyce played. She was there at the right moment, and I truly needed that display of faith and affection. She was real pretty, but I hardly noticed, so preoccupied was I with my endeavor to see this great adventure through. She, herself, was very young, enormously gifted, and perhaps even more aspiring. She seemed to have some serious experience under her belt and was not at all averse to imparting it to me. It was her sincerity that brought me through that frightening period of panic, and I rapidly compiled the strength to continue, gaining more confidence and polish in each glorious moment of that memorable summer. Miraculously, we eventually blossomed into one big happy family. That's not to say that all was peaceful and harmonious. There was so much to learn in so little time. Mistakes were made, and I was quite soundly humiliated, especially in rehearsals where there are margins for error, and I experienced the occasional "boo-boo" in the actual performance. The finished product onstage, in front of a live audience, at times, bordered on disaster (like the time I was supposed to deliver an item to our star, Mr. Rosenblatt, during a sketch, and I walked into the scene empty handed, and empty-headed), and the hell I suffered at the hands of those running the show seemed unbearable. But, my sincere desire to learn was very evident to all, and I soon learned that I possessed a likable quality, which was proven when, early in the season, after my "umpteenth" mistake, which was an obvious blow to the cast's professionalism (audiences don't miss anything) the hotel owner approached Mr. Rosenblatt with a very serious request, "Don't you think it's time to get rid of him?" Quite coincidentally I happened to have been standing near enough to have heard this clandestine conversation, and my self esteem took a giant leap forward when I heard Mr. Rosenblatt's retort, "If the kid goes ... I go!"

It wasn't until half of that glorious, hot summer had passed that I realized that there were actually windows in the trailer I shared with the older musicians. The windows were so easy to open and close (something we all overlooked when we were perpetually griping about the lack of fresh air.) Of course, I spent so little time in that trailer, having, for the first time in my young life, fallen in love ... or, at least I thought so ... at the time we both thought so. A rather torrid romance developed between me n' Joyce, which was only inevitable. True to the "summer romance" scene, we became inseparable, confiding in each other, sharing our dreams and hopes for the future, enjoying every precious moment together, believing that this romantic state of euphoria would never end, and the elders all around us beamed with pride at the sight of the young lovers who were so into themselves. It was an education like I had never had, and I savored every precious moment ... until that sobering finality called Labor Day.

Very soon afterward, we returned to the real world. Those terribly long trips on the subway from Brooklyn, all the way up to the Bronx to be with Joyce, and her long, long rides to Brooklyn (no one owned a car) succeeded in putting the finish sign on "The Romance of the Ages." (How great to be young, and foolish, and so in love.) Of course we saw each other as often as we could, and commiserated together on our failed auditions, and tried hard to continue that beautiful, seemingly never ending idyllic thing that we had going for us during the exciting summer of all summers, but, alas, t'was not meant to be, and, like the couple that shared a water bed ... we drifted apart. I oft-times think of that memorable summer and of how fortunate we all were to be a part of it, and I pray that all good people everywhere have an opportunity in their lifetimes to live a summer like ours was. That was the last time I saw that lovely little girl until about a quarter of a century later as we were leaving New York City's famed comedy club, The Improv. She did not see me, and I would never have recognized her if somebody hadn't told me who she was. She had ultimately married the famous, zany, and I must say, very funny, comedian, Rodney Dangerfield, and, from what I learned, it was a rather stormy, and uneven marriage, in which one or two children were conceived. She had gotten divorced and later remarried. Joyce looked frighteningly thin, almost emaciated. She was still very young, perhaps in her early forties, and very likely, seriously ill, as the dear lady passed away very soon thereafter. What an utter waste. I'm glad that I was so involved with her in her glory days when all she could look forward to was sunshine and roses and such a promising career.

The fall was exasperating, with no nibbles for work whatsoever, and I concluded right then and there that it was all a one shot deal, good while it lasted n' that was that! Luckily for me, I was still liked at the firm I had worked at in the fur district, and my old employers were willing to have me back. Back I went, but my heart was no longer in it. I found what I loved most and vowed to pursue it with all my ambition. I took acting classes with a family of charlatans that preyed upon the unsuspecting, ambitious young, like myself. I even rehearsed for a supposed off-Broadway show that never materialized ... all this while I was holding down a nine-to-five job at Samilson And Romer. The couple that ran the acting school was a self-anointed team that "knew everything," and "everyone," for a fee, of course, and to this very day such ubiquity remains a quasi-necessary part of the learning experience for all budding young actors, who would sell their souls for a chance in the limelight.

My brother Joe, had worked that same summer at another Catskill hotel, as a children's waiter, and had befriended the comedian who was the Social Director there. He was a wildly uninhibited, funny-looking man, perhaps about twenty years our senior who was given to outlandish exaggeration, also claiming that he was the one who taught the incomparable Danny Kaye everything he knew. Joe was naively impressed by this rather likable braggart, and told him about his talented neophyte brother. He was very anxious to meet me, and he also owned a car, which was a real godsend. We became quite friendly, and I spent a good deal of my spare time with this self-styled "star" from whom I learned some interesting things about the business. Of course, there was a price to pay, and that was that I had to listen to his constant self praise, but he was a funny guy, not at all malicious, and he made me laugh. What he possessed in comedic ability, he lacked in the proper use of the English language, about which I'm very fussy. But, when one listens to the horrid mistakes that our popular newscasters make, both on TV and the radio (and they're paid bloody fortunes to flash their ignorance which, in a number of cases is easily surpassed by their engagingly mellifluous voices), I guess that this ingratiating imp could be forgiven. We worked out a hoaky song and dance comedy routine (although dancing was never one of my strong suits ... even though I could be a passable faker), and I used to break up and cringe at the same time when he would seriously announce at some of the benefit shows we did for free, in order to gain experience, "And now folks, we'd like to sing a clever little ditty ...," followed later by statements like, " ... and here's a song that is by farmost the mostest." It was only a matter of time before our relationship would fade, but we did remain distant friends. Meanwhile, because of his age and life experience, this naive young, ambitious comedian was learning a lot from him about the ever present intrigues that go on in my profession, with a pretty good emphasis on the romantic liaisons and the gossipy sexual encounters that prevail. For example, there was a famed instrumentalist, who gave music lessons in his home, not far from where my new "partner" lived, to one of the good-looking young ladies in my neighborhood. We learned from him that he'd been having a hot n' heavy sexual encounter with this innocent looking girl with each and every lesson. In a million years you could never convince my mother, or any of the other neighborhood ladies of this, as they looked upon this "child" as the consummate virgin. Such were the intrigues that existed in the fascinating profession that I was just opening the doors to, and I daresay it looked like it might be fun.

My relationship with my new pal, Phil, came to a sudden stop when I auditioned for a small time lady agent somewhere in lower Manhattan and where I met a singer named Jeannie Reynolds, whose husband Hal, was her conductor and pianist. They were a gregarious couple, also just starting out, and Jeannie had a wonderful sense of humor and a very good flair for doing comedy. They had just accepted an entire season's engagement in what was then a thriving winter resort, which consisted of numerous hotels in invigorating, pine laden Lakewood, NJ. They were in quest of a comedian to complete their staff. Jeannie did the warbling, and Hal doubled as her conductor while he headed up a four or five piece combo. This "gig" constituted a guarantee of about five months of steady work at one good-sized hotel, with opportunities to work at others in the same locale when time permitted. I made the deal, packed my gear, put together whatever material I had accumulated in my very first season up there in the mountains, got a bus on Broadway and 41st in Manhattan, and was on my way to job number two, meanwhile burning whatever bridges I had left in the fur industry forever. Now I was in it for keeps. Show biz ... here I come.

How I survived that first experience as "head man" in those crisp winter surroundings is a credit to my desire and tenacity. I was there, and there was a job to be done. In retrospect, I did it quite capably, with a minimum of material and even less talent. I spent long hours in my tiny quarters, tucked away somewhere in the bowels of the hotel alongside all the other "executive help," preparing nightly programs to deliver to our friendly clientele. That meant doing actual shows in the ballroom, which was our theater. (All the hotels in Lakewood employed either the ballroom, or the lobby, for their entertainment, as none possessed theaters.) I actually surprised myself with my legerdemain in piecing these programs together. The boys in the band, Jeannie and Hal, even a number of the hotel guests, were very helpful with their suggestions, and it was up to me to select whatever I thought would work, a knack that I never, until then, ever had to employ. The successes far outnumbered the failures. (A show that fails, or as we say in the profession, "bombs" is a disaster.) Everyone involved, especially Jeannie, proved to be very entertaining, and we all soon became one big happy family. To enhance our presentations the management would also book some of the already seasoned, and established performers who came in from New York, at least one night a week. It all proved to be a rather winning formula. Aside from show nights I ran game nights where I would involve our guests in some hilarious adult games; I'd have amateur nights when select guests would perform (but only after they had passed my afternoon auditions); I would have "Champagne Hours" which involved having our guests vie for bottles of the popular bubbly in dance competitions, etc. It was a case of learning on the job, and I had to learn quickly, and I did, thanks to the help of all around me.

Though the guests adored us all, management (headed up by a huge, and fiery lady with rings on every finger, a head of auburn colored, meticulously coiffed hair, and sparkling necklaces that rested on her ample bosom) reminded us that we were only the help, and not deserving of guest privileges, aside from our modest quarters (and I was lucky enough to have a room to myself while musicians always had to double up and even beyond.) This, I concluded, rather correctly, was her prerogative and, as I discovered throughout the ensuing years, was the system, the unwritten law of the resorts. We all had our meals in the staff dining room, a simple structure located right next to the kitchen. They assigned a steady waiter to us, a lovable, uneducated young black man who showered us with attention and talked incessantly. Hence the appropriate nickname, "Radio." The thing that stands out most in my memory of that educational winter is our choice of food. It seemed as though the hotel must have cornered the market on mushrooms, and that's all we ever ate. Always the same fare, three times a day (except when we felt "flushed" enough to eat out in some local restaurant or diner). It was mushrooms, mushrooms, and more mushrooms. Most of the time it was twice a day, as we young "night people" only occasionally got to breakfast, but no matter what meal it was, we were always greeted by Radio's sunny disposition. (We always tipped him well but I doubt that it had any bearing upon his delightful personality.) We'd ask, "What's on the menu, Radio?" and we'd all chime in with him as he'd flash that intoxicating smile, and say, "Mushrooms."

In this period of youthful innocence I also soon learned that we, the glorified help, were hated by the other help that had to put in long, hard hours as waiters in the main dining room. They were so envious of the fact that we were able to sleep as long as we liked, and "caroused" at all hours of the night, even carelessly making unwelcome noises as we headed for our rooms. The waiters were generally mature men, locked into their chosen, dead end profession and, except for their obsequious, artificial personalities while attending to the guests, they were, for the most part, sour, defeated individuals whose only recreation, in many instances, consisted of playing the horses via the local bookies or trying to find some feminine company. These were mature men who worked in Lakewood, unlike the waiters and busboys that performed those same duties in the summer mountain resorts. Summertime meant that school was out, and the hotels in the mountains were a boon to those lively college kids, with the great personalities, who were young, and ambitious, and cared very little about trivial matters like sleep. The Lakewood crews were another matter entirely. Little did we realize how many hard feelings were being conjured up in the minds of some of the hopeless, and we went about our way of life assuming we were loved by all, and totally preoccupied with trying to keep up our end of the bargain, which was to keep our guests constantly happy and entertained. The entertainment included daytime activities like Bingo sessions, in-house movies in very inclement weather, arranging for horse driven sleigh rides through the refreshing, pine laden countryside, etc., etc. We did know, however, that, no matter how hard we tried, we were never fully appreciated by management, and in most cases "management" meant gutsy speculators, for the most part fairly successful immigrants, many hardened and insensitive, conditioned by their arduous climb in order to achieve the exalted position of hotel entrepreneur. They all used to refer to us, their very necessary social staffs, by the Yiddish pejorative "umzistike fressers" which means, literally, "people who are fed for doing nothing." Our boss, the buxom Mrs. Silverman, was the personification of just that kind of employer, and she made no secret of her disdain. Fortunately, there were exceptions to the rule whom I would be fortunate enough to meet later on in my life.

The season progressed fairly blissfully, with a few physical, and mostly verbal eruptions here and there. We eventually got the feeling that we'd all be lucky if we finished out the season which was actually twice as long as those highly desirable summer seasons in the mountains. Ominous signs were starting to appear. For one, our drummer, a young man still in his teens, developed an insatiable crush on one of our very attractive, moneyed, season long guests. He had actually made up his mind, that somehow, he was going to get her into bed. The odds against this happening were astronomical. She was, quite apparently, happily married to a fine looking, successful man, they had a couple of young children, and besides, she was a good deal older than the teenage upstart that fancied her. Well, I'd heard about such improbable things happening out of boredom, desire, adventure, or all three, and our drummer actually succeeded in his quest, to the point where they were actually having trysts in a New York City hotel on his days off. This worried us plenty. Our concern, of course was that someone would find out, and there'd be hell to pay for all of us. Fortunately though, nobody uncovered their clandestine relationship, and the daring lovers survived, but for how long I'll never know. Jeannie and Hal had an altercation with the domineering Mrs. Silverman and they moved out into another resort, leaving Hal's band behind, and then I complained once too many times about the damn mushrooms, which led to a confrontation of rather disastrous proportions.

We were having our usual fare one lunchtime in the staff dining room. I had had a particularly long, and hard night, the night before, and I hadn't slept well. I was not in the best frame of mind when the animated "Radio" set my plate of "garbage" down in front of me, and somehow, that afternoon it struck a nerve. I gave vent to all my pent up emotions and yelled, "F'rgoshsakes Radio, bring this crap back to Mrs. Silverman and tell her to shove it up her big behind." Perhaps I was too vociferous, and my timing was way off, as these blasphemous words were uttered just as a waiter was walking through the open, swinging door that led into the main dining room. Luckily, the dining room was being set up for lunch and the guests hadn't come in yet. In a very short while, the maitre'd, a tall, gangly man wearing a suit, with a shirt n' tie, walked into our staff dining quarters and beckoned to me, "Young man, may I see you in the dining room for a minute?" I walked in calmly. The waiters and busboys were in various parts of the dining room setting up for lunch. As I walked up to face the maitre'd, without any warning, he hauled off and punched me on the side of my jaw. I was momentarily stunned, and startled both, and my immediate reaction was to grab him by the throat with both hands and try to throw him to the floor. As we struggled, the dining room staff was in an uproar because of what was going on. A waiter whose face I shall never forget (he had black, curly hair and a moustache that accentuated a sinister sneer, and who must have been fantasizing this kind of an opportunity for a long, long time) broke a wine bottle over a garbage pail and came running towards me with a savage gleam in his eyes, and snarled, as he pointed the jagged glass, "Ya little bastard, I'm gonna cut up that pretty face of yours." It was hardly the time to thank him for the compliment. My head was in an upheaval and the noise in the room was getting louder by the second. All of a sudden, the main doors to the dining room swung open and in stormed the imperious Mrs. Silverman. She took one peripheral look and screamed, "The emcee is making trouble! Call the State Police!" Fortunately for me, the members of the orchestra, sitting in the staff dining room, had been wondering what was taking me so long to come back, and walked right into the commotion just as Mrs. Silverman was bellowing her frightening command. They rushed me down to my room where we emptied all my belongings directly through the window into one of the musician's cars, and swiftly drove me to a smaller hotel several blocks away. There I walked into the welcoming arms of the kindly Breeskin and Jacobs families, for whom I had done some very successful shows in the past, and it was there that I finished out the remaining weeks of the season. Coincidentally, Jeannie and Hal had sought refuge there when they had left, and were now on staff. Oh, I never got paid whatever money had been owed to me at the Ritter. The hotel owners had the law enforcement people in their pockets, and although I actually got up the nerve to go back later on, to collect what was due me, and was rebuffed, I considered myself lucky to have gotten away without being imprisoned. Just coincidentally, perhaps one or two years later I went downstairs into the men's washroom while at Dubrow's Cafeteria and found myself face-to-face with the angry waiter who had threatened to cut me up. There were just the two of us, nobody else. I don't believe that he even recognized me, and the thought hit me that I could exact revenge, if I was a vengeful type. Instead I just glanced at him for a moment, and slowly turned and walked away. Violence is not part of my makeup, but at times like that I wished that it was, except that the past problem was really his and I wasn't inclined to try to analyze why he behaved as irrationally as he did. How does the joke go? The famed Dakota-born orchestra leader who somehow spoke with an accent, Lawrence Welk, was once asked, "Whaddya think of violence?" and he was quick to reply, "I hate violence ... but I like sexaphones ... n' drums."

And so home I went in the spring, wondering what I could do to obtain a decent job in the Catskills for the approaching summer now that I had accumulated, perhaps, enough material and experience, to try to make it as the head man, the Social Director. It would be fatuous to try at any good-sized hotel, but there were enough smaller ones around that would welcome a man like me, so I figured, why not? I was going to make the rounds at the various agencies, this time much better armed, but, as I was soon to discover, the theatrical agencies were not necessary for my next course of action.

I don't remember, exactly, how it came about, and I have a vague recollection that it may have been through an introduction by my cousin Doris' husband at the time. His brother was a popular radio announcer on one of the local New York stations, and he lived in a more affluent area, not too far away from where I lived, in Brooklyn. I spoke to him on the telephone, and he invited me to come to his home one evening, where I could see something that would soon become the rage worldwide. "Have you ever seen television?" he asked me. I said, "No, but I'd love to. I've heard so much about it." "Then c'mon over," he said, "I've got the Joe Louis-Billy Conn fight goin' on tomorrow night on my TV, and I would also like very much to meet you as I've heard some good things about you, and I've got an idea I'd like to kick around."

I remember stopping off at D. Miller's bakery to pick up a cake, and I either walked or took a trolley to Bob Harris' lovely home in Flatbush where I was met by this affable young man with a most distinguished bass-baritone voice, and was cordially introduced to his wife Goldie and their adorable twin little daughters. (The girls were some day going to be the flower girls at my wedding.) And the TV? What a fascinating experience! There was this lovely piece of console furniture that greatly resembled a well-crafted, large, living room standing radio, except that it opened from the top like a liquor bar. He parted the top leaves, and we all peered down onto a screen that was going through the prelims before the eagerly awaited main event that turned out to be a "doosie." Besides being privy to something that nobody else I knew, had, I was treated to one of the most memorable bouts I had ever seen in my life. The handsome, white underdog, Billy Conn, (younger and many pounds lighter than the popular black heavyweight champion of the world) surprisingly was outboxing the champ and was way ahead on points all the way into around the twelfth round of the scheduled fifteen rounder. It looked like the upset of the ages was in the making, and it got to a crescendo when Joe Louis was going to hit the canvas after being battered by a flurry of Conn's combination punches. Suddenly, as Conn bore in on the helpless looking Louis, the great champion uncorked a massive punch that sent the overconfident Billy Conn into "la-la land." It happened as quickly as that, and, as all the reporters present explained it, it was a case of the crafty, experienced Louis (aware that he was quite behind on points, and in danger of being upset) "playing possum" and suckering his eager challenger into a most vulnerable position, and then "WHAM!" ... "The winner, and still heavyweight champion of the world ... The Great ... Joe Louis!"

As we sat around afterward, partaking in the coffee and cake scene, Bob said, "They tell me you're a pretty good comedian, and can handle a season in the mountains with ease. Goldie and I are planning to spend the summer at a hotel up there as solicitors. Through my popularity on the radio I have attracted a following, and in that way my family gets to spend all summer in the mountains. We are currently in the process of putting the summer staff together. We've already got the band picked out, the great Bobby Kaye is the leader, and we just about have the singer, Frieda Starr, in the fold, and, if you feel that you want in, I'd like to have you aboard."

I found out later, that this was an excellent way for Bob to take advantage of his name and popularity, and by getting involved like that, he and his family got themselves an excellent financial dispensation when it came to making a deal for spending the entire summer at a resort hotel. After all, he was a "celebrity" and such things are done all the time. I felt flattered by his surprising offer, and the matter of remuneration was not even discussed at the moment. With my hunger for work and experience, no matter what remained to be worked out by Bob Harris and the hotel owner by way of compensation, it would have been sufficient. We agreed on a handshake, as signed contracts in situations like those were actually useless, and I left for home with an understanding that I would be contacted shortly with all the details regarding the name of the hotel, the travel arrangements, etc.

Memorial Day Weekend constituted the "kickoff" date for the forthcoming summer season, and, since there was a month between then and the July 1st start, that weekend gave the entertainers and the owners the opportunity to "feel each other out." It still left enough time if any changes had to be made, such as a decision to cancel the deal by either party, or both. Very soon after my confab with Mr. Harris I got to meet Bobby Kaye, a handsome, round faced young musician, who sported a well groomed, pencil thin moustache and an abundant head of slick, black hair that rose into a beautiful pompadour, which was all the rage at the time. With his checkered knee length jacket and solid colored pegged pants, he looked like the consummate bandleader. He really looked "sharp." And, from what I observed, he played the clarinet as well as the great Benny Goodman. He also doubled on the alto saxophone and sang as beautifully as any of the big stars of the time. He made quite an impression, and, to my delight, he was soft spoken and good natured. He was married to a rather well endowed blonde whose head of hair was as plentiful as her colorful husband's, and they had an infant son. Later on, when I met the other members of his band, I was thrilled by the thought of spending the forthcoming summer in such good company. We ascertained a rendezvous time with the "hacker" who was to drive us all up to the Royal Hotel in Glen Wild, NY. Just coincidentally, and conveniently, that driver was Bobby's brother Moish, who had a very good paying job as a newspaper distributor for the Journal-American, a cushy, union situation that allowed him enough free time to "moonlight" at other income producers.

Meanwhile, the word got around throughout my neighborhood that I was about to embark on a summer job in the Catskills, as a Social Director. This greatly impressed just about everyone. I dropped in at Vinitzky's fruit emporium one day to purchase some vegetables for my mother, and dear Rosie called me aside and asked if she could speak to me "in private" for a moment. I always had an ear open for that wonderful lady who had been my boss, on and off, for a good part of my early teens. "I heard about your good fortune," she said, "and with another hot summer coming up, and with

Shirley already through with high school and between jobs in the garment center, I'd love for her to get out into the fresh air and sunshine that the mountains have to offer. I wonder if, perhaps, you could find her a job where you're going?" The thought of having that beautiful girl around, just to look at every day, was dizzying. "What kind of a job is she looking for?" I asked. "Anything at all," Rosie replied, "I'm sure that, whatever she does, she'll do well, as you know what a great kid she is, and, I'd feel a whole lot better knowing that you'd be around to look after her." I said, "I'll see what I can do, but I can't make any promises at this very moment," to which she replied, "I understand." I went home thinking, "Wow, that beautiful, personable kid would be an asset anywhere, but who do I have to convince? And, how much clout could I possibly have, and with whom, in order to create a summer position for her?" Like the lyric in the soliloquy in Rodgers and Hammerstein's "Carousel" sung by the character Billy, "I'll try. By God, I'll try!"

"Look after her? That's not too hard to do. She's so lovely." I knew that she had a steady beau for many years. She was now all of about seventeen, and he had been her guy since she was maybe twelve or thirteen. He was currently away somewhere, serving in the Navy. What kind of an environment would this be for a young, single girl with an "almost-fiancee" away in the Navy? "Hey, I'm very young myself. Only a couple of years older than she is. Still in my teens, and, as much as I prefer to think I am, I'm not very worldly. Oh, what the hell, I'll approach Bob Harris n' see if he can talk management into creating some kind of job for her that wouldn't be ridiculous, ... and Bob and Goldie, I'm sure, would love to have that pretty young thing around too, to look after. Let me see what I can work out?" "And then again," I thought, "Maybe she doesn't want to go away? Just because her mother thinks it's a good idea? Well, why don't we wait and see?"

As it turned out, Shirley was thrilled at the thought, and Bob and Goldie had no trepidation about talking the hotel owner into hiring her as a tea girl, or a children's counselor, whichever was more applicable, with either one allowing her plenty of free time for herself. The pay? Mostly tips, and that depended, for the large part, on those guests she was attending to. She should come out quite satisfactorily.

The entire band, all five of them, and the singer, Frieda, a very "hip," heavy set young lady with a magnificent voice that carried into several octaves, and Shirley and I, all piled into Moish's aging "hack" a couple of nights before the Memorial Day Weekend. Our luggage and band instruments were tied down with heavy ropes to the entire exterior of the van, as there was room only for us "beings" inside. It was a comical sight but we were just too excited to notice. We were on our way to the country. It was all so thrilling. "Who knows what's in store for us? We're one big happy family, rarin' to go, ... so move it Moish! Hit the gas! We're on our way!" ... And all the way up we sang the hotel theme song that Bob had taught us, "Gimme the Royal. Gimme the Royal, ... the place of amusement, laughter and joy. Gimme the Royal. Gimme the Royal, ... where Poppa meets Momma, ... and girl meets boy ..." We were all so exuberant that we didn't even mind it when the old "hack" broke down with flat tires, more than once, on precarious two lane, curving mountain highways. The breakdowns necessitated our all getting out n' standing around, shivering in the night air, on pitch black roads, while Moish went about the laborious job of tying, and untying a good deal of the luggage in order to get to the hidden spares, along with the jack, the flares, etc. We all huddled together happily, laughing at Moish's "brilliant preparation," and as seemingly dangerous as our breakdowns were, we were oblivious to everything. A bunch of city kids getting away to those glorious mountains... "Gimme the Royal" ..." "Sing it louder ..." "Gimme the Royal, ... the place of amusement, laughter and joy. .... Gimme the Royal... Gimme the Royal."

It was in that state of euphoria that, somehow, as though it was the most natural thing in the world to do, in the back seat of Moish's broken down hack (that resembled a giant hippopotamus with hives, what with the lumpy luggage sticking out in every direction) that Shirley and I first embraced. It was such a beautiful and warm experience and was followed by a tender kiss, and then another. I felt love like I had never felt it before, and this darling girl in my arms drew closer as our lips touched repeatedly. I had kissed, and embraced a small assortment of ladies before, in my young life, but never had it felt like this, and it was all so reciprocal. As young as she was, she was extremely grown up, and I

Shirley and Van. Catskills (1945)

would gauge, a lot more sophisticated than others her age, and we were throwing caution to the winds, without any forethought about the consequences or whom we may be hurting in the process. After all, she was "taken." She had a guy, and for all I knew, they might have had big plans, but who could even think of that in the passion of the moment. I'm sure that she was not even thinking of him at the time, and as much as I could have written this off as just another amorous escapade that goes with the glamorous "territory" that I was immersing my life into, I felt a love for this girl in my arms that exceeded anything else I'd ever known. If nothing would ever come of that moment, I would still cherish it forever, and ever, and joyfully bask in its reflective glory. I thought to myself, "I love you, my dear, sweet, adorable girl. I hope you feel for me what I'm feeling for you. There could never be another magical moment like this for me for the rest of my life, and I shall remain eternally grateful for the experience."

At long last we arrived in the middle of the night, greeted by a frenzied Bob Harris, who was worried sick over what might have been the reason for our long delay. He showed us all to our respective quarters, a sobering experience to say the least. Though the hotel was called The Royal, there was never, ever, any "royal suite" set aside for the help. Fortunately though, because they weren't overbooked, we all got separate rooms, as shabby and unsafe as they were. After sleeping well into the afternoon, we rolled up our sleeves and went about the business of preparing for the arrival of our guests, most of whom were due on the following day.

Whether it was because we did not fulfill the hotel's expectations, or Bob Harris and the management were unable to formulate an equitable arrangement regarding his family's summer stay (and I suspect that it was a case of the latter), our great expectations regarding the Royal came to an unexpected, and abrupt halt after that weekend. "Not to worry," Bob assured us, and, before long we were all preparing to go up to the Midwood Hotel in Loch Sheldrake from July the first until Labor Day. Best of all, the deal included the tea girl. The only difference was that, much to our dismay, Frieda Starr had accepted another engagement, but, fortunately, we added a delightful singing duo, Jimmy Cosenza and Winnie Stewart. He was tall and heavy set, with a glorious tenor voice, and she was petite and slim, and her soprano notes reached astounding heights. Together and singularly, they made the most beautiful music.

We had a most productive, and successful summer, highlighted by our five piece band's garnering first prize in the annual summer orchestra competition at one of the major hotels (competing against ten and twelve piece orchestras with a stirring, swing rendition of "Las Chapanecas"). The tea girl turned out to be a "quick study," learning all the lines in the skits I presented, and she flourished into the best damn ingenue I'd ever worked with on any stage, anywhere. As she grew in stature, so did our romance, and, as we look back now, it was a summer made in heaven. It was a summer of laughter. A lot of the laughter was provided by our erstwhile, humorous drummer, Herb Gordon (nee Goldstein), who was later to become one of my dearest, lifelong friends. He was both handsome and nearsighted, and also vain. He preferred to remove his glasses whenever he was on the bandstand so that the girls would ogle him. As a result, when he stepped down from his throne in the back after they had finished a set, he would invariably trample the reed and brass, instruments that were sitting on their stands on the floor. There were plenty of noisy eruptions that followed. Fortunately for all of us, no great harm was done, and, for the most part, we remained one great big homogenized group. Herbie was also the band's "lover," and was always willing to accommodate the single ladies that vacationed at the hotel. During one of his trysts, he decided to make an attempt at some kinky sex, and the young lady, whose back was turned away from him at the moment, wheeled around just in time to see Herbie crawling towards her head, sporting a well aimed "protrusion." The dear girl stared at him and asked, "Just what the hell do you think you're doing?" to which he quickly replied, "I'm just trying to look out the window." Soon afterward, this vacationer let us all know what had happened, and until the day poor Herbie was taken away from us by the dread disease diabetes, some forty-five years later, Herbie was always greeted by any of us who knew him well, with, "Hey Herb, been lookin' outta the window lately?"

9 Drafted

At long last, our beautiful summer came to an end, and it was back to reality. Our glory days were over, we said our goodbyes, promised to stay in touch, and headed back to our respective homes. Shirley and I, living just around the corner from each other, continued our summer romance, which didn't escape the eye of her sagacious mother for a single moment. Though Rosie was always quite fond of me, she had to be as perplexed about the matter as we all were. The thought of Shirley's beau, off somewhere in the navy, yearning for the day that he would come back to her, consumed me with guilt, as it did all of us, and we spoke about our not seeing each other again, out of fairness to him, but it just became an impossible task. She was a young girl when they parted, and suddenly she discovered that she had become a young woman. Had he been home, perhaps it would have been simpler to tell him that we had fallen in love. The reality however, was something beyond our control, and, after a great deal of soul searching and serious deliberation, she took it upon herself to write him a delicate letter explaining what had occurred, and how she now felt. I honestly and sincerely felt their pain vicariously, and offered to step out of the picture until such time that he would come home and they could see if they felt the same about each other as they did when he left, when they were both a lot younger, and a lot more naive. Shirley and I could not stay apart, however, and he did come home on leave, and they did speak. Time and circumstances had taken their toll, and the once torrid romance of their youth had come to a sorrowful end. My heart ached for both of them. He was a fine, and gifted young man, and very popular in the neighborhood, and I considered going off somewhere to let things cool, but the fact of the matter was that we were deeply in love. His military obligation necessitated his having to depart, broken hearted, and there was nothing more that could be said or done.

We seriously deliberated the entire, heart rending situation, and, with Rosie's blessings, we decided to get married, though I was still, legally underage, and needed my parents' consent in order to obtain a marriage license. In thinking about it now, how in the world could loving parents allow their daughter to marry a well-meaning, but aimless, underage man, with no real trade other than an ability to charm and make people laugh? Such were the times. We were all children of the Great Depression, accustomed to searching for a way to make a living honestly; a massive, terrible war had just ended, with an astronomical amount of casualties and the entire world was in chaos; the boys and girls that were involved in the worldwide conflagration were about to come home to an uncertain future, and nobody really gave too much thought to tomorrow. (Shirley's brother was scheduled to be returning from China, where he had been ultimately reassigned.) Such was the prevailing atmosphere, and here were two young kids in love. Let 'em get married n' pray for the best. Everybody was doin' it.

Our wedding date, at a large, and popular catering facility on Franklin Ave. in Brooklyn, was scheduled for Christmas night, which was quite a few months away. I went about looking for work and was lucky enough to grab an occasional, low-paying weekend at one or two, local nightclubs. As opposed to the days before the war, there was money around, and neighborhood nightclubs were beginning to spring up all over. I made a connection, through some other neophyte comedians that I had been introduced to, named Bernie Ilson, and Georgie Raymond They worked separately, and both featured record pantomime, where a recording was played behind them while they mouthed the words and made very funny gestures with their bodies, along with funny faces. Lots of successful comedy stars started that way including Jerry Lewis. The club they introduced me to was Dave's Inn, located on Pitkin Ave., in a thriving part of Brooklyn, and it was soon to become one of my favorite spots. Since it was not too distant from where I lived, I was able to fill the small club with friends who brought their dates, so, with whatever little nightclub experience I had, I was able to carry my weight, and became one of Dave's favorites. I remember that they had an abnormally obese waiter named "Davie" who, when he walked by, would block out, at least, half of my audience. My favorite Dubrow "mentor," whose name was "One-Ball Barney," gave fat Davie a very appropriate nickname. He called him "Two Thirds Of The Nation," and even that was an understatement.

While I was struggling, trying to put together a few bucks in these little clubs that Barney referred to as "upholstered sewers," Shirley, who was once a model, was rapidly maturing into a rather stunning woman. She went to work in a successful children's clothing shop in the Ridgewood section of Brooklyn, and was so well liked that she was soon getting promotions. She was making more money than I, which, in reality, was no great feat. We were counting the days until our wedding, and we were having so much fun fantasizing about our future while little by little our friends were starting to wed, and one or two were already having babies. I tried so hard to emulate the romantic things I had read about and seen in the movies. I brought her flowers and sweets, at the slightest provocation, and life was just one big, beautiful rainbow. We had no car, but we managed to get around quite well with all the public transportation that was available. Occasionally a well off friend with a car would pick us up, and we'd enjoy more distant places, like the then pristine Long Island, that sported a marvelous Howard Johnson's ice cream parlor somewhere in Valley Stream, and numerous parks, and lakes. It was truly the good times. The world was becoming our oyster.

I opened my mailbox one gray, early November morning, and found something I had forgotten all about. There was a letter from President Harry S. Truman that started out by saying, "Greetings." Wow! I had been classified 1AL way back when, which meant "limited service," and had forgotten that I was still indebted to our Uncle Sam. It was time to hand in my marker. What timing! I took another physical and passed. (Funny, I wondered, what ever became of "Frayim"?) I was told to report to Fort Hancock in Red Bank, NJ (soon afterward condemned for having contaminated food) in a couple of weeks. I had to break the news to Shirley, who cried bitterly, but we soon settled down and went about formulating a new set of plans. Much to the dismay of her employers who were already starting to groom her as a buyer, Shirley was going to give up her wonderful job and join me wherever I was assigned. The pressing problem was, "What are we going to do about our wedding date?" The invitations had already been sent out to, literally, hundreds of guests, and a good-sized, probably un-refundable deposit had been put down for the orchestra, the flowers, etc., etc. All this presented me with the kind of challenge I thrived on then. I told Rose and Max (the bride's parents foot most of the bill, a rather tidy sum) and Shirley, to go ahead with everything and not let anything interfere with our plans. I told them that, if I would be assigned anywhere nearby I would wangle a pass, and if I were sent far away (much too soon to be sent overseas, if at all), then, "Take my word for it, I will go AWOL! ... but don't worry, I'll be there!"

As things developed, the geniuses that run the army, gave me an 045 MOS (which, in lay language means "clerk-typist." To this very day I still can't type worth a damn), and, after the first, horrible period at Fort Hancock, I was sent to Fort Dix in NJ to work in the separation center, mustering out returning veterans. As Christmas was rapidly approaching, I selected a propitious moment to talk to my chaplain and tell him that the wedding date was all set, and ask for a three-day pass. I was knocked off my feet when he responded by saying, "Whaddya wanna get married for? You're too young!" I couldn't believe my ears! I had even shown him the beautifully embossed printed wedding invitation. It was at a popular Jewish catering hall. He, the chaplain, was Jewish! We are Jewish! I figured it would make some points. How could he turn me down? After all he was my own chaplain. Who needs so many soldiers around the camp on a Christmas weekend? I said, "You're kidding, aren't you?" The imperious officer grinned, and said, with an air of finality, "No, I'm not! Request denied!" It was as though somebody had clobbered me over the head with a blunt instrument. I stormed out of his office, walked aimlessly back to my barracks, muttering to myself, "That sonova bitch! That lousy sonovabitch!" Another G.I., coming from the other direction, walked past me and recognized me. "Whaddya beatin' yer gums about, Harris? Who's a sonavabitch?" I proceeded to tell him what had just happened, and he laughed. "Idiot! That's not the way it's done. I'm Catholic. If I want a favor I go to the rabbi and he bends over backwards to show me what a good guy he is. Go see my chaplain and ask him." You've heard the expression, "No man is an island?" You cannot get along without learning from other, more experienced people. I don't even remember who this guy was, but I could have kissed him. The rest was a piece of cake. I asked permission to see the chaplain, walked in, and the first words out of my mouth were, "Father, I'm not of your faith ... " "Sit down my boy," he replied, with his arms spread wide as though he was about to embrace me, "tell me, what can I do for you?"

The wedding was magnificent. Perfect! Everybody had a ball, and we've got one big, fantastic, leather bound wedding album to prove it. The only regret is that I didn't invite that chaplain, and the helpful soldier, surely, everybody else in the world was there.

We spent an overnight at the famous Hotel St. George, in Brooklyn (where some time much later on, Shirley was going to be briefly employed at the new and popular Stardust Room, as a cigarette girl, in a pretty, tight, short, pink costume.) My father-in-law was flattered when he walked Shirley to the front desk to ask for the room key, and they mistook him for the groom. We then continued on, the next day, to the Hotel Ritter in Lakewood, "under new management" where we spent a one day honeymoon. My old pal Al Sheiner, who was now working there as a waiter, bellhop, and all-around man, brought us a midnight snack. He took a long, long time to leave, and I had to practically throw him, bodily, out of our room. Late the following day we left for Fort Dix.

We had rented a room in a modest house in Bordentown, not far from the installation, and, bright and early the next morning I left my bride, who was going to look for employment, while I went back to camp. We ran into a swarm of bees on that very first day. Soon after I had gone, the elderly landlady knocked on our door complaining that she was not feeling well, and collapsed into Shirley's arms and died. What a beginning for a young bride in a strange new environment. That evening we frantically searched for another apartment, and were lucky enough to find one, and that's where we were to reside for my entire army career. Shirley got a good job, working as a secretary for a local lawyer who later became a judge, and I quickly learned the skills of promoting weekends off, and we would take the train back home to Brooklyn on most weekends to partake in the delicious chicken soup with matzoh balls that Rosie took such delight in preparing for us. Occasionally I would leave camp illegally, with a borrowed pass from a soldier who had already been discharged. It always worked, until that one time that a civilian employee, moonlighting as "security," asked me my name, a long, difficult-to-pronounce Polish name, which I told him, and then he surprised me by asking for my serial number, which I had neglected to memorize (as the name itself was difficult enough). The civilian punk turned me in, which materialized into a court martial, but there again, through the combination of charm and applied legerdemain, I managed to talk my superiors out of that kind of embarrassing punishment. I was learning quickly about man's inhumanity to man, and tried to avoid it at all costs.

A few years back, while the war was going on, my childhood friend, Iggy (a handsome only child who grew up very uncomfortably in a broken home) was drafted into the infantry. While training in blistering hot Camp Croft, South Carolina, he cracked and went AWOL, and hid out in Brooklyn for awhile. I'd come and bring him goodies from time to time. In a very short while he realized his futility and went back to Croft and turned himself in. The omnipotent assholes who were his superiors, punished him by actually placing him in an open dungeon, dug into the ground, and covered only by iron gratings, with the 100 degree sun blazing down on him all day long. His fellow GI's, many of whom were savage, ignorant country boys, would pass by and spit or urinate on him, and practice their expletives. Such great patriots! I wonder how these simple, obnoxious bastards behaved in the heat of battle?

While I was in Fort Dix I fell off a truck and had the occasion to go into Tilton General Hospital located in the camp. During the short while that I was in there, somebody made off with my uniforms which was really no big loss because, when I entered the army I had been issued rough, wooly uniforms that were originally Canadian. Besides being terribly uncomfortable, they rubbed all the hair off my hairy body. I complained to the top Sergeant, a slim, bespectacled career soldier with a thick southern accent. (I think they all had southern accents.) And he said, "Stop yer bitchin' Harris! There's guys bein' discharged every minute and they're depositing their gear in the old kitchen. Go in and pick out whatever you want, n' have the stuff cleaned and wear it." I followed his instructions and came upon a gold mine. I

Van and Shirley's Wedding
December 25, 1945
Franklin Manor, Brooklyn.

selected some beautifully tailored "specials" for myself. I even bought some major's leaves which I wore on my epaulets when I was safely out of sight of everyone, as that constitutes "impersonating an officer," which is a major, major crime (not wishing to pun here). The various service command insignias were still sewn on a number of them, so I got a real brainstorm and filled up a barracks bag with discarded jackets that looked like they would fit my father who was in pretty good physical appearance from working so hard as a helper on a beer delivery truck, and brought them home to him. Pop looked young enough to have been taken for a veteran, and each day he'd deliver beer to customer's homes sporting a different uniform with a different patch on his arm. They assumed that he was some kind of a super hero, and, for as long as he wore that clothing, which was, in essence, a gift from the Sergeant, his tips multiplied considerably. So what began as a petty theft of my uncomfortable G.I. issue, was satisfactorily ameliorated, and also turned into a windfall for my pop.

The war was over, and (except for the instances where some "chicken shit" superiors who enjoyed their momentary omnipotence, were slow to release their positions of power) restrictions were becoming far more relaxed, and, with few exceptions, we were permitted to leave the camp grounds at the end of the day. Realistically speaking, the whole thing was like a stupid 9 to 5 job that you were unable to quit. On those weekends when we couldn't afford to take the train back to Brooklyn, we would generally get together with another couple for Saturday evening, bring in some inexpensive food, and amuse ourselves by reading and acting out a number of the comedy scripts that we had brought along from home with us. This provided us with the joy and laughter that made our situation a good deal more bearable. After awhile they actually began discharging us, and I was out in less than a year.

I shall always respect and admire those who served in wartime, and gave so very much of themselves. The entire world owes them an enormous debt of gratitude, and these heroes, each and every one of them, should never be forgotten, and especially those unfortunate souls who never made it back (a number of whom also came from our beloved

126

neighborhood). I have been with the wounded in the hospitals, I've tried to make them laugh, and have, more times than not, succeeded. I've unashamedly told them how I feel about them, and now, so many, many years later, when I appear before Veterans' groups, I am filled with emotion, and the one word that keeps flashing in the back of my mind like a neon light, is "respect," "respect," "respect." I too, am forever indebted to them. It's very theatrical to wave the flag, sing "God Bless America" and elicit standing ovations by doing so, especially among uncomplicated audiences such as we generally find on cruise ships, but as Abraham Lincoln pointed out so eloquently, "You can't fool all of the people all of the time." Patriotism, especially in our imperfect country that was formed by a desire for perfection, and which still manages better than most all of the others, is a very serious business, and should not be tossed off lightly. If you're gonna do it, then damn it ... ya must mean it! ... And don't, like so many of our politicians, try to hide your own brand of bullshit behind it.

When Johnny came marching home again, so did Big Red, and Julie Woolf. Red, the big, lovable neighborhood scourge, was just as mischievous in the army, where he saw action with an Engineers outfit in the European Theater of Operations, and brought back an impressive load of Nazi souvenirs to prove it. Julie, on the other hand, was in the Navy, patrolling the waters in that same area. Julie was short, and blonde, and built like a fire plug. Whereas most of us were derived from Eastern European Ashkenazi ancestors, Julie was of English Jewish stock, tough as nails, but never flamboyant. I knew him since the early days in Williamsburg, that is, I knew of him. Back then, in elementary school, the two biggest, supposed troublemakers in P.S.147 were Julie Woolf and one, Vincent Lupo. The principal of the school, having had it with those two little ruffians, who barely knew each other, designed what he thought was an ingenious scheme, but one that wound up costing him his job. He placed the two of them in the school's basement with instructions that sounded something like, "You seem to be having so much fun beatin' up other kids, now you can try beatin' each other up," and left them there to do so, and they did! Julie wound up with a black eye, and Lupo lost a tooth, or visa-versa. Somehow the report of this highly unorthodox solution found its way into the sensationalist *NY Daily News*, and there was hell to pay for the man who conceived that wild idea. I can't exactly recall all the specifics of his punishment as we couldn't afford the two cents that the *Daily News* cost in those years. Quite coincidentally, while in his later teenage years, Julie's family moved from Williamsburg to the same Crown Heights area we lived in, and we became close friends. He was an excellent athlete, and although he was basically taciturn in manner, he would easily fly into a rage if he felt that he was unjustly treated in any sports competition. It was generally debated as to who was the bigger hothead on the ball field, Julie, my brother Yussel, or Irving Metz, and in the midst of the action it would be wise not to get in the way of any one of them.

Julie and Red were both in the process of being discharged from the Armed Forces when they each came home for the weekend in their respective uniforms. Both had added on muscle and Red had gotten even taller. The joke going around was, "Hey Red, when are you gonna introduce your pants to your shoes?" When these two were together they made a striking pair, Big Red in his tightening khakis, towering over little, barrel chested Julie in his contrasting navy blues with the bell bottom trousers. Both had driven to one of the famous movie presentation houses on busy Broadway in Manhattan in Red's reconstructed old Buick (a favor to a returning soldier from his loving old uncle "Baldano"). The car was rather unusual in that it didn't have an ignition switch. Red would start it by touching two wires together. It was such fun to watch him start the car up, and when it would start, under Uncle B's watchful eye, the hairless old former GM master mechanic would leap into the air as a gesture of appreciation, and click his heels together as he was levitated, n' shout one of his favorite old-timer expressions, "Oh Martha, save me!" which was a sign of success. If he monkeyed with something mechanical and it failed to respond as it was supposed to, then he'd do the same jump, only as he was descending and clicking his heels at the same time he would yell out, "Shit mother, I can't dance!" Uncle Eddie, nicknamed "Baldano," was quite a character. He owned a bunch of little garages on the same street where he lived, a street we all referred to as "Shitpot Lane," 'cause, somehow, everyone in the neighborhood who had a dog, walked his dog on that street.

The boys had caught a late afternoon movie and stage show, and afterward, strolled into a nearby tavern on 8th Ave. for a short beer. There they befriended a couple of good looking army nurses who'd been sitting there for awhile, bought them a drink, and asked if they would like to go out for a drive. The ladies, replete in their officer's uniforms, and already a bit tipsy from before their meeting, readily accepted, and out they strutted into the fresh night air as the four of them embarked on a walking tour of the brilliant, bedazzling, Manhattan theater district, caught up in the crush of the multitude of revelers that was also enjoying the lingering postwar celebrations, with the excitement of things to come running through their minds. As the night progressed they became even more playful, and, before long, after stopping off for another drink, they climbed into Big Red's "limousine," and the girls giggled with glee as he touched the two wires together and the engine responded with a loud roar. "Great town y'all got here, fellas," they both remarked, 'if they only didn't have so many fuckin' Jews!" Red's eyebrows arched when he heard that, and the corners of Julie's lips automatically started to quiver as his face started to take on a menacing glow. The boys looked at each other for one quick moment, and broke into raucous laughter, deciding right then and there that they weren't going to reform the ladies, but they might as well have as much fun as they could while it lasted, and boy, did they ever.

They had the time of their lives with the well-stacked "pushovers," as they drove back to Brooklyn, fondling, and muzzling, and all else that went with it. While the ladies giggled with delight, they would still, from time to time, continue their irritating verbal assaults upon New York's Jews, while, all the while, the boys would laughingly nod their assent, as their hands traveled recklessly. After a number of stops on dark, lonely roads where they would stop and complete the action, they treated the girls to a lively twirl through the world famous Coney Island, with its exciting roller coasters, hot dog stands, side shows, etc. As they got back into the car to continue on, again the cacophony of "too many fuckin' Jews," which, by then, already had become a bit too intolerable. With a wild, inventive gleam in his eyes, the big red "bear" remarked, "Ladies, it's such a warm night, whaddya say we go to Canarsie for a swim?" The southern belles never heard of Canarsie, but the name sounded intriguing, and they readily consented. Once again, the two wires went "Phtt! and on they drove, singing all the way till they got to Rockaway Parkway, made the right turn up to the pier that juts into the Atlantic Ocean, and turned off the engine. It was still quite torrid out, despite the very late hour, and there didn't appear to be anyone else anywhere in sight. "Whaddya say we go bare ass?" Red suggested. "Great idea," the girls replied, and in a moment their clothes were off. As Red and Julie took their sweet time undressing, deliberately fumbling with their zippers and buttons, Red said, "Go in first. We'll follow you." The squealing ladies dove into the dark waters, and as they happily flapped around in the refreshing water, Red n' Julie scooped up all the clothing, flung the pile into the car, touched the two wires together, and as the car whooshed off into the darkness, he yelled at the top of his lungs, "Fuck you! I'm a Jew!

Nothing ever more came of that incident except that the story has been told, and retold, throughout the years at so many social functions and family gatherings. Somewhere there are two former army nurses reliving that infamous night. So much has happened in our changing society since then, but I would hazard a guess that they're probably still telling the story about how two "sonavabitch New York Jews" literally screwed them.

Meanwhile brother Joe came home from the army after a most successful baseball career with Uncle Sam, where he also doubled as a Military Policeman, guarding German prisoners who were being fed and housed, quite substantially, in Florida. His G.I. buddy, a catcher in the Detroit Tigers baseball organization named Hal Wagner, said, "C'mon Joe, you're good enough to get a tryout with the Tigers and wind up on one of our farm teams." Instead Joe chose to come back to Brooklyn and collect his twenty dollars per week that the US government was doling out to the returning G.I.'s for a total of fifty two weeks, and he spent the next year just loafin' around, giving a lot of his attention to the pool room on St.

Johns Place, next to the Utica Theater, latching on to an occasional job here and there, but surviving mostly on the money he won from betting on the horses, until he met Phyllis, the girl that he was going to eventually marry. Suddenly, like so many others of that turbulent generation, he had to seriously look for the kind of employment that might insure him of a future. His pal Lefty Kossover, a pitcher with whom he had played baseball before the army, caught on with the NY Yankees, and was assigned to their Binghamton, NY farm team, but soon gave up, exclaiming, "Who can work for $160 a month, and ya pay for your own meals? That's not a job for an ambitious Jewish boy from Brooklyn! It's for farm boys who never lived that good." He must've forgotten about the Hank Greenbergs and the Harry Dannings, and the Goodie Rosens, and the likes, ... and one of those farm boys that he had played with during his brief tenure with Binghamton, a "hayseed" they used to poke fun at, and play practical jokes upon, rose to become one of the leading pitchers of his time in the Major Leagues, and a World Series hero for the Boston Braves.

10 Union Blues

Shirley and I were fortunate enough to live with Max and Rose in their four room apartment on Sterling Place, and I scrounged around, grabbing a weekend at some small, insignificant neighborhood nightclub, here and there, until summer came 'round, and I auditioned for a job as a Social Director in the mountains. It was back to the agents at the Palace Building, but this time I came better equipped. Now I had a pretty fair amount of seasoning under my belt. I actually had legitimate credits, having had a two full summer seasons in the Catskills, and a whole winter, fractured as it was, in Lakewood, plus some little clubs that actually paid me in return for my entertaining their patrons. It was a natty little man (as sanguine an individual as I'd ever met, with a shock of wavy black hair that, as full as it was, did nothing to belie his apparent lack of height) ushered me into his office, which was larger and more sumptuously decorated than those I had visited before. Maurice Kurtz graciously invited me to sit down and proceeded to tell me about a client who was interested in meeting a bright young comedian like me with an eye towards running the social and athletic programs for the forthcoming summer at a lovely hotel located on Kauneonga Lake, about a dozen miles from the big and busy Catskill city of Monticello. Mr. Kurtz informed me that his client was a prominent attorney from the Bronx who leased a hotel in that area with his experienced father who was quite a colorful character, and a master at running a hotel kitchen.

My meeting with Carl Schumer, the young lawyer, was an instantaneous success. There was an excellent chemistry that occurred as we discussed our respective ideas regarding the art of "social directing," but, since the life of a resort hotel (with the exception of the two giants, Grossinger's and the Concord, that ran all year 'round) was just the summer months, when it came to selecting the all-important social staff there was truly no margin for error. We agreed upon my Memorial Day Weekend tryout, and Shirley and I passed that with flying colors. I signed a contract to become head man, and, filled with confidence, and more than a modicum of nerve, we packed up my father-in-law's truck with enough clothes, costumes, and other essentials to carry us through ten weeks at the Kenmore Hotel on glorious Kauneonga Lake. So began an idyllic summer that was to be repeated for two additional years. I had, by then, purchased a 1936 Plymouth that was at the point where it had practically outlived its usefulness. (I had to stop the car every thirty miles to add a quart of oil.) From that summer on, Max and Rose spent their vacations on the first two weeks of every summer at whichever hotel I was working at, so that they could transport all of our bulky equipment, which was just too cumbersome for our little excuse for a car. As the summer progressed, I would make several trips back home, alone, on a day off, and, in that way I managed to get all our belongings back by summer's end. Of course, the hotel owners didn't mind our "modus operandi" at all, as it meant that they were guaranteed two extra paying guests, and, of course, Max and Rose were delighted to point out to the other guests that "those two onstage are our daughter and son-in-law."

The Schumers were quite a memorable combination. Carl was the "boss," the titular head, who was the social arm of the family. Tall, well built, and well dressed, sporting a stylish moustache, and wire rimmed glasses, he was every bit the successful barrister. He delighted in taking bows for everything that the guests liked about the hotel, including the programs of yours truly'. His pretty wife Dinah, the mother of their two young children, ran the office meticulously, doubled as the hostess, took care of all the bookkeeping and monetary transactions, and checked the clientele in and out. Beneath her calm and winning smile, beat the heart of a very tough and skillful manager who bridged no nonsense from anyone. She had her pulse on everything that was happening at the hotel, and it was common knowledge to all that Dinah was completely in charge. Of course, thanks to our success with the guests, and our respectful personal deportment, we got along famously with the lady, and my $100 per week, less 10% for the agent Mr. Kurtz, was always paid on time.

"Pop" Schumer, Carl's father, could have been an actor on the Yiddish stage. He spoke with a decided accent, always had a ready laugh, was extremely gregarious, and made sure that he'd wander out of the kitchen in his food-spotted apron during each meal, hoping to accept accolades for his menus from the guests. His quiet, unassuming wife remained in the background. Because of the hotel's proximity to the successful, surrounding summer camps, the hotel, though not as large and glamorous as many of the others, was a welcome convenience for the kids' parents, especially on camp visiting weekends, and, as a result, it attracted an above average clientele in both intelligence and affluence. "Pop" was a lesson in "parsimoniousness." He did things we couldn't believe, like cutting the paper napkins in half and serving a half napkin at each meal. It was very noticeable, and it amazed me that, although the guests were quick to point that out among themselves, and to me, they, for reasons I could not quite fathom, never complained to the management.

"Pop," who sported a full head of hair atop a round, yet leathery face, despite his many long hours spent in the kitchen, was energetic and playful. He also fashioned himself as an actor and, whenever he would wander into the playhouse I'd have to bring him onstage to sing a song and I would shudder as the piano player would fumble all over the keyboard in an effort to find a suitable key to accompany him in. (I kept feeling that it was a payback for what I did to poor Abe Schwartz on my very first job up there.) He also insisted that once or twice during the summer, we present a sketch that he put together that made me extremely nervous. It contained a portrayal of lasciviousness on my part towards Shirley, and had a comic ending, but, as it progressed, he would come up, out of the audience and assail me for doing "blue material" on his stage. I would protest, explaining, "It's only a sketch," but he would get angrier and angrier, and before it was over, he would fire me, and then the members of the band would pipe in with, "What'd ya wanna do that for, it's only a sketch?" and he would fire them too. And, as the members of the orchestra started to pack up their gear, the astonished audience, not knowing that this upsetting sketch was prearranged, would start to add its discomfort. Before the surprise punch line, there was an uproar in the theater. I hated doing that sketch. I was told that, more than once it had caused ominous problems when "Pop" had done it at previous hotels, and, at one time there had been a genuine gangster in a hotel who actually came out of the audience brandishing a real gun, demanding that "'Pop' cool it ... and let the show continue ..."

Yes, he was quite a memorable character, that "Pop" Schumer. Was always the first one up in the morning and generally the last to go to bed at night. He had amazing endurance. One of the things we still talk about is the way he would usually start the day. We had a lovely young college girl working in the office, assisting Dinah with the bookkeeping, whose name was Marcia. We also had a hard working college boy on staff, named Eli, who worked as our bell captain. If they even knew each other it was quite superficially, and, each one slept in a room far away from the other, in distant parts of the hotel. Yet, every morning "Pop" would get on the loudspeaker that boomed all over the hotel, inside and outside, and, in an effort to make certain that these two essential cogs in his organization would be at work on time, announce. "Marcia and Eli ... get out of bed!!" This announcement was heard every single morning, and was a great source of conversation among our guests.

I also got a real taste of how lowly regarded the staff's comforts were, which was a disease that was indigenous to just about every resort hotel up there, as I may have already mentioned. I kept thinking about the famous Broadway producer and director, Moss Hart, who, in his autobiography, described how he had slept in a chicken coop when he was the youthful Social Director at The Flagler, the biggest hotel in the Catskills at the time. Here at The Kenmore, Shirley and I slept in a double size bed that had been squeezed into a closet on the stuffy, hot, top floor of the main building. There was no room for anything else. A dresser was in the attic across the hallway, along with some nails in the wall on which to hang clothing, and it was best to visit that area in daylight, as there were no lights there. Some fun. We used to prepare our clothes for the evening by transporting them to the playhouse dressing rooms, and often scheduled our showers there too. The toilet and washing facilities were all down the hallway and were shared with the lower paying guests, and other members of the staff and orchestra. You had to be young, healthy, strong, and resourceful to put up with such a paucity of comforts, and yet we managed to survive and make the most of it. I guess the management figured that we should be spending all of our time working, without ever resting in our rooms if we had a moment to ourselves.

I must have done well though. Some nights, after the show, we'd go up on the hill behind the hotel and toast marshmallows around a campfire while we sang off color limericks to the tune of "Cielito Linda" while everyone took turns telling dirty stories. I had also saved the management a great deal of money, having incorporated the other members of my staff, singers Dick and Sonny Loren, and the members of the orchestra, and a few, select guests, into so many of my comedy sketches. Ever-reliable Shirley was my ingenue, leading lady, and she also played so many other roles that called for a female character, both straight and comic, onstage. Through my own, inexperienced legerdemain, with the advice of more seasoned performers like Mr. Loren, I managed to present at least four shows per week, continuing that agenda for three additional weeks, before repeating any material. This satisfied the long term guests immeasurably. It was a draconian feat to say the least, and great experience for me as I played so many different characters. On the closing night of the season at the Labor Day midnight supper in the dining room, "Pop" strolled out of the kitchen and announced, "Ve love him very much, and hope to hev him beck again next summer if he's not already in Ollyvoot."

Summer's end filled me with the sort of ambivalence that was going to "dog" me for many summers to come. I was glad that the long hard (but rewarding) summer was finally over, and yet that sinking feeling of apprehension would set in almost immediately. Where was my next job going to be? ... and how long could it possibly last? I wasn't good enough, nor connected enough, to perform in the better nightclubs. There were little neighborhood clubs all over the USA and Canada, but how does one get booked into those things? I was not prepared to "lay off," something that becomes second nature with show people. I did not want to pursue anything legit, for fear that I would have to abort if any opportunity came up in show biz. This sort of problem would haunt me for years to come because the work ethic was part of my upbringing. I knew that I had to support my darling Shirley, who, in my eyes, was growing more beautiful each day, and, I'm sure that she was just as confused as I was. From the money I had made during the summer, I was able to give Max and Rose a good advance in rent payment, which was really a very small amount, but which, at least, allowed me some semblance of self respect. Shirley went job hunting with some reservation, as we could not even project where or when, my next assignment would be, and whether or not it meant our moving away somewhere. That sort of occupational hazard affects all individuals in my glamorous profession, and, as we quickly found out, you must take each day at a time and hope for the best, which is exactly what we did. That's sometimes called "vamping till ready."

The telephone is an integral part of my life. That ring is the catalyst for almost everything that happens. It can denote both acceptance and rejection, and best of all, that ever welcome tintinnabulation, each time I hear it, never ceases to fill me with great expectation. The phone rang one afternoon not too long after we had returned home from the mountains. It was Herbie, the drummer in Bobby Kaye's orchestra, the versatile group that we had worked with on that fateful summer with Bob Harris at The Midwood Hotel. "Van, this is Herb Gordon. We've got a good combo together, and we can get a long term booking at a great club called The Shangri-la, in Astoria, Queens. The job is ours if we can do a couple of shows a night in addition to the dance sets. Bobby wants to know if you wanna be in the band?" "You know I don't play an instrument, Herbie," I replied. "We all know that," he continued, "but we can make you a phantom." "What's that?" I asked." "Well it's like guys you see in the bands at weddings and Bar Mitzvahs. They sing great 'cause they're really singers, and not musicians. During the dance sets they stand n' pluck on a big bass fiddle, but not strongly, as they don't know the right notes. After awhile you get the feel of it and learn to chuck rhythm, and everyone swears you're a bass player, but really you're not. The bass is a very important instrument that you've got to be very good to play properly, but these wedding bands are willing to give up the purity of a good bass in exchange for an entertainer who could help bring in more money. Bobby would like to have you in our band on that basis." "Does that mean that I've gotta buy a big bass fiddle and shlep it around all over? That won't even fit into my farkakte little car." "That's up to you," Herbie went on, "you can do the same thing with a guitar, which is a lot smaller, and lighter. We can slip cardboard into the first frets which will deaden the sound altogether, and you can chuck rhythm, sing with the band, and do your comedy, and we'll even teach you the claves and the maracas, and also how to scratch on a gourd, so that you can look very authentic on the Latin numbers. Whaddya say?" "Tell me where I can pick up a halfway decent used guitar cheap, and when do we start rehearsals?" "Not so fast, we have to get you a union card, and we'll all have to get band uniforms, and you'll have to lay out a little money for that. Tell me you're in, and I'll report it to Bobby, and I'll schedule a date for your music test at Local 802."

"But I can't play well enough to pass any test."

"Don't worry, all you have to do is identify, and play, a few three finger chords for the examiner. I suggest you go over to the Parkway Music School and take a few guitar lessons, and practice till I call you, but don't worry, you're gonna pass."

The school was inexpensive and most cooperative, and even lent me a guitar to practice on at home until I got one of my own. The instructor was a world renowned guitarist and music teacher who had even written instruction books, and right then and there I decided that I was going to study that enchanting instrument for as long as I possibly could. Before I eventually quit years later, I was already starting to play selections by Bach on the guitar. I regret, to this very day, having abandoned that beautiful and soulful instrument. Herbie called me one morning n' said, "Meet me at 802 Headquarters this afternoon, important." I said, "Okay!" n' hung up.

When I got there Herbie was waiting with a sly grin on his face. "Guess what? It's all set, you're takin' the test for your union card."

"When?

"Now. In a few minutes we're going into the room for the exam."

"You didn't tell me on the phone. I didn't even bring my guitar."

"Oh shit! I forgot!

In a flash my resourceful, nervy pal grabbed me by the arm and said, "Come with me." We dashed out into the union hall where musicians were waiting on line to pay their dues. He scanned the crowd and saw a rather mild looking guy standing on line holding a guitar case. He walked right up to him and identified himself, "I'm Herb Gordon, the renowned drummer. I've gotta ask you for a huge favor. I need to borrow your guitar for just a few moments ... PLEASE?" and he snatched the guitar out of the stunned musician's hand, left him standing there, bewildered, as we hustled into the examining room where a frenetic little man who looked like a miniature hawk wearing wire rimmed glasses, and sporting a parrot's voice, bleated, "Okay, who's next?" "He is," Herbie replied, as he opened up the case and handed me the guitar. My legs turned to mush. "Play somethin'," the impatient little man crowed. "Whaddya wanna hear?" I asked nervously. Standing nearby, with one hand resting atop an old upright piano that represented the only piece of furniture in this pint sized room, was a tall, beefy, unfazed gentleman whose presence seemed not only to contrast the high strung little examiner, but also give the appearance of a higher authority. I learned later that the result of my exam had already been ascertained with him.

"Play anything," the little man with the squeaky voice continued restlessly, "play a chord." "G7th," I stammered, as I fingered the guitar frets with my left hand, nervously muffling the sound, and out came "Phtttt." "C'mon, don't fool around," he demanded, "play the damn G7th!" "Okay," I said, as I felt my pores open and the sweat start to overcome me as the blood rushed to my head, "G7th, here it is," and once again, "Phttt." The incredulous little man looked at me and yelled, "C'mon, I don't' have that much time. Don't fuck around!" The big guy placed his hand on the little guy's shoulder and said, "It's so easy, he's only puttin' you on. Give the kid a card." "No, not yet," the frenetic little guy went on, "play another chord!" "C," I said, and quickly my damp fingers went to C and E, and as I placed the third finger down on the string and strummed, again came the sound, "Phttt!" The little guy couldn't believe what he was hearing, and screamed at me, "Didn't I tell you not to fuck around?" and once again, the big fella instructed him, "Give the kid a card." That's how I got my union card, and the only way I could figure it out, as Herbie embraced me and rushed to give the poor guitarist his instrument back, was that what did it all really matter? It was all really a formality, and whether I was a musician or not, it all boiled down to more money in the union coffers, and my presence helped keep six dues paying musicians employed.

The job with the band at the Shangri-la kept me working all the way up until the next summer, when we all took a break and went up to our respective jobs in the mountains. We went back to the Kenmore with an all new staff and orchestra while Bobby and the band wound up somewhere in low, hot Ellenville, in the valley. The advent of air conditioning had not reached any of the mountain hotels as yet (except for the two giants, and Grossinger's had its air conditioning designed, and installed by a highly regarded European engineering company). Ellenville, with its famous Nevele and Fallsview, was still not the most appealing area because of the heat and mosquitoes.

While I played with the band, Shirley and I led a very romantic and somewhat adventurous life. My beautiful cousin Doris had gotten Shirley a job as a cigarette girl at the recently refurbished, and still popular Hotel St. George, in downtown Brooklyn, where we had spent the overnight after our wedding. The hotel had opened up a brand new club which they called "The Stardust Room," and everything was decorated in shades of pink (the drapes, the curtains, the tablecloths, even Shirley's costume, and the orchestra's uniforms). It was really quite a classy place, and although Shirley's salary was meager, her tips were very good, and, for the first time since we got married we were starting to feel a little more comfortable financially. We somehow worked it out so that we had the same night off. (I believe it was Monday, which was generally a very slow night everywhere. Later on, Milton Berle and his Texaco Star Theater on TV turned Tuesday nights away from home into the deadest of them all.) So, on Monday nights I would take Shirley to dinner somewhere on Broadway, dressed in my finest clothing, my band uniform, and we'd take in a first run movie afterward, and the royal family couldn't have enjoyed a better night out. Shirley would take the subway to work and we'd get back home about the same time every night. On Saturday nights she would take the crappy little Plymouth to work and pick me up in Astoria afterwards, and we'd go out with the band for a late bite, and then home. It was truly a fun time in our young lives.

Our band consisted of five men and a girl. She was the piano player, and was really very good. When we would go out for a bite to eat, we felt that the chivalrous thing to do would be to pick up her check, which she would let us do. Later we realized that, as an important "side man" she was being paid more than most of the others. Herbie sat on his throne at the top of the bandstand, way above us all, with his striking set of Slingerland Radio Kings, which he handled magnificently with his drumsticks. In the very front were the guitarist (yours truly, hah!), the clarinetist and leader (who played and sang beautifully), the hot headed trumpet player, Joe Calvin, and the bass player (who was off to the side near the piano). We presented a truly striking group, young, talented, and good looking in our well fashioned gray and black uniforms, black pants, and gray cardigans with silver buttons. We did our job well and actually attracted a lot of repeat customers.

We featured an amateur night once a week for a period of several months and that, too, was a big draw. Our grand prize was a one week booking into the club for the winner. The contestants were all singers and all very good. Among them was a very popular, rather chunky, and quite gregarious local boy with a very strong following, who had a very good voice and used the name, Joe Bari. He got as far as the finals, and when he performed he always drew a large, enthusiastic crowd of fans. When the contest was all over, it was left for us, the members of the band, to select the first prize winner. Being the naive purists that we were, we chose a slender, handsome young contestant with a pencil thin moustache and a really beautiful voice. His name was Danny Cavallero, and I often wonder whatever became of him. As promised, we booked him into the club for a week, and, as gifted as he was, he didn't draw flies. He had no following whatsoever. It was to become a valuable lesson for all of us. You don't pick the one with the most talent. You choose the one who can bring in the money. In this case there wasn't that big a difference between the winner and the runner-up. We should have been observant enough to recognize that the guy who came in second would have been a boon to our business. I do know, however, what became of him. It wasn't too hard to follow his progress. He became a professional, and an excellent one at that. He changed his name to Tony Bennett.

Throughout my career (and I have performed with the biggest and the best), I've often heard musicians complain about their leaders. They say they're strict, they're stern, they're very stingy, etc. The inside jokes have a biting edge to them. For example: Know the difference between a bull and a band? The bull has the horns in the front and the asshole in the back!

Know the difference between a musician and a pig? A pig won't hang around at a bar all night long waitin' to pick up a musician!

Bandleaders must be like baseball managers, football coaches, and the likes. If you're going to be friendly with those who play for you, you'd still better be in a position to show 'em who's boss when it counts. I've known some pretty terrific guys who led orchestras, and when it came to the boys n' girls in the band, the most successful ones were those who were able to "put the foot down" when it was warranted. Musicians and all show people live out of a suitcase, and can be terribly unhappy and morose, and also do some regrettable things when they're away from their loved ones for long stretches at a time. The armed forces have that same disease, but the big differences are that, in a band you're in much happier and safer surroundings, and, you can always quit. A sense of humor will manage to get you through, and a good practical joke, provided nobody gets hurt, is always appreciated.

There was this very classy bandleader on tour with his band. His name was Shaw, but not Artie Shaw. The run was almost at an end, and the boys were at the point where they were uptight and grumpy. Just before coming back to the theater, a number of the guys went into a diner. Unbeknownst to the others, the leader had already conspired with another musician to pull off a practical joke. When nobody was looking, he handed the waitress a flat, rubber hot water bag, and asked her to please fill it up with beef stew, and to quietly give it back to him without anyone noticing. She followed his instructions, and, prearranged, he had the saxophone player slip the filled bag under his belt, and into the front of his pants, and back they all went to the theater to prepare for the show.

As they assembled backstage to put their makeup on and slip into their uniforms, the leader winked at the sax player. That was the signal for the guy to get up and exclaim, "Gee fellas, I don't feel well." Being blase, from all the time they had spent on the road, hardly anyone paid attention to his plea for sympathy, and he clumsily staggered across the oblong room to the sink, with the orchestra leader in hot pursuit. The leader scolded the rest of the band saying, "What the hell is the matter with you guys? Can't you see he doesn't feel well?" And, as they all turned around to see what was going on, the saxophone player pretended to retch convulsively over the sink, and while doing so, with his back to the others, he spilled the contents of the bag in his pants into the sink as loudly as he could. The leader groped in the sink, daintily picking out the food with his thumb and middle finger, while extending his pinkie up into the air, placing each item into his mouth, and joyfully exclaiming, "Look, a whole potato!" "Beef"! "Carrots" ... Needless to say, this ingenious display engendered a bit of regurgitation in a number of the others, followed by explosive laughter when they realized how cleverly they had all been duped. It was a marvelous way to relieve the prevailing tensions, and I've often told this true story to numerous listeners. I keep thinking to myself though, knowing that sometimes there are those who are too lazy to go out into the toilets to urinate, and surreptitiously use the sink, the joke could have been on whom?

Our state of euphoria was coming to an end. We spent close to a year at the Shangri-la, which constituted the longest job I had since coming into show biz. We had been good for the club, and the club was good for us, and, miracle of miracles, nobody suspected that I wasn't a real guitarist, and if they did, they didn't let on. Our boss was a very decent guy, and was very pleased with our work, which included the two-shows-a-night that I took charge of, but the time had come for new faces. Incidentally, we drew good sized crowds, and I was constantly pleased by the friends from the old neighborhood and the new friends, engendered at the resort hotels, that showed up. However, we were given our notice and it was time to pack up n' look for other bookings.

As a group we all got along fairly well. A few changes were made during our engagement. Our lady pianist who was making marriage plans with her fiance, was replaced by a very capable, well-dispositioned male. As I mentioned earlier, the one constant problem in the band was caused by Herbie's refusal to wear his glasses. Whenever we would finish a dance set, Herbie would put down his drumsticks, and he would conceitedly step down, right on Joe Calvin's trumpet. The hot headed Sicilian would let go a stream of profanities under his breath. When we were out of hearing distance of the customers, he would quickly follow up with, "Herbie, I'm gonna kill ya, ya clumsy bastard!"

Herbie managed to avoid these threats until New Years Eve, when a bunch of sailors, just back from Singapore, wandered into the club, and to show their appreciation of the band, plied us with rounds of vodka. After our last set, in the wee hours of the morning, feeling no pain, Herbie and Joe had a real go at it in the dressing room, and somebody's life was saved when Mr. Steinberg, the boss, hearing the commotion, burst onto the scene and sobered us all up, quickly, before too much blood was spilled.

11 "You're not a drummer!"

We were moving about from one club to another, with none of the engagements lasting as long as the Shangri-la did. (I remember one famous jazz club in Secaucus, NJ where a true jazz guitarist sitting in the audience, came over to me. I had just completed a set of thumping rhythm with the fingers on my left hand capriciously roaming over the cardboard-deadened frets, and he exclaimed, "Man, I've been watchin' you for quite awhile, and I'm still tryin' to figure out your style.") It was in-between our engagements that Herbie got a few of us a club date (a one-nighter) that would have a most-memorable bearing upon our relationship for the rest of our lives

Herbie had been recommended to a heavy set Jewish lady who breathed flames, and who was making arrangements for her daughter's wedding at a popular downtown hotel on the lower east side that specialized in Jewish catered affairs. In her own inimitable way, with a colorful, and rather heavy Yiddish accent, she instructed him, "I vant a bend, four or five pieces; a novelty ect, like a good dence team; and a comedian." Herbie assured her that she was dealing with only the best, and so we were booked to play and entertain at a wedding at the Central Plaza Hotel on a Sunday evening.

The band played all the right music (on this gig Herbie was the leader 'cause it was his job) and Bobby played great klezmir frailachs on his clarinet, and even sang a few Yiddish songs. The dance team was a "knock-off" (facsimile) of a very famous dance team named Velez and Yolanda, that appeared in a number of motion pictures. Actually, it was a comedy dance team that was hilarious. The elegantly dressed, handsome couple, would begin by doing serious ballroom dancing, and somewhere along the line he would throw her up into the air and she would come down on his shoulders with her legs around his neck and her billowing skirt all over his head, covering his eyes so that he was unable to see. As he staggered around the floor blindly, the act was choreographed so that his suspenders would snap and his pants would start to fall down. As he attempted to reach behind him to grope at the suspenders in an effort to keep his pants up, his partner would scream hysterically that she was falling, and so it went, as the audience would be convulsed with laughter. This was such a famous and popular act that, very soon, in our unethical profession, notorious for plagiarism, there were many ersatz "Velez and Yolandas" working everywhere, and that evening we were blessed with a highly effective copy. The only one that wasn't laughing was the bride's mother, who didn't get it. She ran over to the bandstand yelling at Herbie, who, himself, was doubled up with laughter, and yelled at him, "Vot kind of a dence team is dot? Look at him. He can't see vere he's dencink... und his pents are fallink down" ... and she continued to describe what was happening, as if nobody else was watching. We were incredulous, but laughing so hard that tears were rolling down our cheeks.

Then it was time I got to do my turn. It was bad enough that the acoustics in the room were terrible, but by then, there was so much noise emanating from the crowd that was so busy eating and conversing, that I had to fight to be heard. When the entire evening mercifully ended (for us, thankfully), the fierce lady paid Herbie in cash, and, as she was counting out the money, doling it into his hands, she kept complaining, "De dence team vuz a disgrace! De comedien stunk! Di bend vas not goot! ... and you, you're not a drummer ... you're a shit! You hear? You're a shit ... you're not a drummer!"

From that day forward, whenever I'd meet Herbie, I would greet him with, "You're a shit! You're not a drummer!" and he would react with a sly and knowing smile. Throughout the ensuing years, whenever he'd call on the telephone, whoever would pick up the phone would ask, "Who's this?" and he'd reply, "It's Herbie," and the next words from that person, whether it was any of our parents, the children, friends, anyone that knew him, would be, "You're a shit! You're not a drummer!" As our children were growing up, from the moment they were old enough to speak coherently, they'd answer the phone when he called with. "You're a shit! You're not a drummer!" ...and he would always laugh accordingly. This went on until he died, many years later. It was a great running gag, and lasted a long, long time.

Many, many years after the episode at that fateful wedding, I was headlining a show at the Century Village in

Pembroke Pines, Florida. Shirley and I had dinner with Herbie and his girlfriend Lillie, the night before. Herbie asked if I could get him into the show. I said, "Of course I would, just show up. I'll leave word with the guard at the gate." This was before those horrid, imperious "Condo Commandos" at the Century Villages began to inflict their embarrassing crackdowns on visitors. When I arrived at work that evening, I said to the security guard at the gate, a gentle, young Black man, with a winning smile, who wore a very official looking uniform, "I'm expecting a friend of mine named Herb Gordon, and his lady friend. Please be good enough to let them in as my guests. He's a musician. When he identifies himself, ask him what he does, and he'll tell you he's a drummer. When he tells you that, please tell him he's a shit! He's not a drummer!" The affable guard caught the gist immediately, and, with an engaging smile he gave me a sort of mock salute and said, "Will do."

A while later as I sat in my dressing room, getting ready for the show, Herbie and Lillie walked in. Shirley, who was at my side, couldn't wait to learn what happened. Lillie was still giggling and Herbie had a big, what Filthy Miltie used to call "shit eating grin" on his face. I said, "Lillie, I want to hear it from you. Tell me what happened." She replied, still chortling that when Herbie identified himself, the security guard inquired, "What do you do, Mr. Gordon?" and Herbie replied, "I'm a drummer." And the guard looked at him seriously and replied, in an affected accent, "Man, you ain't no drummer. You is a shit ... you ain't no drummer!"

In the early days, when we were in Bobby's band together, thanks to Herbie I met some of the finest Black jazz musicians. There were Lem Davis, Teddy Lee, and a whole host of others. They were all fine gentlemen and great musical artists. Years later, when I appeared with the Count Basie band, and later on with Mercer Ellington and the Duke Ellington band, I found them to be highly intelligent, congenial, and hard working, gregarious people. In those early days if anyone would speak unkindly, or prejudicially against the Blacks, Herbie would immediately come to their defense and even offer to fight them. Years later however, thanks to the same kind of venal, low class ignorance that causes bigotry, during a bad time in Herbie's life (when he and his then wife, fertile Renee, who had to have her fallopian tubes tied after she gave birth to their fifth child, were forced to move into a city housing project on Marcy Ave., in Brooklyn), the first to call them all "Jew bastards!" were those people whose reputations Herbie fought so hard to defend.

Herbie died when he was about sixty. He saw good times and bad. Had a great marriage for awhile and that eventually turned into an acrimonious disaster and a subsequent divorce. Way back, when my mother-in-law, Rosie, surprised us all by reaching into her apron pocket and lending Herbie the money to pay for his then miraculous Lempert operation to restore his failing hearing, little did she realize that she was giving him the wherewithal to sustain his livelihood, and actually restore his life. Herbie had great kids, a number of whom became quite successful, and he was lucky enough to live out his life with a kind, endearing companion before succumbing to the ravages of diabetes, too soon ... much too soon.

With Bobby's band in a state of disarray after the "New Years Eve Massacre" in the basement of the Shangri-la, I gave Bobby my notice and recommended my zany old friend Phil as my replacement. The one time "mentor" of Danny Kaye, was still living in his fantasy world, but he jumped at the opportunity to get into a steady job situation. Surprisingly, as long as the bandleader kept him in line, he worked out quite well. I was now free to pursue what? Where do I go for work? Who do I know? I was well aware that, talented or not, in any field of endeavor, one must get help from other human beings. I had accumulated a number of interested, successful friends from among the assortment of guests I had entertained in my short, embryonic career as a Social Director in the Catskills. I wasn't that naive as to sincerely believe every single boast that was ever made to me, but I did select a few successful businessmen who actually ended their vacations by saying, "Kid, if I can ever be of any help to you, be sure n' call me."

One such individual was a gregarious, tall, well-tanned, sartorially splendid middle aged gentleman who smoked the most aromatic cigars, and had a leadership quality about him that was immediately recognizable. He had a highly regarded sales position with the famous Breakstone's Dairy, and was an official in the Dairymen's Union. I figured, what have I got to lose? I got in touch with Abe Certilman, who was to become a lifelong friend. Abe had recently lost a child, and his wife was, herself, waging a brave, but losing battle against cancer, and yet Abe found time for everybody.

"Van! - - How's my favorite young comedian?" was his booming reply to my sheepish "Hello Mr. Certilman," on the telephone. I could just picture his affable smile, as his perfect white teeth closed down on a Havana special. "Since when did you start calling me Mr. Certilman? It's always been Abe, remember? And, how is your beautiful Shirley?" "She's just fine, more beautiful than ever, and sends you her love." "Okay," he continued, as though he had nothing else to do on another of his ever busy days, "To what do I owe the pleasure of this call, and I must say it's really a pleasure to hear from you." I got right to the point. Told him that the summer season was months away, and that I'd, most-likely be back at the Kenmore, n' hope that I'll be seeing him there again, but that, meanwhile, I needed work, and was wondering, with all the people he knew, if he had any connections in show business. "Of course I do," was his instant reply. "Cheer up! I'll get back to you in a few days, if not sooner."

Several days later the phone rang in our apartment, and, not too surprisingly, it was Abe. "Van, here's the scoop. Beckman and Pransky are two of the busiest agents in show business, and they're located directly across from the Theatrical Drugstore on West 46th St. I forget the exact address, it's a small building next to "Variety." It's one flight up. You'll find it. There's always a crowd there. They produce several big variety shows for our union per year. I told them that I might consider going to other agents if they didn't do something for my protege, Van Harris, right away. They want you to come up there as soon as you can. No appointment necessary. Good luck, or, more significantly, Break a Leg!"

There was no waiting around for me, when I got there, despite the bustle of people outside in the waiting room. I soon found out why. I never did get to meet Beckman and Pransky, who were much too big to bother with a small potato like me (Years later, I did loads of business with Johnny Pransky, who also became my very good friend. Once he even sent me to audition for a motion picture role with Paul Muni, which I came ever so close to getting, and, as Johnny gently pointed out, in reply to my disappointment, they gave the part to a studio contract player who was not nearly as good as I was, but "they owed him.") Johnny's partner, Al Beckman, was to die suddenly, and unexpectedly, very soon after my introduction to the office, which sent shock waves throughout the industry.

When I arrived at Beckman and Pransky's, their secretary, a young, attractive lady, quite obviously hardened by her devoted service in a callous profession, was surprisingly gracious to me and immediately ushered me into a satellite office where I was greeted by two friendly young men, not too much older than I. They stuck out their hands and introduced themselves to me. "I'm Roy Gerber," said the taller, well built blonde young man, who, even then, was showing signs of losing his hair, "And I'm Jackie Bryce," said the thin, intense young man with the wavy black hair, who managed to appear cordial, yet had the look of the devil in his eyes. It turned out that they were Beckman and Pransky's young assistants who were given carte blanche to promote whatever they desired and bring more revenue into the office. Roy was, perhaps, the classier one, but Jackie was the "go-getter." He left no stones unturned in order to engender business. We hit it off instantaneously, and, without any questions as to my ability, they started to book me on weekends into assorted small clubs, American Legion halls, Moose clubs, Elks clubs, etc., etc, in Philadelphia and environs, which were only 90 or 100 miles away from NY, and very accessible by public transportation and my 1936 Plymouth (when it was running). I signed no contracts with these two productive gentlemen, just gave them their ten percent commission on each job, and was free to get any other jobs on my own through other connections that I had made, and very soon got to make lots of new friends among the numerous other young, aspiring comedians, singers, variety acts, etc. Thanks to the intervention of dear old Abe Certilman, I was now really and truly in show biz, and was actually bringing home money to my beloved Shirley. It wasn't steady, but it sure as hell had potential, and one job led to another, and soon I had actually created a network of booking agents in little clubs all the way from the neighborhood places in the five boroughs of NY to Philadelphia, Baltimore, Washington, D.C., and many little cities in between. Roy went on to become a Hollywood agent much later on, married and divorced the same lady several times, while Jackie was plagued by a disastrous marriage, he served time in alimony jail, and, one day, he just plain disappeared off the face of the earth. To this very day we often wonder whatever happened to that personable leprechaun. We often socialized with him, and he was always so much fun.

It was then, as a true professional (after all, I was getting paid at the end of each engagement) that I began to discover that the average American audience is not sophisticated, and that the performer shouldn't expect it to be. These people come to be entertained, and the entertainer should find the common denominator, and cater to each individual audience. Even the college graduates are not all that tuned in, so don't go zippin' over anyone's head. You need only look at what comes pouring into Las Vegas every single day, and see that they are basically simple people and the trick is to develop the right formula to make 'em laugh. Today's young adults are totally unsophisticated, and weaned on shock. Toilet jokes have been the biggest laugh getters from the beginning of time, and filthy language is steadily becoming the norm everywhere, which isn't saying much for the future of our so-called civilization. A truly gifted performer, however, can subtly manipulate his audiences and actually induce them to enjoy a higher level of comedy. Don't try it, however, unless you are both, highly experienced, and sanguine. And, the owner of the club, or the producer, can be dumber than all, only don't forget, he's the guy with the money. He's the one that pays you, so don't be a wise ass and cut across his grain. I still remember the immigrant owner of the club I worked in York, PA, complaining to the theatrical agent in Philadelphia, over the phone, "I asked you for a blues singer, and you senda me a black singer!" I didn't make that up. That actually happened. I also learned to keep as far away from management as possible. Just do your job and go home afterward. Though I've worked for some genuinely decent, hard working entrepreneurs, I've also had my share of thugs and ignoramuses, who headed up some of the most successful, and best known nightclubs in the world. I've always disliked these so-called "location jobs" where you're forced to remain there until your contract is ended, as opposed to "one-nighters" where you do your job n' get out. When the owner of one of the most successful nightclubs in all of NY died, there was a huge turnout at his funeral. When an onlooker inquired, "How come so many people?" the answer was one that was first attributed to Samuel Goldwyn, supposedly at Harry Cohn's funeral, "When you give the people something they wanna see, they all turn out!"

Though show biz is reputed to be a fairly democratized profession, I'll contest that, based upon my own early experiences. While the ambitious young comedians sat around Hanson's famous hangout, an eatery on 7th Ave. and W. 51st St. that was the entertainers' mecca for many, many years, and rubbed shoulders with the successful, the newly successful, the pseudo successful, and the bullshit artists who were legends in their own minds, I was scurrying around from agent's office to agent's office looking desperately for work, and, for the most part I succeeded. There were old time agents, holdovers from the vaudeville era, subtly consumed with their pernicious prejudices. There was an Irishman in the Palace Building who booked me because he thought I was Irish. There was an Italian on W. 46th St. who booked me because he was sure I was Italian. The Jewish agents, as a rule, would book anybody, as long as he or she would fill the bill and there was business to be conducted. That is not to imply that, just because the agent was Jewish he was a good human being. I've met some remarkably wonderful people in my life who were agents, but I've also known of, and have also had the misfortune to have done some business with some of the most devious savages. What a business!

There was this one guy that sent me to a club in the coal mining northeastern section of Pennsylvania. I had become a favorite there. (Perhaps because I was told that I was a dead ringer for a popular middleweight boxer who resided in that area.) I had several return engagements and the last time I was there, I had some sort of disagreement with the management (the place was owned by a bootleg coal miner) and it was reported to the agent. When I got back to NY, he called me into his office, and, very confidentially, he put his arm around me, informing me of his client's complaint, and added, "Hey, that's no way to act. We "Degos" (pejorative for "Italian") have to stick together." "I'm no "Dego," I replied, "I'm a "Judea," whereupon a scowl immediately appeared on his face, and he sullenly replied, "No wonder you're so temperamental!" I never worked for that agent again. No great loss!

The Irishman sent me way out to Johnstown, PA to work a weekend at what passed as the fanciest country club in the area. It was during a very slow time for me, and I had a lot of bills to pay at home, and I really needed every cent I could earn. Somehow the word got out to the manager, a gregarious lush, that I was Jewish, and on the last night of the engagement he announced, "A round of drinks for the house, and put it on the comedian's tab." That brought my wages down to virtually nothing, but there was nothing I could do but swallow the bitter pill. I hated him, almost as much as I hated the sadistic club owner in Bayonne, NJ who waited until after the last bus had left NJ for NY on Sunday night, before he'd pay the acts, so that we'd have to sleep in the bus terminal until the first bus went out on the following morning. I never worked for either of those two again, not that they ever asked.

There was this American Legion hall that I worked at in central Pennsylvania. The area was quite inaccessible, so I had to use the car, which was gradually going into its death throes. Part of the deal was to drive the other acts. One act on the bill was a very black, humorous fellow who danced on roller skates. When we arrived at the American Legion hall they sent us to the nearby hotel to check in for the weekend, and we walked into the lobby, where the female owner was tending bar. I was the spokesman, having walked in first, and announced who we were. She was most gracious as we walked over to sign the register. Then she spotted the dancer. "Who's he?" she inquired angrily. "That's Mr. Johnson, our dancer," I replied. "Oh no, he can't stay here," she yelled, "We don't allow Niggers in here!" I was mortified and embarrassed for our fellow entertainer. King Johnson, a veteran of the road, apparently accustomed to such insulting, shabby treatment, and not wishing to make a scene or jeopardize his job, mumbled, "It's okay Van. You guys stay here. I'll find a place in the Black section of town." I said, "Nothing doing. None of us are gonna stay here, and we all stormed out. I don't think the lady even cared. "Funny," I thought to myself, "if she saw how well this guy danced on those roller skates, she would applaud her head off, but he was, after all, a 'Nigger,' and 'she don't want no Nigger sleepin' on her precious beds.'"

I called the local AAA, was sent to an AAA approved rooming house that was cleaner, and prettier than anything else in town. Told the lady in charge that one of us was Black, and she replied, "What difference does that make?" and we all had a very successful engagement at that American Legion hall.

Back home in NY at Hanson's, the place was, as usual, jam packed, and thriving. Hanson's was referred to by many as Hanson's Drugstore. (As I vaguely recall, they did have a pharmacy, but the restaurant portion was the truly big attraction, and what Lindy's was at night, was what Hanson's was in the daytime.) All the emerging young comedians made certain to make their appearances at Hanson's to be acknowledged by the envious. "You did a great job at The Boulevard," you'd hear them say to an Alan King, or "You really killed them at Ben Maksik's," you'd hear them say to a young singer named Vic Damone, and so forth and so on. And, naturally, there were always snide comments like, "Lenny Bruce? "Are you kidding? Where would he be without that cult of his?" And the moment some of these future stars were not within earshot you'd always hear, "Lucky stiff. Got a couple of good breaks. I could put that sonova bitch into my hip pocket." As the great "Shnozz," Jimmy Durante himself, used to say, "Everybody wants ta get inta da act!" while he assumed that marvelous pose where he would cock his head to a side, point his eyes up to the ceiling, flap his arms like a big bird, and mesmerize you with that intoxicating smile. "So dis cowboy said to me, 'What kind of a hat is dat you're wearin' Jimmy?' And I said, 'Don't you recognize a cowboy hat when ya see one? Why dat's a genuine ten gallon hat.' 'No it's not a ten gallon hat,' he said, 'it's only an eight gallon hat.' ... And I said, 'well whadd'ya know ... somebody's been siphoning my hat!'" "Hah! Hah! Hah! I've got a million of dem!" ... And every aspiring comedian in the business did an impression of the most adored, and easiest to imitate, comedian in all of show business, Jimmy Durante, myself included. It's a sure way to get the audience's attention. No need for a sense of humor. Not too much pressure on the mind trying to figure out a joke. It's a marvelous way for a performer to get work, and was never beneath my dignity. Impressions kept me going until I eventually developed the kind of comedy routines I was comfortable with. To this very day I am eternally grateful to the likes of Jimmy Durante, Peter Lorre, Danny Kaye, Frank Sinatra, and Ed Gardner, all of whom I imitated in a routine called "Duffy's Tavern," which seemed to appeal to everybody. It was not too complicated. I expended an inordinate amount of energy which was added to a decent musical background that was written and arranged for me, for nothing, by my dear friend, Joe Gardner (who later became both Tony Martin's and Jerry Vale's pianist and conductor), and, coupled with some bone jarring pratfalls, I even made the simpletons laugh. In looking back, it was a marvelous learning experience.

Comedy, being the eclectic profession that it is, lends itself to artistic theft, and from time immemorial, there have always been those who help themselves to the craft and tools of others by seriously deluding themselves into thinking that they could easily have thought up the same routine, and do it even better. I would venture to say that most, if not all of the post-World War II raconteurs who were populating all the clubs, were doing heaps of army-related material that came from the mind of a wonderful comedian whom many regarded as the best, and most popular G.I. comic to have ever come out of that great conflagration. He was so good, and so appropriately funny that his commanding officers actually allowed him to accept bookings in many of the best Midwest nightclubs while he was still in uniform. His name was Harvey Stone, and he was kinda pudgy, and had a rather prominent nose, and he was very, very funny. When he was finally separated from the army, he was one of the most sought-after comedians in the entire country. They couldn't get enough of him, and the other, ambitious vultures in the business sensed the kill, and borrowed heavily from his act. It got so outrageous that one theatrical agency that managed a parasite who was trading heavily in Harvey Stone's material actually changed its client's first name to "Harvey," so that when an unsuspecting buyer would call and ask for "that G.I. comic, ... What's his name? Harvey something?" they would say, "We know who you mean, Harvey Sands, and you're in luck, 'cause we handle him and we might be able to deliver him a little bit cheaper as a favor to you." Stone got a very good price, but the impostor and others like him, succeeded in undermining him to the point where they eventually destroyed him. He, obviously and unfortunately, did not have the kind of management that it requires to protect such a valuable piece of property. And also, like a lot of funny looking men who are enjoying huge public acclaim, he envisioned himself as a potential matinee idol and had his nose shortened by a plastic surgeon, and after that he was never as funny again. In fact, with that quick, and inventive mind, during those times when he somehow failed to get the laughs he had been accustomed to, he coined the phrase (that was also stolen by others), "I had my nose fixed, and now my mouth doesn't work!" His demise was rapid, which was a real travesty, and not many in our cruel and insensitive business seemed to care. (And to this very day I still wonder, "Where the hell was his management while all this was going on?" He eventually wound up working on cruise ships. This served as the ideal escape for him, as, not only was he plagued by an army of scurrilous thieves, but he had just undergone what was rumored to have been an extremely acrimonious divorce. He actually died at sea, and in attempting to uncover his "next of kin," the name of his ex-wife appeared. The story goes that they asked her if she had any instructions, and she supposedly said, "Dump his body into the ocean!" True or not, somewhere at the bottom of the sea lies the funniest comedian to have ever come out of World War II. He gave pleasure to millions while building a career that seemed unstoppable, only to be fleeced by his vicious peers who rationalized away their sins. They never heeded Shakespeare's brilliant, "To thine own self be true ..." and never really were held accountable in the court of public opinion, and, a number of them, thanks to having had a Harvey Stone around to send them on their way, eventually polished themselves into major stars, who bitch like hell when others do to them what they did to him. It is said that the great Al Jolson, when he was holding forth at The Wintergarden Theater in his heyday, loved and admired by all, would actually send his emissaries around to all the clubs to steal material from clever, but lesser known comedians, and incorporate their fresh material into his act. He, being the famous, and revered star (with all his chutzpah) would then send his lawyers to visit these other performers and warn them to desist from using Al Jolson's material. The adoring public doesn't really want to know about the sordid side of the business. They're paying only to be entertained, and who was a greater entertainer at that time than Jolson? The moral to be drawn here: The public is really not concerned about the infighting that goes on in the business. They come to be entertained, and that's the bottom line!

Meanwhile I was getting one helluva education. Thanks to the great war there was plenty of money around. Unemployment was low, and the liberated woman who proved that she was capable of working at a man's job was getting paid well for it. This created a whole new leisure society. In addition to the better nightclubs, neighborhood clubs were springing up all over, and I was lucky enough to be working in Philadelphia where things were really jumping. I was awed by the abilities of many of the local entertainers and subsequently learned that Philadelphia produced more famous performers, per capita, than just about every other city in the United States. Eddie Fisher was starting to take off like a comet. Joey Bishop was part of the Bishop Brothers. (I don't believe that his partner was actually his brother.) Mario Lanza was starting to make some noise. Virginia Mayo was a young movie star. Of course Ed Wynn and W. C. Fields were the very famous old time stars. So many other future greats were waiting in the wings for their grab at the brass ring. There were neighborhood entertainers who were even more popular than the so-called "stars," and several actually succeeded in reaching all the way up, only to fall back again.

One such individual was a handsome Irish-American named Joe. No need to mention his last name here 'cause his story is tragic, though through no fault of his own. He was in his late twenties or early thirties, married with a family, charming, personable, dressed great, and moved great onstage. He was possessed with a magnificent tenor voice, and everyone in the city of brotherly love was eagerly awaiting the day that he, one of their very own, would become a big movie star. He had worked his way up to where he was now a favorite at Philly's major nightclub, getting repeat bookings there, and his big break was just around the corner. Then, one fateful night, something outrageous happened that would succeed in curtailing his career, something that had nothing to do with him, personally, but would sidetrack his glorious ride forever.

Joe's brother worked as a bartender at one of the bistros in town, and he succumbed to the occupational hazard of so many in his profession. He overdid the libation thing, and one night, after closing time, while in just such a state, he accompanied some "acquaintances" on a ride to somewhere. (The poor guy probably didn't even know where the hell he was at, or where the hell he was going.) He was in the car when the others stepped out to commit a robbery. There was a shootout, and in the commission of the crime, a policeman was gunned down and killed. Joe's brother was among those who were apprehended at the scene, and from that fateful moment on, his once, carefree, but inebriated life was over. He too, had a family, and naturally, it was up to his semi-famous brother to come to his aid. The trial caused a sensation all over the state, and Joe's brother and the others were sentenced to die in Pennsylvania's electric chair. Joe spent the rest of his life attempting to get his brother's sentence commuted. The ensuing publicity didn't help his career one iota, and the tremendous amount of time and energy he expended in his attempt to stave off his brother's execution took a terrible toll on Joe. After years of appeals he succeeded in having the punishment changed to a lifetime in prison, but in the process Joe lost all interest in his career. There went one tremendously gifted talent, right down the drain, or as they say in the business, "into the crapper," all because of his devotion to his sibling. I often wonder whatever eventually became of Joe. It had been a privilege to work with him, and, in the short time that I knew him, I had become one of his most ardent admirers, and, judging from what he did for his hapless brother, he certainly was one to be admired.

Yes, there was some truly interesting talent all around Philadelphia, especially in the vocal department. Though Mario Lanza was being carefully groomed for his comparatively short, and frenzied flight into fame and fortune, there lived a grocery clerk practically around the corner from him in South Philly with the unlikely name of Guissepe

Salvatore Scarricajotele, who mercifully changed his name to Joe Scotti. His tenor voice would send chills up n' down your spine. His was a true and beautiful sound, and once his three little children grew old enough to start to go to school, he prevailed upon his loyal and loving wife, Mary, to allow him to leave his steady, dead end job in the market, and take his chances at earning a living singing. Fate decreed that the theatrical agencies would book us both into numerous jobs, and soon we became an unofficial one-two punch in small clubs all over Philadelphia and the adjoining territories, and we really were great together. In fact, I was living in Brooklyn, making that dreadfully long commute on wheels with questionable reliability, and there were times I would sleep over at his modest home.

It was during that period that I learned how absolutely chauvinistic the first generation Italian-Americans were. Sometimes we would do as many as three, and four shows a night, even in farm communities like Vineland, NJ, where we waited for the last shift of customers to come in, the rugged old immigrant chicken farmers. We would work late and it would be four or five in the morning till we, exhaustedly, got back home. Even those illiterate farmers loved Joe's operatic arias which were anomalous to such clubs. My reliable impressions, especially those of Jimmy Durante and Frank Sinatra, aroused their nationalistic feelings. To say the least, Van Harris and Joe Scotti were one big smash hit in what then, to us, was our Palladium.

I was, somehow, subtly, and otherwise, reminded that religious prejudices were indelible, especially when the patrons were just a few years removed from the old country. I chuckled under my breath when the excited audience would cheer us with, "You two Degos are great!" and would glance over at Joe's apologetic smile as he recognized my practiced indifference. One very early morning while I was waiting for Joe to get his music and other belongings together, so that we could pack in another night's work, I was invited by one of the patrons to the bar for a nightcap. My benefactor was an elderly paisan, tall, mustachioed, and as handsome and rugged as Randolph Scott himself. He still had chicken shit on his boots, but it had dried and the odor was beyond the state of offensiveness. He was delighted to buy me a drink, and showered me with compliments, adding in his Italian accented English, "You're a nica Calabrese boy." I smiled and retorted, "I'm not Calabrese." "What are you?" he inquired, good naturedly, "Napolitan, or Abruzzese?" "No," I answered, "I'm a Judea." His joviality turned immediately to anger. His face turned crimson, and his eyes narrowed to slits. "Don't fool around!" he warned, "You're not a Judea." I asked the leathery old gentleman, who, by then had already downed quite a few whiskeys, as compared to my one, "And what if I am?' He was quick to respond, "If you were a Judea I would take a knife and stick it in you heart." I said, "Why?" He answered, as his face got redder and the slits became even narrower, "Because the Jews matsa Crist!" which I immediately recognized, having heard that damning expression before, "We killed Christ!"... and ignorant people, the world over, were still spewing that venom. At that moment Joe appeared, with his music bag in his hand, and his suit bag thrown over his shoulder, "Ready when you are Van," and out we went into the morning air. I was shaking my head, still in disbelief at what I had just heard. "What's buggin' ya pal?" Joe asked, "Nothin'," I replied, "Let's go home."

It was about five in the morning when we walked into the house. "What're you tiptoe-ing for?" Joe asked, as he stomped in and threw his belongings down on the couch. "Mary," he yelled, "Get up. I'm home." I couldn't believe what I was witnessing. I knew that the kids were gonna have to get up in a couple of hours and that she had to get up with them in order to give them breakfast n' get them ready for school. "Aren't you gonna let her sleep?" I asked in a whisper. "Don't be nuts," he bellowed, "she's gotta make us somethin' to eat. We just got home from work, remember?" By then she had already slipped into a robe, came down the stairs, set the table, and went into the kitchen to prepare some eggs n' coffee, and put up the toast. After the inevitable braggadocio about how great the shows went, we finished our meal and I got up to clear the table. He grabbed my arm and said, "Don't do that. You'll spoil her. You'll spoil it for all of us." She managed an obedient smile and I thought to myself, "I never saw anything like this in my neck o' the woods."

Joe and I worked a lot together whenever I was in the Philadelphia area. His voice was truly magnificent, but he was already well up into his thirties, was short, and getting bald rapidly, and this was not the era of the Enrico Carusos and the Jan Peerces, where talent superseded physical shortcomings. I even took him to audition for the then very popular Arthur Godfrey Television Show, and when he got through singing his magnificent arias (he did a rendition of "The Serenade" from the operetta, "Student Prince" that tore at your heartstrings), everyone in the studio, including the accompanist, applauded. Not surprisingly, he did not get the job. In time we drifted apart, and when I last inquired about him, he was still performing in little clubs, and drinking heavily, to drown his frustrations and terrible disappointments, I suppose.

Another excellent singer I shared the bill with, was a tall, handsome, gregarious Irish-American named Jimmy. He was young, married, in his early twenties, and in his prime. He dealt in popular songs and threw in an occasional Irish lullaby. When he warbled his own inimitable rendition of "Danny Boy," what with so many Philadelphia Irish in the audience, he would stop the show cold. I thought, for sure, he would become a star, and so did our favorite Philadelphia theatrical agent Steve Graham, who would make certain that his hearing aid was in order when he went to hear him sing. Steve was a genuine connoisseur of talent who ran a first class agency with the help of his wonderful children. All the entertainers, myself especially, loved them all. He was beyond middle age, wore spectacles, and was totally dedicated to his profession. He had a hearing impairment, and wore an old fashioned hearing aid, and you could see the impression of its battery through his shirt. He was so good natured that we used to, oft-times, while visiting him in his office, take advantage of his handicap by talking to him, and muting out some words in the course of the conversation. We would roar with laughter as he cupped his ear and kept pounding on the lump on his chest and yelling, "Damn hearing aid! What the hell's the matter with this damn thing?" And his grown kids, his assistants, who were as good natured as their lovable father, would laugh along with the really sadistic practical joke.

The most popular comedian in all of Philly at the time was a husky young Irishman named Mickey. He was big, brash, and very smart. When he'd ride in a cab he would make certain to tip the cabby generously, and would always add, "Remember, Mickey gave this to you." He built up a huge following, and wherever he appeared, he packed the place. He was loved by all, including those ubiquitous racketeers that frequented the better night spots. And he sure gave everyone his money's worth. He was really a very energetic and talented entertainer. He worked the very best places in town, and had "all the right people" among his following. In fact, it was rumored that they were arranging to get him into one of the most important clubs in New York City, and if he did as well there as he did in Philly, it was guaranteed "big time."

The problem with him, as the sages in the business recognized, something that totally escaped any consideration by the locals in Philly, was that a good deal of his comedy material was done in dialect. Some of it, especially the poorly enunciated Yiddish, was in poor taste where excellence was a requisite. The word was all over Philadelphia that he was opening in New York, and even members of his large following came there for opening night. And (true to the predictions by those in the know) when the reviewers observed that he was dealing in small time, offensive dialect material, he was justifiably crucified. He finished the run of his engagement and hurried back to Philadelphia with his tail between his legs. Thanks to his connections and the fact that he was a talented character actor, he eventually got some parts on TV shows and in the movies, but he never really attained the heights that his huge Philadelphia claque had predicted for him.

A few years later, I was struggling in one of those abominable strip joints down on the notorious Baltimore Street in Baltimore, that headlined a stripper who had developed an uncanny knack for twirling propellers, in opposite directions, on her bare breasts. I hated such jobs like poison, and by that time I was seriously questioning the miserable choice of having to leave my love of my life at home in order to try to further my career. After our first week together on the road, where Shirley hung around every night in our dingy theatrical hotel room while I went to work at the Erie Social Club in Philadelphia, we both agreed that we would never do that again. She was just too gifted and vital to spend her life just hangin' around in such wasteful circumstances. She was constantly on my mind, and I was already trying to figure out a way to escape from this outwardly glamorous business that was really starting to tear me up. My salesmen friends whom I would meet from time to time on the road, would envy me for working with all those lovely ladies who remove their clothing in public for a living. Little did they realize that many of these strippers were my best friends and companions. They were also lonely on the road, who also had loved ones waiting for them back home, and were just as ambivalent as I was about the only way they knew to make a living. Some of them, as unhappy as they were, and forever living out of suitcases, were quite well compensated financially, which made it all more palatable.

In this setting, I unexpectedly came across a situation that broke my heart. At the Belvedere hotel, I attended a party hosted by a headliner star named Mickey. He was a most gracious host, with a drink in his hand, and in a very generous mood. "Help yourself to anything you want..." Mickey bellowed to his "valet", who was in the kitchen, "Jimmy, c'mon out here and bring these nice people some coffee." And I could not believe my eyes when I saw who emerged, obsequiously bowing and replying, "Yes boss, coming right up." I did a double take when I recognized my old friend Jimmy, the handsome Irish singer from Philadelphia, who looked very embarrassed when he saw me. I felt so bad that I could have cried. He bowed and scraped all night long in response to Mickey's often crude commands. He answered with a "Yes, Mickey, comin'." It was hardly the time and place for an explanation, but it didn't take much intelligence to figure out that Jimmy (thinking it was going to be great for his future) had sold his soul and hitched his wagon to Mickey's star, performing as his opening act in the show and serving as his lackey at other times. It was a helluva price to pay, but as past history indicates, many a career was launched in just this fashion, and it remains a common occurrence to this very day. The party became quite loud and raucous and I departed. Two days later, on the front page of the Baltimore Sun in big headlines, I read "Popular Entertainer Evicted From Hotel." Many years later, Mickey (after he had appeared in minor roles in a few more movies)

12 The One in the Arena

Luckily, another summer was rapidly approaching, and we had something wonderful to look forward to. Just as I had anticipated, the Kenmore requested us again, and up we went to that euphoric life in the country. As was becoming the custom, my eccentric father-in-law emptied his truck for the occasion, so that he would have room for himself, Rosie, and his darling daughter and her actor husband. Where it was normally about a four hour drive, the way Max drove, it took a lot longer. The Quickway had not been built yet. Old Route 17 required maneuvering through dozens of little towns on antiquated, winding two lane highways. In Max's case, to make it to the mountains in seven hours was considered record breaking. It was quite a scene to see the four of us creeping along on the crowded highway, with other drivers passing us wherever they could, (giving us dirty looks at the same time), while poor, frustrated Rosie bellowed, "C'mon chuchim (sarcastic for "wise one"), move your ass!" It became a habit for them to spend the first two weeks of every summer wherever I was appearing, and they loved every precious moment of it. For us, as uncomfortable as it was, the drive was a good way to get up to the mountains with all our equipment.

For Shirley and me, it was wild anticipation. We had a whole new staff, including a new orchestra and some exciting singers, which I had auditioned during the spring. I don't recall who the girl was, but the male singer was a tall, slender, talented tenor who also was a tap dancer (which was a welcome addition). His name was Charles Julian, and he later gave up a most promising career to marry the girl of his dreams and settle in Tucson, Arizona, where he became a cantor in a reformed synagogue. I had my treasure trove of crazy costumes still in the same cardboard carton in which I had packed them away at the end of the previous summer, and I couldn't wait to put the costumes on again so that Shirley, I, and the rest of our group could perform onstage those absurd comedy sketches that I was unable to do as a "standup" in the clubs. The playhouse was located at the edge of glorious Kauneonga Lake, across the road from the hotel, and between constant rehearsals and the nightly presentations, we spent a major part of our time there. Of course there was no change in our shabby sleeping quarters. It was back to that windowless closet which had room only for our bed, and all the while I kept thinking to myself. "I wonder if Moss Hart had it any better in that chicken coop?" But, we were still better off than the others on my staff who had to content themselves with sleeping in the low, dark attic across the hall. They had to fumble around each night in the dark with flashlights because there were no electric lights. What a ridiculous way to live. Yet the sun drenched daytime held invigorating fresh air, and the exhilaration of recognition of our respective talents, more than compensated for our sacrifices. And huge sacrifices they were. We lived on the top floor of the hotel, where it took ages for the heat of the day that had been baking the roof to simmer down. It was all worth it though. We were in the country surrounded by interesting people who adored us, and we were on the biggest and best damn lake in all of Sullivan County. We were getting paid for it too, with free room and board thrown in. For ten whole weeks, as hard as we worked day and night, this was paradise.

As happy and fulfilled as we were at the end of the season, we were quickly shocked into reality when we returned home and were suddenly faced with the realization that it was back to that grinding routine of looking for work. And if I found bookings, where would they take me, for how long, and for how much? How I prayed that things would be a lot better than they had been before.

And just like after the previous summer, that tiny closet we slept in, once again led to Shirley's becoming pregnant. After that summer, Shirley found herself in the early stages of that condition. Last summer, while getting a ride home from one of our well meaning guests, the car hit an enormous bump that jostled her so that although she was sitting in the back seat, she flew into the air and hit her head on the roof. Whether it was because of that terribly severe jolt or not, Shirley suffered a painful miscarriage in her third month of pregnancy. This time we were going to be a helluva lot more careful. Because of the Jewish High Holy Days, the Kenmore stayed open a whole extra month, so it wasn't until the end of September or early October, that we finally came back home.

While we were away, my pal Jackie Bryce had disappeared, and Roy moved into an office with a new partner, a droll, humorless, but highly intelligent individual named Norman. I was of no great value to either one of them with the kind of money I was making, but whatever they got for me merited a ten percent commission. I'll never forget the time I was sitting home, laying off on a Saturday night, when Roy called and told me that they needed somebody in a hurry at a New York hotel where a fraternal lodge was holding an affair, and it was a last minute thought to hire a "funnyman" but they had no budget. Roy hesitated for a moment when he told me that all they had to spend was eight dollars. "Stop puttin' me on," I said, "who works for eight dollars?" "Honest," he replied, "that's all they've got. Wanna take it or not?" "I'll take it," I said, "but it sure sounds crazy to me." I did the job, and to this very day, we still talk about it. That's how hungry I was to work professionally. Who knows if the agent didn't get more, which, in retrospect, he probably did, but he knew how desperate I was to work, and, very likely he was desperate for money at the same time. Since he collected the money from the client, and he had this unsophisticated chump in his stable, why not make a "killing?" And I was so honest and sincere that I just couldn't see giving him eighty cents commission, so I decided to be a great big sport, and I gave him a whole dollar. This sort of deviousness still goes on to this very day, on a much grander scale, as the swindlers are getting wiser and more daring, but that had to rank as one of the pettiest things that anyone could have done. Sometimes we sit and reminisce about how I once got paid eight bucks for a Saturday night's work ... less ten percent commission... or was it twelve percent? Nevertheless, I was happy to get it. Years later when I became successful, I adopted an attitude. "I don't work cheap. If you want me that badly and you can't afford me, I'll do it for you for nothing!"

And it became a pattern that I would work from summer to summer, grabbing whatever I could get along the way, and I managed to grab a lot instead of sitting around at Hanson's and bellyaching. However it was becoming more and more apparent to me that this was no way to live, especially after

"Danny Boy" made us into a trio very early one Sunday morning in May. It was love at first sight and blossomed into one of the greatest love affairs of all time. Oh how we adored that long, skinny, bald headed infant who would soon turn into the most adorable blonde curly haired little genius we had ever met. By the time he was three, he personally rowed me around Dixie Lake in Ferndale, NY. When he was five, he got up on a two wheeler bicycle for the very first time in the schoolyard after following my instructions closely. He never needed anyone's assistance again. What an intelligent, lovable little man! How did we ever get along without him?

Now with another summer at the Kenmore approaching, how would the Schumers take the news that we now have added an infant to our team? They were not too happy. There was no room in that closet for three. Where would we sleep? They realized that a baby doesn't require much food, but what do we do for housing? After some truly unnecessary hand wringing, they worked it out for us to stay at a rooming house almost adjacent to our playhouse. I'm certain it cost them a pittance, and they rationalized that it was tantamount to a raise in pay, which, by the third summer, I was entitled to.

That was our third and last summer at the Kenmore. (No, Shirley didn't become pregnant that summer. We had a new housing arrangement, and also a baby to take care of, in addition to our frantic schedule.) What a good and memorable summer it was. Once again we had a new staff, and a damn talented one at that. We had Alan Stewart, a fine young, handsome baritone of medium height and with brown, wavy hair. He sang popular music, songs from the Broadway shows, and even some operatic classics. He was a good straight man in all our comedy sketches. The guests liked him, and the women were attracted to him too, which was always a valuable asset to a summer social staff. (I used to chuckle when I would find those ubiquitous notes scribbled and scratched into our playhouse walls, no doubt by frivolous teenage girls, "Van Harris is a hubba hubba.")

There was one beautiful, classy blonde lady who was staying at a bungalow colony down the road, who appeared to be getting back at her handsome husband who only came up on weekends, but whom she was certain was having a fling in the garment center where he worked as a salesman all week.

She would visit Alan quite often, after hours during the week, and he would borrow my recently acquired used car, which was standing idly anyway, 'cause at the end of each day we were just too exhausted to go anywhere but to bed.

I remember getting up one morning and was unable to control the lids on my eyes. Also, when I brushed my teeth, I couldn't control my lips. The water would dribble out of the corner of my mouth, which was decidedly over to a side. I had been sweating like the dickens the night before because I had been involved in an extraordinary amount of physical sketches that included having all my clothes torn off and having a bucket of ice cold water poured over my head. I don't recall why I was showing off. Like they say in the business, "I was on a roll." Then, all sweated up, I stepped into the chilly night air, and I guess that was the start.

The doctor in town diagnosed it as "Bell's Palsy," supposedly a cold in the eighth facial nerve. He gave me a massive shot in the arm of Vitamin B12, and told me to rest. He couldn't assure me when or if, it would go away. How does a Social Director, who's on duty technically twenty-four hours a day, rest? I prepared two nights of all musical programs, where I wouldn't be missed onstage. I got permission to go back to Brooklyn and drove immediately to my chiropractor Dr. Yellin on Utica Ave. He knew exactly what it was, and how to treat it. He did a concentrated number of adjustments on me over the two days, instructing me to keep rubbing my face in a circular motion. By the time I got back, my face was mobile enough so that I could perform again. Miraculously by the end of the week, I was back to normal, as normal as I could be. Whether it was the chiropractic adjustments, or the massive shot of B12, or a combination of both, something worked. It was a frightening lesson, well learned.

The rest of our social staff consisted of a very young, well endowed (physically and artistically) redhead named Rita Michaels, who was very cooperative and a pleasure to work with, and an orchestra, led by one Jerry Gold. Jerry was of medium height, husky and for a very young man, was already starting to lose his hair. He played a pretty fair trumpet and had the good sense to surround himself with competent, albeit neurotic, musicians. His piano player was a very gifted lady whose moods swung widely, but whose ability could not

Danny Boy. Kenmore Hotel, White Lake, Catskills. (1948)

Van and Shirley's family. From left to right. Back row: Shirley's father Max Vinitzky holding baby Danny, Shirley's mother Rose, Van's mother Paulie and father Moishe Harris. Front row: Max's father Moishe and mother Ida Vinitzky, Rose's father Mendel and mother Gussie, Moishe Harris's stepmother Anna.

be questioned. She was good, and she was actually the bandleader "without portfolio". Jerry would tap off the songs, but it was Adelaide who conducted each and every song. Jerry was quite docile about it, understandably. On the drums he had a very tall, likable "drink of water" who was a bit juvenile, hard of hearing, and displayed the most complete set of Slingerland Radio Kings drums that ever graced any stage, anywhere. He spoke with a slight lisp, practiced the drums day and night, and took his music very seriously. He bragged about his German-American father, who was his mentor and idol, and he bragged also that, in the so-called "off-season" he had appeared numerous times with Shorty Carrucio's great dance orchestra (whoever they were). The drummer's name was Ray Starr, and he was such a goofy and likable kid that, despite his shortcomings (and he seemed to have quite a few) you had to overlook whatever mistakes he made. And, as for my comedy sketches, he was a pure natural, even if, at times, he had trouble remembering his lines.

Because it was hard to control Ray's playing, due to his hearing problems, Adelaide would angrily compete with the drummer when it came to volume. To make up for his deficiency, he played much too loud, and by the time that the leader Jerry, would get his attention to simmer down, it was already too late. Adelaide was stomping on the foot pedals while cursing poor innocent Ray out, under her breath. When the singers sang, Adelaide was totally in control. They had to adjust their renditions to her playing or else there would be no synchronization. It got so that when either of the singers would finish his or her act, I would facetiously announce something that sounded like this: "You've just heard Adelaide Robbins on the piano, accompanied by Alan Stewart on voice"... and the audience would roar its approval. She was such a marvelously gifted pianist who always seemed to be angry (no doubt because fate had dealt her a nasty hand by putting her together with a band that was not in the same league with her), and yet she maintained a decidedly sharp sense of humor and was very outspoken. She also had no trepidation about using colorful, unladylike language. On those days when she was particularly obstreperous I would ask her why, and she would reply, unflinchingly, "I've got da curse dis week!"

The members of this band, unlike previous ones, rebelled at not having any electricity in their miserable quarters in the attic. Management was thoughtful enough to find a more comfortable space for the lady. Adelaide shared a real room somewhere with one of the office help. It couldn't have been anything special, but I'm sure it was a lot more livable than what the boys had to settle for. Early in the season they threatened to quit unless they, at least, got some light up there, and I was elected to wire up their quarters (This was another one of the plethora of violations that hotel owners got away with in those years, ... and some owners still do.)

On a July morning, with the hot sun already beating down on the roof, and turning the area directly beneath it into an inferno, yours truly groped around in the dark, cutting and connecting electrical cords into assorted receptacles. I was ably aided and abetted by my volunteer apprentice (the tall, skinny drummer himself, dressed only in his undershorts) who was having a difficult time just trying to stand erect, and who was already drenched to the bone. Knowing how uncomfortable we both were, I tried to work as quickly as I could. For a guy who taught himself some electrical work, (as a child, I was forever experimenting, in an effort to keep our apartment in order during my mother's lengthy stays in the hospital) I was very pleased with the way things were going. Ray's innocent, child-like observations, though at times irritating, served as entertainment, and made the chore a lot more pleasant than if I had to go it alone, especially as uncomfortable as we both were. As I was getting close to the completion of the job, I left Ray in the dark at one end of the attic holding the male plug near the newly installed socket while I rolled the wires to the opposite end, prior to my eventually stapling them to the ceiling. I cautioned the big lug, "Ray, whatever you do, don't plug it in until I tell you, as I've got to strip the other ends and connect them when I get there." Sure enough (and I should have anticipated it) just as I was in the process of splicing the wires together, my eager assistant way over on the other end decided to see if the plug would fit into the socket. I screamed as the sparks wildly flew all around me, momentarily illuminating the entire area. As I dropped the ends to the floor, things once again became pitch black, and out of the darkness I heard this quiet childish voice, softly inquire into the stony silence, "Van, are you dead? Van, speak to me. Are you dead? I hope not 'cause I'll jump off the fire escape and kill myself." (Knowing him as I did, I knew that he meant every word.) Luckily for me, I was able to drop the wires before I became A. C., or D. C., or both. And when I recovered from the shock, I mustered up the most colorful group of expletives (some of which I didn't even think I knew). As the tall, skinny, lovable kid stood there in his underwear, awkwardly attempting to insulate himself against the verbal barrage, while trembling and weeping intermittently, we managed to complete the project. For the rest of the season Ray took such delight in bragging to all within earshot, about how he and I lit up the attic.

Yes, it was quite an eventful summer. Baby Dan, who was all of four weeks old when we took him to the mountains with us, suddenly developed a severe debilitating cough, and it was pitiful to watch this tiny child struggle to breath while being wracked by this seemingly unending plague. The country doctor in nearby Swan Lake diagnosed his illness as whooping cough, quite rare and dangerous in an infant that young. The doctor urged that we take him back to steaming Brooklyn, where at least, the baby would have the comforts of home during his fight to recover. I rushed Shirley and the baby back early in the morning and had to return that same afternoon in order to fulfill my obligation to the hotel. The attitude that the show must go on had already been indelibly ingrained in both of us, and we had accepted it unquestioningly, even though we were both frightened out of our wits by the deadly seriousness of the situation.

It was at that moment that the young mother displayed remarkable strength and endurance. She went without sleep for days on end in order to be entirely available to help the poor baby breathe. With some relief supplied by her ever reliable mother, they pulled the tough little hombre through his terrible crisis. Within a couple of weeks, he was back up into the fresh mountain air where he thrived beautifully for the remainder of the summer.

One rainy early afternoon, I was the first one to walk into our playhouse to set up for rehearsal. I unlocked the big padlock on the front door, stepped inside, and immediately discovered that there was a problem. The bandstand was completely empty. The boys in the band would take their instruments back to their quarters with them at the end of each evening. Of course, you couldn't do that with drums, piano, and other large instruments. However, the bandstand's crown jewels were those shiny new Slingerland Radio Kings and now they were gone. They had disappeared, right down to the smallest foot pedal. Someone had apparently rowed up to the back door that faced the lake and not the well-traveled front road, had broken in, and taken off with our pride and joy. It was obviously a well organized theft that required immediate action. It was bad enough that our whole rhythm section was gone, but we had a show to do that night and without percussion it wasn't going to be easy.

The first thing I did was to call the State Police who had the jurisdiction in such rural areas. A couple of uniformed "Adonises" showed up after awhile. They shook their heads, tried to appear somewhat concerned, made out a hasty report, and were soon on their way; never to be heard from again. I'm sure they would have preferred something a lot juicier, like a raid on an illegal crap game. At the same time, I roused Ray from his sleep and summoned the big goof to the playhouse. "Ray," I said as he listened attentively on the top floor hall phone. "Come down to the playhouse as soon as you can. Something has come up." Of course he was there long before the cops had come. He breathlessly bounded into the playhouse and shouted, "Here I am. What's up?" "Ray," I exclaimed, "look around you. Someone has stolen your drums!." His happy-go-lucky exuberance quickly turned into anguish, and tears started to well up in his eyes. By then the entire staff was preparing to take him around and console him. "Shit!" he cried out, "and I was gonna practice this afternoon!" Of course his reaction caught us all by surprise, but we should have expected something like that from him. That was our Ray...

Time was of the essence so we called "the musicians' friend" (their local union) located some forty or fifty miles south in another county entirely. Once a nondescript union that represented a quiet little area, it became a comparative goldmine as more and more resort hotels cropped up in the adjoining "Jewish mountains", and each hotel hired a band. Somehow that local managed to be awarded the jurisdiction over all of them, enriching a number of people who, in their wildest dreams, never expected such a windfall. The guy on the phone said, "Sure I'll help ya out. C'mon down here and we'll lend you some drums to help you get through till you get new ones." With no immediate alternative, for the next several weeks we had to settle for our shows and dance music being played on the kinds of weather beaten drums that are carried on one's chest in high school parades. Such generosity. How fortunate the musicians were to have it. Hey, that's what they pay their dues for, right? ... How lucky can you get?

The saga continued when, on the following morning, a huge black automobile pulled up in front of the hotel. Ray, who had been wild with anticipation, squealed with delight. "It's Poppa!" he shouted. "Poppa is here ... I just can't wait to see him!" Neither could we. Eli, the all-around bellhop, graciously opened the driver's door and out stepped a diminutive man, officious and reeking with confidence, wearing what looked like something right out of the Swiss Alps: patent leather shoes, high woolen socks that came up to and over his knees, lederhosen (long Alpine shorts held up by wide suspenders), and a peaked Pinnochio hat, with the little feather on the side (all representing pure rugged individualism). The sight of father and son embracing was something to behold. Nature never ceases to amaze me. Ray was, at least three times the height of his illustrious father and it was quite a comical sight to see Poppa with his arms wrapped around his little boy's knees, while the dutiful son had to bend almost in half in order to plant a tender kiss upon the top of Poppa's head. We watched all this with amazement, and Ray took delight in introducing his tiny hero to all of us. I detected a trace of a German accent, which lent credence to the way he was dressed. He had driven up to the hotel to console his son, and also lecture him on the virtues of protecting one's valuable property, which I rightfully guessed was insured. After some polite, preliminary banter, Poppa excused himself by saying, "Koom, kind, ve go for a valk," and off they strolled down the road. It was a sight to behold, Poppa in full control, lecturing unceasingly while looking way up into Ray's kindly face, gesturing with his hands and wiggling his index finger at him admonishingly, and all the while Ray answering, "Yes Poppa ... I know that Poppa ... "

September was upon us once again, and we were filled with the usual ambivalence. On one hand we were happy that the long, concentrated summer (with its daily rehearsals, highly charged shows, and all the other social activities that I was responsible for from early mornings well into the nights) was over. Yes, we were young and energetic, but that didn't insulate us against fatigue, and boy, we were tired and happy to come back home to our loving families... happy to just relax and spend more time with the baby... and to lie in a bed that was so much more comfortable too.

On the other hand, we were filled with fear and apprehension. The show biz year starts and ends in September. Whether it's legit or variety, the summer is usually a guarantee of work, be it summer stock, state fairs, resorts, or whatever. When the big boom is over, it's time to go lookin' again. The audiences are no longer on leisure time. They too are back at work, narrowing their recreation allotment down considerably so that the performer has to maneuver for his best shot. Summers are Saturday nights every night. September is a reminder that for the next ten months you're going to really have to hustle for work... unless you're lucky enough to get into a Broadway show, a motion picture, a steady TV show ... "the big time." But it's like a guy wearing a cast on his arm or leg whose skin is itching underneath it, and the only way to relieve it is to scratch. Just like "the big time" it's always within reach, but impossible to get to.

And so I started making my rounds of the numerous bookers' offices almost immediately upon our return. I was a little bit more experienced by then, and name recognition (no matter how limited) in a business that has no secrets, is a decided asset. Of course, there's always the thought of giving up this tantalizing business if something more secure would avail itself, especially when one becomes a parent. It then becomes incumbent upon him to make certain that his new responsibility is welled cared. Babies are so endearing, and our little bugger was growing cuter and smarter every day. It became more and more difficult for me to tear myself away from the two people I loved more than anything else in the world, and it got so that I accepted the out-of-town engagements with more and more trepidation. Not that these jobs were plentiful, and most of them were only on weekends with minimum remuneration (and almost always, that was less ten percent). I started to look at some of these assignments like jail sentences. The only true compensation was the approval of the audiences. There are no sweeter sounds to the ears of a comedian than those of laughter and applause. Being honest with myself however, I couldn't wait for the engagement to end. There were many times that I would find myself going home, half asleep on one of those tedious "milk trains" (stopping at every single stop) for what seemed like hours on end, and my thoughts would depress me. Sometimes I was fortunate enough to be distracted by other performers and agents who were on the same train, but when I was alone, the realities would really start to sink in and they were terribly depressing. There I was, with a pocket full of money, so that I could pay my bills and buy whatever was needed, and visualizing the sweet smell of the baby's breath and his delicious gurgling sounds, while I was holding his lovely mother in my arms. Then came the realization that it was all so temporary, and that very soon I would have to leave again so that we could all survive.

This same feeling of despair was not indigenous to show people alone. Many were the times when I would drive to some small city, and as I would be unpacking the trunk of my car before checking into some fleabag, inexpensive hotel, somebody else would be pulling up next to me doing the same thing. He'd generally say something like, "Hi, I'm with such-and-such company. What company do you sell for?" Traveling salesmen who spent their lonely lives on the road became my friends. And, when they'd learn that I was not a member of their dreary profession, but a "glamorous entertainer", they'd be delighted to make my acquaintance, and would often spend their evenings at the dumps where I was performing. After their tongues were loosened by drink, their conversations would sound very much alike, "I make a damn good living at this, but I can't take this shit too much longer. I've already told my boss, this is my last trip!" And the same guys, each time a little more shopworn, would be making the same complaints when I would meet them again, weeks. months, and years down the line. I kept saying to myself, "Am I any different? Isn't the same damn thing happening to me?"

There was an instance when a stranger ambled up to me after I had concluded my first show of the evening and I was just hangin' around at the bar accepting my accolades. In reality, I was always happy to have someone to talk to. I also had a drink in my hand because it was expected of me, but I could never get used to the real stuff, so unbeknownst to all, except the bartender, it was filled with water. And smoke? ... I smoked a lot in those years, as did everyone else, but I was fortunate enough to dump that addiction some time later. You could see from this stranger's clothing that he was a class act. His style was impressive. His choice of words was good, and his cigar smelled expensive. He had no trouble blending in with the crowd and said to me, "Excuse me, but I really came over to tell you how great you were, kid." By now I was already accustomed to such congratulations and had already developed a knack for accepting them gracefully and unostentatiously, which always helps to enhance one's popularity. Actually I was just trying to be myself. I have met so many phonies in my profession who live for such moments, and who really make a big show of accepting compliments while managing to hide their obnoxiousness. They are actors, and they do it quite well, and there's no one any the wiser for it.

We all soon found out that this man was one of the great industrialist Henry Kaiser's right hand men. He proceeded to tell us how generous Mr. Kaiser was, but that he'd forsaken his wife, his kids, ... everything, by being so devoted to his boss and traveling all over on his behalf at his slightest whim. As whatever it was that he was drinking was starting to take its effect, he unexpectedly impressed us with a sudden show of bravado by exclaiming, "I've had it with him! He's ruined my life! I've ruined my life with my loyalty. I can't take it any longer. Watch me fellas, I'm gonna quit ... right here and now." And, to our amazement, he approached a nearby telephone, made a collect call, identified himself, and asked to be put through to the boss. We all stood with our mouths open as we listened to this man firmly tender his resignation, and in a very short while, his air of confidence disappeared completely, and we heard him continue, "But Henry, I don't care how much more money you'll give me, I've had enough of this. I'm all worn out. Er, what's that? That much more,

Henry? But Henry, I'm suffering from burnout. So much more Henry? Wow! You certainly are a generous one sir. Yes sir. I'll take care of that matter. You can be sure I'll take care of it, ...and well. Yes sir. See you in the office when I get back!" This guy was for real, and he was one of the lucky ones who must've spent a helluva lot of time on the road for Mr. Kaiser. But unlike so many of the others, if he played his cards right, he could soon accumulate enough to retire on comfortably, long before his peers (if he didn't suffer a breakdown first).

The longer I stayed in the business, the more I developed a desire to get out of it. Yet every time I saw a great comedian on TV, or at any one of those presentation houses on Broadway, I envied him so, and I kept saying to myself, "With a little bit of help, and a little bit of luck, I could do that." I am convinced however, that a lot of it, if not all, is still "who ya know." I envied the really excellent American comedians, not the nightclub variety that was rapidly springing up. A number of the new, so-called "stars" spoke English poorly, or sloppily, or both. The desire for excellence was gradually disappearing from life, and the stultifying age of mediocrity in the arts (particularly in music) was slowly starting to take hold. The elitists, for lack of a better description, were slowly disappearing into the woodwork. Vulgarity was slowly seeping into our everyday patter, and it was only going to proliferate. It seemed like fewer and fewer people dared to be great. I read once that, at those times in history when there was an unusual abundance of truly great leaders all in the same generation, somehow, mysteriously, the stars in the heavens were in a certain juxtaposition, and that has never happened again since the thirties and forties. How convenient it is to be an observer and not a participant. I once read somewhere:

It's not the critic who counts. Not the one who points out where the strong man stumbled or how the doer of deeds could have done them better. The credit belongs to the one who is actually in the arena. Whose face is marred by dust, and sweat, and blood. Who errs, and comes short again and again. Who strives valiantly. Who knows the great devotions, the great enthusiasms, and spends himself in a worthy cause. Who, at best, knows in the end the triumph of high achievement, and who, if he fails, he fails while daring greatly... So that his place shall never be with those cold and timid souls who know neither victory... nor defeat.

I've always hated nightclubs, and that was the area from which all the newly successful performers were emerging. A great many of these flourishing bistros, cleverly cloaked in the guise of respectability, were owned and run by unsavory characters who had ties to unscrupulous operations. I had no desire to get involved with such people. In fact, they frightened me. And they, a good number of whom were uneducated, unsophisticated, but, to their great credit, had developed remarkable native intelligence when it came to the art of making money. Most had no sense of humor and wouldn't know good comedy if they fell on it, but they did know what brings in the customers and they were the kingmakers. They had working agreements with some unscrupulous and scurrilous theatrical agents, a number of them cleverly cloaked in respectability in major agencies.

13 Kirby

It was just after having appeared at a busy Pittsburgh nightspot, owned by some Jewish thug, that I made the decision to get out of show business. I was determined to look for some kind of "legitimate" job and try to settle down "and live happily ever after" which in reality, was a fantasy. I would die without show business. Besides my beautiful family, there was nothing in the world that I loved more than performing. It's intoxicating ... "The smell of the greasepaint ... the roar of the crowd." It transformed me from the ordinary to the special. Vain, but true. There was magic in "theater"... at any level. This was nicely exemplified when Shirley and I appeared at some "toilet" in the mountains on a Memorial Day tryout, before we began to have a family. It was a hotel that catered to Jewish immigrants, as they all did in those days, and the packed house was abuzz with excitement. The great Michel Michelesko was going to appear there on a Saturday night. We'd heard the name, but we had never seen him, and we wondered what all the fuss was about. We had heard that he was an excellent singer and actor, and the older and even the middle-aged ladies were all agog over his pending appearance. It was almost as though they were the older, Jewish bobbysoxers awaiting the appearance of their own Frank Sinatra.

That Saturday morning a limousine pulled up to the hotel, and an elderly man (showing signs of the beginnings of a pot belly) with a full head of grey, wavy hair, and wearing rimless bifocals, stepped out to the applause of anyone and everyone who was standing around on the front porch. It was the star himself, Michel Michelesko. Shirley and I looked at each other. We couldn't imagine what they saw in him. To us he appeared old, even a bit stooped, and certainly not glamorous. That evening, after my comedy warmup, I introduced "the star of not only the night, but the whole weekend ... the great Michel Michelesko!" Mr. Michelesko, as he prepared to go onstage, had removed his glasses, tucked in his stomach with a small girdle, applied lipstick to accentuate his full, sensuous lips, and applied a pancake makeup that gave him a healthy looking tan. He put on a beautiful tuxedo wore patent leather shoes. After the exciting introduction I gave him, he nonchalantly strolled out onstage to tumultuous applause. He had a great Yiddish Theater orchestra, well rehearsed, providing his background, and he sang like an angel. Women actually fainted. He was beautiful in every way. The magic of show biz ... we really and truly learned something that we would never forget.

Some regular weekend patron at a nightclub called "Rogers' Paraglide" (owned by a number of Italian-American brothers named Rogers) made me an offer I was tempted to accept. I had worked at the Paraglide as much as they would have me, which was fairly often but on weekends only, and this customer used to frequent the place a lot, and we became quite friendly. He worked for one of the big baking companies out on Long Island in Hempstead. He convinced me that I could make a great living as a bakery truck driver, and the hours were such that it would free me to work in clubs on weekends. The pay was steady and good. I was just about ready to throw in the towel in exchange for a guaranteed salary and perhaps a more normal life. We made up to meet at the club on the following Saturday night. I had been booked in there for the weekend, and it was most convenient for us to talk about the details between shows.

I brought my father along that night for him to hear what this man had to say, and Pop sat at the same table with him until the show was over. As I was changing back into my "civvies" backstage, Mike Rogers came hurrying into my dressing room and said, "Van, get your father n' get out the back door, right now." Somewhat startled, I asked Mike, "Why? What's the problem?" He replied, "Your friend's been drinking sidecars all night, and he's bombed pretty good, and he's run up a good-sized check. He's fumbling around for the money, which I don't think he's got. He said something about your making good for him, so before you get stuck for the dough, I'll send your father back here, and the two of you, get the hell outta here, right now ... before it costs you money!" We took advantage of the boss' sage advice and departed. That was the very last time I ever saw the guy in the bakery business. He never even called on the phone.

That weekend while thumbing through the "Want Ads" in the newspaper, my eyes fell upon something that looked very alluring, the kind of "come-on" that's still ingeniously being placed right up until this very day. In larger-than-usual sized bold print it said, "Men, are you accustomed to making lots of money? We are looking for bright people to train and employ for a very prosperous future in an exciting profession. If you are interested, report to the Grand Ballroom of the Hotel Victoria at 9AM Monday. We promise you a golden opportunity."

This intrigued me greatly, and bright and early on Monday morning, with a newspaper under my arm, I apprehensively slipped into a back row seat in this rather large auditorium that smelled of freshly made coffee that was free for the asking to all the many curious men of assorted ages, sizes, and manner of dress, who were starting to fill up the seats. The very front three or four rows were occupied by a chorus of cheerleaders who were loudly chanting short, enthusiastic slogans, and poems, about something called "Kirby." At the end of each cheer they would leap up in the air and applaud wildly. Obviously, they were all members of the organization and the only ones there who knew each other, while we others, sat somewhat confused, wondering what was going to happen next. After awhile, someone mounted the stage and thanked us for showing up and advised us that what we were about to see and hear would possibly change our lives forever. He asked us to please be patient as we were awaiting the imminent arrival of their commander-in-chief.

Suddenly there was a burst of applause, a highly charged and speeded up resumption of the chanting, and one of the men leaped out of the group of sycophants onto the stage and wildly announced, "Fellas, here comes the man of the hour, the man of the day, the man of the year, the man himself ... here comes Big Al!" While they all drummed their feet on the floor till the sound reached a feverish crescendo, a tall, well built man who appeared to be in his early thirties, casually dressed and sporting a full crop of brown hair (swept into a pompadour in the front, and a "duck's ass" in the back) strutted confidently out onstage. He had the pale complexion of one who spends his lifetime in the bedroom, which was accentuated by the spotlight that shone on his face. He hesitated for a moment as he took one big peripheral look around the room, and then opened his mouth, revealing large white symmetrical teeth. He began to speak, and all the while his devoted followers kept chanting, "Al! ... Big Al!" over and over again. He raised his large, bejeweled hands and motioned for them to desist. A hush came over the audience as he began, "Fellas, I came out of the United States Marine Corps with nothin' but the suit on my back and a couple of bucks in my pocket. I tried doing assorted jobs with a minimum of success, and one day as I was walking down the street, feeling very disconsolate, I bumped into an old buddy of mine who was lookin' very prosperous ... like I'm lookin' now (or haven't you noticed) Ha! Ha!" And they all broke out in a chant once more "Al!" ... "Big Al!" ... "I asked my friend how come he was lookin' so good and he said he owed it all to Kirby. I asked, what's Kirby? and he said come with me and I'll show you. After I found out, I joined the Kirby organization and with a little bit of personality (and there he staged an exaggerated wink, while the edge of his mouth curled down to a side), I soon worked my way up to the top, (and then he started to gradually raise his voice) ... and now I own a Cadillac convertible and a Lincoln Continental. I live in a very fancy pad, ... and I get all the ass a guy could ever want!!" ... and at that point, bedlam! Uninhibited, but organized chanting reached a feverish pitch ... "Al! ... Big Al!" ... "Let's hear it for the king himself."... "Al! ... Big Al!"

As we all looked around bewilderedly, he continued on. "All of you assembled here this morning can have the same opportunity I had, only I want to warn you that we are very selective. In a moment, my aides will be passing among you and they will be distributing test papers and pencils. If you answer the questions and pass the test we will take you one step further and reveal what Kirby is all about and then indoctrinate you into our organization for the opportunity of a lifetime. Those of you who are not interested in going any further can leave now, and thanks from the bottom of my heart for showin' up. The rest of you can remain and take this short test and hand in your papers. At the end of the test we will give you a phone number to call after seven this evening. By then we will have gone over the test papers and we will inform you as to whether or not you passed. Those of you who passed will then be given further instructions. Once again, thank you, and I'm looking forward to seeing all of you again soon.".... and off he went as his cronies broke into a loud, inspiring a cappella version of "Onward Kirby," sung to the tune of the college marching song, "On Wisconsin."

The so-called "test" consisted of some rather simple gibberish, and just like many of the others (except for the wizened ones who had already experienced such crap), I figured that I was there already and I had gone through the trouble of having invested time and travel expenditures, so I might as well try to see this thing through. I handed in my completed paper and walked out into the rain, diagonally across the street to Hanson's drug store to see if anybody I knew was around. No question about it, I was still being drawn to the womb. I even made the rounds of a few agents to let them know that I was available for the weekend or longer. I then went home and reported to Shirley about what had gone on. "Kirby?" she asked, "what's a Kirby?" "Search me?" I replied.

That evening I called the number they had given me, and a man's voice with a decided speech impediment answered. I had barely identified myself when he said, as if he was reading it off a sheet of paper, "Congratulations, you have passed the test. Report tomorrow at 9AM to ... " and he gave me an address somewhere on Braddock Ave. in Jamaica, Queens. The following morning I got into my new Ford, two door sedan (the first new automobile I had ever owned thanks to Shirley's grandfather having lent me part of the cost, which I paid back in a very short time), and I was off to engage in the next chapter.

When I arrived at the given address, it turned out to be a large, somewhat empty store, except for a makeshift platform at one end and rows of folding chairs. A number of the other "lucky winners" were already there, while others, like myself, straggled in. Of course, up front was that same loud gang of chanters from the previous morning, except that, this time they distributed song books as we entered, and then asked us to join them as the launched into a whole slew of college marching songs that were all revised so that all the lyrics became parodies about Kirby. Soon a number of speakers were individually introduced by the "house emcee," while the delirious chanting proliferated, and each speaker told us of their fantastic successes with Kirby. One guy, sporting a moustache and smoking a pipe that gave off an intoxicating aroma, told us of how successful he had been as an accountant for a big firm, but it was nothing compared to the great success he was enjoying since having joined Kirby. Another man, with an Eastern-European accent, told us of how well he had done selling assorted items, home to home, directly to housewives, with liberal time payments, but Kirby took him away from that sort of drudgery and made him into a proud and affluent man. And on and on they went, each one different than the previous speaker, and each testimonial followed by the revved up Kirby "glee club."

The convincer for me was when a simply dressed young man who spoke real "Brooklynese" and who seemed to be bothered by some sort of facial tic, revealed, "I used ta woik on a garbage truck." In my comedy-oriented mind I said to myself, "Yeh, and I got paid twenty dollars a week and all I could eat." He next told us of how, by joining Kirby he and his family now live quite well, and his wife is no longer embarrassed when people ask her what her husband does for a living. I figured (and I'm sure that the others thought so too) that if this guy could make it, then anybody could.

After all the talks were over (and, by the way, Big Al wasn't there, nor did any of us ever see him again), we were informed that we were all being treated to lunch. We piled into our respective cars and the caravan snaked its way to Andre's Restaurant, somewhere on Jamaica Ave. There we were served the usual roast beef fare, and afterward we were asked to come into the big back ballroom where we lined up in rows, standing with our feet slightly spread apart, army style, and each of us was handed what looked like a full barracks bag. An articulate man stood in front of us, and in the manner of an army sergeant, he asked us to empty the bags in front of us, and as we did so, he informed us that all that the apparatus which resembled a good sized octopus, was the world's greatest vacuum cleaner, the Kirby. It was tricky to follow his instructions and put all the various parts and attachments together, but he eased our minds by informing us that we would be well supervised, and that we would be visiting the fertile new Levittown area of Long Island, which was loaded with new homes. We would work in teams with a group leader and other, more experienced salesmen. "The product is more expensive than other vacuum cleaners, but that makes our commissions higher, and because it's so effective, it's a very easy sale." He instructed us to sign a receipt for the Kirby and take it home, study it, and meet on the following morning back on Braddock Ave., with the Kirby in hand. We would be assigned to our individual teams, be given some preliminary tips, and then we'd be on our way to "reap our rewards." My head was spinning as I drove back home. I was already envisioning putting some large amounts of money into our coffers. That is, if it was going to be as easy as the guy said it would be. In fact, that night I called my pal, my singer and straight man at the Kenmore, Al Stewart, who was experiencing the same rigors in show business (only he didn't have a wife and child to worry about at the time) and I told him all about what was going on. This interested him greatly, and about a week later, he went through the same ritual and also joined Kirby.

On the following morning, amid those ubiquitous college marching songs that were supposed to inspire us, one of the leaders got up on the platform and described the various types of housewives we would encounter. He mimicked their behavior and reactions, and applied unflattering nicknames to each. Some of the simpletons laughed, which was to be expected I suppose. I was too concerned about getting started and rushed out into the street ahead of most of them, rarin' to go. The weather was quite cooperative so we drove out to a central meeting point on a quiet street somewhere in the rapidly expanding, ex-G.I. city of Levittown. We got out of our cars, broke off into six-man squads, and followed the instructions of our seasoned leader.

The modus operandi went like this: We worked in teams, and whoever concluded the sale got the commission, with those in superior positions getting their override. There was enough to be made on the sale of a single Kirby vacuum cleaner for everyone to share in the profits. We were all dressed in suits, with shirts and ties, which gave us a bit of an air of authority. The first team of two would ring the doorbell and some happy young lady (happy to be living in the sunny suburbs with her retuning lover and child, or children, or whatever) would come to the door. We would greet her by handing her some sort of bogus ticket from what looked like a raffle book, and some advertising for popular daytime TV shows. Before she could say a word, we'd cheerfully blurt out, "Hi, we're with 'Bride And Groom' and 'Queen For A Day.' You've heard of our shows, of course, haven't you?" As the surprised, and generally impressed, lady would stammer, "Y-yes?" whoever was the spokesman on that caper would continue, "If you are selected, you will be receiving a call, and they will be asking you a few simple questions about Kirby, and if you can answer them, you will be awarded a prize." Naturally, the puzzled lady would reply, "A few questions about a Kirby? What's a Kirby?" The answer came back, "Oh, I see you're not familiar with the Kirby. Will you be home for the next few moments? There are representatives in the neighborhood, and in a very short while they will be coming through here, and it'll take only a moment of your time for one of them to familiarize you with the amazing Kirby." Usually the flustered woman, caught completely off-guard by this ingenious ploy, and probably welcoming a break in her newly acquired housewife monotony, would say, "Okay," and the die was cast.

In a little while, after the contact men had returned to the pack, to point out the "mark's" address, a new team of vultures (one experienced and the other the novice, like myself) would arrive, equipment in hand, concisely packed into an impressive looking, large, fancy container, and before the bewildered lady could say another word, the "octopus" with its various parts was out on the floor. We started off by running the powerful sweeper over the occupant's present mattress, as the strength of the appliance automatically sucked up grey matter that looked like a large accumulation of dust, which was, in reality, part of what the mattress was made out of, but which the unscrupulous salesman was quick to point out, was "dead skin" that the family had been sleeping on all this time because an ordinary vacuum cleaner is not capable of drawing it out like the Kirby, and only the fantastic Kirby, can.

A savvy woman would say things like, "I have to talk it over with my husband when he comes home," to which there was always the ready answer, "Of course, please do, and we will be back again in the neighborhood tomorrow and the next day, and if your husband wants to see a demonstration we'll be happy to send one of our guys around in the evening." To the question, "I just bought a new vacuum cleaner, what am I supposed to do with that?" there was always the answer, "We can't give you what you paid for it, and, as you can see, it's really worthless, but we'll take it off your hands as an accommodation and throw in as much as we are able to." Then, of course there were always the very many who would say, "Sorry, can't afford it, but thanks anyway," which was the majority. However, sales, and especially door-to-door sales, depend upon perseverance, tenacity, and the law of averages, and I quickly learned that only the callous and desperate survive.

I hung in there for a month. Al Stewart, who worked with another group in another new Long Island area, also lasted a month. I sold one Kirby. Al sold none. The straw that broke the camel's back for me was when I was invited in for coffee to some dear lady's home prior to my making the presentation. I noticed that her eyes were quite red, and became nosey enough to ask her if she'd been crying. She told me that she had just lost a child to some sort of kidney disease, and being a religious Christian, she was coping with the acceptance of her tragedy, and was thankful that she had, at least been blessed with her older child, an adorable friendly little girl who stood at her side listening to all that was being said. She instructed the little girl to "keep the nice man company in the living room, while I prepare some coffee in the kitchen." This prospective sale was taking a longer than usual amount of time, and as I was sitting and chatting with the little doll, the doorbell rang and in walked one of my superiors, "Harris, what's takin' ya so damn long?" The lady of the house invited him to join us for coffee, and he accepted, and while she went back to the kitchen he plopped himself down into an easy chair, waiting impatiently, as I continued my conversation with the six-year-old. She wandered over to my grumpy overseer and asked, "Would you like to hear me sing 'Jesus Loves Me'?" and was met by a low barrage of expletives that I couldn't believe I was hearing. That was it for me! We politely had our coffee when the lady came back into the living room. I excused myself by telling her that I've got to rush to another appointment, and quickly concluded my visit. I thanked the lady for her kindness, said goodbye to the little girl, and rushed outta the house. "What the hell was that all about?"I asked him. He nonchalantly shrugged his shoulders and tossed it off with, "Whadd'ya beatin' yer gums about? I'll betcha dollars to donuts that, that was not gonna be a sale anyway." That evening, still fuming in disbelief of what I had witnessed, I handed in my kit and asked when I could pick up the commission they owed me for that one sale. A week later I came back to the store in Jamaica, picked up my check, and on the way home, depressed and preoccupied, I sideswiped a cement wall with the car, inflicting some damage to a fender and losing some chrome. I had the car repaired and the bill came to exactly what my commission had been. The Pennsylvania Dutch have an expression, "Ve grow too soon oldt undt too late schmardt." How right they are! Once more, it was back to the drawing boards.

People would often say to me, "Wow! You certainly have the gift of gab. I'll bet you'd make a helluva salesman. You're a natural!" I decided, after several aborted experiences, that in order to succeed in sales one must have a certain amount of unscrupulousness. I sincerely believe that. One of my truly interested neighbors made a connection for me with a firm that sold new and reconditioned typewriters, adding machines, and assorted business equipment. I made "F.M." my partner for two very important reasons: He was good natured and likable company; and he also had a car, so we took turns with our automobiles. We sold a few items to retailers, but once again something occurred that shook my faith in humanity. A retired insurance salesman, the father of a couple of kids that I used to play ball with, had bought a grocery store in a poor area, and asked me if I could get him a cash register with a "non-add button." I had never heard of such a thing, but inquired from my supplier, and, sure enough, I fulfilled the man's request. I naturally was curious about the "non add" and was appalled when I found out that a famous company was actually manufacturing a cash register that you can add all kinds of monetary charges (that don't show up in the itemizing at all) but are added into the total. The thought of this thief, cheating poor, trusting, and oft-times ignorant people out of countless dollars with the aid of a machine that was made by a reputable company and supplied by me, was just too much to bear. Right then and there, I decided that I was going to remain in the business I knew best, where I didn't have to cheat anybody and (sink or swim) I was going to do my utmost to survive. Despite the many hardships that were to follow, I have never regretted that decision. I'm happy to boast that none of our four children are engaged in professions that require any sort of larceny or underhandedness, and for me, show biz provided the moral concept that I demanded.

14 The Village Club

Shirley was pregnant with our second child (she had miscarried in her third month between each of our boys), and to prove that we could make it on our own, and especially with things about to become a little more crowded, we moved out of Max and Rose's comfortable surroundings into the only thing we were able to afford, a small basement apartment in East Flatbush (a bit more upscale neighborhood around the corner from Shirley's high school alma mater, Samuel J. Tilden). Of course many a tear was shed by the loving grandparents, but like with everything else, they soon became accustomed to the change which actually provided them with more tranquility, and us with just a wee bit more self respect. Besides, the trip from Rochester Ave. to East Flatbush was a very short one which became a most-enjoyable Sunday expedition, usually for all four of them. Like all the basement apartments in the clusters of one-family homes that were rapidly proliferating, heating in cold weather was a constant problem. The landlords could never get it through their heads that heat rises, and, until a few years later, when, we again moved, to more suitable quarters, there was a never ending demand for more heat while the frustrated owner would point to his own (upstairs) thermostat, and exclaim, "Whaddya talkin' about? Look at what my thermostat reads! It's hot as hell up here!" It took awhile for both, the landlords and especially the unfortunate tenants, to realize that those apartments were, in realty, actually meant to be only basements.

Al Stewart, in the meantime, had teamed up with a lovely blonde soprano named Ruth Barbour, and they started to perform in better places that included a number of theaters and clubs in Toronto and Montreal, plus the popular little French bistro located on W. 46th St. in Manhattan called the Bal Tabarin. Al recommended me wherever they had played, and as apprehensive as I was, I was pleasantly surprised by my acceptance, and even subsequent return bookings.

The Barclay Hotel in Toronto was a real class place, and they welcomed me with open arms. The management treated this very new (virtually inexperienced in such elegant surroundings) young comedian, both courteously and generously, and they even added a song and dance spot for me in the show's finale. It was a lovely rendition of "Singing In The Rain," which I did with a flair. They even had hot towels and refreshments waiting for me when I got off the stage. This was truly "star treatment." To add to my delight, part of Shirley's family resides in Toronto, and her cousins insisted that I stay at their home, an offer I readily accepted. I still recall how old fashioned Toronto was in those years. Women did not smoke in public, and electricity was on "half-cycle," not nearly as luminous as the lighting in the states.

Shirley's cousin, Lou, whom everyone called "Luscious," was a big, handsome man with a moustache, wide shoulders, and a most-engaging personality. The whole family, including the elders and the children, was charming and friendly. "Luscious" ran a bookmaking operation out of his mother's tailor shop on Spadina Ave. No, he didn't manufacture books, he made book! He was a bookie ... a gambling man, and if anyone in Hollywood was looking for the perfect type to cast in just such a role, he would have been the ideal actor. He was very soft spoken, yet tough when he had to be, and had a quick, calculating mind.

We took a walk on busy Spadina Ave. one afternoon, and while we were crossing the street I was almost run down by a car carrying about five young men in their twenties. "Luscious" had the presence of mind and the reflexes to pull me out of their way onto the sidewalk as they applied their brakes with a loud screech, and jeered, "Next time watch where you're walkin' ya Jew bastard!" "Luscious" whispered to me in Yiddish, "Shtay du," which means "stay here," and walked right up to the driver, who had a cigarette dangling from his lips. In very even tones "Luscious" inquired, "Do I take you on one at a time, or all of you at once?" He then proceeded to lift his right leg, and with his size 12 shoe he bashed in the front door. "Take a good look at me," he said, "if I ever see any of you guys around here again I'll kill you!" The car roared away, and my respect for this mustachioed giant with the wide-brimmed hat, just soared.

I did so well at the Barclay that they wanted to hold me over for several more weeks, but by then I was filled with longing for home, and I offered a typical show biz excuse,

"Sorry, but I've got other bookings in the states to fulfill ... Perhaps another time." As I recall it was a terribly long train ride from Toronto to New York. And, as for "Luscious," I would see him from time to time at family gatherings in Brooklyn. Being in the profession that he was in, he had to be very careful about how to handle his investments, and the worst possible fate befell him. He had invested in several hotels with two dear and trusted friends. He had the major amount of cash invested, but for legal reasons his name could not appear on any of the agreements. He and his partners were quite young, and in the prime of life, yet both of his partners died suddenly and unexpectedly within months of each other, and their wives inherited the hotels, and "Luscious" was "aced out." He philosophically swallowed that bitter pill, and just went along making a living the only way he really knew how, ... right out of momma's tailor shop.

My next stop, thanks to Al who interceded with a nice little agent named Jack Lewis, on my behalf, was a one month booking at the Bal Tabarin. I had my good nights and my bad ones, but, miraculously, the management liked me. We had a lovely line of girls who did wonderful French production numbers in glorious costumes, and we also featured a singer who included sultry French ballads in her repertoire, plus a young, energetic tap dancer. The audience had its nightly regulars that included businessmen who were having affairs with some of our beautiful girl dancers, and transients from all over the world. The price was right, the food was good, and the drinks were not "watered,"... and the show was very entertaining. Like I said, I had my good nights and my bad ones, and I knew just which they were. I still recall an item in the famed reporter, Walter Winchell's daily column that read, "I saw a young comedian last night who was so bad that I'm gonna do him a favor by not mentioning his name." My intuition told me it was me, and to this very day, I believe it was, and am thankful that he did what he did.

One evening Johnny Horcle, one of the two brothers who owned the Bal, came into my dressing room and asked me to do him a favor. In his colorful French accent he said, "Van, there's a lady out there who saw your show and asked if you would do her the honor of dancing with her. She's had a few drinks and she claims that she's Dean Martin's first wife." I complied with Johnny's request. He introduced me to this rather nice looking, well dressed young lady, who, as he had forewarned me, had had quite a few drinks. As I danced with her she became teary and spilled out whatever was in her heart, telling me that this so-and-so deserted her and her five or six kids, in Steubenville, Ohio, and went on to become a star and carouse with beautiful women, etc., etc. She was pleasant enough, and I listened attentively as we danced, and she had the presence of mind to quit when the effects of her drinking were starting to take their toll. I graciously danced her back to her table, and went back to my dressing room with another story to tell Shirley when I got home. One of the great advantages of being in my beloved profession is that so many interesting things are constantly happening, and it makes for such fascinating conversations to share with a woman like mine.

One of the outstanding "side effects" of working at the Bal Tabarin was that "F.M" would occasionally drive me to work in his Model T Ford, right onto the sidewalk, up to the door, at night, with that 6 volt bulb hanging from the top, all lit up. I would wear a tan homburg, and equally tan wrap-around camel's hair coat, and our doorman, in his exquisite uniform, replete with fancy epaulets, would hold the door open for me as crowds would gather at the spectacle, and he would bow gracefully as he helped me down from the running board, and say, "Good evening Mr. Harris," as Miltie would sit there with a great big shit-eatin' grin on his face and a delirious look in his eyes. We certainly knew how to work the crowd.

Summer was still off in the distance. The thought of going back into some of those horrible little clubs was appalling. It really was not the little clubs that bothered me, as the audiences were generally wonderful (except the strip joints that attracted the drunks and degenerates), and the club owners were, for the most part, decent, hard working people. It was the reminder of what being on the road meant: the fleabag hotels, the lonely hours, the great distances, and time away from home ... all for what? For that moment of glory and adulation onstage? It just didn't seem like it was worth it. The longer engagements were like prison sentences. I kept a calendar in my suitcase, and marked off each dreary day. I remember standing on a bridge in downtown Baltimore after my last show of the evening, hoping to, perhaps, hitch-hike a ride back home and catch a train back in the afternoon in time to get to the club for my first show. There was a ray of hope with every approaching car, and it continued to fade with each one that passed me by. I kept thinking to myself, "If they only knew that the guy they're passing up is the well-dressed hotshot comedian that everyone adores at Club So-and-so?" ... Finally, around three o'clock in the morning, shivering in the night air, and deflated, I turned around and quietly went back to my hotel. Such was the lot of the small time performer ... this one anyway.

The great little agent Jack Lewis, did everything he could to hold on to his prize account, The Bal Tabarin. In fact he operated the spotlight there, free of charge, for every single show, on every single night, so that he could be in a position to ward off any of the parasitic theatrical agents that would drop in from time to time in an effort to steal the Bal away from him. It was while I was "on notice" at that Gallic bistro that I took a chance and asked Jack if he was able to get me another NYC location job after I left. He said, "Funny you should bring that up. There's a place in "The Village" (Greenwich Village) that's lookin' for a comic-emcee to start next weekend. It's a pretty rough job. They feature a couple of strippers along with the rest of the show, and they sometimes draw some rude outta town crap, y'know, the small town guys, away from home on business, and lookin' for ass. There are some damn nice "kids" (show biz for performers) in the show, and they all have to "mix" (drink with the patrons), but y'know ... it's part o' the job." I said, "Jack, I'm willin' to give it a try. How 'bout it?" The good natured little, soft-spoken agent smiled, and replied, "Ya look a little too clean cut for the job, but tell ya what, and by the way, it doesn't pay a helluva lot, I'll book you in for next weekend, and let's see how ya make out." I couldda kissed him right then and there.

The Village Club turned out to be a rather spacious, square room that could very easily have once been a garage. It was located on the street level on a rather well traveled avenue on the west side of NY's Greenwich Village. As you entered, you came into a small foyer with a hat checking room on the left that had a large, steel mesh window that moved up and down. The glass was opaque so that when the window was down you were unable to see what was happening on the other side of it. That window was down more times than up, and when it was down one would always hear some sort of commotion going on, with whispered conversations accompanied by giggling and lots of groping and fumbling. The lady in charge of that area was a dark haired beauty who looked and dressed like a gypsy, replete with large, metal, hanging earrings, and her plunging neckline gave one an instant desire to reach in and fondle those loaded torpedoes that appeared to pulsate the moment you set your eyes on them. Her winning smile accentuated her friendly demeanor and served as an ideal welcome into a den that promised lots of interesting fun in store once you stepped through the beaded curtains into the main event. Maizie, the hat check girl, was your introduction to this bustling den of iniquity, and an indication of things to come. If a male customer was willing to make an arrangement with this sultry lady, he could have stopped right then and there, and spend the rest of his stay behind that clouded window, interrupted only when he was forced to hide behind a screen whenever she would have to check in ensuing patrons. She was hot stuff, our Maizie, both lively and daring. Her bright eyes shone and her large white teeth gleamed, as she would part her sensuous lips and recite, "Good evening, it's a pleasure to see you here. You're entering into one of New York's liveliest bistros. Have a good time."

This converted garage featured simple chairs and tables with checkerboard tablecloths, and they were set up so that they framed the rectangular dance floor on which the shows were also presented twice a night. In a corner of the room, stood the bandstand, upon which was an upright piano. Five capable, middle aged Dixieland musicians who, besides playing dance music, accompanied the floor shows. The spotlights that shone on the bandstand were subdued in hues of mostly red and blue, and the smoke that billowed from the musicians' cigarettes gave it an evil aura. The entire back wall, adjacent to the bandstand, featured a very busy long and casual bar, with one short, grumpy bartender who had tatoo'd arms and who hated anything and everything that was progressive. The girls in the show, when not onstage performing, were constantly assembled at that bar, mingling with the customers, 'cause that was part of their job. On the other end of the bar, in the corner, stood a small upright piano that was highlighted by a strong, single pinspot, and that was where the "relief piano player" performed when the band took its break.

The laws of New York clearly state that a place that serves drinks must serve food, so there was a kitchen, but, there really wasn't a kitchen. It was a door that had the word "Kitchen" artfully painted above it, in attractive, colorful, flowing letters. A small, skinny Filipino named Jimmy, heightened by a huge white chef's hat, wearing a large white apron, and flashing the most ingratiating smile, highlighted by a number of gold teeth, stood imperiously in the doorway. Unbeknown to our customers, most of whom got drunk pretty quickly, that door marked "Kitchen" led out to the side alley of the building, and when our affably obsequious waiters would hand Jimmy an order slip and yell out the order at the same time, like, "Jimmy, one t-bone steak, rare," he would yell back, "One rare t-bone steak comin' up," and dash through the door, into the alley, cross the avenue to one of the cheap, fast food restaurants nearby, and, upon returning, would place the food upon the fancy porcelain plates that he had stored in a shed in that alley, and present the waiter with his quarry. Of course the law enforcement people were on to this hilarious scheme, but they happily looked aside thanks to those regular Friday night "paydays." Of course the shouts of "My compliments to the chef" would punctuate the smoky din throughout the evening.

This was the place that Jack Lewis placed me into for a weekend tryout, and where I was destined to perform, and learn my trade, for the next four years, even with allowances to take the summers off to go work in the resorts, thanks to the munificence of two of the most wonderful entrepreneurs I ever had the privilege of working for. It was strongly inferred that the club was actually the property of a combine headed up by a gentleman whose name was synonymous with Village nightclub ownership. We, the employees, never saw the fabled landlord. We answered directly to Les and Dave. Les was a former waiter, of medium height and stocky, who preferred to wear expensive looking sports jackets, had a winning, sincere smile, and was very liberal with his help, very likely because of his own hard working background. In fact it was Les who hired me. On my opening night, both shows, early and late, exasperated me. I had never been confronted with that many inattentive people in my life. I did all that I could to get their attention, and barely made a ripple. In observing the other performers, who were very adept at what they did, I soon realized that that's the way things were going to be. The audience came to drink, eat, and carouse, and the two-shows-a-night were incidental. The singer, the dancer, the strippers, and the comedian who introduced everyone, we were all just somethin' to look at, not necessarily to react to. We all did our best to maintain our respective dignity and self respect. By the time the second show came around my adrenaline was flowing, and I actually took on a few hecklers, with mixed success. When the evening was over Les walked up to me with that disarming smile of his, and I figured to myself, "Oh, oh, here it comes ... he's gonna tell me that I'm not quite right for the place." Instead, and much to my great surprise, he said, "Kid (he hadn't taken the trouble yet to learn my name, probably because so many come and go, so there's no use getting to know 'em) ... kid, ya handle yourself pretty good. Tell ya what I'm gonna advise ya, ... don't fight with the hecklers and I think you can work here a long time."

As things turned out, these words were most prophetic. The Village Club became my home, and his tall, thin, droll, and somewhat taciturn partner, Dave, whose scowl belied his gentle manner, also became my supporter, my confidante, and my good friend. It was a most difficult learning experience, but, as the shows multiplied I became ever more sanguine, although there were some terribly rough nights, I actually acquired the knack for holding an audience's attention, even an unruly one. I had a shabby dressing room upstairs, all to myself that was located directly above the checkroom. There I would sit n' strum the guitar I was still in the process of learning, which helped to overcome the sounds of wrestling, and heavy breathing that was coming from below.

The intrigues that went on were most educational and maturing. When I was downstairs at the bar I learned to keep my patience in tow while the bartender was constantly mouthing off about our government being in the hands of the communists, while the customers were doing their best to cop a feel of the girls in the show. The girls were all pretty and they had perfected the art of spitting back the liquor (that the customer paid for) into their water, or ginger ale chasers, while, at the same time, smiling pleasantly, they would be removing the guys' roaming hands from inside their dresses. They were big pros, these kids, and generally very good, fun, intelligent, knowledgeable, and trying so hard to appear relaxed. With very few exceptions I grew fond of all of them. It turned out that I became part of their family for four years, but at the end of each night I would take two subways and a bus, home to my loving wife and son in Brooklyn.

As the first summer rolled in I got up enough nerve to ask Les if I could have ten weeks off to take my family to the Catskills where I was guaranteed a good job as a Social Director. Much to my delight (somehow I wasn't too surprised) he said "Yes, why not? We're not all that busy in the summer anyway." ... Les got someone to replace me for all the summers while I worked those four years at the club. He even went so far as to let me work at the club right up until the day before I left, and arranged for me to resume working the day after our return from the mountains. What a guy!

His life was no bed of roses, as he was married to a Scandinavian beauty who towered over him, and who was very jealous. They had about four or five children, and she fantasized that he was cheating on her. Their arguments at home erupted violently, and throughout my tenure at the club, we all would shudder as Les would come into work with adhesive bandages on various parts of his anatomy, especially his face and head. Through it all he never lost his composure, but our hearts went out to "the boss" and yet he wasn't the type to look for sympathy.

One evening as I was standing at the bar, talking to Lorraine, our lovely chanteuse, and Jerri, our erstwhile tap dancing opening act, my pal Rafael, our most colorful and personable waiter, strolled over to me and said, in his own delightful Spanish-accented English, "Van, there is a South American gentleman sitting on my station who has just told me how much he enjoyed your performance, and he would like, very much, to speak with you. I will come along too just in case he has any trouble with the English." Rafael was an excellent waiter, who got special dispensation from Les and Dave. In his youth, he had fought for the Loyalists against Franco, and his younger brother was killed in that conflagration. Rafael was outspokenly political, and he was highly intelligent and artistic. He had a wonderful sense of humor and laughed readily, at times raucously. He also possessed a beautiful, flowing handwriting, which I discovered when we corresponded during the summers, and yet the checks he presented to the customers were all scribbled in practically illegible figures.

The majority of our customers were out of town tourists who knew very little about tipping. When Rafael first began working at the club he would cry when he would see the paltry gratuities that many of these unsophisticated bozos left for him. After a conference with Les and Dave, Rafael was given permission to scribble "Svce" at the bottom of the check, and put an additional 15% next to it as his tip. No one, and especially the inebriates, ever questioned the "Svce" especially as unintelligible as it appeared, and in the event somebody did, he would hastily thicken his accent and make the explanation even harder to understand. In that way, Rafael was assured of a decent living, and soon thereafter one or two of the other foreign waiters who were nervy enough to try it, did the same. It was a great demonstration of self preservation.

Rafael escorted me to a corner table near the rear of the club where a well dressed, intelligent looking gentleman who appeared to be in his late fifties or early sixties, sat alone with a bottle of expensive wine set before him. He addressed me in broken English and immediately Rafael put him at ease by changing the conversation to Spanish and performing as his interpreter. From the Spanish that I had studied in school, I was impressed to see that they were both employing a good deal of Castillian, which indicated to me that this visitor was a man of breeding and most likely important. They did all the talking, and I tried to fathom what they were saying, which required a good deal of patience on my part, but after awhile the conversation was concluded with a handshake and a "hasta la vista." After the man had left, Rafael explained to me that the gentleman was the former President of a South American country. (I don't exactly remember, but it may have been Uruguay or Paraguay.) The comedy sketch that I had just performed, called "Take It And Shove It," (though he had some difficulty in trying to understand a number of the nuances) had him in stitches. "Take It And Shove It" was a satire on a radio quiz show, and I portrayed an eager listener, sitting at a table and bantering with the voice coming over the airwaves, which was in the process of informing me that I had just won 64,000 silver dollars, plus Hawaii, Guam, and the Philippine Islands. It was truly laugh provoking and, at times, was capable of reaching profound hilarity. This gentleman recognized that if I could do that bit in Spanish, he would like to book me into a theater in his country. Strange things like this do happen in my profession, and Rafael, eager to represent me (and already envisioning a long run in South America, including money and glamour in a nation where he spoke the language like a gentleman) assured the man that it was a cinch. In parting Rafael told the stranger that he would use his scholarly expertise and rewrite the entire scene in Spanish so that I could soon memorize it, and they agreed to meet back at the club some weeks hence, when all was ready.

Once Rafael had explained everything to me, "con gusto" the sudden acceleration of events became somewhat dizzying. Though life went on as usual, and Rafael and I came into work nightly, I continued to query him, at home, on the telephone, at various hours, as to how his writing was coming along. He would always answer confidently, while injecting outrageous laughter, "Magnifico!" "I makee a few changes to makee eet more funny een Sponish ...Hoh boy, ... ees eet going to be great!"

After many weeks went by the long awaited moment arrived. Rafael arranged for the man to rendezvous with us at the club one night so that he could apprise him of our superb progress by reading him the script, and, hopefully, afterwards, start to set the machinery in motion. Though I didn't fully comprehend what exactly was shaping up, I must admit that, I too, had become mesmerized by my pal Rafael's enthusiasm.

The first show that night played quite well, despite the unruliness of the crowd, and the hysterical laughter of the gentleman from South America could be heard above all the others when I launched into "Take It And Shove It," with my adrenaline flowing because I knew that he was in the audience. Between shows, when things quieted down and Rafael and I both caught a moment, we sat with the former "Presidente" and Rafael proceeded to read his carefully prepared script to him. I watched, wide eyed, for his reaction, and suddenly my heart began skipping beats as I saw the man's face turn red, and glow redder and redder with each passing word that was coming out of Rafael's mouth. Finally, when he could tolerate it no longer, he grabbed the script out of Rafael's hand, flung it to the floor, and cried out, "Eef you do thees in my country ... I THROW YOU EEN JAIL!" ... and he maintained just enough composure to ask for his check, then stormed out of the club, stopping long enough to get his coat at the checkroom, while Maizie displayed some exceptional charm.

Rafael and I, still reeling from what had just occurred, sauntered back to my upstairs dressing room where I closed the door and asked him, "What happened? What did he get so upset about?" Rafael flashed a sheepish, semi-quizzical grin, "I no understand. I makee it more jazzy. I know Sponish people, and in South America they likee more dirty, so I makee more funny dirty. I no like 'Takee And Shovee.' Ees too quiet. I changee in Sponish so it say "Takee ... And Eeef You No Likee ... Shove Eet Up You Ass!"

There was the whole sordid story. It taught me another valuable lesson. When was I ever going to stop learning? Although I loved that devilish Spanish waiter Rafael like a brother, right then and there I made up my mind to personally be in control of everything I was going to do thereafter. It was a lesson well learned, and in retrospect, as embarrassing as it turned out, it was funny ... very, very funny. And, g'wan, I never couldda done that damn thing in Spanish anyway.

Friday night was "payoff night" at the club. Every Friday evening, between the first and second shows, the police captain from the local precinct would sit on the far end of the room with dour Dave, with a full bottle of libation set up in front of him, while a gregarious sergeant with the brown wavy hair and handsome Irish puss, would be doing likewise on another side of the room with Les. I never saw the actual passing of the green, but this ritual, which occurred every single Friday night for as long as I was there, was insurance against any and all unforeseen indiscretions that could materialize that might cause costly predicaments or might even involve the State Liquor Authority. As long as our friends on the force had things under control, there was no need to put other superfluous parasites on the payroll.

These two friendly cops were like old friends after awhile, and they too, became a part of our one big colorful family, complete with revolving strippers (the only acts that we would change every month or two). There was this very young, naive German stripper who was truly built, like the saying goes, "like a brick shithouse." Her name was Ursula, she was blonde and beautiful, and for whatever reasons she had attached herself to me. We enjoyed each other's company a great deal, but that was as far as it went. We were both married folk. She was married to a prizefighter who was constantly in training. He had brought her over from Germany, and because he was almost always in the process of staying in pugilistic shape, he was forced to overlook those burning desires of hers in order to be in fighting form. (This might be a myth that was later roundly shattered by the likes of Sugar Ray Robinson and a number of other "greats".) I remained her good friend and confidante, and convinced her that our piano player was a real nice guy, and he was nice enough to drive her home after work many a night, which, I assumed, made up for her athlete husband's lack of attention and gave her some desirable satisfaction.

Like I said, she was very naive and trusting, and was forever inquiring. One Friday night, out of the blue, she posed what she believed to be a serious question to me. In her quaint "Choiman" accent she asked me, "Von." (She insisted on calling me "Von," instead of "Van," though they both have the same meaning, "son of," and, at times I'd been accused of being just that ...) "Von, my luff, I vorrk here already sree monts, undt I don't know who iss boss. Who iss boss?" I was surprised by this sudden query, and then gave it some thought. We were such a free wheeling operation, thanks to the liberal demeanor of both Les and Dave, that rank and order of importance had no real bearing as long as you did your job. "Oh," I replied, and then, for some reason, I felt playful, "ya wanna know who the boss is? Ya see that little fat prick sitting there in the hound's tooth jacket and talking to the police sergeant? He's the boss!" I rarely, if ever, use profanity in public, and especially in front of ladies, but the "hipsters" Lorraine and Jerri, were standing nearby and overheard the conversation, so I thought I'd show off a little, and, sure enough, they had to muffle their giggles. "Prrick?" she repeated, "Vass iss his name, Prrick?" I said, "Yes, Prick!" and before I could say another word she was walking towards his table. She broke right into their conversation, looked directly into Lester's eyes, and asked, very innocently and honestly, "Are you da boss, Mr. Prrick?" For the moment Les was startled, as was the policeman. "Wha?" "What?" Les good-naturedly stammered, catching on quickly as he looked off in the distance and saw me and the girls standing there laughing. "Yes, who told you my name?" She pointed to me and replied, "Von. Von-Emcee" (She heard the others refer to me as the emcee, so she thought that was my last name.) "Von-Emcee told me you are da boss, Mr. Prrick." By now the handsome police sergeant was doing all he could to contain his laughter. Les hesitated for a moment and said to Ursula, "I'm not the big boss." He next pointed to his partner who was sitting across the room engrossed in what looked like a serious conversation with the captain, "He's the real boss, my partner, Mr. Ballser!" "Vass iss his name, Mr Ballser?" she asked. "Yes, that's his name, Mr. Ballser. Why don't you go over and say hello?"

She casually strolled over to where tall, lean, baggy-eyed Dave was sitting, and interrupted him with, "Excuse me, you are Mr. Ballser, da boss?" Now we three in the corner near the bar and Les and the sergeant at their table, were all in hysterics. Dave, being the sophisticate that he was, realized that she was being serious, and followed her question with, "Yes, I'm Mr. Ballser." (He went along with the joke, as did the captain, who was smiling from ear to ear.) "But who told you I was the boss?" She turned and pointed to a laughing Les, and blurted out, "Your partner, Mr. Prrick!"... and that guttural "rr" sent us all into convulsive laughter.

It was moments like this that helped make what was otherwise a fairly grueling job so much more palatable. The money wasn't great, but, thankfully, it was steady. And, there was enough interesting camaraderie to make up for some of the most difficult audiences one would ever encounter.

15 Boys of the Neighborhood

In early March Shirley had given birth to cherubic little Andrew, and now we were four. Danny had a brother, and soon he found out that he was no longer "king of the hill," and, believe me, it took a lot of adjusting on that little man's part, especially when non-thinking friends and relatives would come to see the new baby, and they momentarily forgot that, until that moment he had been the apple of everyone's eye.

We were still living in that basement apartment, battling over heat in the winter because such apartments apparently were not truly designed for habitation, and mildew in the warm months for exactly the same reason. But we were not alone. Lots of young families lived in just that fashion as that was all that we all could afford. In fact, when Andrew was born, we didn't have the money to get him and Shirley released from the hospital. Fortunately for all of us, our family and friends contributed enough in monetary gifts so that right after the "briss" (I tried to convince the mohel to make it painless by trying Crisco for shortening), I visited the hospital's cashier, and (with the gifts we got) paid the bill, and home we happily all went.

Another good feature about The Village Club was that, as long as there were some empty seats, my colorful friends from Pitkin Ave. were allowed to come in free of charge. It became habit forming. On many Friday nights I would be sitting, between shows in my dressing room, part of which faced the main avenue, and hear the familiar sound of Filthy Miltie's "arroogagah," which was the claxon horn on his trusty old Model T Ford. I'd run down the stairs to meet him, and always find him seated at the wheel with a different crop of characters all around him. Some nights it was those four that hung around him that he named The Bee, The Brow, The Bug, and The Bear (a quartet of nondescript guys) who clung to him whenever they could. Other times he would bring Sidney The Gook who was the spittin' image of Danny Kaye, only though he'd scribble Kaye's name whenever somebody would stop him and ask for an autograph, he was not an entertainer but instead worked on a cement truck. Or else there was Jake The Blade, or Looie The Burglar, or Joe London, or Hemo, or Henny The Glazier — all good, honest neighborhood young men who worked at virtually anything in order to make a living., They were all good guys with the possible exception of Looie, who was shady, and who soon after joined the Merchant Marines. One day, he disappeared at sea, never to be heard from again. And let's not forget Bob The Pirate, who was born with a withered arm, which was no handicap to this good looking young man who could wipe out any opponent in the game of handball, and who, with that one trusty arm, became a car wrecker by profession.

Another outstanding member of that illustrious group was the one called "Herbie The Nibbler," who was forever hungry and possessed an appetite of inhuman proportions. Whatever restaurant he would dine in, he would stop the show. He would outeat ten human beings and still crave more food. Chinese dinner for five was a lark for him. His voracious appetite led to a battery of tests at various medical institutions and nobody was able to come up with a reason for it. He had no tapeworm (Barney used to say, "He hasn't got a tapeworm. He's got a snake!"), and he was fairly slender, of medium height, and as he pointed out, "The way I've gotta eat, I can barely support myself." He always carried a bag of sunflower seeds or raisins, or both, just so he wouldn't pass out between meals He would tag along with anyone who would tolerate him, and Miltie was among the most tolerant of them all. Whoever Miltie would bring, they were all welcome at our nightclub thanks to the generosity of my liberal bosses, and the visitors would filter into the crowd quietly and respectfully.

One night I ran down at the sound of the claxon, and Miltie was sitting there with a grin on his face, with a few of the characters around him. But, sitting in the middle of it all, oblivious to the world, was the one guy in the neighborhood who stood out like a sore thumb. He always appeared to be in a constant state of a semi stupor, and had actually been in and out of mental institutions. He was really harmless. Bearded, haggard, and wan, he looked like Jesus Christ himself. He was nicknamed The Phantom, and he enjoyed whatever freedom he was able to recognize and appreciate, only because his poor, long suffering parents opted for caring for him at home as opposed to having him cruelly incarcerated somewhere. "F.M.," I exclaimed, "Aren't you pushin' things a bit?" Miltie, eyes staring up at his forehead and looking like a kid who had just surreptitiously stolen a piece of candy off the plate, replied, "D'ya think we can get him in?" I said, "Miltie, you're forgettin' that it's still a place of business and there are plenty of well dressed people in there that are payin' good money." Miltie persisted, "Whaddya say, ask Lester." I said, "This one you're gonna have to ask for yourself." I walked back into the club alone, got to where Lester was sitting with his Friday night companion, and informed him that Miltie was waiting outside in his Model T with some new characters. Les, who loved to walk out there (if for no other reason but to play with the horn) said, "Van, I'm a little busy now. You tell him they can come in." I insisted, "Les, there's one among them that you'll have to approve of. I won't have him come in until you clear it." Les tried to look a little disgusted, excused himself for the moment, and walked out into the foyer towards the front door, muttering under his breath, "You and your farkakte friends. I've seen them all. How much worse can this guy be?" I said, "Les, you'll have to tell me." As he walked out into the street, still carrying on, with his head down, he suddenly looked up, square into the eyes of The Phantom. He gasped and exclaimed, "Who the hell is he?" ... and Miltie placed his right hand over his heart, adopted a most angelic look on his face, and replied, "A little respect ... he's our savior."

Of course he was allowed in, along with the others, with an admonition from Lester, "Try to shuffle him in fast so that not too many people see him." As it turned out, it was the late show, and it was not heavily attended that night, and whoever was there was drunk, so it didn't much matter. To top things off Miltie asked me if I would introduce The Phantom, and, for the moment, I actually lost my head and brought him up on the floor, only I used his proper name, which very few of us, including me, actually knew. Amid the din, the smoke, the babble, and all, I said, "Ladies and gentlemen I would like you to meet a guest ... all the way from Brooklyn ... Harold!" The introduction was greeted by total indifference, and with the aid of a push from Miltie and the others, he stumbled out into the strong spotlight. Bewildered, he shielded his eyes, tried to peer around the room, and blurted out, "What a nutty place this is." ... How utterly prophetic.

Miltie and his Runyonesque recruits all hung out on a bustling and particularly well known corner in Brooklyn called Pitkin and Strauss (Strauss St. was once called Douglass). It was truly a wonderful corner, filled with a tremendous variety of young people, and mostly good ones. Author and historian Rich Cohen, in his revealing book about the Jewish underworld, points out that a lot of Brooklyn boys, commencing in the thirties and forties, had favorite corners the way people have favorite cities today. He goes on to say that, for more than a few kids, trouble was first encountered on the corner. Established gangsters recruited from corners, and it was from corners that young men went into gambling, extortion, and killing. "When you went to the corner you didn't have to go anywhere else. The world, sooner or later, came to you. Each group of kids had their own corner. If they went to a strange corner, they took their chances. Some corners were friendly, some not so friendly. In Brooklyn every cool kid had in his head a map of friendly corners stretching from here to home. On summer nights a group of pals might make their way clear across the borough, friendly corner to friendly corner, until they reached their home corner, where nothing could touch them."

My corner, Rochester and Sterling, and the adjacent, Rochester and Park, constituted the two sweetest corners in the whole wide world, (as is evidenced by the unbelievable success stories still being told about what became of the magnificent boys n' girls who emerged from there). Great kids, guided by devoted parents who may not have experienced the true feeling of loving each other. There were constant familial verbal battles among our elders but nothing ever became physical. Striking one's mate was verboten, a complete "no-no," a disgraceful act that was looked upon with scorn and derision. In my total recollection there was only one such set of parents in the neighborhood, and they were Joey's mother and father.

Joey was an only child whose mother supported the family via a freelance beauty salon operation, set up in her apartment. We never learned of his father's vocation, and for all we knew he barely worked at all, but we did know that he

FM with wife Natalie and son James

was not adverse to raising his hands to Joey's mother, and that was whispered about in many a household. Joey himself appeared well adjusted outwardly, but it was obvious to all of us, his good friends, that he was just dying to break out of his environment, and he was forever angling for something. He was interested in making money, and the quicker the better. He had a penchant for gambling and always carried a deck of cards, but how much could he possibly make from us, his friends? We were basically all poor kids, and pennies didn't add up to much. In the candy store he developed a way to beat the pinball machine by guiding the steel ball with a heavy magnet, but he never anticipated its strength, and only succeeded in drawing it through the glass and breaking the machine, which caused the storekeeper to declare his establishment "off-limits" for all of us for awhile.

His restlessness led him to other, more exciting corners, deeper into Brownsville, and he soon satisfied his urge for money by consorting with petty young thugs. We had all heard numerous tales about his underworld escapades, and, some years later, when he surprised me by showing up at The Village Club one night, looking so nervous that his eyes wouldn't stop darting in every direction while the slight facial tic that he had developed seemed to compete with them in counterpoint. He had been in prison, and I knew why, and whatever possessed him to visit me could have sent him right back. He was out on parole after having served more than half of what I had heard was a seven-and-a-half to ten year sentence, and being in a place that served intoxicating beverages could very easily have constituted a parole violation. I was shocked to see him, and asked him, "Joey, what are you doing here?" He replied, "I heard you were working here, and I desperately need a few laughs, so here I am." Well he got his few laughs that night, and enjoyed the bonus of watching our beautiful strippers take their clothes off, even more. At the end of the night he thanked me profusely for my hospitality (thanks, once more, to the generosity of Les and Dave, who waived his tab, which I offered to pick up), and, much more relaxed than when he had sauntered in, he hugged me hard, and disappeared into the night, and I never, ever saw him again.

His downfall had begun when, as a teenager, he fell in with that bad bunch on that nefarious corner. Before long, they took him along on heists and other such varied and dangerous capers, and soon he was wearing better clothes and flashing some pretty fat rolls of bills. He even visited me in the mountains several times, and while there, he asked me if I would give him the blackface makeup that I used in my occasional minstrel shows, a request that I had no trepidation about complying with. Subsequently, I found out that I had inadvertently been an accessory to his crimes, as he and his cohorts had been hijacking loaded trucks, at night, in blackface, and the victims had described the perpetrators as black males.

What sent him away however, was a wartime stunt that he had pulled in which the victim was actually to blame too, except that his role was overlooked by the authorities. Joey had called this "mark," a dress manufacturer, to inform him that he could supply him with a good amount of black market dress material, and they had arranged to meet in the lobby of the office building that his firm was located in. He was instructed to have $10,000 in cash on hand for the transaction, and he must have been desperate for the material because he actually did as he was told. Joe arrived on time, only instead of the cloth, he had a gun and he relieved the prospective buyer of the money. The story made the front pages of all the tabloids and Joe got away Scot free ... so he thought.

A couple of months after the crime was committed, Joey was a front seat passenger in a car that was headed east, to Brooklyn, on Canal St., on a balmy summer evening. There were about five young men in the car, all innocents, except for Joey. In what might aptly be described as a "one-in-a-million" circumstance, the driver stopped at a red light, and who should, coincidentally, pull abreast, on the passenger side, but the man he had robbed. I'm sure that Joey's face was indelibly inscribed in the victim's memory, for the moment he spotted him he rolled down his window, leaned hard on his horn, and gave chase on that crowded street, while screaming at the top of his lungs for the police, or anyone. Amid the turmoil that followed, the savvy driver made a hard right into Chinatown, where Joey, not wanting to implicate the others, leaped out of the car when it paused for a moment, and raced around frantically, looking for refuge. Fortunately for the others, the car got away, but the man's frantic cries for help attracted a number of policemen, and they scoured the area looking for Joey.

As Joey later related it to me when I met him coming out of the Utica Ave. subway station, he had dashed into one of the many old tenements in bustling Chinatown, raced all the way up to the fifth floor and knocked on a door with a believable story already formulating in his mind. When nobody answered, he managed to bash the door open with his broad shoulders, and seeing no one there, he quickly squeezed himself under a bed. A tenacious plainclothes detective with the instincts of a bloodhound, had wandered all the way up there, opened the door which Joey had had the presence of mind to close, but was then unable to lock, and peered around cautiously. Seeing no one around, he was about to leave, when he spotted Joey's shoe sticking out from under the bed. He reached down to where he surmised that Joey's head would be, and dragged him up by one ear. Joey pointed to where the ear had been stitched. The skin was still raw and the sight of it made me wince. When they booked him, they contacted the police precinct that Joey's "resume" was in, identified their captive, and inquired, "Whaddya know about this guy?" "Bad actor, with a long list of violations," they were told, "Don't go easy on that punk!" Joey removed his shirt and showed me where he was burned, numerous times, with lit cigars, during his interrogation. There were red welts all over his back, the size of quarters. It was out n' out police brutality. Who knows if Joey didn't say, or do something during his interrogation? What would warrant one's inflicting such physical violence upon someone who has not harmed you personally? I kept thinking to myself, "Poor Joey...look at what his misguided ambition has done to him. A long stretch in Sing Sing for a bright Jewish boy from such a cherished neighborhood. Some reward ..."

16 Dixie Lake

Summer was just around the corner and our thoughts turned to another season in the mountains that included our new baby and we were all eagerly looking forward to it. I got a telephone call, out of the blue, from an agent named Abe Lyons, who booked the staff at the famous, star-making Pocono Mountains resort, Tamiment. The producer and director of the popular original shows up there was the great Max Liebman, and such luminaries as Danny Kaye, Sid Caesar, Imogene Coco, Dick Shawn, Carl Reiner, Howard Morris, Mel Brooks, Woody Allen, Neil Simon, Carole Burnett, and a whole host of others, were all illustrious graduates of Liebman's Tamiment productions. Lyons, whom I had done a few minor jobs for in the past, asked me if I would be interested in joining the Tamiment staff for the forthcoming summer as a "fifth banana." "That's the bottom of the totem pole," I pointed out, "but who am I to be choosy?" I envisioned a fairly rapid climb up the ladder, along with some marvelous experience, in the company of ultra talented performers and a director that I could learn a lot from. "What does it pay?" I asked, enthusiastically. "Not very much," he replied, "but look at the opportunity I'm offering you." "What's not very much?" I continued cautiously. "Two hundred and fifty bucks for the whole season, with room and board thrown in, of course." I quickly calculated the loss of income in my mind. I got a thousand for the season at the places I had worked at, less ten percent to the booking agent. He was offering me a quarter of that, less his ten percent too, I would assume. "What a petty, bullshit business," I thought, "but who knows what could come from such a sacrifice?" "Of course, you know that my wife n' kids come along on my summer deals." "Sorry, no family ... it's just you alone!" Stunned, I said, "I'll have to discuss this with Shirley. I'll call you back." "You better do it fast," he said, as such offers are at a premium. I'll be waiting for your reply."

When I hung up I gingerly approached Shirley, telling her of the offer I had just gotten on the phone, and added, "But that's ridiculous. The money stinks, and I'm not gonna leave you and the kids alone in hot Brooklyn all summer. I'm gonna tell him to forget it." Shirley surprised the hell out of me by saying, "Listen, it could really hasten your career and open the door to bigger and better things. It may well be worth it. I'm willing to stay home with the kids if it will help us in the long run." I've loved this woman from the moment I first set eyes upon her, and this noble reaction made me adore her even more. I was moved to tears. But, the thought of leaving her and our darling little boys for the summer, was just too much to bear. I said, "Look, I'll follow this thing up further. Let me pursue it a little more, and once they're interested, maybe I can con them into throwing you all into the package since I'm willing to make such a financial sacrifice," and we left it at that for the moment with my mind racing around trying to figure out how I was going to approach this terribly tantalizing dilemma.

I got Abe on the phone the next day and said, "We've given it some thought, and if you are ready to go further, so am I." "Hold on," he surprised me, "we've gotta send someone to see you perform, to see if you're right for the place." "Twenty-five stinkin' bucks a week, with no family included, and I've gotta audition yet too?" I thought. My blood started to boil but I composed myself and continued on, "Okay, what's the next move?" "Where can our man catch you?" he asked. "Well, I'm appearing nightly at The Village Club, in the village, but it's basically a strip club and the audiences are generally not too sensational, and I can't guarantee that he'll catch a decent show. It may not be the right place for him to catch me, but that's all I can offer you." "Let's leave the decisions up to him," Abe replied. "He's an experienced man who is one of the producer's assistants, and he has a good imagination. He'll understand any adversity. He's quite capable of making the right choice. Where and when, can he see you?" I gave him the travel directions and hung up.

We agreed that the scout, one Monroe Hack, would come to see me on the late show (the worse of the two nightly) on the only night that was convenient for him, the coming Friday. On that given night, a stocky, ruddy-complexioned, middle-aged, bald gentleman, with horn rimmed glasses, smoking a pipe, and wearing what looked like an expensive Harris tweed sports jacket, casually, and confidently, strolled into the club. Maizie, with her uncanny sixth sense, didn't even try to come on to him. The crowd was, as luck would have it, sparse, and unruly, and, as I sat him down right in the middle, up front, my intuition told me that I was going to be in for a very bad time ... and I was. The drunks in the audience barely paid any attention to the other acts, including the usually eye-catching strippers, and when I went into my "piece-de-resistance," the sketch where I showed off my comic acting ability ("Take It And Shove It"), I tried so hard that, by the time I was through I was drenched from head to toe. The room was noisy, and I couldn't even tell where the laughs were coming from, if at all. Occasionally I would manage a quick glance at him to try to gauge reaction, but he just sat there, impassively, imperiously, and unsmiling, puffin' large amounts of smoke out of his pipe that quickly blended with the rest of the pollution that consumed the atmosphere. When the show ended I hurried to my dressing room to dry off and then bounded back down the stairs eager to find out what he thought. He, at least, had the decency to wait for me to get back to him, though he did express impatience when I approached him. "Well, Mr. Hack," I tried to apply some charm, "Whaddya think?" He then annihilated me with an answer that I shall remember for the rest of my life. He looked at me coldly, and said, very deliberately, "You oughtta get out of the business!" ... and out he went into the night.

I was a grown man. A husband, and a father of two little boys. I had earned the respect of my devoted family and so very many of my friends, and even my employers. My self confidence was shattered by those seven destructive words. I wandered up the stairs to my dressing room in a daze, and buried my head in my hands, and sat there for what seemed like an eternity, reliving the entire evening in my mind. "What did I do?" What else could I have done under the circumstances? What did I do to hurt him? Why in the world did he behave so cruelly? Why couldn't he have been more gentlemanly and let me down more easily?" He could have said, "I'll let you know," and then find some kind of an excuse like "I didn't realize that they had already hired somebody else." Instead, he just savaged me, callously and sadistically, and it took me a long, long time to get over it, though I never really did.

Again Barney's prophetic expression came into play, "Time is a great healer, but a lousy beautician." Many, many years later, when I was, perhaps at my zenith, having had some fairly important television stints under my belt, and enjoying a rather busy career in club dates (one nighters, mostly corporate), in addition to having scored nicely in a few major nightclubs, I was booked into that same Tamiment resort hotel, as the evening's headliner. Like with all the other resorts, they had changed their show policy. Max Liebman had been long gone, having gone on to a magnificent career in television, and the hotel was no longer presenting "book" shows, but, instead, strictly variety shows that featured a comedian. I was their "star" that particular evening, and, as I was sitting in my dressing room, waiting for the singer to get through with her musical rehearsal so that I could go on with mine, a somewhat stooped, stocky, ruddy complexioned, bald, older man, with horn rimmed glasses, and puffing on a pipe, gently approached me and introduced himself. He quietly said, "Hi, I'm Moe Hack. It's my job to see that these dressing rooms are kept clean and in order, and that the acts are comfortable. May I get you a drink, Mr. Harris? Or a cup of coffee, or a sandwich?"

I was startled. For the moment that entire incident at The Village Club flashed in front of my eyes, and I must have appeared as though I had lapsed into a catatonic state. Obviously he didn't even remember that moment that had gone crashing down on my head as it must have been so insignificant to him. I recovered my senses quickly enough and blurted out a quiet "No, thank you," and as the old man walked away he called out, "Well just holler if you need anything." I struggled to regain my composure. I was going to appear onstage in a little while. I had to be bright, and fresh, and charming. Yet, I could not get that now ancient incident out of my mind. How that scene had played in my imagination, over, and over, and over, throughout these many years. How I hated that man for what he had done to me, and now, so many years later here was my chance for retribution. Retribution? What retribution? Fate had already played a hand. What would I gain by bringing it all up, and attempting to crush him? I know some very successful people in my profession who would have delighted in vengefully tearing him from limb to limb, but they are who they are, and I am what I am. I sat there in a trance for a moment, then picked up my music books and walked onto the stage, "Hey guys ... ready to play my rehearsal?"

In retrospect, my not having gone to Tamiment that fateful summer was a blessing in disguise as we, eventually, wound up at a summer resort that can only be termed as "delicious." But, in the meanwhile, the shenanigans at The Village Club were getting wilder all the time. Our intermission pianist, a handsome, rugged, ex-marine left his job at the club, and he was replaced by a gay lady who looked, and spoke, and sang, like Tallulah Bankhead, and she belted out the dirtiest ditties I had ever heard, and her off-color jokes were hilarious. As crass as she was at the piano, she was a gentle soul offstage, and we were all delighted to be around her, both on and off the stage. Both her personalities could aptly be described as "intoxicating." Her name was Joy, and if ever a name was appropriate that was it. When this slender, middle aged beauty would doff her cigarette holder and assume a pose reminiscent of FDR at his finest, and then tinkle on the piano, and break in with a dirty limerick, she was positively evil, and everyone just loved it. An example of her "blue artistry":

> There once was a young man from Brighton
> Who thought that, at last, he found a tight one
> He said, "Oh my love ...it fits like a glove
> She said, "Oops! Yer not in the right one!

... and roar they all did. And her jokes: Two old maid sisters. One finally has sex with a man. The other is disappointed in her, and reprimands her and tells her she's ashamed of her. "That's disgusting!" The no longer virginal old maid sister says, "Sis, you don't know what you're missing, it was wonderful." "Hmph," says the other sister, "what's so wonderful about giving yourself to a man?" "You won't know until you've tried it," says the other sister. "The only way I can describe the feeling is that, when it happens it's like a flock of wild geese, flying." The other sister finally finds herself a guy, and against her better judgment, gets into bed with him. While they're going at it she keeps complaining, "What's so great about this? It's disgusting!" (and here Joy actually inserted lurid descriptions, complete with sound effects). And she continued complaining while they're wailing away, "Terrible!" "Ridiculous!" ... and she's breathing harder ... "I can't see what on earth my sister saw in this. Like a flock of wild geese flying ... What on earth did she mean by that? ... Whoops ...THERE THEY GO!"

By the time the first of July would roll around in those years, it was time for a breather though, and my family looked forward to it. I had no trepidation about taking that break, knowing full well that my job at the club would be waiting for me in the fall. This time we connected with the most considerate, and cooperative hotel owners I had ever met in my life, and thus began a rewarding relationship that was destined to go on for three exhilarating, productive, and most-enjoyable summers. It didn't start off great at Colton, Herring, and Chaddock's Dixie Lake Hotel, up in Ferndale, NY but as my sagacious old timers at Dubrow's were quick to point out, "A bad beginning oft times leads to a damn good ending ..."

Dixie Lake was a picturesque little resort hotel located in a remote corner of Ferndale, NY, not far from the back end of the famous giant, the world renowned Grossinger Hotel. Dixie Lake was owned by a lovely, intelligent (a rarity at a number of Catskill hotels in those years) and caring family. A beautiful lady named Lillian Herring reigned as head of the domain while her hard working husband produced all the heavenly baked goods that were ingeniously made right on the premises. Fay Chaddock, her sister, and her husband performed numerous chores that kept this thriving vacation spot going all summer long, and Sid and Sylvia Colton, Mrs. Herring's daughter and son-in-law were in charge of all front office affairs plus maintenance, at which Sidney was very adept. They were all very social, and sociable, and ran their lovely establishment with great affection and respect for their guests and also their staff, which they looked upon as family. The natural lake, constantly supplied with fresh fish by the State of New York, was a great source of pride, and attracted a good many fishermen and their families. We featured excellent home cooking, and good, all around social and athletic programs, and I was in charge of both those departments. Staff had all the privileges that the guests had, except for the same kind of housing, which was understandable, as decent guest accommodations meant income for the proprietors. As with all the other resort hotels, rooms were allocated for staff that wouldn't exactly be considered as prime for paying guests. Shirley and I, along with Dan and baby Andrew, were housed in our playhouse, directly behind the stage back wall. Amazingly, the boys slept beautifully despite all the loud music and commotion that went on there nightly. They adjusted extremely well into their new summer surroundings, and Dan, as young as he was, became an ardent boatsman in an instant. It became an attraction for the guests to come down to the lake and observe this blonde, curly-haired little freckle faced tyke rowing his proud dad all over the place. Those were heady times for all of us, and the confidence displayed by management made for a most euphoric existence, after a few complications.

Of course I worked very hard putting things in order and ran into a brick wall almost at the very beginning. Our orchestra, which had been there for one or two prior summers, had some important previous commitments back in New York, and we had to find replacements for them, and the leader's wife, who was the staff singer, just for the busy, July 4th weekend, which signaled the opening of the new season. We were fortunate enough to acquire suitable substitutes that included a pretty and talented young chanteuse named Betty Fain, who, at her young age, was able to boast of having already been on staff, a few years earlier, with the recently emerged comedy star Sid Caesar and had also done some important engagements with the famed orchestra leader Skitch Henderson. Of course she was only available to us for that weekend, and we were very fortunate for that. In fact, my gregarious, trumpet-playing old friend, Marty Chess, dropped by to visit us that weekend, and brought his pal, a humorous fellow named Lenny Falitz along. Lenny, observing our demure young thrush onstage, asked, "Could you introduce me to that lovely looking girl?" which I readily consented to, and thus began a romance that led to a better than 40 year marriage, and an everlasting friendship for all of us.

Upon the return of our regular staff and orchestra, I immediately launched into the frenzied job of concentrated rehearsals that included as many comedy sketches as I could put together, as we had to embark upon the unenviable, yet satisfying chore of presenting four different variety shows per week, for four continuous weeks, before we could safely start repeating material. We assumed that, except for those wealthier and more fortunate vacationers who could afford to stay for an entire summer, no one really stayed for more than an average of two weeks, or three, or at the very most, four. That meant a total of sixteen different shows, not all as strong as we would have liked them to be, but with a little bit of improvisation, and lots of theatrical legerdemain, aided by lots n' lots of personality, we managed to put it over.

The problem arose when our regular singer (the bandleader's wife) balked at having to do so much acting. I pointed out to her that Shirley was taking the brunt of it all, and that acting in these scenes was part of her job. Apparently she was not required to do as much with prior Social Directors, and she defended her uncooperative stance by pointing out, "I was hired to sing." As the days went on, it became more and more laborious to get the haughty lady to conform, and when I insisted that, for the sake of the total success of our shows she must act too, she really upset me when she blurted out, "So don't pay me!" Of course her husband was in full agreement with her, and it got to the point where they handed me an ultimatum, "Either we do it our way, or we quit!"

After a heated conference with the affable Mr. Colton, in which I was both surprised and extremely pleased, to learn that he would go along with his Social Director, upon whose young shoulders rested the entire season's programs, we accepted their resignation, which didn't give us a whole lot of time to adjust, as they wanted to clear out as quickly as possible in order to search for another job immediately. This was not an uncommon occurrence during those summer seasons as there were always changes being made everywhere, but this was the first time that this ever happened to me, and my apprehension, though difficult to contend with, managed to raise my adrenaline level to the point where I even surprised myself with my ability to endure. Word was sent to our theatrical agency that we needed a new band and a singer, and we were blessed with an enthusiastic young band, and a beautiful, and slender young lady singer from somewhere in the state of Georgia, gifted with an inordinate amount of talent, and the most delightful southern accent to boot. She was an elegant lady whose name was Sally, and besides having a rather full, and lovely repertoire, she was crafty enough to arrange duets for herself and Dick, our tall, handsome tenor, and we all felt blessed by the fortunate turn of events. Of course, the original band, shocked by management's hazy acceptance of their threat to resign, didn't leave without a fight, and lodged a complaint with the union. Luckily for us, however, that "nouveau riche" group of country bumpkins up there was more adept at collecting dues than solving disputes, and all the potential grief soon dissipated.

Our splendid summer season gave birth to two ensuing ones down the pike, and after our third season, as friendly as we became with the family, and especially the younger, lovable Coltons, we mutually agreed to part, for the sake of giving the repeat guests fresh faces to look at. We went on to Zalkin's Birchwood Lodge (another marvelous family of owners) for one season, while Dixie Lake got itself an entirely new staff. Of course, each season we would change our singers and musicians in order that they all could, hopefully, attempt greater pursuits. It was a great game we all played, as the challenge of starting summer seasons anew, with new people to indoctrinate and to perform with, was exhilarating to say the least. After one memorable season at Zalkin's (where our third son David was conceived), I fatuously flexed my muscles, and told the most-accommodating Zalkin family that they needed a bigger, and better baseball field, and that I had decided to go back to Dixie Lake again on the following summer. Of course we remained great friends with all those wonderful people I had worked for. Unfortunately for all, shortly before that fourth season at Dixie Lake was to begin, that pretty little hotel, located in that picturesque, bucolic corner of Ferndale, burned to the ground, leaving behind a few small buildings, and, of course, that inviting lake, and it all became a NY State recreational park, free to the public, and especially great for those who enjoy good fishing.

Meanwhile that first season at Dixie Lake engendered an interesting friendship that was destined to endure for quite a long time. The young, enthusiastic, four-piece band that was

227

sent to us, as a replacement, turned out to be a most welcome addition to our staff. Though they were still quite inexperienced they were all proficient players, and, best of all, so eager to learn, ... and learn they did. They spent long hours in our playhouse rehearsing the singers and myself, and spent hours putting together appealing overtures and also individual musical performances in our shows. They also participated in our comedy sketches, and quite adeptly. The leader, a handsome pianist with a winning smile and a shock of brown wavy hair, did all that he could to endear himself to us. Morty was his name, and the other boys were very dedicated to him, and we all breezed through the season with very little difficulty. Though I was just a few years older than he, I became his father figure, and our relationship carried even into the off-season. Coincidentally, he lived several blocks away from us in the Flatbush section of Brooklyn with his mother, father, maternal grandmother, and a very friendly black standard poodle. Morty was an only child and the apple of everyone's eye. They fawned all over him and his precociousness. His ability to play the piano was a great source of pride to all. When he introduced his "summer boss" and his wife to them, we were immediately accepted with great affection, and quite soon thereafter we were regular visitors to their home. His mother taught school, and his father worked in a large grocery store, and precious little grandma enjoyed the pleasant task of looking after him most of the time. Of course there were occasional crises, such as his threat to not go on to law school when he had finished college, and at times like that the family would summon us to intercede, as he valued our opinions highly. I convinced him that, as taken as he was by show biz, and as much as he could pursue a career in same, it would be most beneficial if he would acquire a law degree and have that highly respected profession as a backup just in case he did not realize those dreams that were obviously already forming in his mind. It was after numerous heated discussions that he acceded to my sage advice, and though he never went on to practice law, his family, proud as it was of his ability to entertain, felt a lot more secure once he received that precious educational document. In the ensuing summers he and his dedicated little band, worked at assorted resort hotels, greatly improving with each passing season, and on those mid-summer "benefit nights" where they sold tickets with all receipts going to them as a reward, I was recruited, from wherever I was appearing, to be their "piece de resistance," their star.

Peacetime conscription was still in effect at the time, and much to his surprise, Morty received his "greetings" from Uncle Sam and was drafted into the army. He served for a couple of years, and from his letters and reports I received from his family, he used his musical prowess to great advantage. When he was eventually sent to Japan, he put together a seven piece entertaining orchestra that was the talk of his division, earning extra money playing parties at officers clubs, and even private affairs. He was able to convince the Seagram Beverage Company to sponsor him, and soon "Morty And His Seven Crowns" became one of the most popular American G.I. groups in Japan. Throughout it all he kept corresponding with me, telling me that he was using a lot of my comedy material to great advantage, and thanking me over and over again for all that I had taught him. Though our own adorable progeny was giving me n' Shirley so much pleasure and growing up rapidly, we felt as though we had a grown son overseas who was doing so much for us to be proud of too, and we conferred constantly with his parents and grandmother, who were also overjoyed by his accomplishments.

At the time he was discharged from the army, my own career was at a stage where it was shifting into a higher and more profitable gear. I was one of the most sought-after club date (one-nighters) comedians in the business, the niche that, of all phases of the comedy profession, was most satisfying to me, and most suitable to our lifestyle. (I traveled extensively, but was never away for long.) I received a call one Saturday afternoon as I was preparing to do two separate engagements that evening at two of New York's leading hotel's main ballrooms. It was Morty on the phone, and instead of sounding jubilant, there appeared to be a sense of great sadness and urgency. "I'm home," he said, "and I must see you right away." "Home on furlough?" I asked. "No, home ... home! I've been discharged! I served my time and I'm back, ... and please, I've gotta speak to you, it's very important." "I've got two shows to do tonight, and the scheduling is very tight.

D'ya wanna tag along? Wanna hang out?" "I'd love to ... can you pick me up?" "Sure thing ... see ya around 6:30!"

Instead of an ebullient young veteran who had made the most out of what generally is considered a miserable penance, I found a pale, nervous, thin, sad-faced individual waiting at the door. We hugged each other and got into my convertible Cadillac. (All my life I dreamt of owning a convertible Cadillac and going back to the old neighborhood, Rochester Ave., to show everyone how well I had done, but by the time I was able to afford one, there was nobody left there.) We headed for the always exciting island of Manhattan.

"Morty," I said, inquiringly, "What's wrong? I hope you don't mind my telling you, you look awful. Is everything okay? Are you okay?" For the rest of the night, before the shows, after the shows, and in-between, often with real tears welling up in his eyes, he related his tale of woe: While serving in Japan he had fallen deeply in love with a Japanese girl, and had married her in a Shinto wedding that was acceptable by the Japanese, but not sanctioned by the United States Government. He described his adorable and adoring wife, as the greatest thing that could ever happen to any man. "I was crazy about her," he continued. "I cannot put in words what a love affair it was. She was everything that any human being could ever ask for. We were both so in love. How blessed I was to have her for a wife ... my darling wife." "So what happened?" I continued. "I thought that my parents would be thrilled for me and give us their blessings, but when my father found out that she was Japanese he told me that that was unacceptable, and prevailed upon my commanding officer to put an end to our marriage, and every time my papers came up for my return home, they refused to recognize that she was my wife, and I could not get discharged with her as my mate. Meanwhile my father threatened to kill himself if I brought her home, and to tell you the truth, I often thought of killing myself rather than to leave without her." "So what did you do?" "I had to leave her there and return home, an empty shell. I give my father the respect that I am supposed to, and he's much relieved, but I am a dead man, Van. I cannot go back. I don't know what to do. Each passing moment is torture. What should I do? Not to mention my darling's feelings back in Japan, ... I feel like my life is over ..."

My heart was breaking for him. Funny how you can separate your emotions when you go onstage to perform. What marvelous therapy to get in front of an audience and forget everything around you except what you are involved in onstage, and that's to entertain the waiting audience. "Life must go on," I told him. "You've gotta get back to work immediately, and build a career. You've got so much to offer. Go to it Morty!"... And then I, once again, had the occasion to invoke Barney's great and prophetic line, "Time is a great healer ... but a lousy beautician!"

Morty tore into the business with a vengeance. He corralled his ex-bandmates and formed a musical comedy group. I even helped them to get an agent, and they helped themselves greatly by employing a writer-director. I wasn't too crazy about the act he wrote for them, but it did have a polished, professional touch, and they became good enough to work in the then busy lounges in Las Vegas. They called themselves "The Four Frantics," and they actually started making money though it meant being away on the road for long periods of time. He stayed in touch with us, and lo and behold, he called us one day and announced, "Guess what? I'm getting married!" He had met the girl of his dreams in Las Vegas, a beautiful young blonde "shiksa" (non-Jewish female) who was converting to Judaism in order to please his father, and the wedding was going to take place at the famous Brooklyn nightclub, The Elegante, that was owned by Don Rickles' affable and colorful manager, Joe Scandori.

Morty's family invited us to their home to meet the prospective bride at a pre-nuptial celebration, and everyone was in a grand mood with the food and drinks being served up almost as though it was the actual wedding itself. There was a lot of hugging and kissing, and then Morty announced, "Guess who's gonna be my best man?" I looked at Shirley. She looked at me. And then came the surprising answer. "I've asked Johnny Ray to be my best man, and he's accepted." Johnny Ray? The singer who just had a couple of hit records? Hey, that's quite a star ... for the moment, anyway. To say I was disappointed would not be entirely truthful. I was never much for parties, or even being in the limelight. The only time I really enjoy being the center of attraction is onstage. Morty's unexpected announcement shouldn't really have been taken as such. Our boy was really hooked. He was now in show biz all the way. He was now rubbing shoulders with the stars. That obnoxious caste system that prevails in our ambitious profession had reared its head. We enjoyed the wedding as much as everyone else did. A good time was had by all. We wished the bride and groom all the best, and now it remained to be seen what would happen next.

Morty would check in with me whenever he'd come back into town and soon he was telling us how jealous his wife was. In fact, she was doing something that is not acceptable in the trade. She sat in the front row at each and every one of his shows, and became consumed with rage if and when, a female patron would converse with him. As he later described it to me, one night, during a run in Montreal, she flew into such a tizzy that she overdosed on sleeping pills and the hotel's doctor had to be bribed handsomely not to report the incident as an attempted suicide. That proved to be the straw that broke the camel's back, and very soon thereafter they were divorced.

As time went by the "Frantics" broke up. Two of the boys had fallen in love with ladies who wouldn't tolerate the road, married them, and settled into other, more acceptable lines of work. The third partner, thanks to having an uncle in the motion picture business, moved to Hollywood where he became a force in the rapidly expanding field of TV commercials. Morty tried his hand at being a single, and much to my surprise, was the #2 act on a five act bill that I headed on a club date in Elizabeth, NJ. He had become my competitor, and, I was certain, with his ambition, angling for a way that he would get top billing on some future dates. I couldn't fault him for trying. After all, that was the name of the game. We did become lively competitors, but never on the same bill again. He took on a male partner, and they headlined shows at the resorts on different occasions, as I did at other times. He married again, and this time his father felt as though he had died and gone to heaven, which may have been a portent of things to come, as, not much later the poor man actually passed away. What had made him so ecstatic before his demise was that Morty married a dyed in the wool, true blue Jewish-American girl. Eventually they became the parents of two sons, and Morty's mother and grandmother reveled in their newly found status as grandmother and great grandmother respectively.

Morty, still consumed with ambition, hit the road a great deal. I'd run into Morty from time to time, and we would greet each other with respectful, but usually curt salutations. I offered my sincerest condolences when he told me his beloved and caring grandma had passed away. She was such a lovely, devoted lady. And so it went, two formerly good friends would meet like ships passing in the night. A quick hello, some small talk, and a hasty goodbye.

Fate decreed that he and his partner would accept the positions of Social Directors at a nearby Catskill resort hotel when Shirley was somewhere in the middle of her years as full fledged Social Director at Lebowitz's Pine View. Both Morty and his partner, and I, had a unique arrangement with our respective hotel owners. We were free to go to the other hotels to work the circuit, only I had Shirley to cover the whole gamut for me while I was out entertaining at the other hotels, and I must say, she did it magnificently. I don't know what Morty's system was, but whatever it was that they were doing, it must have worked. I was startled when I ran into Morty. He was pale, and wan, his clothes hung on him. He actually looked quite seriously ill. He told me that he had cancer and was going into the city to get cobalt treatments twice a week, and true to our profession, it didn't bother him while he was performing. Some time before the summer ended Morty passed away. He was, perhaps, in his early forties, had lived a short, oft-times frenetic, but always interesting life. We didn't attend his funeral as we learned of his death some time afterward, ... but I'm sure that many nice things were said about him. They generally are at such times.

A short addendum here concerning my staff at Dixie Lake on that first, memorable summer. I never saw that elegant singer Sally again after that season. I never forgot her name because she had left such an indelible impression upon all of us. I did learn, however, that she had gone back down south to her home, and she did marry. Quite a few years later, when I was appearing at the #1 nightclub in all of New York, The Royal Box of the Hotel Americana, a couple of Air Force pilots wandered in and watched the show. It was just around the time that the war in Vietnam had ended, and those two were distinguished veterans of that horrible and senseless conflagration. They were both cheerful, hearty souls, laughed uproariously at my jokes, and afterward asked the Maitre D' to see if I would come over to their table and join them. I was delighted to sit with them and even more so when one of the fly-boys, Jim, with just a trace of an engaging southern accent, introduced himself as Sally's husband. He told me that she had always spoken very flatteringly about me, and that she had never forgotten that euphoric summer at the Dixie Lake. In fact she knew that, in his travels, he did get to NY, and she instructed him to come over and introduce himself should he ever see me appearing anywhere. I thanked him for the regards, sending my very best to her in return, and after awhile we parted. Roughly about a year later Shirley and I were knocked off our feet when we read in the front section of our NY newspaper, with graphic photos included, about how Sally, for whatever insane reasons had possessed her, had shot her husband and two young sons to death. I don't know what happened to her after that. It was so long ago. Life's peculiar turns never cease to amaze me.

17 Evolving Into Club Dates

Back once again, after another exciting summer in the mountains, I was greeted by Les and Dave at the club with open arms, and things continued along as though I'd never been away. One fateful evening in late fall, Lester approached me casually and said, "Van, we've gotta talk." I could sense from his air of apprehension that it was going to be serious, and, truthfully, I knew that the time had finally arrived for just that long awaited moment. "Kid," he said, in his amiable manner, with his head cocked over on the side, ever so slightly, "ya know just how much we all love ya here, but in this crazy business of ours, things can't go on the same way forever. I think it's time for us to make a change, ... to look for someone fresh and new to replace you." I wasn't even upset. I had been fortunate enough to have gotten away with a helluva lot more than I had ever anticipated when I had tried out on that first, fateful weekend so long ago. "Les," I replied, "how much of a notice d'ya wanna give me?" Without even giving it a second thought he came right back with, "How's two months? Will that give you enough time to get your things in order, and find another job?" "Great," I said, as I threw my arms around him and hugged him. "Les, I doubt that I'll ever find many more like you n' Dave as I go through life. How lucky I've been to have worked for you."

The months went by quickly enough. In fact, towards the end it seemed as though they were flying by, and too quickly. Jack Lewis, the pleasant, soft-spoken little agent, who had been collecting his ten percent weekly for over four years, and suddenly looking old and sickly as a result of recent prostate surgery, assured me that he would be looking around for other work for me although there weren't very many choices to be had, anywhere. Nevertheless, as turbid as my immediate future appeared, having been out of circulation, thanks to a steady job, for such a lengthy time, I felt somewhat secure knowing that Jack was sincerely searching.

What he finally came up with, without missing a beat when my grand tour in the village had ended, constituted what might very well have been one of the darkest months of my life. 52nd St., in NYC, had, at one time been the jazz capitol of the world, almost like New Orleans, with one music club after another. A peculiar metamorphosis had unexpectedly occurred however, and every great jazz club was turned into a degenerate strip club, inhabited by well dressed bums from all walks of life, who came to drink, stand as much as three deep around the bar, and ogle the steady procession of strippers who pranced, practically naked, before their eyes. They displayed their wares on the platforms that were erected above, and slightly back from the busy long rails that the inebriates held on to. Each one of these clubs needed a comedian-emcee to introduce the girls and tell some jokes along the way. Of course nobody listened, and those moments onstage were hell for that person, and it was my misfortune to have been booked as one of those scapegoats. I thought to myself, "Oh God, how did I ever come to this? And, how much longer can I keep this up?" The shows also included a rather dissipated looking singer who had once been a beautiful girl, and who, despite her time worn vocal impediments, presented herself very professionally and energetically, and had an uncanny phrasing ability. She became my friend and confidante, and I really enjoyed her company, and the company of the strippers, when we were taking breathers in the dressing room before and after our continuous performances. My outlook became so bleak that I actually felt that it was the end of my rope. I was bewildered as to what to do to extricate myself from this miserable existence. I couldn't recall ever having been so unhappy.

My good, well-meaning friends, who still envied the "glamorous profession" that I was involved in, tried to bolster my confidence by patronizing the club whenever possible, and I was embarrassed when they came in and saw what was going on. My devoted Shirley suffered along with me, but what on earth could she do other than sympathize with my plight. The bills had to be paid, and I was trapped. Then one evening early in the week, the boss, appropriately named "Rocky," came over to me and announced, unceremoniously, "Kid, you're through on Thursday night. I won't be needin' ya anymore." I was stunned by this sudden and unexpected proclamation (though secretly I felt a sigh of relief). I exclaimed, "Thursday? Rock, you're not giving me enough time to visit the agents and look around for another job," to which he immediately snapped back, "Look at yer contract. It says "two day notice," I'm not runnin' a charity here!" I protested, "But Rock, gimme at least till Saturday night. You're taking the bread outta my children's mouths." That statement unearthed whatever kindness he may have possessed, and his mood quickly turned to benevolence, and he blurted out, "I don't take no food from no kids. Ya can stay till Saturday night! Ya can stay as long as you like 'cause Rocky ain't that hard that he takes food outta kids' mouths." My anguish was overcome by a smile of relief and I said, "Saturday night would be enough, n' thank you Rocky. I really appreciate it." ... and he walked away.

As luck would have it, on Saturday night, while all the usual bedlam was going on at the show bar, a good sized group of nicely dressed ladies and gentlemen wandered into the club and demanded to know if they could be provided with food and drink, and a show, away from the noisy bar. Rocky, rather flustered, led them to a spacious back, seldom used, banquet room. He alerted the chef to whip up whatever he had that was good, tidied up a few waiters, and instructed the band to set up in that room as quickly as possible to play civilized dance music and accompany a show. He then knocked me off my feet by inquiring, "Kid, can you tell some jokes?" Here I had been busting my chops for a month trying to get the attention of those bums at the show bar, and he, the boss, wasn't even aware of who, or what, I was. What a crappy business! What a stupid, nonsensical profession this really was ... and the whole world thinks it's glamorous? What a big bunch of unmitigated crap!

The group was the entire staff of Ridgewood Electrolux. All the employees were out on the town, courtesy of management who was enjoying with them. Of all the places to wander into. It was like God had sent them to me to save my life. I rolled up my sleeves, got the girls together, told Dottie, the singer, that she was gonna be a star like she once was, and prevailed upon a few of the select strippers to give it all they've got, only classy, more ladylike. "Pretend you're at the Follies Bergere, and not teasing those bums at the bar and mesmerize them, really and truly get them to eat out of your hands." A quick, talkover rehearsal with our experienced band who now also had a chance to prove their worth, and we were on our way.

Probably for the only time ever, this club was going to appear like a real nightclub, ... and what a glorious job we all did in order to make it so.

Rocky stood in the background rapt with attention, hypnotized by what he was witnessing, and when the audience laughed and applauded, he laughed and applauded along with them. When the evening was over he graciously bowed and accepted the party's plaudits. He grew in stature as they each filed out and thanked him for everything along the way. At the end of that surprising evening, as I said goodbye to all my temporary good friends, Dotty, the singer, wistfully thanked me for having created one of the very best days of her present being, and Rocky paid me in cash. He actually put his arms around me and said, "Thanks kid! If you ever have the good fortune to really become somebody important in this business, and you work at any of the big clubs, call Rocky. I'll come down with the biggest party you've ever seen, just to show them all what a following you've got." Many years later I appeared at the famed Copacabana, and also the even classier Royal Box of the Hotel Americana, and if Rocky happened to be in the audience, I'm absolutely certain he wouldn't have remembered the obscure young comic who had the nerve to have upbraided him by telling him that he was taking the bread out of his children's mouths.

And so it was back to the drawing boards once again, only this time I had been out of circulation for four years. That meant four whole years of not having to make the rounds while a number of my peers were still hanging around at Hanson's Drugstore, still complaining about those who were steadfastly climbing up the ladder when they should be enjoying that success. It's a disease that exists in all walks of life, only I'd never seen it to the extent that it seems to prevail in the arts ... and especially the performing arts. And there I was, wondering if any of the agents would remember me, and also, how many of them would still be around. All I knew was that I had a wife and babies, who depended upon me for sustenance, and as intangible as my chosen field of endeavor was, it was my sworn duty to make a living via that route, and, hopefully, a damn decent one. To further inspire me, Shirley's Aunt Dorothy, and her husband, Uncle Herman, had discovered a lovely new housing development called Harbor Isle. (Some of the local anti-semites soon dubbed it "Hebrew Isle," despite the fact that, although a number of the new residents there were Jewish, it had a very fair distribution of residents of assorted ethnicity.) They purchased a lovely corner plot, on which to build a new, split level home, on our behalf, by plunking down a deposit of all of fifteen (yes, that's what I said, "fifteen") dollars. Harbor Isle was part of the town of Island Park, which is a lovely seaside community on the south shore of Long Island, and a great place for young families to raise kids. Dorothy and Herman were childless, tragically having lost two babies in their infancy, and from her early childhood on, Shirley was treated as though she was their own daughter. I used to kid them all by maintaining that Shirley was Dorothy's illegitimate daughter, and that in order to overcome her shame, she allowed her older sister, Rosie, to raise her as her own. This became a running gag throughout the years, and judging from the kindnesses that those two heaped upon my Shirley, this fable of mine could very well have been accepted as having been true.

Now, along came my chance to fulfill every poor, apartment dwelling Brooklyn girl's lifelong dream of owning her own home, and, by God, I wasn't gonna blow it. And, as our lives seemed to be shifting into a newer, and more hopeful phase, my luck suddenly took on a new look along with it. In making my rounds, seeking employment, I came across a breed of agents that I had never been able to do business with before. They were called "club date bookers" and they were busy little bees who packaged, and sent variety shows to the various organizations that were thriving all over, and especially in all five boroughs of New York. That covered the multitude of fraternal groups like the Knights of Pythias, Nights of Columbus, Odd Fellows, the assorted Masonic lodges, Elks, Moose, etc., in addition to unions, and corporate functions. There was a multitude of such groups, and they met on virtually every single night of the week. They kept the entertainers and musicians in business for a long, long time, and the various hotel ballrooms in New York City were constantly in use, not to mention the various meeting halls, school auditoriums, and catering establishments that were an integral part of the big, all around picture. And let's not forget the plethora of religious institutions (especially the synagogues), and, of course those sumptuous country clubs located all over the United States and Canada. Some huge affairs were also held in theaters. There was one old large theater in downtown Reading, PA that specialized in just such affairs, presenting some large variety shows several times a year on behalf of the Masonic Order, and I was destined to become one of their fortunate regulars.

It was a lively, and lucrative new world that I had discovered, and, luckily, it discovered me. There was one bright young agent in the theatrical district, who, like a number of his peers, not only booked club dates, but was also one of the pioneers that convinced the Catskill hotels to abandon the up-till-then practice of social staffs with their sketches and their other assorted variety displays, in favor of travelling variety shows consisting of a comedian, a singer, dancer, ventriloquist, acrobat, instrumentalist, etc., etc., etc. Such packages (and the hotel owner was free to determine the size, in addition to what he was willing to spend) could circulate, virtually nightly, from hotel to hotel, and provide the people with new, fresh entertainment every single night if desired. This system changed the face of entertainment up there, and not only did it prove to be most satisfying to the hotel guests, it created an abundance of employment for all the acts.

Like a travelling salesman, I would make my daily rounds with these enterprising booking agents and would smile politely (in spite of my anguish) and say, "Thank you," as they would dismiss me with a curt, "Got nothin' for ya today kid. Try me another time." Most of them did not have secretaries so it was easier to just fall in on them without having to manage your way past a self styled guard dog. I did just as they offhandedly advised, and kept coming around again and again, but with no success, until that lucky day that I happened to fall into Jack Finck's rather busy little office and he was stuck for an act. "Ya workin' this coming Saturday night?" the nattily dressed, slightly built, very glib young agent asked. I hastily lied, "It just so happens that I just got a cancellation." "Good," he said, "I need a comedian for a Pythian lodge in the main ballroom of a good hotel here in center city," and at that point I could actually sense the wheels turning in his scheming mind, "It doesn't pay much but it's a good chance for you to show me how good you are." Then he turned to the equally well-dressed, moustachio'd gentleman who was sitting nearby, and said, "Harry, I'd like you to attend the affair and gimme a report on this kid." Harry, who was Harry Eaton, the producer of the "Colored Waters" exhibit at the recently concluded World's Fair in Flushing Meadows, and now an associate of Jack's, smiled and said, "Sure thing Jack, I'll be glad to do it."

Harry and I became instant friends after that fateful Saturday night. Like all club date agents he approached this untried new comedian with an air of skepticism, but as he watched me ingratiate myself to the audience and then proceed to royally entertain them, his apprehension very quickly disappeared, and he relaxed and laughed along with the rest of them. For me, it was a most exhilarating experience. Here was an audience of well dressed, well behaved ladies and gentlemen, out for a good time on a gala evening, intelligent and, best of all, sober, and the business of entertaining them was a piece of cake. It was totally unlike the transient boozers that I had been dealing with in the clubs over the past several years, and, in retrospect, I was truly grateful for having had the opportunity to have gotten through to such staunch opposition. They made a performer out of me, and this marvelous contrast in audiences, in my mind, was spectacular. This was not those captive audiences that are so easy to charm in the resorts. This was a one night shot, and I was a stranger to them, and they very soon showed that they loved me, and I loved them for it, and I gave them my all, and what a thrilling victory it was.

Needless to say Harry gave Jack a glowing report, and soon after Jack himself went along on ensuing engagements, and watched with glee as I demolished his audiences. I had found a very comfortable and rewarding, home in "club dates" and Jack became my representative, not only providing me with whatever dates he produced, but he began talking me up with the other agents, and, without any signed contract, and for a fee of ten percent of what the other club date bookers paid me, he gave me a new lease on life. I had an agent who truly believed in me, treated me with respect and importance, and Shirley and I occasionally even socialized with Jack,

Harry, and their loved ones. There was also a life-size cutout of yours truly standing in his office, which made quite an impression upon the other performers who would come by, and I was delighted to learn that they were even starting to talk about me in Hanson's, which was actually located downstairs in the same building as Jack's office.

That summer, instead of going away as a Social Director, I took my family to a modest bungalow colony, and I did one-nighters, which was now the fad, at the various hotels. Shirley and the boys had a relaxing and enjoyable summer, especially with having our Brooklyn friends, Lenny and Etta, and their children, in the bungalow next door. Truthfully though, we missed the action of those crazy comedy sketches, and the hilarious game nights, and the frantic preparation that went into providing those nightly programs at the hotels when I was the Social Director, but, in essence, this was a lot easier, and the pay was better.

Our colorful friends would come by and stay awhile. "F.M." and his soon-to-be bride, Natalie, would appear, naturally, in vintage cars that would attract everyone's attention. Gootch, who had become a ladies shoes importer, came up on a number of weekends, and I would help him peddle the hot item of the day, "Wedgies," at the various surrounding colonies on Saturday and Sunday afternoons, which provided us with extra money. It was a most interesting summer to say the least, and the thought of coming back home to a rather thriving club date industry, with an agent who was looking out for my interests, was comforting indeed.

Jack and I had a productive arrangement going, and soon we were being called by other club date bookers from all over the country in addition to those glamorous one-nighters at the great New York City ballrooms. There were exciting places like the Hotel Astor, the Waldorf Astoria, the Roosevelt, the Commodore (with the most horrible acoustics in the world, and yet continually busy), the swank Hotel Pierre, the Plaza Hotel, Manhattan Center, etc., etc, etc. It looked as though, for as long as it would last, I had really found a home. There was one nagging problem however that we were going to have to confront very soon.

Jack would collect all the outstanding monies due me from the other agents I worked for, deduct his commissions, and then present me with the remainder via his own, personal check. At times he would ask me to hold on to the checks a bit longer to give them "time to clear." At other times he would make excuses like "I haven't gotten paid yet," and, perhaps worst of all, sometimes his checks would bounce. I forgave him all those trespasses because we got along so well, but it did offer me a good deal of discomfort, and played havoc with my covering my own expenses. Shirley never complained, though it did make for some awkward situations, but eventually he did make good, so we just had to live by making adjustments.

Outside of that annoying idiosyncrasy, Jack was a fun guy to do business with, as long as business remained brisk. The so-called "straw that broke the camel's back" occurred when we purchased that first house in Island Park. I had alerted Jack to the fact that I was going to meet with the lawyers to close the deal and had to have a certain amount of money (money that I had earned some time back, with which he was still in arrears), and he assured me that there was nothing to worry about. Shirley and I met with all the concerned parties on a lovely spring morning, filled with joy and anticipation, and at the conclusion of the signing I handed the builders' representative two checks signed by my dear friend and agent, and we drove back to Brooklyn to make arrangements with the movers to proceed to our dream house in the almost imminent future. The excitement among all of us, Shirley and I, and our three little boys (though David was an infant at the time, and I couldn't imagine what he was so happy about, yet he too must have sensed everyone's joy) was overwhelming. We were in the process of achieving the "American dream" and kept pinching ourselves to assure ourselves that all this was really happening to us.

Several days later I received a most disheartening call from the builders' lawyer telling me that both checks had bounced. It was a kick in the solar plexus. I caught my breath, did all I could to appear unruffled, telling them that it was some kind of a mistake, and asked them to please deposit the checks again. As soon as I hung up I called Jack and did all I could to contain my anger as I related what had just happened. He remained as cool as a cucumber, and without missing a beat he answered, "Tell 'em to re-deposit."

This time the checks made it, but I came to the sorry conclusion that I would do all that I could to maintain our friendly relationship, but that I would have to take on a different manager, one from the many that were already romancing me, one that was known to be solid and ethical. I found just the right guy in a grey haired, one-time vaudeville tap dancer named Nat Dunn. Nat ran a very busy club date agency, and was fortunate enough to have had an articulate, dapper, handsome, sincere, and dedicated assistant named Harrison Bob Fuller, who was also a former vaudevillian who had performed in a song and dance act with his lovely wife, Jane, which they called "The Midshipmen." Nat was really good, and Bob made him even better.

As I had anticipated, Jack did not become acrimonious. (I had a feeling that he knew that we could not stay together forever.) We remained good friends even years later when he actually became a player in one of the giant, worldwide theatrical agencies, and was probably continuing to practice the same petty deceptions, which seems to be a requisite with so many in that shark-infested profession.

My family loved Island Park and Shirley and the children treasured every precious moment of living about a mile from Long Beach, which was situated on the Atlantic Ocean. I worked quite steadily, doing the one-nighters when they were available, and also accepting steadier location work when that presented itself. There was one club in Philadelphia that was always very busy, specializing in catered affairs, and just as with that club where I had worked in Greenwich Village, I was booked in it for one weekend and stayed about four years. I drove all the way from Long Island to Philadelphia and back, nightly, on an average of four nights a week, which was a draconian feat, but I was young, and, I guess I was strong. I must have been strong 'cause I did as many as two shows a night, and my average performance per show ran about an hour, or longer. The owners, a very colorful family consisting of an older father and two married sons ran a very successful club, and showered me with bonuses and gifts because I was "so good for the business." It was a profoundly happy relationship, but the long, demanding commute was taking its toll, chipping away at my energy, and I began to seriously consider a "better way." Besides, Shirley was once again "with child," expecting the arrival of a long-awaited little girl named Madelaine. (I loved that name. It belonged to my favorite English teacher at Thomas Jefferson High School in Brooklyn, Madelaine Quinn, a vivacious Rosalind Russell type, and it was also the name of one of the adorable little flower girls at our wedding ... There's something so lovely, and feminine sounding, about that name, Madelaine. How pretty that sounds ... "Madelaine.")

It's not easy to maintain a stable existence in a profession like show business. The work is rarely steady, and filled with rejection. You are constantly "on call," waiting for the phone to ring, praying that it's a job, and oft-times being asked to pack your bag n' leave immediately for an engagement on that same night. You have no time to get sick, or tired. The show must go on, and somehow, once you're onstage, you forget about anything that might be ailing you, physically, or mentally. What a miraculous experience it is to be an entertainer, a real entertainer, and not some jackass who's in the business 'cause he can't stand a nine-to-five job. Believe me, it's harder than a nine-to-five job, and there are no pensions or benefits. You make your own. If you're a variety act, as I am, you're a Gypsy, an "independent contractor." Unless you're in a movie, or part of a cast in a Broadway show, or on TV, you pay your own way, building up some sort of plan for your old age, and health insurance, that is if you are disciplined enough and sagacious enough. What a business, ... but I wouldn't trade it for the world. Intangible as it may be, realistically speaking, in what other profession can you feel so free? In what other profession do you receive such acclaim when you're good? Tell me, where else can you get such instant gratification? In what other profession do you have enough "layoff-time" to play with your kids and also shower your partner with love and affection, and be able to make time to share your family's triumphs and travails? Would I recommend it to anyone? You bet I would, if that someone has the talent. Without the talent you deceive yourself. You're a fool. How do you know if you have the talent? Ay, there's the rub. Ya gotta hang in there. Work, perfect your performance, and, hang in there. After awhile you'll know if you're any good. If you're not, then look for somethin' else and get out while the getting is good. If you've got the product to sell, eventually they'll recognize it and buy it. If you don't have it, and you've tried like hell but to no avail, then go into somethin' else if you still can. It happens all the time. But, if you're good, and the audiences let you know you're good, then milk it pal, and savor every precious moment you're in it. It's not easy, but it can be so deliriously gratifying. Someone once said that, in order to be in show business you've got to have the heart of a lion, the brain of a fox, and the hide of a rhinoceros ... but most of all, the hide of a rhinoceros. I have appeared onstage the day after a hernia operation. I once fell offstage, ten feet into an unoccupied orchestra pit, in the presence of a thousand people, and clambered back onto the stage with a torn suit and the muscle around one of my knees all torn up, and to resounding applause. I've gone to work immediately after a head-on automobile collision. I've gone to work the day after an eye operation. I've worked numerous times with high fevers. I've lived by the adage that "the show must go on." I've driven and flown in all kinds of dangerous weather. I love my work. The show goes on if I can help it, and yet, with it all, I've never shirked my responsibilities and my devotion to my family. I love it! Maybe I'm nuts! Why must the show go on? Figure it out for yourself. If you don't go on, for one thing, ya don't get paid! That could be a very valid reason, n'est ce pas? It's more than that though. It's dedication, and if you can make people laugh and even for that brief moment help them forget their common, everyday cares, you, my fortunate friend, are a very blessed individual, and are doing something genuinely good for all mankind, and don't you ever forget it! Count your blessings!

I discovered my natural habitat in the field of "one-nighters." It far surpassed living on the road out of a suitcase. No matter how far away I travelled, and my work took me from coast to coast, and as far north as western Canada, I was still able to come back home soon after the job was concluded (many times even on the same night). I knew that I was deluding myself by overlooking the fact that the road to true success was by taking long term engagements in clubs and theaters, but the price you paid for being separated from your loved ones constantly, just didn't appeal to me, and I put the thought out of my mind, refusing to accept the truth, that

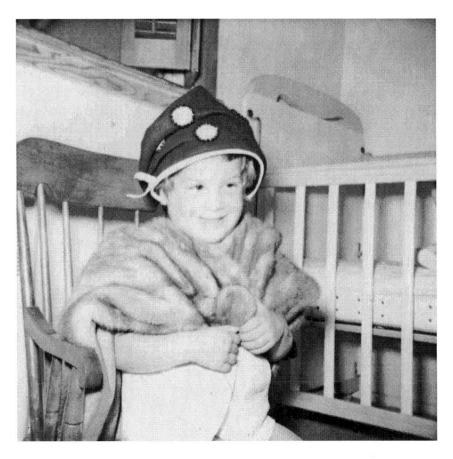

Madelaine (1960)
a.k.a. "The Grat"

the only way to make it would be by attaching yourself to a proven star, as an opening act, and then being exposed in the important places. That was not the life for me, and I revelled in just what I was doing, setting aside all thoughts of future glory, with the underlying thought that "I'll cross that bridge if ever I come to it. Perhaps there is some kind of magical osmosis out there that will enable me to become successful without having to take the recognized route of its day? I'll just have to wait and see."

Oh, I enjoyed sharing huge, one-night variety shows with some of the most prominent performers, but I was not, officially, their "opening act." I didn't have to live with them or cater to them. On such shows we were all separate entities. We did our own things and went our own separate ways afterwards, and I preferred it that way. Our business is filled with horror stories about ambitious young comedians who attached themselves to a "star," and, until such time that they were able to accumulate enough public recognition and strike out on their own (if ever at all) they were forever subservient and obsequious. From what I observed of a great number of our famous people, so very many of them are driven, narcissistic, insanely egotistical, rude, selfish, devoid of manners, and so much else that makes trying to just be their friend, both impossible and frustrating.

An acquaintance of mine, a successful, and highly regarded, club date ("one-nighter") comedian, and a very devoted family man, accepted the assignment of going out on the road with a world famous, handsome, attractive young recording artist. He was to be the opening act for this "glamour boy," who, himself, had a wife and children somewhere. The comedian assumed that all he was required to do was his stint onstage and then pass the baton on to the "star." His intentions were sincere, and he performed his contracted job well. He very soon found out that he was also expected to be the star's hand maiden, gopher, pimp, psychiatrist, and the repository of his tantrums, and all the other craziness. Onstage the star was loved and admired by all. Like all gifted people, and particularly those in the glamorous professions like theater and sports, he should have paused and given thanks for having been blessed with the unique and profound abilities that had made him into such a huge attraction, but, instead, he refused to control his human frailties, and became the monster that those who truly knew him recognized. The poor comedian, after trying his utmost to survive under the unanticipated pressures that were heaped upon him, and on the verge of a nervous breakdown, was just fortunate enough to find the propitious moment to blurt out his confused resignation, and rush back home to his family in a furious effort to try to regain his self respect. And, the glorified star couldn't have cared less. There were many more eager beavers just waiting in the wings to give it a try.

18 The Stars

My pal Joe, a serious and brilliant musician, a composer and arranger, and a gentleman who was a feature player with no less than three symphony orchestras, threw in with a few recording artists and travelled on the road as their pianist and conductor. He did it for the monetary compensation, which is good, but he paid an awful price as a result. To date he's been married four times, has fathered three children who have had a goodly share of extraneous problems which caused their parents no end of grief, and he is currently trying to put his life back in order, teaching music in an inner city public high school, while battling a serious and debilitating illness.

I was booked on an elegant club date at a country club in suburban Detroit one Saturday night, and through a chance conversation on the phone with Joe, while back home, I learned that Joe was going to be on the road during that time, at a famous night club in the city of Detroit, conducting and playing piano for a famous recording artist on an extended run. Joe had a first class accommodation at a downtown hotel and insisted that, instead of my booking a room somewhere, I stay with him overnight in the rather commodious suite that the star had provided him. Since Joe is a dear friend with a great sense of humor and an engaging personality, I readily consented. So, after my show, I took a cab to the club that Joe was appearing in, and sat in the background with Joe, the star and his entourage, and I observed all that was occurring as they were just relaxing between shows.

The star had a "road manager," a slim, gregarious, Latin-type, who travelled everywhere with the star. He was both charming and glib, and his oversized nose actually lent an aura of character and sophistication to his magnetic personality. He was of medium height, slim, and had excellent sartorial taste, with a dash of a loose, colored hankie casually placed to add an attractive flair. It was obvious that the ladies were attracted to him, and he was genuinely enjoying the role he was cast into. In addition to attending to all travel arrangements and accommodations, his job consisted largely of keeping the star happy. The star was a rather withdrawn, and somewhat sour individual. His offstage demeanor was a total antithesis to the pseudo-hip, glamorous individual that he projected onstage while in the spotlight. Back home, according to his press releases, he was a dedicated family man, wealthy from his numerous hit recordings, and clearly devoted to his wife and children. It was obvious to me that he was miserable on the road, where, because of his success, he was forced to spend so very much of his time.

His performance was excellent and he finished the evening to wild cheers from the audience. It was his closing night and we were all scheduled to leave for the airport in a limousine early the next morning, so Joe and I bid all a goodnight and off we went to his room. I slept poorly because Joe had to finish writing several arrangements for the star for a forthcoming recording session and kept the light on all night. Joe was also in a constant battle with obesity, and the whirring sound of his malted machine as he kept preparing his "Weight-Watchers" formulas, added to my discomfort. He worked diligently throughout the night, and into the wee hours of the morning, and was forever excusing himself by explaining, "Ya don't get paid for doin' nothin' ya know."

Joe had been the conductor and pianist for a truly major old time star who was currently in the throes of salvaging what remained of a once glorious reputation. Both he and his hugely talented wife, though they didn't work together, were also movie stars and known the world over. He still possessed a beautiful voice and although he was now having difficulty when it came to reaching his high notes, he was clever enough to gently gloss over them without attracting too much attention to his shortcomings. He still looked good for his age, and the older ladies in the audience still fawned over him, vicariously reliving their own youth as they watched him perform.

His wife was as beautiful as ever, despite her years, and it was to her credit that she spent so many hours out of each day diligently exercising each and every part of her still fantastic physique, in a gallant and excruciating battle to defy the vagaries of aging. To her many fans and admirers she was the miracle of the ages, and still managed to snare an occasional role in a motion picture.

Joe had to live with these people and fulfill his professional obligations to them. He found them pleasant enough to live with and learned to get out of the way when danger lurked. The uncomfortable part of the arrangement happened when the singer had too much to drink. It was then that he took on a dark, and unexpected side. He was a chameleon, and only those who knew and worked with him were aware of it. When he was sober he was quiet and reserved, but when he was drunk, watch out! Like the wealthy benefactor in one of Charlie Chaplin's silent films, he had two separate and distinct personalities, only this star's behavior was the opposite of the character in the Chaplin film. The character in the film was beneficent when inebriated, and ugly when he was sober, while this guy was just the reverse. Nevertheless, Joe made his living from this semi-tyrant, and, studiously avoided his rampages, for which, surprisingly, the star would apologize whenever he was made aware of his erraticism.

One of Joe's "stars" was booked at a resort hotel in San Juan, Puerto Rico, so, naturally, Joe was part of the package. Engagements at such glamorous resorts were among the perks that went with the job, and Joe, whose foremost hobby was "fishing," was delighted with the opportunities that Caribbean waters accorded him, especially in the winter when conditions were far different back home in New York. With an abundance of hotels, all of which featured gambling as an additional lure to vacationers, San Juan was ready made for entertainment, and a good number of celebrated performers dotted the landscape.

Among those appearing at the time was a glamorous recording artist from Great Britain, who was very well known for the enormous amount of sex appeal he exuded, which apparently, was a characteristic that he was able to employ very successfully in his act. The few times I watched him work I was overcome with sympathy for the poor fellow when I observed how a cordon of police had to surround him, and escort him back to his dressing room at the end of each performance, in order to stave off the hordes of screaming females who were clamoring just to get close to him, and clutch at him. He was like an animal being put back in his cage, before harm could befall him, and, although I admired his magnificent ability, I just couldn't help feeling sorry for the guy.

In the daytime he would loll on the beach, disguised in large sunglasses, and surrounded by bodyguards and sycophants, in addition to his immediate entourage. Word came down that there was going to be a big banquet in his honor, later that evening, in the grand ballroom of the hotel, and a number of the other attractions in town were invited, which included Joe's boss, and, of course, his loyal conductor. The star decided that it would be a marvelous diversion to see how many young ladies he could take to bed that night, after he finished working, so an idea was conceived to have his honchos fan out all along the beach and approach every attractive female and ask each one if "she'd like to have sex with 'so-and-so' that evening." There were many more "yeas" than "nays," and later that evening a bevy of beautiful ladies who made up the afternoon recruits, was seen having dinner in the ballroom to which they were invited, while the "celebrities in town" were sitting at the dais, with the "king" himself, perched delightedly in the middle.

As Joe related it to me, "his majesty" scanned the assembled "smorgasbord," and told his advisors, "I'll take the one with the dark hair at that first table; "the blonde at the next one; the cute one with the curls at the next; the sultry lookin' one with the bangs at the next;" and so it went, on and on, and all the while Joe was filled with disbelief at what he was witnessing. "And what happened to the rejects?" I asked Joe after he had related this unbelievable story to me. "Oh," he replied quite casually, "his flunkies tried to make out with them while trying to impress them by telling them that they were very close to the "head man." So it wouldn't be a total loss, some stayed on ... and the others just went home."

Though I managed a number of "location dates," in a few of the better nightclubs, I've never considered those exactly memorable. I've had my share of big bands that I appeared with on club dates, cruise ships and the likes, and I found that experience to be most pleasurable. To this very day both Shirley and I cherish the friendship of our musician friends. We have generally found them to be erudite, fun loving, interesting, dedicated, hard working, and, in addition to the many more superlatives, just damn good friends.

I'll never forget the time, in Atlantic City, when the Harry James Orchestra was being featured on our show. Harry James! The Harry James! I grew up loving his music. When we were kids we danced to his wonderful music, featuring that outstanding trumpet of his, and we even collected his recordings. Here I was, sharing the bill with the great Harry James! Before the show I walked up to him and said, "Hi Mr. James, I'm Van Harris, the comedian on the show. How would you like to be introduced?" and he looked right at me and said, "Mr. Harris ... I'm going to be introducing you!" I couldn't believe the scenario. Harry James, one of those many greats that I had admired throughout my youth ... and he was going to be introducing me! It was like a dream come true.

I consider it a privilege to have appeared with Harry James, Count Basie, Mercer Ellington ("The Count's" kid), Warren Covington, Les and Larry Elgart, The Jimmy Dorsey Orchestra, The Guy Lombardo Orchestra, (headed up by my good friend, Art Mooney), both Skitch Henderson, and Milton DeLug (when I did the Johnny Carson TV Show) and numerous other such notables, in addition to the countless "unknowns" who rate among the most talented musicians on this planet.

Among the singers, the late Sergio Franchi was one of the most confident, and gifted people I had ever met. He had a wonderful disposition, as did his sister, also a fine singer, Dana Valery. They must have come from wonderful parents. They were both so classy, so obviously well bred. Poor Sergio, he died so young, in the prime of his career, from brain cancer. What a loss, not only to our profession, but to all mankind in general.

I'll never forget the time we were booked at the Westchester Civic Center in White Plains, NY for a huge Sons of Italy affair. I was scheduled to do the first half of the show, and he the second. I approached him backstage and introduced myself, "I'm Van Harris, and I'm opening the show tonight. How would you like me to introduce you?" "Introduce me?" he bellowed, in that distinctive half Italian, half Russian accent of his, "Dere are two tousand Italians out dere! Dey know me ... Dey don't know you!!" And then he did something that endeared him to me for life, something that, at least 90% of the insecure stars never do. After the opening overture by the orchestra in the pit, he strolled out onstage in his street clothes to tumultuous applause, and when the roar died down he said, with that big, intoxicating smile out front, "My friends, I want you to meet a pal of mine. Be nice to him. Here's Van Harris!" It was all so easy after that.

After my stint, during intermission, I went automatically to my rather nondescript dressing room to change. I still remember the surprised looks on Shirley and her friend Mary's faces when Sergio burst into my dressing room, with a handful of admirers behind him, and shouted out, as he took me by the hand, "Van, this is not your dressing room," and proceeded to lead us into his spacious dressing room, filled with "goodies" like wine, after shave lotions, an abundance of clean towels, etc., and he continued, as he motioned for us to sit, "This is yours and mine!"

The next time I saw him he was appearing at the famed Royal Box of the Hotel Americana in NYC, not much after I had appeared there with Rosemary Clooney. After witnessing his great show with Shirley and my dear pal from Detroit, "Col. Guano," at my side, I picked up the phone in the lobby and called up to his suite. His lovely manager Marian Billings answered. (The poor lady was destined to contract the fatal Lou Gehrig's Disease not too long after.) And I said, "This is Van Harris, and I'm downstairs in the lobby with my wife and a friend. I just wanted to tell Sergio how very much we enjoyed his performance this evening." "Why don't you come up and tell him in person?" she answered. What a wonderful gesture. We walked into his suite and he was sitting in a chair with a sheet around his neck, and his beautiful sister, Dana, was giving him a haircut, and he was giggling, and complaining that she was tickling him. How gracious he was. A welcome addition of fresh air to our oft-times stifling profession. Even the way he handled hecklers. As we watched his performance earlier, some drunk interrupted his act, got to his feet, and while reeling, blurted out, "My wife is in love with you and I'm gonna kill you." Instead of reacting negatively, the surprised Sergio broke into a great big grin and addressed the audience, "Folks," he pleaded, "dees man wants to keel me. What should I do?" The entire audience broke into laughter, and started to yell at the heckler, "Sit down you bum, and don't interrupt the man. He's great!" For anyone unfamiliar with the tricks of the trade that certainly would have been a magnificent lesson on how to handle a pest.

Unfortunately, not everyone was like Sergio. There was this Black singer and dancer who had made an excellent name for himself on the Broadway stage, and later on TV. We were booked on a show for a big Jewish fundraiser at a lovely theater in Toronto, Canada. The agent, who was also the producer, had invited Shirley along to that breathtaking city, as his guest. Before the rehearsal, we were all treated to dinner at a posh restaurant by the owner of the theater and the lovely lady who was directing the show also joined us. The star had not shown up yet, and in his stead was his "road manager," a young African-American who came dressed like he was going to play in a sandlot basketball game, dirty white sneakers and all. He was also rude, and what was planned to be a delightful, leisurely dinner experience was marred by his presence.

The star arrived in town before the show, with his hands thrust deeply into his pockets, looking and behaving like he could use a shave and a decent bowel movement, in any order. He was surly, snippy, and very uncooperative. In fact, when we were introduced, I stuck my hand out and said, "Glad to meet you," and he only thrust his hands deeper into his pockets while he hunched his shoulders and scowled, "What does that mean?" After that I refused to ride in the same limo with him and his road manager, who had also tried to inject the fact that he was a Black Muslim during our conversation earlier at dinner.

Everyone went out of his way to be polite to the star, but he was impossible. The show? It was great! He was great! He killed the audience, dazzling them with his footwork and his all-around versatility. He appeared in a white suit and, at one time in his act he even pulled out a little gold mezzuzah that he was wearing around his neck, telling his adoring audience that he had gotten it in Israel when he appeared there. He really knew how to pour it on, and handled his audience quite expertly. All the while I kept wondering what his road manager might have been thinking while he was praising his Hebrew religious symbol in his effort to endear himself to his public.

Several weeks later we appeared on the same bill at the War Memorial Auditorium in Syracuse, NY. He seemed a lot more friendly and relaxed than he was in Toronto. I refused to go near him, even at the party at that show's producer's home after the show. I was told, when I got back home, that he complained to the agent that I had refused to talk to him. "Why?" he asked. Several months later I spoke with another comedian who had spent lots of time with this guy on the road, as his opening act. I described his anti-social behavior in Toronto. The comedian shrugged his shoulders and exclaimed, "He must've been on cocaine at the time."

The same agent that had booked me into Toronto and then Syracuse, had put together a show with an actor (who once was the lead in a successful TV series, starred in the national company of a hit Broadway show, and was now doing club dates before opening in a show in his home state of California) and myself. We were scheduled to appear at the historic Philadelphia Academy of Music, home of the renowned Eugene Ormandy and the famed Philadelphia Symphony Orchestra. It was ascertained that I would do the first half of the variety show, and the star would do the second half. Partly due to my popularity in the "City of Brotherly Love," where I practically got my start, we sold out, and I was thrilled. Just before the show was to go on there was a commotion. It was the smiling star (he smiled to my face, anyway, and was always so friendly in the agent's office), demanding that I do only half of the first half of the show, and he does the other half of that first part. Then he comes back and does the entire second half. I felt as though someone had hit me over the head with a plank. I looked at the agent waiting for him to say something, but he just shrugged his shoulders apologetically as if to imply, "What can I do with this egotistical sonovabitch?" There were two reasons why I just didn't turn around and go home: One was that I had so many friends in the audience; and the other was that the money was good, and I had come all the way to Philly, and I wasn't about to give it up.

The show went on, and it played well. When I concluded my portion of the show, obviously prematurely, the people were yelling for more, but I did what I had to, and he finished with a flourish, banking largely upon his reputation and his acting abilities, and was smart enough not to belabor the jokes, which he finally may have sensed, were best used as "throwaways." We all drove back to New York together and he said nothing more about his unreasonable demands. On the following day he even called me at home to tell me what a splendid job I had done. This guy was the personification of the term "chutzpah." He mentioned that he was going back to California to appear in a show, and even extended an invitation for me to be his guest at the show should I find myself in the LA area for any reason.

About a month later Shirley and I, and my brother Yussel, went to California to visit our children, friends, and some former business associates. I remembered the actor's kind offer and called his office and his secretary informed me that he was out, and would be back later in the day as he had a performance in his show scheduled for that night. I told her we were on our way to visit some friends down near San Diego, and asked her to please remind him of his kind offer, and asked if he would please put away three tickets for us for that evening's performance. I added that I would call her late in the afternoon, as soon as we got back to LA. When we returned in the late afternoon I got her on the phone and was informed that he said he would be delighted to see me at the show, and that he had put aside three house seats at fifty bucks apiece. I was stunned, but I should have known better. I just hung up, and, of course, we never went. About three weeks later his show opened in New York to unanimously negative reviews. It closed in one week. Couldn't have happened to a nicer guy!!

19 Discord at the Concord

On a snowy Washington's Birthday Weekend, very soon after a triumphant, and exhilarating one-month engagement at the Royal Box of the Americana, I was booked into the famous Catskill resort, The Concord, where, by that time, I had probably appeared, in any given year, more than any other comedian in the business. It was the first night of that important weekend, and I was asked to open the show for a very popular and highly successful, husband and wife singing team that also deals in humorous banter. The snow had been falling steadily all throughout the day, and the guests were very tardy in arriving. We were unable to present the show on time, as the audience was slowly filing into the large Imperial Room Night Club in dribs and drabs. The stars were edgy, and couldn't wait any longer and insisted to the management that, regardless of the situation, we "get the show on the road." On I went, with practically no one in the house, and I labored until I finally had gotten together some semblance of an audience. From the wings I kept hearing a lot of angry muttering, which was steadily increasing in volume. After about twenty minutes of battling to get some attention from the audience that was still slowly filing in, I was shocked to hear, "Get off already!" I stayed on about another ten minutes for my own self respect, and by then the lady in the wings, in a shrill voice, was exhorting the "show booker" (a member of the family that owned the place) to "get him the hell off!" I walked off, stunned and embarrassed, and asked the man in charge what the ruckus was all about. Instead of thanking me for doing my best in a valiant effort to set the stage in face of the annoying obstacles, he was surprisingly angry, and yelled, "You stayed on ten minutes too long. You'll never work this place again!" I was mortified!

There was a hiatus of close to a year before I began to work at the Concord again, and I've been appearing there quite steadily ever since. When I had come offstage on that fateful evening, my manager described the terrible tantrums the lady was having while I was on, and how she was screaming at the booker to take me off. I swore that I would never work with these rude and vulgar people again (not that they would ever want me to). The memory of that ugly night at the Concord has haunted me for the longest time, and whenever I think about it, I try to invoke the adage, "In order to survive, ... the heart of a lion, the brain of a fox, and the hide of a rhinoceros ... and most of all, the hide of a rhinoceros." Such indignities are all part of growing up, and you become a better, and stronger person because of them. No matter how small, and insignificant they eventually become, they never quite go away.

Interesting, how an accident of fate can overturn the good relationships that are such a necessary part of gaining success. Until that unfortunate incident, I was both, socially, and artistically, on extremely good terms with the Concord's "Charge d'Affaires." He was an extremely bright individual, from a rather accomplished family (one of his brothers was a famed Broadway choreographer, another a renowned psychiatrist) and except for his tendency towards sadistic humor, he was well suited for his rather important job. When one considers the amount of talent that was presented on his stages at that busy resort hotel and the cost, it certainly was no job for an inexperienced neophyte. Thanks, however, to his familial relationship, he had the advantage of starting out young, and learning on the job. For that matter though, the hotel also started out young and also "learned on the job," as it was growing into the "monster" that it had become. Though it never attained the warmth, and all around "hotelmanship," that its older competitor, the world-famed Grossinger's had, it was definitely an important "force" to be reckoned with.

Phil, our protagonist, had no trepidation about socializing with the performers. I, more than once, had the good fortune to attend several celebrated parties along with him. Since I was residing on the south shore of Long Island, in an area not too far away from where he lived with his wife and young children, such occasional get-togethers were convenient. They lived on the bay in an opulent part of town, and, right across the road, in a most respectable part of what was referred to as 'the five towns" lived the well known harmonica virtuoso, Blackie Schackner, who was also a big favorite at the hotel. Blackie, in addition to being an outstanding instrumentalist, was also an accomplished composer and arranger, who also had several important movie scores to his credit. This curly-haired, short, stocky, and loquacious, individual (built like a fireplug) was one of the handiest people I'd ever met, and he had a great sense of humor to go along with all his other attributes. He kept his lovely home in tip top condition, and was also available if he was needed by others to help with challenging repairs. He would often invite you to his home to show you what he had built, with his wife and two children standing by beaming their assent. He was also a tough little guy who brooked no nonsense, and was known to have hurled garden tools, at any drivers who were foolish enough to recklessly speed through his quiet, residential area.

Phil, his wife Jane, and the kids were getting ready to leave on a picnic one Sunday morning when the little boy's orthodontia suddenly broke loose. Here they were, all set to go, and this sudden emergency occurs ... and on a Sunday morning yet! "Whereinthehell are we gonna find an orthodontist on a Sunday morning?" It didn't take too long before the flashbulb lit up in Phil's head, "Blackie! Of course, let's call Blackie! He can fix anything!" Jane stood there incredulously. "Blackie?" "To fix his braces?" "Are you kidding?" We've gotta try," replied Phil, "We've got no alternative." Blackie, who had performed the night before, and had gotten home late, didn't quite appreciate being awakened so abruptly, and by such an outlandish request. He soon arrived at their home, carrying a ping hammer, several pairs of pliers, a soldering iron, and whatever else he thought he might need for just such an emergency. After studying the little boy's problem, in a jiffy he did the repair, and soon all was in order, much to everyone's delight. They thanked him profusely, and in the next moment everyone was out the door. Blackie smiled to himself knowing that what he had done was above and beyond, while at the same time thinking to himself, "He can't say no next time I need a date at the Concord."

That very same night, upon returning home, Phil and Jane discovered a puddle on the kitchen floor. Upon further examination they noticed that one of the water pipes had sprung a leak. Phil, scratching the back of his head, looked at Jane. Jane looked back at him, and together they blurted out, "Let's call Blackie!" Luckily for them Blackie was not working that evening and was home relaxing. When the phone rang with the new request, Blackie hesitated for a short while, and then answered, "Hey, wait a minute. I'm a dentist... I'm not a plumber!"

My rapport with musicians is legend, and yet I suffered a vicious financial setback at one of the resorts thanks to the spinelessness of the orchestra leader, a drummer who apparently was determined to "even the score" because I had the audacity, in an extremely frustrating moment, to point out, onstage, that he just wasn't doing his job. It has been my habit to allow the bands to leave the stage for at least a half hour after my opening "chaser," so that they can take a break, and not have to sit around onstage looking bored because they had heard the act so many times before. Even if you change your act completely, throw in all new material, they're only interested in their end of the job, and not in being entertained. Orchestras are known for displaying their displeasure when they're forced to sit in the background and do nothing while the acts are performing. I purposely reserve the musical portion of my act for the latter part of my show so that these guys can have a breather, a welcome respite.

Many's the time that the musicians, blasé, and undisciplined, hesitate to come back on time, and, on rare occasions they don't return at all, leaving the performer all alone onstage, non-plussed, and trying to formulate a way to get off gracefully. Of course, nothing escapes the eye of the audience, and so you're left with a less than desirable finish. Because of my good natured relationship with the musicians, especially in the Catskills, they do take advantage of me. One particular week I was embarrassed three nights in a row at three different hotels, as I stood onstage bewildered, asking, out loud, "Well, where the hell is the band?" Of course I cover up their slovenliness with funny remarks, or a little animated ad-lib dance, or song, making it appear as though its all part of the act, and sometimes I'm forced to sing "a cappella", which, to me, is the worst possible course to take.

That last time, after having exhausted my little bag of tricks, and after actually having sung a rather intricate song "a cappella," I became enraged and asked the people in the audience for their sympathy as I launched into a tirade about "people not being there to do what they're paid to do." I thanked the audience for their kind indulgence and concluded my performance. When the show was over, as I sat in my dressing room, changing back into my "civvies," the disgruntled orchestra leader burst his way in, flung my music books down on the table, and scowled, "Ya didn't hafta bad mouth the band like that!" "You owe me a big apology," I quickly shot back, but he didn't hang around long enough to even listen.

To get involved with co-workers in such a fashion is very unpleasant, and especially if the antagonists have known each other for years, as we did. Instead of doing the gentlemanly thing, and attempt to reason it out, (though, as I saw it, the only solution was his apology), he ran to the hotel manager (a relation of the family that owned the place) and distorted the entire picture, claiming that I had said unkind things about the hotel in my act.

The next day my agent called me at home, starting his conversation off with, "I see you really ruffled some feathers last night ..." I was flabbergasted! Floored! It wasn't as though I was dealing with someone who didn't know and respect me. I had appeared at that hotel many, many times for many, many years. I was one of their favorites, and also their "troubleshooter." Once when a popular British comedian was filming a tour of the US, which was later presented on the BBC, he asked if he could feature an American comedian at that hotel for one segment, and, of all the performers they could call upon, they selected me. I was highly regarded, and was sure that they appreciated all that I had given to the hotel, artistically, throughout all those years. I tried to call the manager after my agent's admonishment, but he was "not taking any calls" (an old, show biz trick employed by some of the glorified mailroom graduates at the theatrical agencies). I next wrote him a letter explaining what truly had occurred, and sent a similar one to one of the owners with whom I was convinced that I had an excellent rapport. None were answered, or even acknowledged. The result was that I was no longer employable at the hotel, which constituted a big blow to my ego, and, without any doubt, to my income. Upon searching around for an explanation, I subsequently discovered the astonishing reason for their obstreperousness. It came by way of a season-long guest who was very, very close to the management of the hotel, and who also had first hand knowledge of just about every little intrigue that went on. The indelible answer came as a huge and shocking surprise. The explanation, reiterated by others supposedly "in the know" was that the orchestra leader (a big favorite of management) had been maneuvered over the heads of other, more qualified people, into that exalted position. He had a very special personal relationship with the manager. Both he and the manager indulged in the use of drugs (not too surprisingly) and the bandleader was the manager's supplier! As good as I may have been for the hotel, how dare I tell off the manager's drug supplier? Like the guy in the off-color "dog-doo" story, I didn't see it, so I stepped in it!! Another lesson in just how fragile my noble profession can be. I stepped on the "druggie's" toes, and, instead of the user, it was I who "paid through the nose." It was a very bitter lesson to be learned, and, in thinking it over, it could happen to just about anyone. As the inimitable Jimmy Durante used to say in times of pending defeat, "Wot a rotten developement dis is!"

20 The Hide of a Rhinoceros

In my lifetime in the field of comedy I have been fortunate to have rubbed shoulders with some of the most colorful and fascinating performers in the world. These blessed people are all unique, and their experiences could fill volume upon volume. The following is a true story regarding an incident that occurred in the life of one such individual, a tall, rather good looking, well dressed, articulate comedian named Emil Cohen. He was, and still is, a huge success in the field of Jewish-American entertainment, though he's reached the stage in his life where he regards himself as "currently in the state of semi-retirement" (one never fully retires from "show biz." As is often heard from the mouths of entertainers, "When I open the refrigerator and the light goes on, I immediately go into my act"). While his family was growing up, for years on end, he, his devoted wife Lillian, and the boys would regularly shuttle between the famous Jewish resorts in the Catskills in the summer, and those busy places in Florida in the winter, where they also maintained a residence.

Soon after hanging up his American army uniform at the end of World War II, he discovered that people really paid attention when he would say something funny, and especially if that wit had a Jewish flavor. He launched into a career of entertaining wherever large numbers of Jews congregated. He was soon to become the best, and most sought-after Jewish-American comedian, and for many years he would perform on the busy "synagogue circuit" helping to sell Israel Bonds, performing for organizations such as United Jewish Appeal, and wherever he appeared he would have them screaming with delight at his funny antics, and highly amusing interpretations. He was a STAR in synagogues all over the United States and Canada. This not only brought him the recognition that he longed for and deserved, but also had a tremendous effect upon his bearing, the way he carried himself, and his all around demeanor. Having performed in so many Jewish surroundings, and having consorted with so many rabbis, he soon began to take on an air of ecclesiasticism. He actually began to imitate his friends, the rabbis, in so many ways. If, for instance, you would be introduced to him, he would not only shake your hand wholeheartedly and enthusiastically, but he would add a verbal blessing, offer prayers for your soul, and go through an assortment of applied benedictions. He became what I would call, "a vicarious rabbi." I would not be the least bit surprised if he even had the title "clergy" stamped on his driver's license.

It happened during one of the many summers that he and Lillian were residing at the world famous Grossinger Hotel outside of Liberty, NY. He was engaged to perform on a Saturday night at a Jewish resort hotel in Atlantic City, NJ. (It was just around that time when Atlantic City was in a state of transition, going from the glamorous resort of yesteryear to the glistening, sparkling, modern east coast gambling mecca.) Emil nervously waited for sundown, so as not to violate the Sabbath, and with a cold sandwich for company, he leapt into his trusty Cadillac, and whooshed down the Quickway in a gallant effort to drive the two hundred miles to his destination. Given the time allotted, every minute counted, and being a veteran of such pressures, he was up to the task, rarin' to go. We show people are faced with such deadlines constantly, and, after awhile it becomes part of your blood and you actually look forward to such challenges. Saturday night, heading south on Route 17, with most of the traffic going the other way, with a little bit of luck, he might even salvage enough time to have a cup of coffee before going on. Not paying too much attention to his speedometer, and playing with the buttons on his radio in an attempt to get something civilized in an area notorious for rock n' roll and lots of "hillbilly music," he was suddenly made aware of flashing red and blue lights twirling in a circular motion all around him. He came to a stop on the shoulder of the road. As he turned off the engine to await the friendly greeting of a bear in a grey uniform wearing a very official, and imposing domed troopers hat (that made him appear even taller than the mountain that he was) our resourceful friend, in his mind, was already formulating his spiel. The officer requested his license and registration and a plethora of miniature police courtesy badges and cards practically tumbled out of his wallet as he complied. As the policeman stood there perusing the identification that was just handed him, Emil spread his arms out wide and immediately launched into his benediction, "God bless you officer. May God bless you for the dangerous and useful work that you have dedicated your life to. May the lord bestow his countenance onto you, and all your loved ones" ... It had all the earmarks of an ancient and mysterious chant penetrating the still night air, interrupted only by the sounds of cars whizzing by. The NY state trooper stood there patiently, looking very officious, with his hands on his hips and his feet, slightly spread, and firmly planted on the ground, and waited out the indefatigable Mr. Cohen, who, by now had reached quite a crescendo. When it appeared as though he was all through, the trooper quickly handed him back his credentials and snapped, "Okay, you can stop all the crap now buddy ... Your wife had called for us to head you off ... YOU'VE BEEN CANCELLED IN ATLANTIC CITY!"

The "club date" business certainly provided me with lots of adventure, and a huge assortment of experiences. I became very proficient at applying myself to just about every assignment that was handed me, and quickly learned how to tailor each and every one to fit the occasion, and the audiences were quick to show their delight. I had found my niche in a business that I was rapidly becoming ambivalent about, and suddenly I looked forward to every date with relish. Times were good. There was lots of work around, especially for a craftsman like myself. Word of my ability spread quickly, and my club date manager was only too happy to accommodate all buyers, and set up my busy schedules. Wily, grey haired, Nat Dunn, the old tap dancer, and his charming assistant, the ever reliable, and impeccably dressed Bob Fuller, were having a field day handling my many dates. Coupled with the other successful performers they were managing, the office soon became the talk of the show biz neighborhood.

I worked large, sumptuous affairs, along with an assortment of variety acts, at the finest hotel ballrooms, and theaters, all over the country. No job was too small for me either. In addition to those large shows which were generally presented on weekends, I also did many lectures and one-man shows for corporations and fraternity groups, and even did "stag" shows, with some of the most glorious strippers in the whole wide world. I even did "put-ons," where I was accepted by the unsuspecting onlookers as: a retired law enforcement officer; a member of the State Dept.; a merchandising genius (where I employed "double-talk"), an English professor; a minor league athlete with a dazzling future; etc., etc., etc. Those were truly heady days, and, in retrospect, I was fortunate enough to be involved at a time when that kind of show biz industry flourished. There was a whole generation of fun loving, involved, informed, intelligent people out there, of assorted ages and sexes. (Those afternoon sisterhood luncheons were a great source of income, and artistic satisfaction, both.) I was there to fill all their requirements. Among my proud accomplishments were shows for the handicapped. I loved entertaining sightless audiences, having quickly discovered that their imaginations were far more acute and sensitive than those of us more fortunate. I even did free shows at Veterans' hospitals whenever I worked in the vicinity. These shows were most gratifying experiences.

I was taken aback the first time I was confronted by an audience composed of the hearing and voice impaired. The "normal" director of the group advised me to go right ahead and treat them like any other audience. "Just do your act. There will be someone at the side of the stage interpreting everything in sign language as fast as you can dish it out, so just proceed as though nothing is any different." I was amazed at how well it went. The lady standing at the side of the stage delivered my material with ease and excellence, and the assortment of sounds that greeted each punch line, after its initial surprise to my ears, became exhilarating. I was so inspired that, after a very short while, I ad-libbed that she was "lousing up my jokes," which she immediately related to them, and the laughter only increased, and it became one big, ever-so-satisfying party for all. That was my first such experience, but certainly not my last. Oh how I learned to love those challenges.

Probably the most difficult assignment that was ever handed to me was when I was asked to emcee, and perform, at the Roosevelt Hospital in Montrose, NY, which, at the time, was the largest Veterans' psychiatric facility in the Northeast. The members of the audience were males, veterans of several wars, who sat, in various positions, in their bathrobes, in this huge auditorium. A number of them were peering over newspapers at what was going on onstage, and of course, the reactions were indescribably scattered. Once more I was advised to go ahead as though everything was normal, but this one was really tough. The agents that booked the show demanded a ninety minute show, and, instead of using "sight acts" (acrobats, magicians, erratic dancers, and other novelties), which would have been the perfect menu for just such a crowd, they presented me, along with two tap dancing sisters, and a female vocalist. That, and the orchestra, was the whole show. The reactions were as expected, ranging from "good to "poor" to "virtually non-existent." As for my comedy, I tried to be as visual, and vocal (employing sound effects) as I could, and I very soon discovered that the majority of the audience didn't understand punch lines, but found humor in certain words that, for reasons known only to themselves, elicited laughter. The other acts did a combined total of somewhere between thirty and forty minutes, and I was left with all the remaining time. Though I even sang to keep things going, and added a careful bit of audience participation, I don't think I ever labored so hard in my life. However it came out, I got the job done, but I couldn't help but question (to myself, of course) why it was not a properly planned show. I had to content myself by accepting the fact that it was the agents' problem, but, having been an integral part of the whole picture, I couldn't avoid having some feeling of guilt. There we go again ... "the heart of a lion," "the brain of a fox" ... but if you're going to survive, don't leave out "the hide of the rhinoceros."

I did a stag show for the Volunteer Fire Dept. of a medium sized upstate NY city at a nearby Catskill resort hotel. It was a big weekend outing that they plan for all year long. They feature a fancy dinner for the husbands and wives, followed by dancing to a big band, on Saturday night; and an all day carnival, along with rides, prizes, and assorted goodies for the children on Sunday afternoon. Then the men return that same night for dinner, followed by a stag show. I was appointed to do my "blue material" (for an all male audience I also throw in interesting sports trivia which they seem to enjoy just as much as the dirty jokes) and I also emcee the show. The show consisted of yours truly, a very provocative belly dancer who really knew how to work a male audience by getting very close to them and even sitting on their laps, and a pretty, but quite young and fairly inexperienced strip teaser.

The men in the audience were a compendium that appeared to cross all economic strata, but primarily blue collar beer drinkers, and were all quite well dressed, most with shirts and ties. I had no problem entertaining them, and was quite pleased with our rapport. I opened the show well, did some appropriate material to start with, and, after a short while I presented the belly dancer. She was in rare form and really did what she was expected to do, raising their libido levels quite capably. I then went on again to do the bulk of my act, and, when it was finished, and they sat back quite contentedly, I introduced the stripper. She was young and, having witnessed how well the belly dancer had done, I figured that she might just go out n' try to top her seasoned performance. The young lady's good looks overcame the fact that her wardrobe was not exactly of the dazzling sequined caliber that some of our more successful strippers wear, but, from where I was looking, she was a good choice to finish the evening. I stood outside the dressing room in the back of the ballroom, chatting with someone, while the young lady was doing her job, and I would glance over my shoulder every once in awhile to see how she was doing. "Wow!" ... "She's really pourin' it on," I thought to myself. As I turned my back on the festivities once more, I was suddenly surprised by some sort of commotion, and turned around just in time to hear her yell, "Help me!" as the men, many of them intoxicated, and aroused, were surging towards her in a mob. I did the gallant thing (blame it on my upbringing) and stood in front of her to protect her from the oncoming hordes, frantically shouting, "Help me! Somebody help me!" while thinking, "Are these guys crazy? I also became frightened by the moment, and wondered if we were going to come out of this thing alive.

Out of the corner of my eye I spied a big, handsome man, with broad shoulders, and a very imposing demeanor, sitting there, glancing around and taking in the whole sordid scene, astonished by what he was witnessing. I'll never forget his face. He looked like Randolph Scott and the Lone Ranger, all wrapped up in one. I looked directly at him as I yelled, once again, frantically, and certain that I was about to be trampled, "Help, somebody. Please help!" In a moment, this giant of a man was up on his feet. He banged his hand on the table so loud that the sound reverberated around the room, and in a determined, and very arresting voice, he shouted, "All right! Cut it out! Everybody, back to your seats!" It was like a miracle. Like the film snapping in the projector while showing a movie, everyone and everything froze in midair. Sheepishly, and shaken out of their raging stupidity, they turned around and all returned to their seats. The young stripper went back into her dressing room where the poor, frightened thing had a good cry. I calmed her down and went out to look around for my benefactor but he was nowhere in sight. The crowd was starting to disperse, and soon all disappeared in a fairly orderly manner just as though nothing had ever happened. I sighed a sigh of relief, picked up my music from the members of the orchestra, who were still shaking their heads at what they had just seen, and said my goodbye's. Who was that powerful stranger? Hadda be somebody very important to command that sort of instant respect. Or, was he a mirage? I'm afraid I'll never know. Oh well, ... all in a night's work.

Sascha was a superb instrumentalist. He was pure magic on the violin, and he knew it. Instead of becoming part of a symphony orchestra somewhere, this slim, swarthy, good looking fiddler figured out that the variety field was the only way to go with his intoxicating charm and restless personality. He adored being the center of attraction, had an eye for the ladies, and it wasn't beneath him to lie about his accomplishments. Wherever he went he became an instant favorite with the audiences. He was a charming rogue in constant demand on cruise ships, in resorts, on club dates, and at the gambling meccas. In fact, gambling was his biggest pleasure, and he would wager a bet on just about anything. He was addicted, and if he were able to work in Las Vegas or Atlantic City for the rest of his days he would have been in all his glory. Everybody loved Sascha, except the musicians. He was sadistic with them. He would go out of his way to torment them, and had no trepidation about insulting them if he wasn't pleased with the way they played for him. Actually, the bands that backed him were generally superb, but somehow he would become belligerent in rehearsals and he took delight in battling them. He was, to the best of my knowledge, half Italian and half Hungarian, and was born overseas, and though he was not very tall, he took on gigantic stature when he played. His full name was Sascha Tormas, but after awhile many that worked with him scornfully renamed him "Sucha Torment!" He had to be a schizophrenic, so friendly and playful on one hand, and so downright belligerent on the other, but he was an artist, fortunately involved in a field where such erratic behavior is generally overlooked. He was a mean practical joker who actually carried extra orchestral parts, and many were the times that he would berate a musician for the way he was playing, jump up and down like an angry Rumplestiltskin, and shout, "You stink"! "You can't play!" and tear up his music chart into little pieces, as the poor musician would gasp unbelievingly. Little did he know that Sascha carried duplicate parts for just that sort of ruse. He bragged incessantly, and even when he would introduce himself onstage, he would begin with a most impressive untruth. In his charming European accented, partially broken English, he would say, "Mine ladies and gentlemen, I have just return from Caesar's Palace in Las Vegas, where I appear with Liza Minelli, and I close the show because she say is too hard to follow me." And the rubes in the audience, would believe every word he was saying, and were greatly impressed. We, his peers in the business, all saw right through his facade, yet we enjoyed watching him "snow" the crowd, as only he could.

When he appeared in the Catskill hotels, where the audiences, for the most part, were Jewish, he would always finish his act, by playing a very exciting, dramatic version of the movie theme from the motion picture "Exodus." He would make certain that, as he energetically bowed the closing bars of the arrangement, the hairs on his bow would snap and fray, and he would frantically race to the end, seemingly unconcerned that he was playing under what the audience assumed was an unanticipated handicap. They would gasp as the hairs were wildly waving about, and he would continue to smile and plunge on to the end, which was a long chord that was sustained while the orchestra played the Israeli national anthem, "Hatikvah." Then, while sweating profusely, he would leap high into the air, waving his violin and shouting, something he had learned from his Jewish friends, "Long live Israel!" The audience, with its passions so aroused, would go nuts. He was a sensation in the Catskills and had learned all the "shtik."

One Sunday evening we were booked on the same show in Detroit by one of the Motor City's busiest agents, Lenny Borovoy. It was one of the major events of the year, Danny Thomas' St. Judes Hospital Fundraising Dinner, and was held at a fine catering establishment that once was a popular nightclub called The Latin Quarter. It was a black tie affair that featured one of the best known society orchestras in town, plus a three act show consisting of yours truly, Sascha Tormas, and the handsome, gifted singer, Jimmy Randolph, who starred in the leading role of Sky Masterson in the all Black version of "Guys And Dolls" on Broadway. The audience was comprised, almost entirely of the finest of Detroit's Lebanese-American community, something that our pal Sascha never bothered to find out.

After an elegant dinner, and dancing to the melodies of a great sounding band, the lights were lowered as the guests sat back and relaxed. The talented musicians launched into a rousing overture comprised of familiar show standards, which was followed by a dramatic roll on drums, and over the sound system came "Good evening ladies and gentlemen ... Welcome to Danny Thomas' 10th Annual St. Judes Hospital Fundraising Event. Tonight we have put together a wonderful show for your entertainment pleasure, ... and to start the ball rolling we present the magnificent voice and talents of the Broadway star of 'Guys And Dolls' ... the incomparable... Jimmy Randolph!" And on went this tall, extremely well tailored, magnetic singing star, and he, as they say in the business, just "fractured them." I went on next, and it was a very easy assignment for me, especially when the audience had already started tittering as I was introduced. I too, was a big hit!

Now came the closing act, the "piece de resistance," "the supreme musical genius, Sascha Tormas!" He mixed his selections beautifully: show tunes, standards, novelties like "The Hot Canary" (always a big crowd pleaser), a sterling rendition of "The Hungarian Rhapsody," etc., etc., and then the rousing finale, "Exodus." He could do no wrong. He had them all eating out of his hand. First the beautifully arranged prologue, then the haunting and exciting theme, and, at last, the stirring end. When the bow snapped, the expected gasp, then the acrobatic leap into the air, and as the orchestra filled in the last chord with the melody of "Hatikvah," he thrust out his floppy bow in one hand, and magnificent antique violin in the other, and at the top of his voice, never suspecting the ethnic makeup of the audience, he shouted, "Long live Israel!" To this very day, I still cannot remember whether the audience applauded, yelled, or both. All I can recall is the picture of fat little Lenny Borovoy, sweating profusely, charging towards Sascha as he came offstage, grabbing him by the arm and hastily hustling him up the stairs to his dressing room while screaming hoarsely in that unique voice of his, "Let's get da fuck outta here!"

21 Pine View Hotel

Such many and varied club dates constituted the major portion of my work, and was most gratifying, financially, and artistically. Residing on the east coast with my family, I had the advantage of having a place for us all to go in the summer, while remaining steadily employed at the same time. There were those ubiquitous Catskill resort hotels, many of which had even graduated into year 'round attractions. At one time, hard as it may be to believe, it was rumored that as many as four hundred of them, ranging from gigantic to tiny, flourished in that desirable area located around a hundred miles from the "Big Apple." Of course there were county fairs and cruise ships, and a few other alternatives for the entertainers, but why go there when we had "the mountains" as we referred to them.

Whereas, in the beginning, the hotels featured social staffs that stayed all summer and worked feverishly to supply the guests with a variety of entertainment, things were changing rapidly. Someone conceived that bright idea of circulating "packages" of performers from hotel to hotel, and conveniently staggering the showtimes, thereby providing the people with new, and different entertainers on every show night. It was a simple, yet brilliant concept that provided lots of employment to the acts and the agents, both. A great new industry was flourishing, and the owners enjoyed the fact that they no longer had to house and feed large staffs. The entertainers became transients, and they were provided only a free dinner and overnight lodging when desired, and the system really worked out very well.

The only steady entertainment staffs consisted of an orchestra and a likeable, capable Social Director, who could mix well with the people, do a workmanlike job of presenting the acts onstage, and also prepare the weekly entertainment schedule. His most difficult job was to fill in those nights when there were no shows, with novelties like: game nights; dance contests among the guests (often referred to as "Champagne Hours" because of the bottles of that sparkling beverage that were presented to the winners); amateur nights; square dances (where they'd bring in authentic "callers" from the outside); etc., etc. etc. The Social Director was very important and worked hard, long hours because it was his job to keep the paying guests occupied day and night. (Rainy days were "murder.") There were even a handful of entrepreneurs up there whose business it was to present movies at the hotels.

In the past, the dining room staffs and children's counselors consisted of college boys and girls earning tuition money by working summers in the mountains. That too began to change when hotels stayed open all year, and the college kids, who were available in the summers only, were no longer there. This led to an influx of people from the Caribbean and South America, who moved into the nearby towns, with their families, and filled the void. Capable year 'round Social Directors were at a premium. The hotel owners, who really had to practice some legerdemain to keep their places functioning, were content to settle for a good Social Director during "prime time," which, of course, was the summer. The ensuing seasons would have to be attended to when the time came.

Shirley was a premier Social Director. She had learned the craft well from our having worked together during all those early summers. The occasion arose for her to display her capabilities thanks to a unique and interesting deal that I struck with a college professor, who along with his brother, mother, and sister, owned a "different" summer resort hotel in the Catskills. His name was Mickey Lebowitz, and he headed up the Sociology Department at Fordham University, a Jesuit college, in New York. The hotel was called, "Lebowitz' Pine View," and it was located in Fallsburg, NY. What made it "different" was that it was one of the possibly three, Catskill resort hotels that catered to a strictly Orthodox Jewish clientele.

I never knew that Pine View existed until it showed up early one summer on my schedule as I worked the circuit. It surprised me with its rather large capacity, and I'd never before appeared before an audience where all the men wore yarmulkes (skull caps), and, a number of the ladies, because of their orthodoxy, wore wigs. They were extremely well dressed, (even the wigs were highly styled and quite natural looking), and they were, for the most part, younger than the guests at the other hotels. I thought that, because it was a religious crowd, they'd be very stiff and difficult to entertain, but I quickly concluded that, as long as you don't say, or do, anything that was "off-color," or ridicule their beliefs, they could be a very receptive bunch, and I was right. I also noticed, while watching the performers who preceded me onstage, that this group preferred to be treated with respect, and that they were quick to let you know it, if they didn't like you. I must've done well 'cause they booked me back again on Labor Day weekend, which was very important, as it constituted their last hurrah of the summer. I left feeling good, and thankful that I didn't have to spend my summers living with such people whose strict, religious beliefs took precedence in everything they did. It also scared me to see how downright rude many of them could be to the acts they didn't care for. That was really surprising, and, I must say, quite unsettling.

After a subsequent, fruitful year of highly diversified, and mostly exciting club dates, another summer was just over the horizon. It became a ritual for me to work out a deal for all of us to spend our summers in the mountains, and once again I made the rounds of the agents' offices, in quest of such an arrangement. It was not going to be easy this time, as our brood now included three children. It sure as hell wasn't gonna be easy to convince some hotel owner to employ a Social Director who comes with such heavy baggage, in the form of four extra dependents.

Sidney Colton, of Dixie Lake, was more than willing to have me n' Shirley back, kids n' all. However, just around recruiting time, in early May, quite unfortunately, the main building of his picturesque empire somehow caught fire and burned to the ground, leaving that lovable family out of business, not only for the summer, but as it turned out, forever. Bob Zalkin would have loved to have us back again, as we had established such a fine rapport in that one memorable season when I was there with Shirley and only Dan and Andy, but he was well aware of the fact that he really had no staff rooms for a family of our present size, and because his lovely inn was not very large to begin with, it just wasn't cost effective to give up a couple of guest rooms to the Harrises. So, with both Dixie Lake and Zalkin's Birchwood

The Three Musketeers: Dan, Andy, and David
at the Pine View Hotel. (1956)

The whole family. Pine View Hotel. (1962)

Lodge out of the question, (as exciting as it may have been to see if I could pull off a minor miracle and actually find a hotelman who was willing to accept us) I approached the task of getting us set up for the summer with a great deal of apprehension.

Avuncular Jack Segal, the theatrical agent who probably booked more summer resorts than all the others combined, phoned me, and said, "Van, would you be good enough to drop into my office? I have an owner who is interested in you. He's aware of your situation, but he would like to talk with you nevertheless. Could we set up an appointment?" It was then that I met Dr. Milton Lebowitz, known to all of his family, friends, and employees, as "Mickey."

Tall, good-looking, bespectacled, articulate and intelligent, and about eight or so, years my senior, he was a pleasure to converse with. I learned that he was one of the brothers who owned and ran, that very Orthodox hotel where I had done so well, on the previous summer. Having heard from Mr. Segal all about me, he assured me that the hotel was large enough to accommodate us, that is if we were willing to reside in fairly decent "staff quarters," and wanted to know just what sort of monetary arrangements we could equitably arrive at, considering that it's not exactly cheap to feed a family with three growing boys. My offer turned out to be most intriguing to him, and one he found hard to refuse, but, while I was presenting it to him, he asked, as he shrugged his shoulders, "How the hell am I gonna explain it to my brother and the rest?" I said, "Hold on, maybe this whole thing can't work? We are not religious, and not about to change, just to get a job. I've never lived among people who are religious to the extent that your guests are. They look like pleasant enough people, but, with their rules and regulations, we're apt to step on each others toes. My kids and I are not about to wear yarmulkes. If we can get by with rudimentary instruction so that we don't offend anybody, and at the same time no one makes us feel uncomfortable, then maybe we can talk further. But, I really and truly don't know just how suitable it will be for you, your family, your guests and us?"

A great big grin appeared on his face as he began to delineate the situation. "First of all," he began, "I'm not religious myself. Though I was raised in an orthodox family, I do not practice religion. I run the kitchen at the hotel, surrounded by people wearing yarmulkes, except for the Orientals, Blacks, and Hispanics that work there. To pacify my family, I wear a hat, but it's a Luftwaffe cap that I got from one of the POW's we captured when I served in the E.T.O. We have other secular individuals employed who are not required to cover their heads, and just so your boys won't feel like outcasts in our day camp, let them wear baseball caps." That sounded fair enough to me, so I presented him with my demands: "I'll run all your activities for you, both social and athletic, and will hire the staff, including an Athletic Director to work under me, and the orchestra, and whomever else. I don't want any salary. I must be free to run out and work, whenever, and wherever, my agent books me, so that I can make a living. On the nights that I'm not away, and there will be plenty, I guarantee that I will perform, and with the aid of Shirley and the orchestra, and if we bring in a "guest artist," like a singer, an instrumentalist, or any other kind of performer that I might request, you will have excellent shows virtually every evening. You can bring in the "stars" supplied by Mr. Segal on Saturday nights and special occasions, and you will be covered in every respect. I'll try to engage an Athletic Director who is also able to emcee the shows when I'm not there. But, we must be treated with respect. I will not tolerate anyone yelling at me or members of my family, or being treated rudely in any way. Agreed?" He was a bright, intuitive gentleman, very well accustomed to responsibility, and making right decisions. He sensed my sincerity, believed in my ability, and shook my hand, "Agreed!"

The Catskill resorts, then, (and now), with few exceptions, were owned, and sometimes leased by families who were harsh in many ways, insensitive towards their help, and often delinquent in making payments for purchases of food and other merchandise, and even for taxes. Their notorious reputations were legend, and yet, when push came to shove, most of them managed to ante up, but there occurred some terrible and disgraceful failures from time to time that left many a supplier in ruins. Also, their behavior towards their employees oft times left a lot to be desired, but for every crude and crass scoundrel, there were always some gentle and thoughtful souls that were very well respected and loved. One old time waiter up there explained it very succinctly to me, when I complained to him about the boorish indiscretions of some of the hotel owners, "They all had the same mother."

The Lebowitzes were way above average in intelligence. Nat, the older brother, who ran the hotel with his capable wife Evelyn, was a retired high school principal. His sister Ruth was a large, gregarious lady with a delightful sense of humor and a storehouse of knowledge (which was reflected in her colorful young twin offspring, whom we affectionately labeled, "The Katzenjammer kids," after the delightful comic strip characters). She did the bookkeeping and was in charge of all the expenditures. Mickey ran the kitchen and dining room with an iron fist and a no-nonsense, at times very tough, attitude that was grudgingly respected by all the waiters and busboys, who were motivated college kids, working summers to help them get through school, and well on their way to wondrous careers as doctors, lawyers, scientists, educators, or other highly respected professions. Mickey's wife Ruth, a Canadian import, had nothing to do with the running of the place, but her mere presence added a welcome touch of class. Mama (Minnie) Lebowitz, a magnificent octogenarian and widow of Max Lebowitz, a highly regarded, and multi-talented gentleman who founded the hotel, was the titular head of the entire organization. She was loved and admired by everyone and anyone. She brooked no nonsense from anyone. She was an engaging conversationalist, a crackerjack poker player, and the most "dead on" swatter of flies that the rustic Sullivan County area had ever known. (She was rarely seen without an old fashioned fly swatter in her hand or conveniently handy.) All in all, the Lebowitz family was one that was highly impressive, and a refreshing anomaly among the plethora of Catskill entrepreneurs.

The hotel catered to a fairly opulent, "Modern Orthodox" clientele, that is to say, very few of the "shtetl types" with the extreme "black hats, sidecurls, and long black coats," but the guests were fundamentalists just the same. They observed every extreme religious ritual, and were very rigorous in their enforcement. The Lebowitzes, who were very orthodox themselves, with the exception of Mickey and Ruth (and, at times, sister Ruth), believed in "laissez faire," and looked away if a member of the staff would inadvertly violate the canons of the religion that they all cherished so seriously. Everyone respected the Sabbath, kashruth, the very holy days, etc., with a fervor.

We, the select social staff that made the place tick, were almost entirely secular. Everyone knew it, and did not say or do anything to offend us, as we, in return, were mindful and respectful of their feelings and behavior, even though we would, among ourselves, oft times be astonished by examples of extremism we had never before known existed. Not surprisingly, with such a staff of honest, dedicated, fiercely independent personalities, and all smart enough to recognize where we were at, with no need, or desire, to violate the house rules, the hotel was run like a well oiled clock, and the Lebowitzes greatly appreciated it.

I headed up the Social staff and was in charge of all recreational facilities, which meant not only what occurred onstage, but all the athletic activities, including the pool area and our basketball team that included outstanding stars from the various colleges who were working at the hotel in assorted positions (waiters, busboys, bellhops, lifeguards, or counselors). It was essential to field a strong team to compete with the squads from the surrounding hotels, which amounted to, at least, one night a week of exciting entertainment for our guests. Basketball was a huge attraction in the mountains.

We had four extremely well maintained clay tennis courts, the proud domain of Leo and Sue Richling, a fine looking, mature husband and wife duo, who, in addition to being incredibly good players, were superb instructors. They turned the courts into one of the busiest facilities in the hotel. Leo was a product of the New York City public school system where he taught high school "Art."

Our dance instructor, Sam Janus, later went on to become a world renowned psychologist and the author of best selling books on, of all things, "Sexual Behavior" (i.e. "The Janus Report"). He too, had his family with him, and his wife served as his assistant. In ensuing seasons they were replaced by a couple of school teachers, Marty and Dora, the personification of grace on the dance floor.

The people that ran the refreshments and sundries shop were also from the school system. Herman and Peggy

Saunders were loved by all despite the fact that he spoke in a growl and had one of the most unattractive, and oft-times most unfriendly little dogs I'd ever seen. In defense of "Checkers" though, I must point out that he loved children and only flashed those menacing teeth at grownups. Herman was a culinary genius, and a very popular teacher at the New York High School for Food Trades.

We employed Art Instructors who gave daily classes to our guests, and they too were drawn from that vast pool of New York City educators. Stanley and Eileen Marlin went on to become extremely successful Interior Decorators. Dick and Rhoda Klein, their successors, were already well on their way to "Stardom" when they replaced Stanley and Eileen. Dick was the principal of a Bronx high school, and eventually went on to that same exalted position at the NYC High School of Music and Arts, which was later moved into a new building at the Lincoln Center complex and renamed Fiorello H. LaGuardia H.S. (after our long ago famous, and most colorful Mayor). Dick gained further fame as NY's youngest retiring H.S. principal and went on to become Provost of the New World University in Miami, and also a leading consultant in the formation of numerous other such unique fine art and performing art establishments the world over. Eventually the Kleins gave way at the hotel to Larry and Judy Anzelowitz, also dedicated art teachers from a Bronx high school.

Among our troubadours and folk singers who performed daily on our vast front lawn, were Lenny Levine, a tall, versatile, animated buffoon who eventually became an important professional in the entertainment industry, and Herb Gold, who, in addition to accompanying himself on the guitar, was a prolific songwriter. He, later on, moved to southern California and became a famous psychologist, Dr. Herbert Goldberg. His area of expertise was in "Male Behavior," and he appeared on NBC's "Phil Donahue Show" no less than seven times.

I personally hired our Orchestra Leader, a serious and gifted young pianist named Joe Gardner, whom I had discovered playing at some nondescript hotel in Loch Sheldrake a number of years back. Joe came up with an excellent band, and the travelling acts that performed at Pine View were delighted with him. He also provided us with a full-fledged concert every Thursday night. In addition to a "star vocalist" that we imported through our booking agent Mr. Segal, Joe invited musicians from all the surrounding hotels to come and sit in, for free, in a big, symphonic production, for which he orchestrated all the parts. I still remember how nervous I was when he incorporated a simple saxophone part for me while Shirley played the violin, which she had studied when she was a little girl. He went on to play "First Bass Fiddle" with the Indianapolis Symphony Orchestra, and later on held the same position with the Baltimore Symphony Orchestra. In both instances, with the symphony world being what it is, he was forced to become an Encyclopedia Britannica salesman on the side in order to support himself and his young wife. It wasn't until a number of years, and one wife later (in addition to three young children), that he really started to make a living by becoming the pianist and conductor for two outstanding pop singing stars. He also wrote their arrangements. This "stroke of good fortune" succeeded in losing him his family, which, like with so many others in the field, found it impossible to keep up with his peripatetic lifestyle.

On my first important weekend at Lebowitz's Pine View Hotel, July 4th, something happened that set the tenor for our future relationship with the family. It was a balmy summer early evening, and we had moved the piano out on the side terrace, adjacent to the dining room, where the orchestra had been set up so that the diners could go out and dance "under the stars" between courses. A sudden, and unexpected rainfall occurred, and all went scurrying for shelter. The musicians ran inside with their instruments. Even the drummer had to perform quick and assorted acrobatics in order to get his collection of percussion equipment out of harm's way. The large, cumbersome, upright piano stayed however, and got drenched. The rain eventually subsided, and the remainder of the evening was spent indoors where all the action moved to the playhouse area with its grand piano onstage. The upright on the porch, however, remained wet, and wasn't attended to until well after dinner when a couple of busboys rolled it back through the dining room into the lobby.

As soon as the Lebowitz boys had finished attending to their frantic chores in serving up the special holiday dinner, they sought me out. (I was preparing to drive to some other hotel to perform, which was in accordance with our agreement.), They literally read me the riot act about "not seeing to it that the piano was protected during the squall." I was nowhere in sight when the rain had come down. As far as I was concerned, everything was in the hands of the orchestra, also new on the job, and there was absolutely no need for me to have been there. Now both Mickey and Nat cornered me with fire in their eyes, and excoriated me for not taking care of their property. I listened briefly and politely, and explained the situation, adding, "If that's the way you're going to react when an unavoidable disaster like this happens, I think it would be best if we packed up n' went back home. I promised you a full measure, Mickey, but I can't work for you guys if you're gonna treat me like some sort of bimmie." Nat, the older brother, never having actually spoken to me before, turned around and walked away. Mickey quickly turned the conversation into something like, "Sorry, it's been a tough meal and hot as hell in the kitchen," and continued on, "We'll dry the thing out n' get the tuner to look at it in the morning."

Later that evening Mickey and wife Ruth, attended the first big "travelling show" of the season. (I forget who the "headliner" was.) I got back from my show, which, as it turned out, was not too far away, very soon after the Pine View show was over. That was when I inquired how the show had gone over, and Mickey minced no words, employing a couple of choice expletives, in telling me what he thought of the Athletic Director I had hired who had assured me what a great emcee he was. It was in that historic moment that a twenty-five summer future at Pine View was forged. Shirley, in all her glowing beauty and exuberance, with a wondrous wardrobe of evening gowns to boot, was appointed the full fledged emcee, and our Athletic Director spent a part of the season doing what I had actually hired him to do, which was to organize all daytime activities for our guests, and make himself useful whenever, and wherever needed. He left very soon thereafter to go on to what he referred to as "greener pastures." The basketball team remained under my aegis, and very soon I had to release the two "stars," who refused to do their daytime jobs because, as they lamely tried to explain, "Man, we're here to play basketball, n' the rest is window dressing." I replaced them with two terrific young players who had, just coincidentally, come looking for "any kind of a job that would also allow us to play basketball." They turned out to be superb players and assets to our rapidly formulated staff. In fact, they stayed on at Pine View for several seasons. I appointed one of them to captain our basketball team, and it was an excellent choice. Incidentally, one of the "stars" that I had to let go, eventually went on to become a major player in the National Basketball Association, which was good for him and the league, but, to us he was still worthless.

We had a marvelous summer at Pine View with very little conflict, if any. Shirley did magnificently. I had a great number of outside shows, and we were still able to give the Lebowitz family a goodly share of our unique and hilarious "in-house" shows. Our children, sporting their baseball caps at all times, just loved it! The children's day camp, run by a young orthodox couple, Moish and Dinah, both enormously charismatic, witty, and prolific, was the best hotel day camp I had ever seen, and each and every child that had the good fortune of attending, was blessed. They presented original plays and standard fare (that was expertly revised) by those two earnest directors. Our eldest son, Dan, had a preoccupation with sports and nature and science, and received a great amount of each at the camp. Middle son, Andy, already a piano virtuoso (and a favorite student of Joe Gardner) was getting deeper and deeper into dramatics, and had the leading role in all the plays, much to everyone's delight, and particularly his own. Little David and even littler Madelaine, were both very young, but even they were greatly affected by the magical Pine View Day Camp.

Throughout the season, the elder Lebowitz brother, taciturn and very able, and I maintained an arm's length from each other. I felt that he was unsure of my feelings about the religious extremism that was at the center of everything, and he might have assumed that I was merely on good behavior in an alien environment, so very little conversation passed between us. All of the executive staff socializing with management was with Mickey and Ruth, who were as irreligious as we were, and it was a most enjoyable relationship that continued after the summer. At the end of that summer, as I was putting away the assorted sound equipment and other stage accessories, Nat happened to be standing nearby. I casually inquired, "Where would you like me to store this stuff, Nat?" and he replied, "Put it where you'll find it next year." That answer was the catalyst for a relationship that was destined to endure for twenty-five summer seasons.

And so, for the next quarter of a century my schizophrenic existence in show business continued. All year long I played for audiences of assorted stripes and colors, everything ranging from gridiron dinners in Delaware to golf outings in Jacksonville, to the Daughters of Isabella in Boston, to Imperial Oil in Saskatchewan, and so forth and so on. Came the months of July and August it was back to the Jewish womb, the Catskills, and particularly Lebowitz's Pine View, which, thanks to Shirley's dedicated abilities, became our summer home. Our position there was so secure that several times we were even able to take some weeks off to perform on cruise ships in the Caribbean and to Europe. Whether we were there in person, or not, all hotel activities were attended to meticulously.

We were young and strong, and worked terribly hard at times, and our children revelled in the sunshine, surrounded by everlasting friends in the Catskill's greatest day camp. As they grew older, one by one they all went away to sleep away camps where they adjusted beautifully. The only one of our children who had trouble with the sleep-away pattern was our youngest, Madelaine. She had made up her mind that if she wasn't going to like something right away, then she was going to leave. She did that at Camp Anawana, where both Andrew and David had become "Superstars," and we succumbed to her pleas to take her back to Pine View where she virtually grew up. The following summer she attended Captain Carling's All-Girls Equestrian Camp in northwestern Connecticut, and the first week there she pleaded with us on the phone, every day, to take her back home. I decided to give it some time, and she remained there. By the first visiting weekend she had already skillfully mastered the art of English horseback riding (very little saddle, if at all), and she and her favorite horse were daringly leaping over steeplechase fences. She had also become the camp entertainer and comedienne, and was one of the most popular girls in the camp. She loved the place and was ready to go back on the following summer, but by then, Captain Carling had become ill (through no fault of hers), and the camp was disbanded.

Sundays were toughest for us. The hotel was a beehive of activity on that day with guests checking out while new ones were pouring in. The bulletin board had to be in order early in the morning in order that our incoming patrons would be apprised of the entire week's activities. That meant, in addition to laying out our nightly plans, we had to huddle with the theatrical agent, who arrived bright and early every Sunday morning to present his bill for the past week and get paid (in full, if he was lucky). Shirley and I both labored hard the night before. She had her big Saturday night show at Pine View, and I had mine (sometimes as many as three in one night depending upon what the agents were able to work out). We generally met afterwards with the Saunders and the Richlings, and unwound over a fresh cup of coffee at Forim's Pharmacy in South Fallsburg, or at Malman's in Woodbourne, before retiring. We slept fast, and arose early in the morning to get the kids off to breakfast in the children's dining room, and immediately began our hectic day.

My Saturday night jobs were not always in the vicinity. They could have been just about anywhere. There was one Saturday night that I performed in Santa Monica California, at the Santa Monica Civic Auditorium, for Mickey Katz (Joel Grey's illustrious father). I left the hotel on Saturday afternoon. (The car was always parked outside the gates on the Sabbath, as there was no driving permitted on the grounds on the holiest day of the week.) I drove all the way down to Kennedy Airport in Queens. There I met several members of the cast and we flew to L.A. (where it was three hours earlier than our east coast time). We did our show, which was a huge success, and afterwards I caught a "red-eye" back to NY. I drove back up to the mountains where the sky was already starting to get light, slipped quietly into bed where I slept for an hour or two, (luckily my obstreperous little dog Alphye never barked at me, though he flexed his muscles at just about everyone else), and soon the guests were greeting me on their way to the dining room for breakfast while I was assembling the bulletin board in the lobby. In a million years they would never have suspected where I had been during the night. In answer to the question, "How did your show go last night?" I would smile and reply, "Great! Just great!" This happened more than once in the years that I was at the Pine View. If it wasn't California, then it was some other distant place, but I managed to work it all out. Ah ...youth!

In selecting our performers we had to make certain that the comedians' acts were clean, and that no songs were performed that had any anti-Jewish religious overtones. There were always zealots among our guests who would cause a riot if they witnessed anything onstage that they found offensive to their piousness. For years one obnoxious young rabbi kept complaining to management that Shirley should keep her forearms covered when she appeared in those elegant gowns onstage, but Evelyn and Nat Lebowitz kept putting him off by humoring the poor despot.

There was a time when a very popular quartet sang the theme from the hit Broadway show "Jesus Christ Superstar." During the afternoon rehearsal, the piano player pleaded with them to just change the lyrics to "Super Star! Super Star!" instead of using the name "Jesus Christ." No matter how much he tried, he couldn't convince these naive young people that it would cause a disaster if they persisted. That evening they stood on stage, thunderstruck, as the entire audience walked out on them, while some self-styled "Rebbetzin" (female rabbi) stood facing the stage, furiously wiggling a forefinger at them, and upbraiding them for not having the good sense to delete "what is offensive to Jews." This was the stuff that Pine View was made of, and one had to step gingerly around all the rules and regulations in order to avoid such embarrassing confrontations. There was no sense in fighting fundamentalism.

On the holiday called T'ish B'ov, which is the commemoration of the fall of the Temple of Zion in biblical times, and falls out somewhere in the middle of every summer, the Orthodox don't eat meat products for nine days prior to that very holiest of days. Many don't bathe during that time, and many don't wear leather products because they are derived from animals. The men wear sneakers and they don't shave, and the grownups and the children sleep without pillows. This ritual never affected us or our youngsters, but we certainly were made aware of the custom. And, when the big day is over, they celebrate by having a hearty meat meal, and go back to their normal way of life (as normal as their restricted lives can be). After that meal we present a show, which usually consists of one performer, generally a raconteur, a ventriloquist, a puppeteer, or anything in that order. The show would take place in an anteroom to the lobby because a number of our guests would remain upstairs in their rooms attending to what they had neglected to do during those nine holy days, like showering, shaving, etc., etc. Therefore a smaller, more intimate entertainment area was more expedient.

One of the "house toomlers," an above middle aged comedian who resided at a nearby Catskill hotel, implored me to book him into our hotel to perform on that night. I informed him that Mr. Segal does all the booking, but he pleaded with me to put him in and agreed that all monetary arrangements could be made through our agent. I was totally unfamiliar with his work, and, warned him that, because of the nature of our difficult and reserved audiences, he must work "perfectly clean." He readily agreed, adding that he performs only clean, and the stage was set for his debut. Just before showtime he called me aside and uttered, "Look, I work clean, but sometimes the audiences laugh dirty." I couldn't quite comprehend his ambiguous remark, but it was showtime, and I gave him the benefit of having the good sense to do as he was told. I introduced him to the eagerly awaiting audience, and on he went. His opening line was: In Egypt they have built a university and named it after their former king. It's called "Farouk U.!" ... and it was downhill for him after that. I didn't hang around to see how he finished up. I handed the thankless job over to poor Shirley, and walked away, knowing, full well, that there'd be hell to pay on the following day. My work was cut out for me, and, in my mind I began furiously organizing my plan of attack.

I decided to schedule a lecture with audience participation, on the huge front lawn that afternoon. Perhaps the most popular subject that Orthodox Jews love to discuss, in addition to religion, is the State of Israel, so that was the theme I chose. Of course it drew a very large audience, and the contributions from our guests were very knowledgeable. Things were humming along beautifully, and, at what I deemed a "propitious moment," I craftily injected, "And what did you bright and wonderful people think of the show last night?" That question gave birth to a delicious war that went on for some time, with opinions, both pro and con (much more of the latter) reaching a feverish pitch. Among the expressions were: "The management ought to be ashamed to present that kind of crude performer at a hotel of this caliber," while the more forgiving would answer with "Nobody forced you to listen. You've got legs. You could have gotten up and walked out." My staff and I were all smiles as the debate got hotter and hotter. I kept whispering to my Art Director, who was standing alongside of me, "What a wonderful catharsis." At last, one elderly lady, taking it all in while sunning herself at the same time, and who kept waving her hand furiously for all to give her our attention, was eventually recognized. She got up off her chair, drew herself up to her full four feet ten inches, deliberately walked up to a number of the debaters, and in an adorably Yiddish accented voice, summed it all up by reciting, "I heard what you had to say," then turned and repeated, "I heard what you had to say," and went further, "And I heard what you had to say. "I heard what all of you had to say," and then she capped off the entire afternoon's histrionics by exclaiming, "Just remember, everybody's gotta make a living!" It brought down the house.

Our basketball games were very heavily attended by our guests, by guests from surrounding hotels, and by guests from the hotels of the opposing teams. The games were held outdoors on a midweek night, and we had the perfect setup for them. We had a professional size basketball court, located adjacent to the swimming pool. The pool had a strong wire fence all around it, but that didn't keep an errant ball from bouncing over into the pool in the middle of a game on some balmy evening. It would evoke great laughter from the fans sitting in the stands when, invariably, one of our lowly subs, sitting anxiously on the bench, waiting for his brief chance to get into the game, would climb over that enclosure and dive into the pool in his Pine View uniform, in order to retrieve it.

The entire scene was exciting, filled with assorted cheering from both sides in the grandstands, and the children who were old enough to stay up late really considered themselves very lucky. Herman and Peggy Saunders, also had a big night, serving up kosher hot dogs and hamburgers (which was no violation of the kashruth regulations, as dinner, just a few hours earlier, was a meat meal). From their enclosed food shop under the solarium, they also sold lots of other goodies like candy, popcorn, and everything else that went into making it one of the most festive nights of anyone's vacation. Yes, basketball was a staple indeed. Too bad that a few years later the gambling syndicates discovered the summer basketball circuit, and numerous scandals emerged. Players threw games, there was point shaving, and eventually the N.C.A.A. ruled that any college players caught playing summer basketball in the Catskills would automatically be declared ineligible to play for their schools, which also meant, in most cases, a loss of scholarship. The beautiful bubble had ingloriously burst.

Of course each hotel took great pride in its team, and players were recruited from all over the country. The athletes loved the idea of playing and also working and earning money. Klein's Hillside fielded a team comprised of players who were not averse to spewing anti-semitic epithets. During a game between Pine View and Klein's Hillside, one of those giants lost a contact lens on the court and all the players could be seen crawling around on their hands and knees until one of them finally came up with the elusive little culprit. In the meantime, while one of the boys was crawling around, he didn't realize that his shorts had split on the bottom, and it caused quite a stir when the fans gave notice to what was hanging out through the opening.

We beat them in a very close, and emotional game that was marred by fist fights because of the opposing team's belligerence. The game had to be stopped several times. Our center was quiet, soft-spoken, 6' 5" Charlie Rand, who worked as a bellhop, and was the son of a Protestant minister from Northport, L.I. Every time he would go up for the ball, the opposing team would yell, "Get the big Jew under the boards," and they would elbow the hell out of him, even pummeling him below the belt. As he came off several times to rest, bloodied and beaten, and I towelled him off and served him orange slices to chew on. He bewilderedly asked me, "What have they got against me, Mr. Harris?" and all I could answer was, "I guess you're learning what it's like to be a Jew, Charlie."

He was the tallest man on our squad, and little Frankie Townsend was the shortest. Charlie was from Suffolk County out on Long Island, and Frankie had graduated from an inner city high school in Manhattan. Charlie was white and Frankie was black. Both worked as bellhops. Both were extremely good looking. Both were very personable and highly intelligent. Charlie was 6 ft. 5, and Frankie was about 5 ft. 7. Together, and, of course, with the aid of all their other superb teammates, they made up one helluva team. When the very formidable Kutsher's team came to play us, we even beat them. They sported the great Wilt Chamberlain, out of the University of Kansas, at center, but little Frankie ran rings around the big guy that night. What a player he was. You can well imagine my profound grief and chagrin when, some years later, I picked up the NY Post and saw Frankie's picture on the front page. I had lost track of Frankie Townsend after Pine View, and I imagined that, with his superb talent and intelligence, he easily breezed through college on a scholarship. He never made it to the professionals though, and I'm certain it was because of his size. That's the only reason I could think of for what I read on the front page of the Post. I'll never forget the main story, in big red headlines, "Ted Kennedy's Friend Drowns at Chappaquidick in Auto Mishap." The item beneath the headline, that made me cry, was a photo of a handsome, well dressed young man, accompanied by a detective, and the caption read, "Drug Kingpin Sentenced to Twenty Years in Prison." It was our Frankie.

22 Jewish Ways

It would be hard to describe the complexities and diversities that we learned about, concerning the behavior of the Orthodox Jews during our long tenure at Pine View. It was not at all uncomfortable to live there (except towards the end when the European faction began to take hold in greater numbers). The guests, and most of the staff, were basically modern American in every way, and behaved like average Americans, both young and old. We all shared the same love of sports, music, literature, and politics. Our political discussions used to get hot and heavy, but were always of above average intelligence. The only difference in demeanor was evident when religion became a factor. Though they were born in this country, the welfare of Israel seemed to take precedence over just about everything ... Orthodox Israel, that is. It all boiled down to religion being first and foremost on their minds, and that was something we secular ones went along with, and respected, only because we were living in their home. We witnessed a great deal of dogma that, at times, seemed absolutely incredible to those of us who were not steeped in their ways, but we just closed our eyes to all the severity, some of which we found downright offensive. But, in thinking it all over, the assets outweighed the liabilities. Fundamentalism is just that, fundamentalism, and Harry Truman would have summed it all up with, "If ya can't stand the heat, then get outta the kitchen!" It got so that, though I wasn't at all required to do so, I even wore a yarmulke (skull cap) at every meal so as not to invite questions from those who did not know who I was. I did not consider it as any sort of hypocrisy. It went with the territory. It did not change me. The way I looked at it, I was just being respectful. Had I been working for Catholics, or Buddhists, or any others, I would have shown similar respect.

For those not familiar with the workings of Jewish Orthodoxy, it must have appeared strange to see our ever busy red clay tennis courts constantly crowded with players who all wore yarmulkes, while some of the more extreme ladies played in skirts down to their ankles and sleeves right up to their wrists. Even though regular tennis attire was acceptable, the die-hards stood their ground, sartorially, ignoring the fact that their clothing encumbered them, and they looked ridiculously out of place. Shirley had even groomed a number of the ladies to strut their stuff in an authentic French can-can presentation, on stage in our theater, on some of our Saturday nights, and not too many objections were voiced. And even if there were any naysayers, the sight of those beautiful ladies, prancing around in flimsy costumes, kicking their shapely legs high into the air, and pointing their derrieres at the audience in that raucous world famous finale, brought out such hysterical cheers and laughter from the audience that it overshadowed everything. Much, much earlier, that very morning, that same chorus line sat in the synagogue with their heads covered, silently and seriously communing with their God, while being separated from their men ... which was the custom. Yes, Pine View was an education in itself.

For every stern disciplinarian among the rabbis and other elders, and heads of families (and the Orthodox are masters in the art of familial multiplication) there were also true "tsadikim," holy men who were gentle and kind and respectful of the dignity of all. This was best exemplified by our "mashgiach" (the rabbi appointed to ascertain that all dietary laws, and customs, are strictly enforced, which included the separation of meat and dairy utensils) a soft-spoken, elderly, cherubic little gentleman with a well groomed pointy beard. His name was Rabbi Poplack and he brought sunshine into everyone's life. He was the first one up in the morning, and spent the day diligently going about his duties, while dispensing cheer and good will to all who came close to him. Everyone adored him, and especially the children. He was our "poster boy." Say what you will about extremism and other "craziness," he was the one who levelled the playing field. He was the true holy man, and we were privileged to have had him as our representative. Our dear Rabbi Poplack, he really gave the place class. The clergy, like so many organizations, unfortunately, also has its share of pomp and incompetence, therefore it is all the more refreshing to find one as modest and unassuming as our diminutive "surveyor of our silverware," so absolutely loved and respected by one and all.

There were a few other rabbis who left indelible impressions upon us. One was, perhaps, the most gifted athlete I had ever had the pleasure of competing with, and against. His name was Bernard Rubinstein, and his pulpit was the Midway Jewish Center, a large, popular Conservative congregation located in Syosset, Long Island. He was tall, good looking, muscular, intelligent, humorous, and when he vacationed with us, his magnetic personality always managed to draw crowds. I had first met him years earlier, at another hotel, when he was playing on an opposing team in a heated softball game. I covered center field, and each time he came to bat, he drove the ball way over my head. I became so frustrated that I lost my composure several times and hurled a few expletives in his direction. It was then that a teammate of his called me aside and whispered, "Cool it! The guy's a rabbi!" The rumor was that, in his youth he was actually offered a tryout with the then NY Giants (when they played at the Polo Grounds up in Coogan's Bluff) but, unlike some of the few Jewish professional baseball players in the major leagues, he refused to play on the Sabbath, so that took care of that.

We became very close friends almost immediately afterward, Bernie and I, and our wives got to know each other too. He took his calling very seriously, and, for years, he would phone me just before the Jewish High Holy Days, to listen to his wonderfully prepared sermons so that I could give him an honest critique, add or subtract anything, and also inject appropriate humor into them wherever possible. I felt honored, as he was well aware of my "extreme secularism"' and yet he respected my personal beliefs totally. It was a mutual admiration society that lasted for many years. When my dear pal Bernie died of cancer while in his late forties or early fifties, he left behind an envious legacy, in addition to a beautiful wife and three winsome daughters. Shirley and I were grief stricken, as were all who knew and loved this great human being. His was a funeral for all times. Upwards of a thousand mourners swarmed into the towns of Syosset and adjacent Plainview, to pay their respects, with his tearful, loving mother, and two devoted brothers (also rabbis), looking on, in addition to his darling Gladys, and their little girls.

Where have you gone our darling Bernie? We miss you terribly. You were truly one of God's chosen people.

Despite my lack of personal religious adherence, I have rubbed shoulders with clergy and lay persons from assorted denominations with whom I engendered significant human relationships. Among them are some gifted musicians, Charlie and Dorothy Scardino, (he, a first class bassist, and she a renowned pianist), who are both Protestants. I wouldn't trade them for the world. Ditto Tony Sheldon (real name Scelba, and also a genius at the piano), and his devoted wife Edith, two of the most outstanding Catholics I have ever had the pleasure of knowing. Dear, dear Mary DiCara, the caring wife of banker Sam, who I met when I did an interesting tour for the South Dakota Bankers Association. Both Sam and Mary are Chicagoans of note. She marched barefoot in some sort of Catholic ritual in church, to pray for our son Dan's recovery while Dan was lying in the hospital in Riverside, California, having been critically injured in that plane crash. I even had the good fortune to sit at the dais at a costume jewelry affair that I performed at in Providence, R.I. with the then Provost of Providence College, a Jesuit school. His name was Father Murray, and he was my height and weight, and appeared to be exactly my age. We sat and discussed our respective youth, and upbringing, and, from the sound of things, we could have been twins. Both from different ethnic backgrounds, and both from entirely different regions, and both a million miles apart religiously, and yet we had so much in common that it was eerie. It was one of the most interesting, and memorable experiences that I could ever remember. We all have a great deal to learn about each other. Unfortunately, in our mad scramble to survive, we rarely ever get the opportunity. I am all the more grateful for being part of a profession that has opened such a window into the world for me.

If one wants to be elected to high public office in the city of New York, or even the state, for that matter, it is essential that he, or she, carries the Orthodox Jewish vote. It constitutes an enormous block of voters who come out to vote, and generally vote as one, and has had very strong effects on all past elections. That is not to imply that the Orthodox Jews, apart from their secular brethren, who, as a rule, are independent voters, control the elections, but, as all politicians are aware of, they have a very strong voice, and should be courted. I recall the time that handsome, debonair John Lindsay (perhaps a little too liberal for their tastes, as the Orthodox tend to be conservative) was running for Mayor of NYC, and it was incumbent upon me to walk him around that huge lawn where our guests assembled, and introduce him personally to all, then follow up with a flattering introduction, from which he launched into a well prepared speech. His good looks and boyish charm ("If you've got it ...flaunt it!") carried the day, and, in fact, helped sweep him into office. Mr. Lindsay rather enjoyed the manner in which he was treated that afternoon, and, as we dined afterward, he thanked me and added, "Any time I can be of any help to you, feel free to call." I took it as just another offhand political promise, but during the time he served as Mayor, I had the occasion to bump into him at various political affairs that I performed at, and I must say, he had an acute memory, and greeted me like an old friend.

I came close to having to call him only once: Our friend, Eddie Hershman (he and his brother were the owners of Goya Guitars), and his wife, were leaving on a vacation aboard the cruise ship, S.S. France, from New York. Shirley and I went to see them off. It was a lovely late spring day, and the west side pier was swarming with people. I had to make a phone call to check in with my agent, so I asked Shirley to go ahead and told her I would meet her aboard that huge luxury liner, in the Hershman's cabin. When I got through with the call, I looked for a way to board the ship and somehow managed to get lost, and wandered aimlessly through what looked like a large airplane hangar until I actually found myself practically standing on the edge of the Hudson River itself. I realized that I had made a mistake and turned around to go back, when I was startled by a tall, husky middle-aged man who approached me. He quickly confronted me with, "What the hell are you doing here?" I smiled, hoping to get a similar reaction from him, but did not. I thought it was obvious that I was just a visitor who had lost his way. "I'm lost," I quietly replied. "How do I get onto the France?" Instead of helping me, he scowled, "D'you realize that you're in a classified area? How did you get through security?" Instead of allowing myself to be intimidated by him, my comedic mind prompted me to quip, jokingly, "If a guy like me can get through just like that, it gives you an idea of how good your security is." Instead of laughing, the big lug flashed a badge and instructed me, "Come with me." Having nothing to fear I tagged along until we got to the front of the enclosure, the point where I had entered, and we were met by another burly giant. "What's up?" inquired the other man. I was getting the feeling that this ridiculous game was getting too serious, and that these two terrible examples of New York's Finest, in plainclothes, were starting to toy with me. "Goldberg here, is questioning our security." "Goldberg?" I thought to myself, and immediately saw red. Maybe it's because I'm soft spoken, and I displayed a sense of humor that he automatically assumed that I was Jewish. Guess he's not accustomed to meeting people like that in his line of work, and if he was going to hurt somebody, perhaps the way he was conditioned, it would be more fun to hassle a Jew. The second man also took out a badge, placed his large hands upon my shoulders, looked me square in the eye, and commanded, "Let me see some I.D." I pictured calling my friend, the mayor, or going there in person to report these two bastards, and that kept me surprisingly sanguine. Instead of complying, I did a quick about face and his hands dropped off my shoulders and I walked straight ahead, out onto the street, without looking back. Not a peep from either of them, nor any attempt to follow me. "Goldberg?" I kept saying to myself over and over again, "Those filthy anti-Semitic bastards! Trying to scare me, ... and they're cops!" My knees suddenly got weak as a delayed reaction, and I talked myself into remaining poised as I finally found my way aboard ship and onto the Hershman's cabin. Shirley greeted me with, "What's the matter, you look pale?" I looked at her, the Hershmans, and several other well wishers that had assembled, and said, "Please sit down, everybody. I have a story to tell you."

In another election campaign Mario M. Cuomo was not as lucky however. To the best of my recollection it was a primary race for the mayoralty, and, as charming and impressive as that eloquent young man was, the odds that day were against him. It was a dark, cloudy afternoon that had followed a rainy morning, and the guests, having been indoors for a part of the day, had anticipated that the weather was going to change for the better, so they towelled off the lawn chairs, took out their newspapers and their assortment of chessboards and scattered around in the fresh, but still moist air. They were all very polite to this fairly unknown, swarthy young Italian-American with the engaging smile and surprisingly intellectual demeanor, responding amiably to his eager handshake, and waiting to hear what he had to say. The gods conspired against him that afternoon, for, no sooner had he launched into his prepared speech, when the skies opened up and a sudden rainstorm sent just about everyone scurrying for cover. He, in his business suit, and I (in a warmup suit, or shorts and a t-shirt, I don't recall which), both held our ground as the rain's intensity lessened, and resumed, alternately, as he determinedly continued on. Huddled under trees and overhangs from buildings, they intensely tried to catch every word he was saying, despite the odds against him, and I watched him go right through to the end, with the rain rolling from his forehead down to his nose, and dripping into the puddle which he was now standing in, hell bent upon getting his point across, while his shoes were starting to curl. It was a most empathetic sight and he was greeted with enthusiastic applause (little did we then suspect that we were listening to a young man who would some day go down in history as one of the great orators of our time). No, Mario didn't win that year, but he certainly won over some fans, I, most assuredly among them.

23 "Yo Dawg is Dead"

Rabbi Poplack may very well have been the first one up in the morning, but the kitchen staff, headed by Mickey Lebowitz (Luftwaffe cap and all), surely had to be right behind him, so as to get the hotel ready for another busy day. We resided in the former main building of the Pine View, a three-story relic that had been moved up the hill, and replaced by a newer structure that was built on the same spot where it once stood. The old "main" was now "executive staff quarters," and, for the love of us, we could never quite figure out how, or why, guests would have paid good money to spend vacations housed in such a slum. Such quarters for staff were not atypical in the Catskills, and we all accepted it, as long as the rooms were clean and the beds were made, with the linens changed, regularly, by the housekeeping staff. The walls were cracked, with the wood lathe actually showing through in various parts, but the building was sturdy, and presumed safe. There were not enough closets for our clothing, so we had no trepidation about hammering large nails in the walls, to hang Shirley's large assortment of gowns, in addition to my stage attire and other various and sundry items. As we boasted to our neighbors (the Art Director and family; the dance instructors and family; etc.), who also did the same thing, "It added charm to our surroundings." The children thought this was all "sensational." They loved it.

Our "suite" faced the front of the building, and the side, which was situated on a part of a hill and had a fire escape. The entire building looked down upon the rear end of the kitchen, which might as well have been the rear end of a cow. We all joked about the ambiance, but considering the amount of time we all actually spent in our rooms, it truly didn't matter too much. We were all up in the country with its heaping supply of fresh mountain air, and we loved it.

Early one Saturday morning, after I had performed at another hotel the night before, and had gotten back quite late, I was awakened by the sound of desperate choking, and a loud, grating voice, with a deep southern accent, yelling, "Van Harris ... Wake up! ... Yo dawg is dead!" The voice grew louder as it kept repeating that same message, over, and over.

It took awhile to get out from under my slumber and put my thoughts together. I managed to quickly slip into a robe and rush out on the fire escape where I saw our mutt, Alphye (his name now spelled fancy because I had been training him for use in my act onstage), hanging from the fire escape on his chain, barely a sound coming from his throat, and in the last jerking moments of life. I immediately released the chain and he tumbled to the ground where he remained stiff and motionless. I realized that Shirley, in her desire that the dog wouldn't wake me early, had gotten up out of bed and put him on his chain leash, which she attached to one of the vertical bars on the fire escape. In her stupor she did not realize that she had placed the chain in the "choke" position, and after she had gone back inside, the playful pup fell through the bars and had hanged himself. The voice that roused me belonged to Johnny Bizell, a happy-go-lucky, very black, and very bald young man, with gold front teeth, who was Mickey Lebowitz's right hand man in the kitchen. Mickey had, just coincidentally, walked out into the back very soon after Alphye had fallen through the bars, saw him dangling, and yelled for Johnny to go quickly and rouse Van Harris. Johnny's loud, raspy voice certainly had its effect. In fact Alphye might even have heard it, despite his condition.

As Alphye lay there, apparently dead to the world, and I stood by helplessly, Herman Saunders, the "candy store man," who was out walking his ugly dog, Checkers, came rushing over and I pleaded with him to help me. He quickly turned Alphye over on his back, and started to press hard on his chest. Alphye, surprisingly, responded, and labored to breathe, while all the while, blood and bile came gushing out of his mouth. I rushed down to the lobby, grabbed the Sullivan County telephone book, looked up the local veterinarian, who was located about fifteen, or so, miles away, apologized for awakening him so early in the morning, and described what just had happened. He instructed me to wrap the dog in a warm blanket and get him right over to his office, "the sooner the better." It was the Sabbath, and my car was all the way down the hill, outside of the hotel gates, which were closed on Saturday. I wrapped Alphye up in a blanket, and charged down the hill with the poor, sick little dog in my arms, still gagging and coughing up blood, while Shirley stood on the fire escape in her robe with tears rolling down her cheeks.

The good doctor was ready and waiting, and came through like a champion. He concluded that Alphye had cheated death by a whisker, gave him a massive injection of an antibiotic to ward off infection, and advised me to keep the little guy warm, and under wraps for a few days. "He'll tell you when he's feeling perky again." Alphye recovered quickly enough and life at Pine View continued, but Alphye, with whatever went on in that canine head of his, from that moment on, would forever associate the sound of Johnny's voice with a frightening time in his life, and he would bare his teeth, bark furiously, and pull on his leash with all his might in an effort to go after him. Oft times, when we were out of the building, we would attach Alphye's leash to a long rope, and tie him to a post in front of the building. He was playful and posed no threat to anyone, and especially the children, who would stop to pet him. But, when we heard him display anger, we knew that Johnny was somewhere nearby (as he entered and exited his major place of business, the kitchen, through the back of the hotel, which looked up the hill at our quarters).

Johnny was a friendly, happy-go-lucky young man, who smiled a lot, laughed a lot, and talked a great deal. Very soon after the near fatal incident, I found Johnny and thanked him for saving my dog's life. He reacted with a mammoth smile that accentuated those 32 kt. gold front teeth, and poo-pooed. "T'was nuthin' ...really nuthin'," I replied, "Don't be so modest, Johnny, I'm gonna give you a reward." One night during the following week I had a club date somewhere in the Big Apple, and stopped off at home where I plucked an unopened bottle of J&B Scotch out of the liquor closet, and also picked out a very slightly used maroon colored suit out of my clothes closet. I wear my suits only onstage, and rotate them frequently, so they never get very worn. I sized Johnny up and figured that he was exactly my height and weight, or very close to it. The following day I presented Johnny with the suit and the bottle of "hootch," and I thought he would faint from the excitement. That following Saturday night I had a show to do nearby, so I was leaving the hotel after dinner, and, as I stood in my room, packing, and preparing to go all the way down the hill to my car, I watched Alphye suddenly go crazy as we both heard that familiar raspy voice calling out to me, "Van Harris!" "Van Harris!" I stepped out on the fire escape, and there stood Johnny, at the bottom of the hill behind the kitchen. He had already gotten through working and was all dressed up in that maroon suit, and was carrying the bottle under his arm. When he saw me, his smile and his eyes lit up the night, as he waved the bottle in his hand to show it to me. He was heading out to "downtown South Fallsburg," which had a fairly large black population. Apparently he had a date, and he was in his Sunday best and rarin' to go. Once more he called out, "Van Harris!" and as I acknowledged him, standing there, all "spiffed out," he waved the bottle once more and bellowed, "Mmmm! Mmmm! ... Ah hope yo dawg do it again!"

There were many times that summer when I heard Alphye go nuts while I was in my room and he was tied up outside. I knew that Johnny couldn't be too far away, and, sure enough, there came the familiar sound of his unique voice. He was smart enough to stand far enough away, so that Alphye, couldn't get close enough to take a bite out of him, and I'd always hear him seriously trying to make friends with the angry mutt. He'd keep reminding him with conversations like, "Alphye, why do you hate me? I saved yo life." I found myself laughing hysterically when I overheard him, after numerous attempts at conciliation throughout the long summer, finally throw in the towel, in disgust, and exclaim, "Yo foget ah saved yo life, Alphye," ... and then a thoughtful pause, and ... "Ah shouldda let you die!"

Our postal address was "Fallsburg," which consisted of one post office, a barbershop and an Italian restaurant. The village of South Fallsburg, which was located just four miles away, was the busiest little town in all of Sullivan County. In its heyday, the four block span that made up the main street, boasted three drugstores, a liquor store, a shoe store, two or three very busy restaurants, a bar and grill, a shoe repair shop, a bank, a movie theater, a post office, and, right next to it, the police station. In those halcyon days, considering the concentrated amount of hotels and bungalow colonies that were situated between the two towns, South Fallsburg was the hub, and a beehive of activity from early morning throughout the night. Those that lived in the rundown, ramshackle apartments on the outskirts of the town were people of color, the families of mostly unskilled hotel workers who had migrated up there when all the many resort hotels were humming. Now, with so many closures constantly occurring, unemployment was rapidly proliferating, and the welfare rolls were having a disastrous effect upon the local taxpayers. Meanwhile, those poor souls, heads of families who seriously wanted to work, were forced to sit around idly and watch their children become affected by the horrible vagaries produced by poverty. There were drugs, and drunkenness, and prostitution, and, of course, crime, fighting, and arguments that sometimes reached horrible proportions. Good natured Johnny, with that ever present smile in addition to that sunny disposition, worked at Pine View for about three or four summer seasons, until he had the supreme misfortune of having gotten into a meaningless dispute in town one hot summer night and he was beaten severely. It must have been quite serious because we had heard that he had to be sent to the hospital. No one knows, for sure, whatever happened to Johnny after that fateful beating, as he never came back to the hotel again. Such mindless savagery. Not only did it inflict untold suffering upon a poor soul, but it succeeded in leaving a rather large void in all our lives. After that, every time I'd hear Alphye bark outside the house, I'd run to the window to see if it might be Johnny standing there, but to no avail.

Not all of our guests were Orthodox. A number of them came back year after year because there was an awful lot to enjoy at Pine View. The facilities were quite good; the social staff was excellent; the athletics were many and varied, with a large emphasis on tennis and basketball; the swimming pool was large and well maintained; the food was excellent and the dining room service quite good; the children's day camp was superb; and the theater presented the same talented performers that were seen in most of the other good hotels, including the "giants," Grossinger's and The Concord. The only exceptions were the handful of extremely high priced superstars that only the huge hotels could afford. My personal secular friends vacationed there because Shirley and I were there, and they always had a great time, especially with the personal attention we gave to them. Dave and Martha

Gincel, whom we had met many years before at one of the other hotels, were, by now, an older couple, but they savored every precious moment of their annual two-week summer vacation with us. They were childless, and Martha was content to bask in the sun on that great lawn, converse with the other guests, and enjoy other people's children, including our active brood, vicariously. Dave, on the other hand, even at his advanced age, was still a crackerjack athlete who participated in everything. Years back he was a shortstop on our hotel softball team, and a damn capable one at that. The years had not slowed him down. Our sons, who knew him well, used to get such a kick out of watching this grey haired gentleman, in his seventies, hustle some unsuspecting young athlete into a friendly game of 5-3-1 on the basketball court, for money. Dave would stand around the court, alone, purposely handling the ball awkwardly while waiting for some unsuspecting sucker to come along. He'd actually entice his opponent by missing a few baskets the first time he had the ball, and, once his adversary ran up a little score and the ball was eventually delivered back to Dave, then the old timer would roll up his sleeves and proceed to toss every ensuing shot right through the basket with such precision that the ball would barely make a ripple in the net. Soon a crowd would gather, and cheer wildly as the old man took on all comers, even those who seriously thought they could outplay him. He would handily annihilate each and every one of them. He was a pistol, our Dave, a picture of athletic grace, a most unforgettable character if there ever was one.

Joe and Evelyn Force were among the most famous of the elite group of family photographers that reigned supreme on the Grand Concourse in the Bronx, which was then still the jewel of all the Jewish enclaves in the city of New York. Joe and Evelyn were not religiously inclined but they were constantly in demand for weddings, bar mitzvahs, and the likes, by the entire Jewish population, and also those gregarious Italians along Arthur Ave. They both had an excellent sense of humor, and, through their business, they were minor celebrities wherever they went. They loved Pine View and vacationed there often, and hung out with us, the executive staff. Joe was a lifetime smoker, and he had reached the stage where the dread disease of emphysema was already starting to destroy him. His doctors forbade him to smoke any longer, and Evelyn watched him like a hawk to make certain that he obeyed, but poor Joe was so hooked that he'd hide anywhere to "cop a smoke," wherever and whenever he could.

We were all sitting in the stands, watching a basketball game one exciting summer evening, and Joe was cheering more rabidly than most. It was so nice to witness the great pleasure he derived from rooting on our Pine View gladiators. Came halftime we all got up and stretched our legs and walked around a little. The second half began, and Joe was ominously missing. We peered around to see if he had, perhaps, taken another seat, but he was nowhere to be found. About 150 yards or so, up the hill, there stood several enclosed, old-fashioned toilets to accommodate those, especially the people at the swimming pool, who didn't feel like walking all the way to the main building to relieve themselves. I had a feeling that he might be in one of those stalls and wandered over just to satisfy my curiosity. As I got close I heard violent coughing interspersed with a hollow sounding, desperate call for help, and quickly opened the door to where the noise was coming from. There was Joe on the floor, his lit cigarette smoldering nearby on the ground, and he was gasping for air. I hurriedly pulled him out. By this time, Evelyn and Shirley, and a few others who had been following my movements in the dark, rushed over to help. We managed to resuscitate him, but the poor soul was so debilitated after that, that Evelyn had to take him back to the Bronx the very next day to see the doctor.

The following winter Joe had gotten a lot worse and was taken to St. Joseph's Hospital in Woodhaven, Queens. At that time Shirley and I were booked to work on a cruise ship in the Caribbean, and, just before we left, I called Evelyn at home to inquire as to how Joe was feeling. She told me that his emphysema had gotten a whole lot worse, and that the medics at St. Joe's informed her that people with his breathing disease could not withstand surgery to try to clear their lungs, as they cannot tolerate anesthesia. They suggested that she save her money, and take him out of the hospital, "He'd be happier dying at home."

We couldn't get Joe out of our minds throughout our cruise, and one afternoon, while sitting around on the deck and chatting with a psychiatrist couple from NY (Dr. and Mrs. Claire) whom we had befriended, Joe's plight crept into our conversation. The male Dr. Claire advised me that he knew all about the inability to apply anesthesia in such cases, but he had a colleague at Flower Fifth Ave. Hospital, named Dr. Ernst Rockey, who had had a great deal of success in treating that illness. He described him as a middle-aged, bald-headed surgeon who spoke with a Hungarian accent and who looked like Otto Preminger. The procedure he used was to first hypnotize the patient and while he was under hypnosis, Dr. Rockey would cut a fenestration into the base of his neck, which, once healed, would allow a sterile tube to be pushed down into his lungs, and whatever was accumulated as a result of the lung's having lost its elasticity, would be suctioned into a special receptacle machine. That procedure would be repeated as often as needed, and would offer untold relief. We immediately contacted Evelyn, and she arranged for an appointment for Joe to see Dr. Rockey.

The unique operation was performed and it added an additional five or six years to his life. Of course his quality of life was greatly diminished, but they both did manage to salvage some sort of livable existence. Whenever I appeared on Johnny Carson's "NBC Tonight" show, I knew that Joe was in bed watching, so I'd manage somehow, to communicate with him surreptitiously. For example, if I told a funny story in which I had to mention a street address, I would say something; "So the guy jumped into the cab and said take me to 2200 Morris Ave. in the Bronx!" That was Joe's address, and he knew that I was saying hello to him in our own sneaky way. If a character in a story needed a name, "Joe" was always a good choice.

As time went on, Joe's condition deteriorated to the point where poor Evelyn had to carry him whenever he wanted to get out of bed and move about. He and she never lost their sense of humor though. When things had reached their nadir, Joe was admitted to Flower Fifth, and Shirley and I came to visit him. His devoted wife was holding his hand while he was lying there and laboring to breathe with the suction machine at the side of his bed attached to his throat with tubes, working overtime and churning like a steamboat. He managed a smile when he saw us walk in, and pointed to a pad and pencil that was lying nearby on the table. I handed him the pad and pencil, and he scribbled the words, "How are the children?" and handed the pad back to me. I took the pencil and wrote back, "The kids are fine," and showed it to him. He quickly grabbed the pad and pencil out of my hands and wrote, "Schmuck, I can hear! I can't speak!" Joe Force died later that night, no doubt with a big smile on his face. He managed to get in the last laugh, he was so good at that.

It's hard to imagine that we spent twenty-five summers at Pine View, and all that after a one season "tryout" on alien turf. An awful lot went on during that era, and the business of adjusting from a Jewish summer to a universal existence, year after year, for all those many, many years, one would think would be a draconian feat. Yet it was easy as pie, and as natural as breathing. It helped make my life and the lives of my beloved family that much more interesting. Of course, as the children grew older they all went their separate ways, but they were so much more worldly and sophisticated thanks to our experiences. To go on about our children would require a whole other book, so I'll leave that to them, in the hope that they will be kind to me in their reminiscences. I have no doubts whatsoever as to what they will say about their astounding mother, whom my friends have facetiously dubbed, "Mama Teresa," after that saintly nun who, just coincidentally shares her very same birthday.

As for Pine View, as with everything else, the climate changed. We started to get a different clientele, and in this age of fundamentalist revivalism, it became impossible for us to live there any longer. Newer, ultra-ultra religious guests started to vacation there, many from Europe, and quite a few with what I call "a shtetl mentality" A lot of the newcomers were not all that well versed in English and couldn't comprehend the humorous nuances in an American comedian's repertoire. Some of the mothers, and particularly the grandmothers, came here with eastern European customs and habits that I personally found offensive. I got tired of admonishing some of our newer guests to take their baby grandchildren up to our indoor bathrooms to urinate instead of having them piss off to the side of the pool. We have been to Israel quite a few times, and I consider myself to be very fortunate that we consider some of our Israeli brethren among our dearest friends. The whole world rightfully admires how the inhabitants of Israel rose from the ashes and created that magnificent and historical homeland. Yet, I had the occasional misfortune to try to accommodate the few boorish, obnoxious Israelis that decided to come to Pine View on vacation, and it was a trying, oft times impossible, and thankless chore. Perhaps they had to be tough to survive, but not while they were on vacation in the Catskills.

The Russians are to be admired for having endured communism, and survived Stalinist terrorism, and for having sacrificed so much and stood up so valiantly against the Nazi hordes, not only from Germany and Austria, but even from their own savage country. So very many now reside here in our great free nation, but I think I would die if I had a steady diet of them as audiences. It never ceases to amaze us all how quickly these new American citizens succeeded, and a good number of them now populate the Catskills. They have brought with them their own customs and cultures, and they deserve their own entertainment. American comedians and foreigners, like the Russians, are not a mix, and I, for one, do not wish to expend the time and energy that it requires to bridge the virtually impossible gap. Bless them all, I'm not interested in trying to entertain them. And from where I'm looking, they are rapidly becoming a force in the mountains, and the glorious Catskills as we once knew them, are no longer. They are forever changed. The king is dead. Long live the king! Oh yeah?

24 Changing Stables

I continued my hectic career as (at the risk of sounding immodest) "The King of Club Dates," gave it my all (up to my very last ounce of energy) and loved every waking moment. I became hot! People in the business were talking about me, many with praise and admiration, and always those with envy. Of course, there were also detractors, but that's to be expected in an industry inundated with perniciousness. A number of agents were looking to spirit me away from Nat Dunn and Co., and were promising me the moon. I loved the life I was leading, as it gave me comfort, money (never the astronomical amounts that the big stars got, but enough for me and my family to live comfortably on), and, more importantly, the opportunity to watch my beloved children grow up. We resided in lovely homes, in nice neighborhoods, always drove a good automobile, and I wore super clothes onstage. We had many good friends and gave some damn good parties. I remained loyal to my friends, including my dear pal "F.M." and his wife Natalie. Inevitably we lost touch with some of the boys n' girls that we grew up with (like those in my old athletic club, "The Hurons," where, for awhile, guys like Alvino would occasionally sound me out).

I never failed to show my respect to those old timers who were my mentors at Dubrow's, and especially Barney, who was rapidly getting older, and besieged by personal problems. Barney never married. He had an identical twin brother named Monty, and adored him. Monty had a wife and young son, and "Uncle Barney," with his crazy, uninhibited antics, (like donning that Frankenstein mask when paying the highway tolls and scaring the hell out of the toll collector, while, at the same time, blurting out "Two adults and a baby!"), endeared himself to all. One day Monty's wife decided to walk out on him, with the little boy. This struck a nerve in poor, disappointed Monty's brain, and shattered his self esteem. He moved in with his bachelor brother Barney, and Barney took good care of his distraught twin. One afternoon Monty said, "Barney, I've run outta cigarettes. Do me a favor and run downstairs to the candy store and pick up a pack for me." The devoted Barney complied with his request. He wasn't gone very long, but long enough to allow Monty to fulfill a deranged plan. When Barney returned to his cramped apartment he could never have anticipated the devastating shock that awaited him. In the short while that Barney was gone, his twin brother Monty had hanged himself! Barney would never forgive himself for having left Monty alone like that. In one brief moment his entire life became shattered. After that, Barney would never be the same again.

Barney suddenly detached himself from everybody and everything. He rarely went out into the street, didn't answer his phone calls, and just plain disappeared. I recall bumping into a mutual friend and inquiring, "Georgie, has anybody seen Barney lately?" and Georgie replied, "I came across him on Schenectady and St. Johns. I said hello and asked him how he was doing, but he never acknowledged me. Just kept rolling his eyes around as though he didn't recognize me. I'm afraid that poor Barney has lost his mind." Very soon after that I heard that Barney had been sent away to Pilgrim State Mental Hospital, out on L.I., and we were all very saddened by the disheartening news.

During the following four or five years I continued to work fast and furiously, and I thought of poor Barney often. I really missed him and his zany antics. Many performers would ask me where my funny sidekick was. I told them the truth, and they too were extremely sympathetic. We would meet on club dates, and between rehearsals and showtime we would sit around and reminisce about the many times, and many ways, in which he used to make us all laugh. For example, when we worked banquets there were always a number of "no-shows." Barney, who had accompanied me to work, would stroll out into the dining area and find an empty seat n' sit himself down and eat. His tablemates would stare at this slim, sallow looking individual with the pock marked face, slicked down hair, and bloodshot eyes, and wonder who the hell he was. At such affairs people are not necessarily seated with others whom they know, so they're reticent about asking questions. They generally introduce themselves, then go about eating and conversing. We, the show people, would peer through the stage curtain and watch, in hysterics, as he would first, remove his hat, revealing a small, striped prison skullcap that he had been wearing underneath, then turn his head away very quickly and insert a tiny flashlight bulb into one nostril, so that it looked like he was in need of a napkin or a handkerchief to wipe his nose. He would stare straight ahead, impassively, and devour his meal while the others at the table would look on, shocked, and in disbelief. No one had the nerve to ask him to leave, as no one was certain whether or not he belonged. In that way, Barney, the bachelor, would obtain for himself, an excellent meal, without anyone suspecting that this guy was a free loader. After awhile some of the booking agents caught wise to my funny friend's exploits and warned me not to bring him along on club dates anymore, while other, more imaginative, and fun loving agents, figured, "Let him come! He's not really hurting anyone, and he's so outrageously funny." We all really missed Barney when he became ill and wondered when, or if, he'd ever come back.

In the meantime thanks to a kindly booking agent named Herman Fialkoff, I was doing more radio on WHN's "Caravan of Stars," and rubbing shoulders with extremely talented actors who added immeasurably to the colorful and unique historical and philosophical vignettes that the show presented in one action packed hour every Sunday at noon. Its producer, Sholem Rubinstein, plucked me out of his vast collection of performers to emcee a brand new ethnic TV variety show that he had put together called "Club Tel Aviv." It was sponsored by Pabst Blue Ribbon Beer and appeared on station WATV. We were on one afternoon a week, and the show ran for a year. Our guest artists were from all over, and it made for some very interesting TV viewing. I was really coming into my own.

Early one Saturday morning I received a surprise phone call at home. It didn't take more than a moment for me to recognize the voice, and I yelled, "Barney! Where the hell are you?" "I'm at my sister's," came the excited reply. "Y'know, I've been away, but I'm okay, and back again. Any chance of seeing you soon?" "Great chance, I answered, "I've got a gig at the Hotel St. George in Brooklyn tonight. How would it be if I picked you up around six?" "Great!" he said, "This is where she lives," and he filled me in with the details.

He was dressed and waiting outside when I pulled up to the house, gave me a good, hardy handshake, hopped into the car, and off we went to downtown Brooklyn. We talked all night, before the show and afterwards, and a few of the other performers who had recognized him were delighted to see him back. "Y'know, it's been quite a few years." "Yes I know," I nodded. "I saw you on television briefly while I was there," he continued. "They had the TV on and were twisting the dial. I caught a glimpse of you and yelled, 'Hold it, that's my friend Van,' but y'know, they were all nuts, and wouldn't listen. I did catch more of you some time later on. Hey, you were pretty damn good." I said, "Thanks Barney, comin' from you that's quite a compliment," and we continued to catch up into the wee hours of the morning. "I'll tell ya somethin'," he confided, "after Monty died I crawled into a shell and didn't wanna come out of it. I didn't want to talk to anybody or see anybody. I'd sometimes be standin' on the street, and if anybody I knew would pass by and try to say hello, I would just stare straight ahead and roll my eyes around in my head."

Barney would accompany me to work from time to time thereafter. It was like old times, except that he couldn't sponge on his sister, so he had to go out n' get a job. Jerry Jacobs, the exterminator, put him on as his assistant, and from then on he was dubbed, "Barney The Ratcatcher" in our Runyonesque neighborhood. I did confer with him often enough, but his work and the effects of his recent illness tired him out and he had to ration his nightlife somewhat. Eventually, as he grew older, he virtually disappeared. I would inquire from mutual friends if they had seen him, and if so, how was he doing? Fyvush Finkel, who, along with his highly intelligent wife, a social worker, was in the midst of raising a couple of very talented sons, would report to me on Barney's whereabouts from time to time. Fyvush, was a product of the Yiddish theater (He was one of the "younger set.") He was busy performing in national companies of "Fiddler On The Roof," playing every important role from "Lazer the Butcher," right up to the leading role of "Tevye." He was from our neighborhood, and was extremely gregarious and very well liked. "Run into Barney lately?" I inquired of him, after not having seen Barney in a rather long time. "Yeh," was Fyvush's reply (he had an intoxicating grin on his face whenever he spoke, which was his trademark). "He's left the area. He was living in an apartment, all alone, on Kingston Ave., and he's been mugged several times. Whoever it was, hurt him, but didn't kill him. This last time, his brother-in-law got disgusted and insisted that he leave the place. They moved him down to Florida to the old Blackstone Hotel. It's a residential hotel in South Beach that's gone to seed somewhat, but it's not expensive. Barney is now living there."

Several years later, while I was in the midst of a run at the condos in the Miami-Fort Lauderdale area, we went out to dinner one evening with our dear friends, Ben and Sylvia Ripka. Ben had once had a very successful cleaning and laundry business in the wealthy and fashionable Sutton Place section of Manhattan, and he had recently retired to Lauderhill. There were many prominent theater people among his high-class clientele, and he made certain to put my theatrical brochures into each and every one of his completed bundles. Talk about Public Relations. Anyway, we decided to go way downtown in Miami Beach, and had a scrumptious meal at the Famous Restaurant on Washington Ave. It was a lovely, balmy night, and as we stepped out of the restaurant my eyes focused upon a building that stood directly across the street. I said, "Shirley, do you see what I see?" "What do you see?" she asked. "Look across the street at the neon sign, it's the Blackstone Hotel!" "Do you think he might still be there?" she asked intriguingly. "We can go in and take a look, can't we?" I replied. Ben and Sylvia stood there wondering what we were talking about that got us suddenly charged up. I said, "Kids, how would you like to meet one of the world's most colorful characters? Are you game?" "You bet," they chanted in unison, "We're with you all the way."

The four of us crossed the street and walked into the front door of the Blackstone, and came upon a scene reminiscent of the asylum segment in the cult classic, "King of Hearts." There was a large assortment of mostly older people, dressed in what could best be described as "summer bizarre." Some were standing, some were wandering around, and others stretched out in worn armchairs. There were also a number of canes, crutches, walkers, and wheelchairs in evidence. Some people were talking, some were trying to read, but most were busy gazing at a rather large TV screen that was blasting away in decibels that were meant to accommodate the hearing impaired, who were probably also well represented. The smokers contributed their share to the atmosphere, and in the middle of all the din and fog, sat a balding, burly man in a semi glass-enclosed booth, dressed in an undershirt, with a half smoked cigar clenched between his teeth. He had a microphone on a table in front of him, so I figured him to be the "Concierge."

I approached him casually and inquired, "Would you, perhaps have a Barney Glassman registered here?" All the while Ben and Sylvia stood wide-eyed at what they were witnessing. Shirley, on the other hand, was not the least bit surprised. Her uncanny intuition had actually forewarned her that the place might turn out to be just like it was. "Of course we do," the husky man bellowed, in reply to my question, "let me see if I can page him for you." "BOINIE GLASSMAN," and he repeated the name several times in order to cut through the noise, "BOINIE GLASSMAN, come to da boot ... you have visitors." No reply. After awhile he said, "He must be up in his room. Pick up a house phone on da wall over dere, and ask da operator to connect you wit Boinie Glassman."

I bade Shirley, Ben, and Sylvia to sit down on an empty couch that was located against the wall, and picked up a phone and asked to be connected with Barney Glassman. The phone rang, and rang, and rang again, and just as I was about to hang up disappointedly, someone picked up, and in a muted voice, answered feebly, "Hell-o." I wasn't certain whom I was speaking to, and quickly injected, "Barney, is that you?" Only his close friends knew him as "Barney," and his voice suddenly brightened a little. "Yes, this is Barney (he sounded weak though), ... Who is this?" "It's Van ... Van Harris!" "Van? ... Where are you calling from?" "I'm downstairs, in the lobby with some people. C'mon down!" There was a hesitation, and then, sounding as though he was in pain, he answered, "I can't, I'm sick." "Too sick to come down to see your old pal?" "Yes, I'm afraid I'm too weak. I won't be able to make it." "What's wrong, Barney? What's ailing you? "I don't know, I'm just sick. I've been like this for a long time." "Barney, Shirley is down here with a couple of my friends. She's dying to see you." He loved Shirley, and I could actually picture his eyes lighting up. "Shoiley?" That's the way he pronounced her name, in pure Brooklynese. The name

"Shirley" is a windfall for anyone who speaks Brooklynese. "Shoiley is downstairs?" I replied "Yes, and she's anxious to see you. Put on something nice. I want you to impress my friends." "Okay," he said, "I'll be right down."

I stood back from the elevator doors, patiently awaiting his grand entrance. Shirley, Ben and Sylvia sat in eager anticipation. My friends had never met Barney. The elevator door opened and out stepped the man of the hour, woefully thin, yet surprisingly suntanned, and wearing a brightly colored Hawaiian shirt, white slacks, and open sandals, with no socks. He walked towards me slowly, and he smiled. His lips parted revealing nothing but gums, except for one lonely, discolored upper front tooth. I thought to myself, "What a perfect face for a comedian." Then an ingenious thought struck me. I greeted him with, "Barney, if they ever put a price on your head ... take it!" That started his juices flowing and he came right back with, "If you ever change your mind ... try to get a better one!" "Hey Barney, the stork that delivered you should have been arrested for smuggling dope!" "Oh yeah," (He was all well again, and gathering strength as he went along.) "Ya better close that yap of yours or I'll press the down button on your elevator shoes!" Now the contest was in full swing, and Ben and Sylvia stood there gaping, with their mouths open. Shirley, on the other hand, recognized what was going on and was delighted by the metamorphosis that was occurring.

"Hey Barney, you've got great lines but they're all in your face!"

"Yeah? These are my father's jokes ... are you one of your mother's?"

"I'd put a curse on you but somebody beat me to it!"

"Someday you'll go too far ... and I hope you'll stay there!"

"You're the kind of person I'd like to have over when I have the measles."

"Was the ground cold when you crawled out this morning?"

... and on and on it went with Barney gaining more and more strength with each putdown. It all ended with a laugh, and he put his arms around Shirley and hugged her. Next he shook hands with the amazed couple, and we all sat down n' talked for a while. When we were all through he said, "Come,

I'll walk you to your car," and he walked briskly beside us as we went out into the night air. We all continued to chat and laugh all the way to where the car was parked. As we were parting I said, "Barney, I have to be back in Florida in about a month from now to appear at the Miami Theater for the Performing Arts with Eddie Fisher. It's practically around the corner from here. I would love to see you backstage." He answered with a quick, "You bet!" and we all shook hands and parted. All the way home Ben and Sylvia couldn't stop talking about the miraculous transformation they had just witnessed.

A month later I came to work at the Miami Theater for the Performing Arts, but Barney didn't show up. I called the Blackstone and was told that he had moved out and was now living at a place called "The Colony," ... a little south of here, on the beach. I picked up a phone backstage, got information, and called. They connected me with Barney's room, and the phone rang and rang. I waited patiently till someone picked up. It was Barney and he sounded terrible. "Barney," I said, "it's me, Van. I'm at the theater. I thought you'd be here. What's keepin' you? C'mon over. It's a great show. You'll love it! I'm waiting for you. Put on some nice clothes and c'mon over." "I can't," he barely answered, "I'm sick." "D'ya want me to come over to you after the show?" "No, I don't wanna see anybody, I'm sick." That was the very last time I ever spoke to Barney. I tried to call him at the Colony some time after that, but was told that he was no longer there. "Where was he?" Nobody knew.

My career was moving into high gear. Club dates, resorts, after-dinner engagements for assorted industries, cruise ship dates that took me n' Shirley all over the world, etc. etc. Agents were starting to take notice, and a number of them started to romance me. I kept hearing, "You're too good for the 'one-nighters,' and the Catskills should be used only as somethin' to fall back on when there's nothin' else ... It's time to make your move." I did not want to go out on the road with so-called "singing stars." It was against my nature to become a lackey, a gopher, and everything else that the opening act becomes. I considered it a terrible price to pay just for more important exposure. I loved working with these stars on one-nighters. I appeared in better surroundings and drew large, enthusiastic audiences. When I performed in hotel ballrooms and theaters, for dignified agents like Neal Kirk or Dick Lyons, I would be on the same bill with some of the most celebrated acts in the business, and these clever agents would arrange the shows so that everyone received a piece of the action. Each act had its own slot, was accorded a respectable amount of time for the good of the show, and all played out perfectly. And, when the show had ended we went home either that same night or the very next day, depending upon where we were. I was willing to appear on the same bill with stars in nightclubs, but only in NY, where I was happy and it meant something, but never on the road. If that meant inhibiting my career, so be it. I was not going to waste my life away on the road. I had too many people that I loved at home, and was much more productive there too. Many performers love being away for assorted reasons. They can exercise their freedom, if that's what they're looking for, enjoy a free swinging life away from certain encumbrances, drink all they want, eat all they want, and really live it up, while growing older and oft-times grouchier, each day. I spent enough time on the road in my early days, and I learned to hate it. It was not for me. One of the good young comedians I had been friendly with, cast aside his wife n' kids to go out as an opening act for a major, major star. He enjoyed all the wild escapades that appearing with that person had to offer, and entertained worldwide in some of the very best places. He died of a stroke around the age of fifty. Man, that's livin'!

Charlie Rapp, the biggest, and busiest agent in the resort industry at the time, approached me, and suggested that he could enhance my career with an eye towards TV. Since he was a booker and not a manager, and didn't want to create a "conflict of interest" situation, he suggested that I sign with a successful triumvirate that he had connections with, and he would handle me through them. I knew who they were, and I was impressed by their accomplishments, but I also knew that one of the group had been indicted for racketeering and I wasn't about to get involved with such an organization, so I politely told the avuncular Charlie, "Thanks, ... but no thanks!" Charlie was quite prescient though, as he foresaw the potential in Jackie Mason whom everyone in the industry was poking fun at because of the way he spoke English. Charlie said, "I guarantee that some day they will all be imitating him," and he was right. Charlie handled Jackie through his lawyer nephew, Bob Chartoff, and the rest is history. I don't go along with Mason's attitude, and he makes my skin crawl when he does some of the Jewish things that he's famous for, but I must admit that he is brilliant, original, and very, very funny.

Several other managers approached me. (I was currently with Nat Dunn, happily, busy, but with no signed contract, and going nowhere career-wise. Nat never promised me anything more than just club dates.) I was truly ready for a change. We do make wrong decisions in our lives, and that's just what I did when I left Nat, and signed a three-year contract with David Jonas, another club date manager, who approached me like I was the most desirable comedian on earth. I had just done a successful date in Greenwich Village to which I had invited Mr. Jonas, and he waxed ecstatic after the show. I was changing in my dressing room, and he was talking a blue streak: "You're all that I have been looking for. I have already proven my ability in handling club date comedians, as you very well know, but you're different. I can see you as a major American star. You've got what it takes. Listen, I can sign up as many club date guys as I want to, but I don't want any more. I want to go to the top with you. I'll get you writers. I'll mold you. I beg you, sign with me and we'll go all the way together." My friend, Stan Earley, the continuity writer for "The Ted Mack Amateur Hour" on TV, was standing at my side and heard all this. I replied, "I appreciate your interest but I'll have to think it over. I'll let you know." David left saying, "What is there to think about? I'm offering you the moon." He was waiting outside when we walked out into the street, and as Stan and I got into my car, he reiterated, "I can make you into a star. Don't be a coward. I'm giving you a great opportunity. Don't blow it!" As we drove away I turned to Stan and asked, "Whaddya think?" He replied, "Man, he's really hot for you. If I were you I'd go for it!"

Nat Dunn and I parted amicably, and I signed with David Jonas. He was a very capable agent. He called me every day to ask how I was doing, and he connected me with some club date agents I had never worked for before. Meanwhile he added my own lengthy list of bookers to his repertoire. But, all I ever got from him were club dates, and more club dates. I asked, "Well, when are we gonna start workin' on the big time?" He said, "Don't worry, I've got some things in mind." That's the way it went for months.

One day I came into the office and found my friend, Mac Robbins, a popular and successful club date comedian, sitting in the waiting room. I was surprised, and happy to see Mac. I asked him, "What are you doing here?" and he shot back, "What am I doing here? I could ask you the same thing." I said, "Mac, I signed with Dave a few months ago." He replied, "So did I." Then it hit me. This guy is signing up the best working club date comics. All that stuff he enticed me with was a lot of crap. He wants to control the club date market. He probably has no other connections. No doubt Dave was good at what he did, but so was Nat Dunn.

I let a few weeks go by and then sprang an ultimatum upon him. I said, "Dave, where's the writer you promised me?" He hesitated. "Uh, I've got someone in mind ..." I said, "Dave, if you don't come up with a writer immediately, and we don't proceed with those grandiose plans of yours, and I've got a witness who heard it all, then I'm afraid I'm gonna have to get out of my contract with you."

He did come up with a writer, a brilliant, but erratic former science teacher in the New York City school system, named David Panich. He was a prolific writer and wrote some very witty material that I truly was able to take to. It was, for the most part, intelligent, even intellectual. Panich was a blessing in disguise. When I use the word disguise, I mean what I'm saying. He was "off the wall," but a brilliant writer. A relocated Californian, he lived in an apartment in Lefrak City, in Queens. On our very first meeting, arranged by Jonas, I was to meet Panich in his apartment. I came to his high rise in the middle of the afternoon, rang from downstairs, and on the intercom he shouted, "C'mon up!" When I got off the elevator, there he stood in the hallway of this huge apartment house, stark naked, with a devilish grin on his face, stuck out his hand, and said, "I'm Dave, ... Let's go into my pad." (For the moment I was reminded of something I had read in Moss Hart's book, "Act One," in which he described how Jed Harris, the famous Broadway producer, whom he had gone to see with an eye towards having one of his plays produced, met him at the door of his hotel room standing stark naked. It was a ruse that he had employed in an effort to weaken a potential client's resolve. Only the brilliant George S. Kaufman did not fall prey to his diabolic attempt at disarmament. When he greeted Kaufman in the same manner, Goerge S. nonchalantly walked past him remarking, "Don't look now Mr. Harris, but your fly is open!") Of course I was nonplussed by Panich's appearance, but recovered very quickly and walked into a rather dishevelled apartment. It had all the earmarks of a man who lived alone. David was about my age, slim, and a bit shorter than me, and quite animated. He quickly donned a robe and said, "Come into the bedroom for a minute. I wanna show you somethin'." I did as he asked and there, hanging on the wall over his unmade bed was a holster with a loaded 45 in it. "I was mugged several times when I taught school in a bad neighborhood. I keep this piece loaded and ready for protection. Nobody is ever gonna mug me again." David was quite an eccentric. I soon found out that he had suffered several nervous breakdowns, and he was due to encounter several more during the time we were associated. In fact, a year, or two, later, he was sent away to Camarillo State Mental Hospital in his native California, from which he emerged after awhile. He was an excellent writer. Trouble was that he sold a number of the same things to other comedians whom he had also been writing for. That's an unfortunate malaise among many comedy writers, and produces some very embarrassing situations for their clients. For as long as it lasted, which wasn't particularly long, we enjoyed a good, productive relationship until he went back to the west coast where he wrote for several television variety shows until he died, a few years later, at a rather early age.

Jonas never got me anything but club dates and I was becoming more and more frustrated having now been enriched by some newer and better material, and I began searching for a higher plateau, knowing that my contract was nearing an end very, very soon. Enter Jerry Cutler into the picture:

Tall, good looking, warm, friendly, and somehow always appearing a bit rumpled, he was a pleasure to be with. I first met amiable young Jerry Cutler when he was a kosher caterer at an uptown hotel where I had performed on a club date. He had an excellent sense of humor to go along with his rabbinical credentials, and he was highly intelligent and articulate. Jerry, married, and the father of three lovely daughters, would have preferred to have been a comedian, instead of serving up banquets, but his first allegiance was to his growing family, so he stayed with what he was most successful. He was an honest man who told it like it was, and a compliment from him was sincere, and with me he was always generous in that respect.

He was coming out of that tiny, cubbyhole office, located on the same floor that Jonas was on, when I pleasantly bumped into him. It was then that he told me all about Buddy Hackett's paying the rent for the place as a favor. "Say," he added, "would it be all right with you if I tried to help you out with your career?" "I don't see why not," I replied, figuring that here was another friend with noble intentions, which will probably very soon disappear. "How 'bout some coffee," I asked. "Okay with me," he added, then gave me a grin and a wink, "as long as it's kosher." We sat downstairs at the "Chock Full O' Nuts," and spent a very pleasant hour just discussing the business in general. The chemistry was excellent, and we also laughed a lot. When we were about to part, he said, "Van, Rosemary Clooney is opening at the Royal Box of the Hotel Americana, right here on W. 53rd. It's the best room in NY, and I know for a fact that she hasn't got a comic yet. You would be ideal. How would it be if I called Eddie Risman, the booker, and tried to get you the gig?" "I'd love it!" I replied, while thinking to myself that nothing was going to happen because every comedian in town, and his agent, would be after that plum engagement. "I'll call you as soon as I hear," he said, and off we both went.

The Royal Box was brand new, and very popular. It had opened only a few months before with the legendary Ella Fitzgerald, and she packed 'em in. "Clooney ought to do the same," I thought. In fact, they closed the room after Ella's engagement in order to rearrange the layout. It was geographically awkward for performance (something to do with the sound system, and the manner in which the tables were arranged). Ella did great in spite of the handicap it presented, and after she left, the engineers knew just what to do, and straightened things out so that it would be much better for the following attractions.

The Americana Hotel, owned by the famous Tisch family, took NY by storm. It boasted a number of ballrooms, of assorted sizes, and I had already done a couple of dates in the beautifully appointed Grand Ballroom. There too, there was a problem that had to be corrected. Alan King had done a club date in that Grand Ballroom when it first opened, and the backstage was not accident proof yet. He walked off the stage to tumultuous applause, into the wings, and toppled off the edge of the stage there, falling quite far, and cutting his leg so severely that he had to be rushed to the hospital to get stitched up. I was told that Alan's "colorful" reaction to that unsettling tumble could be heard all the way down to Times Square.

My most recent club date there was still fresh on my mind. It wasn't only because the show was big, and wonderful, and extremely successful. It was because I had bumped into an old, and valued friend who was playing the drums in the rather large, and excellent orchestra. He was Joe Gardner's drummer during Joe's years at Pine View, and we had spent some very enjoyable summers together. I didn't recognize him. His name was Harvey Klotz, and his brother Phil was the saxophonist in that same band. Harvey was big and round, had a huge crop of wavy brown hair, and was a superb drummer, in addition to being a very funny guy. What made him even funnier was the misfortune he had of being terribly cross-eyed. Now, here he was, so many years later, sitting up on that stately throne in the rear of the orchestra, and playing the hell out a magnificent set of percussion instruments. When the show was over, and I was changing in my dressing room, he casually strolled in and said, "Hello Van. Remember me?" He looked familiar but I couldn't quite place him at the moment. He continued, "It's me, Harvey ... Harvey Klotz!" "Harvey!" I screamed, "I didn't recognize you. What did you do to yourself?" He had slimmed down to the point where he was actually svelte. His hair was wonderfully coiffed, and he was sporting a suave, pencil thin moustache. He really looked handsome. He went on, "No more 'fat boy' stuff for me, and no more Harvey Klotz. I'm now known in better circles as Harvey Leonard." Then came the biggest surprise of all. I kept thinking to myself, "There's something else about him. It's bothering me. What is it?" Then he pointed to his eyes and they were perfectly congruous, and it all came back to me in a flash. He commanded, "Dig man!" I asked, "Dig what?" He said, "Take a good look ... I had my eyes tuned!" If there was ever an example of desire and perseverance, it was Harvey Klotz ...oh, excuse me, ... Harvey Leonard! What a guy! I went home feeling real good. I was so proud of Harvey Klotz. He knew what he wanted and he went after it with a fervor. I felt so good about Harvey Klotz Leonard who even went so far as to have his crossed eyes surgically corrected.

A couple of days had gone by since my talk with Jerry Cutler and I hadn't heard from him, and I was ready to shrug the whole thing off as just another of my many disappointments. The following morning the phone rang. It was Jerry, and I could sense the excitement in his voice. He said, "Van, I got hold of Ed Risman, and I got him interested, only he doesn't know you and he said he'd have to see you work before he makes any kind of move." I felt my brief elation fly out the window. I said, "Same old crap. It's the old cop out. He's gotta see me work, and it's gotta be at his convenience, right?" Jerry said, "Right, and I made it very easy for both of you. I spoke to Mort Sunshine, the head man at Variety Clubs International. That's all guys in the motion picture business, and they've got a luncheon scheduled in the Georgian Ballroom of the same Americana next Tuesday afternoon. I volunteered you to do a free show, and then I invited Risman to come see you. Even if you're booked on a gig for money somewhere on Tuesday, it's more likely that it'll be at night, so you won't be giving up anything. They're a successful, fun loving bunch of sober guys, and all quite intelligent. It should be a snap for you. See you later this week and we'll go over our plans for Tuesday. I was walking on air, and saying to myself, "God bless you Jerry, for coming into my life."

Tuesday afternoon rolled around and I reported to the appointed place before showtime. Mort Sunshine was a terrific guy and treated me like a star. The crowd was well dressed and orderly, a very good omen. I was there. Jerry was there. The audience was there ... but no Ed Risman. Jerry didn't panic. He took the elevator down to the main floor and walked into Risman's office. Only his assistant, Dick Towers, was there. "Where's Ed?" Jerry gently demanded. "He's in the hotel luncheonette having his lunch," was Dick's reply. "Could you tell me where it's located?" "Sure," Dick replied, "it's around the corner from the reception desk." "Thank you!" said Jerry, and out he dashed to the luncheonette. He found Ed Risman nonchalantly sitting there, and munching on a sandwich. Jerry had great chutzpah when it counted and he knew how to use it. He walked over to where Ed was sitting, grabbed him by the arm, forcing him to his feet, and said, "Mr. Risman, you're supposed to look at my client's performance. He's up at the Georgian Ballroom and about to go on, so please, I don't want you to miss him." The surprised, and somewhat flustered Mr. Risman, took one more swallow of his coffee, dropped some money on the table, signed the check, and out they ran to the elevator.

I saw them walk in, and if they were close to me I would have hugged them. I did an inspired performance and the audience laughed and cheered all the way. As far as I was concerned, I was a smash. I watched Jerry huddle with Risman in the back of the room, and then they parted. Jerry came over to me and had a disappointed look on his face. I inquired, "What's going on?" "He's hedging," Jerry said, "He says you're very good, but this was a male audience, and he's gotta see how you do with a mixed group, and, it's gotta be soon, and, more importantly, convenient for him." I surprised Jerry by exclaiming, "No sweat. Just so happens I've got a date in the Grand Ballroom of the Hotel Astor this coming Saturday afternoon for the National Hardware Assn. ... men and women." Timing and luck are two very important ingredients in my profession (in every profession) and this time I had both going for me. Jerry gave me a great big smile and said, "Don't worry, we'll be there, even if I have to wait outside his door in the morning." The Hotel Astor is no longer in existence, but for many years it was a famous NYC landmark. The Astor Roof was home to many of the famous big bands, and the Astor Grand Ballroom was among the most beautiful hotel ballrooms in the world and was noted for it's near perfect acoustics. Risman came to see me there. He liked what he saw. Early on the following week I signed a contract to open with Rosemary Clooney at The Royal Box about three weeks hence.

Though my contract with Jonas had technically expired by then, he was continuing to provide me with club dates, so I continued to give him his 15% commission on those dates, and I gave Jerry 15% commission on the Royal Box date with a promise to make a deal with Jerry on everything once I weaned myself away from the Jonas office. Jerry also signed me with the William Morris Agency, which meant another 10% to them, but Jonas got nothing from the Americana engagement because he had nothing to do with it. We also hired some big, fat guy to do my PR. He came highly recommended to Jerry, and was supposed to start planting my name around in the newspaper columns and make connections with the columnists. He was a bad mistake, totally ineffective, and lazy. Before I opened, we had to discharge him, which made him very unhappy, and also left me with no prior newspaper coverage. To our great dismay it also turned out that the guy who covered the show for the trade paper *Variety* was a friend of his, and, as a result, he gave me a very ambiguous, lukewarm review that didn't help me much at all.

Opening night was very exciting, sold out, and many of my friends were among the revelers. We did a brisk business for the length of the engagement, which was about a month, and the Tisch brothers (they were also members of Variety Clubs International) treated me like royalty, giving me a lovely suite to use at my convenience. I used it as a dressing room and preferred to commute to my home in Teaneck, NJ nightly, which was only a half hour away at the most. One night a friend of mine named Ham Morgen, who was a cameraman on the Ed Sullivan Show, was working a day and night assignment at CBS. He lived all the way up in Westchester, and was dog-tired, so I generously offered my suite to him to sleep in, for which he was eternally grateful. After all it was my place to use as I please, and it pleased me greatly to do a friend a favor.

Shirley came in on Friday and Saturday nights, and did a commendable job visiting the tables of our many friends who loyally patronized the club. It soon came to our attention that whenever she sat down at someone's table, although she didn't eat or drink there, the waiter would slap a cover charge on the bill, which was actually criminal. This was done on

25 The Zenith

Needless to say, The Royal Box of The Americana was a big step up for me, and coupled with a flattering review I received in the then NY Herald Tribune, for the first time people in my industry were starting to take notice of me. Rosemary Clooney was at her charming best, after a somewhat shaky first night. She was suffering the effects of a very recent acrimonious divorce from her famous actor husband, Jose Ferrer, but being the marvelous trouper that she was, she pulled herself together and demolished the audiences.

I was off on Sundays, and the club was available for private affairs. Jerry advised me that NBC was having a dinner there on one of those Sundays, and they wanted to know if I would entertain and also introduce their new talk radio people who were slated to begin programming very shortly. The people at NBC wanted to know what my fee was and I instructed Jerry to tell them that it would be my pleasure to work that evening for nothing. They were rather surprised by my magnanimous gesture, but didn't object at all, and joyfully accepted it.

As it turned out, a great many of NBC's business people attended the lavish affair in which they were unveiling the new cast of daytime, and nighttime, radio talk show hosts. Among them were Tom Snyder, Bill Mazer, Joe Pine, and a number of others who were going to infuse NBC's radio broadcasting with color, controversy, and other attractive ingredients. Besides performing for those in attendance, I also introduced these new celebrities. I learned a little about each of them and added a modicum of appropriate humor as I brought each one to the microphone. It all worked out very well and everyone was pleased.

Jerry, who had brought me to areas that I never knew existed during all the time that I was trapped in the unimaginative little world of the club date managers, called me, all excited, early on the following morning. "Van, I would like you to go over to such n' such address, on Fifth Ave. this morning to broadcast a comedy turn that will be beamed to our armed forces overseas, and then meet me in front of 30

Rockefeller Plaza at 1:30. We've got an appointment to meet with Jim Grau, the head of broadcasting at NBC, at 2 o'clock." The show for the armed forces was very exciting to me, reminiscent of the glory days of radio, where one sat at a mike in a bare room, and aired whatever it was he was instructed to do. I was interviewed by a well experienced interrogator, and followed up with a short army routine, and felt flattered when I had actually engendered laughter from the person I had been talking to, and the few engineers that were present. It was so exhilarating. Though I was paid nothing, I still felt so important, ...like this is the sort of stuff that really counts, ... and I left there on a real high.

I met Jerry at the appointed hour and he looked as though he had just jumped out of bed with barely enough time to get dressed. Luckily for him, his curly hair didn't require too much combing, for it appeared like he had quickly run his fingers through it in a hasty effort to try to make it look neat. That was typically Jerry, and it was all part of his charm.

When we got to Jim Grau's office, for whatever reasons, Jerry asked me to wait in the reception room while he went in to see him. The door to his private office was left open, and I was able to see Jerry and Jim gesturing, and laughing out loud. (I guessed then that Jerry wanted to display some of his own comic ability with Grau all to himself.) The contrast that the two of them presented made me laugh. There stood Jerry, in his rumpled blue serge suit, looking somewhat like a burlesque comedian, evoking smiles and outright laughter from the tall young, handsome executive with the crew cut, who was dressed impeccably in an expensive looking grey flannel outfit. After they had talked awhile, Mr. Grau handed Jerry a carton of sorts, they shook hands, and he walked Jerry out so that he could say hello to me and thank me for helping to make the previous evening such a huge success. "Jerry has something to tell you," he said, "and that thing in the box is for you as a gesture of our appreciation." We all shook hands and parted. As we were riding down on the elevator I remarked, "That guy sure has class." "More than you can imagine," Jerry replied, "You're doin' the Johnny Carson Show next Tuesday night!" I almost fainted! "Could all this be happening to me? ...Or was all this some part of a beautiful dream?"

Shirley and the children couldn't believe their ears when I got home and told them what had happened, and they were so impressed by the large portable Zenith radio that was in the package. We were walkin' on air and just like in the movies, after the newspaper reporters had just witnessed the verdict in an important trial, the rush was on to the phone. The kids were anxious to tell their friends that their daddy was going to appear on the NBC Tonight Show, and Shirley had to call her family and I mine. The excitement was intoxicating.

The TV show was quite an experience. I met with several of Johnny's "talent coordinators" at around four in the afternoon, and we sat around a table, they with legal pads and pencils in their hands, and they made notations as I did about twenty minutes of a monologue. There was a mixture of laughs and comments along the way, and when I was all through they huddled for a very short while. Then the man who was assigned to me and would be my supervisor for all of my ensuing appearances on that show, asked me to look over his pad with him. "This is what I would like you to do tonight," and he pointed to the jokes that they had selected. Of course this meant my having to quickly learn a whole new six minute routine of jokes that I was accustomed to doing, but never in that sequence before. "We tape at 7:30 tonight, in front of a live audience, then you can go home and watch the results on your own TV at the usual 11:30. Get back here about 6:30 for makeup, etc."

Now the trick was to talk to yourself for the next couple of hours and go over the abbreviated routine in your mind, over and over again in order to be prepared. "If only I could find someone to do this shortened six minute routine in front of, that would be a marvelous rehearsal. But, who do I know around here?" Suddenly the thought struck me. "My cousin Sylvia, and her husband, Bill, have a retail jewelry store on 47th and 6th, only three blocks from here. Perfect, I'll do the bit for them. I hope they'll also have some of their customers in the store. I know they sell to all the hookers who live in and use, the hotel next door. Maybe they can round up some of the girls to be my audience." I got to a telephone booth and got my lively, animated, pretty cousin on the phone and told her what my plan was. She got all excited and said, "Just gimme a little time to round them up. They all can't be too busy this time of the day, and c'mon over. We'll be waitin' for you!"

I excitedly started to walk in the direction of her store when I heard someone honk his horn and yell out my name. I turned to see who it was, and, surprisingly, it was one of the guys from the old neighborhood who drove a cab for a living. I yelled out, "Goldie, have you got a fare in there?" He said, "No, where do ya want me to take you?" I replied, "Nowhere, but I'd like you to pull over to the curb for a moment. I've got something important to tell you." Good natured Goldie parked on 48th St., not too far from a fire hydrant, and asked. "What's up?" I quickly proceeded to explain to him what was happening and asked him if I could sit in the cab while the motor was running, so that he wouldn't get a ticket, while I do the six-minute routine I was going to do on the Johnny Carson Show that same evening. Goldie was impressed. "The Johnny Carson Show? Wow! You've really made it kid! Shoot it to me!" I went into my routine, hesitatingly, of course, because of the newness of the format, but Goldie caught all the funny lines and laughed uproariously. He was one of the guys from the corner. He had a sharp sense of humor and knew a funny line when he heard one. "Great!" he said, just as a meter maid was starting to approach the parked cab. My plan seemed to have succeeded. It was my first attempt and I got a favorable reaction. Now I was ready for cousin Sylvia and her hookers. I thanked Goldie and he wished me luck as he drove off, elated.

I walked into the store and dear Sylvia had already set the girls up in rows of chairs, theater style, awaiting my entrance. Bill was busy waiting on a customer. My theatrical cousin (she was really very pretty and looked like an aging Judy Garland) addressed the assembled audience with, "Ladies you're in for a real treat. The star of tonight's Johnny Carson show on television, here he is ... I give you my talented cousin ... Van Harris!" There was an honest-to-goodness round of eager applause, and I launched into the routine that I had just done for Goldie, which I had continued to go over in my head as I walked to Bill and Sylvia's place. The ladies reacted with laughter and applause, and, as a result, I became more sanguine and was ready for action when I got to 30

Rockefeller Plaza awhile later. Of course the butterflies were already nibbling away at my stomach. Everybody connected with the show, from the producer on down, was just wonderfully cooperative and friendly. Ed McMahon was an absolute doll, and we became quite conversant while I was having my makeup applied. Skitch Henderson, the renowned orchestra leader, was also a delight. The talent coordinator who had been assigned to me (a gentle human being named Sy Kasoff) treated me as though I was his own personal ward. I felt very much at home. Those ubiquitous butterflies were a result of my mind tormenting me. It's not unnatural for one's inner voice to keep reminding one that there will be millions of people watching, "So you'd better not crap up!" The trick is to say, "Scram! You're bothering me!" Sitting around in that well known "Green Room," under those conditions, and waiting to go on, is tantamount to going to the electric chair, especially if it's your first time. No matter how friendly and reassuring the other guest artists are (and, as I recall, the great country star, Eddie Arnold, and his manager, were both so refreshingly inspiring), the turbulence doesn't go away until you get that first laugh. Well, I got out there and got my first laugh quickly, and many more. Johnny himself was laughing loudest of all, and, at times his staccato laughter sounded like an unstoppable machine gun. I still enjoy watching the videotape of that show, taken from the original kinescope, and listening to Johnny Carson's hardy reaction to my humor. I walked off to deafening applause, and my talent coordinator, who was so very pleased with the way I followed his every direction, including the entrance and exit, and camera technique, hugged me and said, "Great! ... Just great!" Jerry was in the wings, beaming, and smiling from ear to ear. Even the usually undemonstrative guys from the Morris Agency seemed delighted. I did well, so well that I was invited back four more times that year.

Johnny Carson didn't know I was alive. He missed two of my next performances because he was spending an inordinate amount of time in court, battling his first wife, the mother of his then three children. The twice more when he and I were both there, they ran out of time, so I just got paid n' didn't go on. I complained to the producer and he tried to placate me by telling me that there was a young Black comic around who had been waiting to go on five times already, and still hadn't gotten his chance, and the kid's name was Flip Wilson.

My next time on, the brilliant and precocious comedian, Henry Morgan, had replaced Johnny for the night. He was hilarious and furious at the same time. Among his guest artists that evening were two young British actors. One was Rex Harrison's son, Noel, whose wife unashamedly breast fed their infant while we were all waiting around in the Green Room. The other was Shirley Knight. They were both dressed like "Hippies" and each had an iconoclastic attitude, and each one was extremely taciturn, answering Morgan's questions with a terse "Yep," and "Nope." At one point Henry got so disgusted that he threw his hands up and appealed to the audience, "How would you like to be sitting in my place? Yep! Nope!" he mimicked them. I did very well in my spot, thanks to a change of material that was again rehearsed in what had become my favorite rehearsal hall, Bill and Sylvia's jewelry store on W. 47th St., with its very select audience.

The fifth, and last time that I was on that show was after Skitch Henderson was replaced by a talented and virtuoso pianist and accordionist named Milton DeLug. Tall, slim, and bespectacled, Milton was disarmingly friendly and a privilege to work with. I was having my makeup applied (by now the butterflies were virtually a thing of the past, as I was feeling very much at home on the show), when my big bear of a pal, Ed McMahon, accompanied by Milton DeLug, came bursting into the room in a frenzy. Johnny had been unexpectedly detained in a court in Connecticut once again, and there was nobody to take his place. "How would you like to take over for Johnny tonight?" Ed surprised me. My adrenaline shot all the way up. "Would I!" I exclaimed, "Let's do it!" He and Milton laid out the plan. "We'll present you early for the usual six minute stint, and afterwards we'll call you over to where we're sitting, and Milton will ask you some questions about domesticity, or somethin' to that effect, to which you'll reply in your own witty way, and then you'll take over the rest of the show, introducing the rest of the guests, etc. We'll be right next to you to guide you in case there are any awkward moments." Everything was set and I was rarin' to go.

Unfortunately for me, the fine Broadway actor who played the role of the psychiatrist in "Teahouse of the August Moon," Larry Blyden, was also on the show. Larry was a seasoned veteran of The Johnny Carson Show, and really knew his way around. He had been interviewed prior to my doing my spot, and apparently had made up his mind to stay on, and take advantage of Johnny's absence. He had done an unusual amount of foolin' around before I got to my turn, and chewed up a lot of prime time. I finally got to go on, and when I was through, Milton was in the process of summoning me to the dais when there was a tinkle on a cymbal, which indicated that it was time to cut to a commercial. After that commercial very little time remained for me, and so the plan had to be aborted. When the show ended there were apologies all the way around, which gave me no solace whatsoever. My big chance never happened.

That was the very last time I appeared on that show, for several valid reasons, foremost of which was that my talent coordinator had departed from the show to join an ill fated TV venture in Las Vegas. He took on an exciting assignment to become the head man of a new night variety show featuring Bill Dana and Don Adams, that emanated from there. Sadly, that show evaporated rather quickly, mostly because of the fierce competition.

Jerry, meanwhile, had to move out of the tiny little office that he had occupied, and also had to seriously think about his future and the support of his family. I had severed my relationship with Mr. Jonas, and was now steering all my club date requests to Jerry. I had also left the Morris Agency, having been lured to the then new Ashley Famous office by an agent who caught my act at The Royal Box and promised me the moon. I learned, very soon afterward, that, although he was in some sort of executive capacity, he had very little clout with that office, thanks to a running feud he had been having with an irritable superior, and I did what I had to do and tendered my resignation. Now it was just me and Jerry, and the industry was still very much abuzz with the excitement that we had stirred up together.

I increased my commissions to him in order to give him a little more breathing room, which I could hardly afford to do, as I had a rather large family of my own to attend to. There were a number of performers who would gladly have thrown in with this "miracle man," who seemingly had come out of nowhere, and I urged Jerry to take them on, so that he could enhance his income. He was surprisingly stubborn, saying, "I don't need any deadheads. Right now I wanna concentrate only upon you."

I found out that my friend, Eddie Hershman, and his brother, partners in the successful Goya Guitar Company, had decided to go out of business, and that Eddie was interested in becoming a theatrical agent. Eddie was actually a neophyte in the variety field, having had contacts only with musicians. However, Eddie had money, and opened a rather sumptuous, well equipped office in a brand new building on W.57th St., a good show biz address. I talked to him about taking Jerry in as an associate and he jumped at the opportunity. Jerry, on the other hand, was reluctant. (Some guys are just "one man shows.") I finally convinced him that it would be an excellent opportunity, and the marriage was made. It was ideal for Jerry, as he didn't have to put up any money, and Eddie was an easy enough guy to get along with, and very eager to learn. The office was a pleasure to walk into, and it really began to percolate, but I could sense that Jerry was not happy. Somehow the chemistry just wasn't there, and after giving it a halfhearted try, Jerry left. Eddie hung on for close to a year and discovered that the agency was not his cup of tea, and he, having been a businessman all his life, had no trouble going into something else. Jerry packed up his brood and moved to southern California, after having attempted a few short-lived ventures connected with show biz. Until Jerry's departure I was still busily doing club dates, and once he left I gravitated back to my protective womb, the ever busy Nat Dunn (club date) Agency.

Jerry, believe it or not, took advantage of his diploma and background when he got to Hollywood, and there he established the Synagogue of the Performing Arts, where he served as Rabbi. He later divorced his lovely wife, Hannah, and soon thereafter married an enchanting young widow, of Scotch- American descent, who converted for him and made him an outstanding partner. His three daughters grew up to be beautiful ladies in every respect, and his new wife, Jeff, who is a writer and a producer, bore him two more adorable daughters. Shirley and I visit with Jerry and Jeff when we're out there. His is a "roving synagogue" (actually it's Temple Beth Ahm, and they lend it to him for his once monthly services), and he numbers some very famous motion picture and TV personalities among his colorful roster of congregants. We happened to have, coincidentally, dropped in when he was conducting services one Friday evening. He had recruited the fine baritone from back east, Hale Porter, as his cantor, and at the time we attended, I was told that Monte Hall was the President of his congregation and that Lorne Greene was the President Emeritus, and that Walter Matthau had been one of the previous cantors. Jerry, who also reviews movies on the local radio, maintains a very strong popularity, and has never lost his devilish sense of humor. The license plate on his car bears the word "Baytsim," which actually means "eggs," but every hip Jew can tell you that it's slang for "testicles." "The night we were there he had just gotten over a hernia operation and he opened the evening services by exclaiming, "I would like to read you a telegram that I received from the Board of Directors right after my surgery. It says, "Dear Rabbi … The Board of Directors wishes you a speedy recovery by a vote of eight to seven." We still visit each other whenever we can, and I've even managed to do some club dates for him while I was out there.

Nat Dunn, for reasons of his own, suddenly decided to discharge his "right arm," the elegant Harrison Bob Fuller, so loyal and dedicated all those many years, and aging handsomely. He replaced him with one of his star client's young brother. The client was comedian Morty Gunty, and his brother, Elliott, married, with a son and a daughter, up until that time had been a caterer at the old Bronx landmark, The Concourse Plaza Hotel. The entire industry was stunned by the news. It couldn't have happened at a worse time for Bob, as his teenage daughter had been going through some difficult emotional problems that were tearing Bob and Jane apart. It was a very trying time for all of us. We loved Bob dearly, and we also felt compassion for young Elliott, who needed the job and was vaulted into it at Bob's bitter expense, thereby making him appear the "heavy."

Perhaps no more than a month had gone by when word got out that Nat Dunn, tall, grey, charming, and fit, had suffered a serious stroke. His wife, Annie, had called an ambulance immediately, and he was rushed to a hospital paralyzed on one side, from his face all the way down to his leg. He could barely speak, and when he managed to, it was with extreme difficulty. His thoughts immediately ran to saving his business, and being fearful of Elliott's inexperience, he had Annie call Bob to ask him to come back. Jane answered the telephone and informed Bob that it was Annie and that she wanted to speak to him. Bob knew about Nat's stroke, and refused to come to the phone. Jane offered up some sort of excuse and hung up. The story has been told of how Annie called again and again, for many days, and Bob refused to pick up the phone. The way Jane later described it to me, he just sat there, rigid, and let it ring, and ring, what seemed like forever, while desperately fighting off all temptation to answer. All the while the tears kept streaming down his cheeks. His profound pride prevailed. It was killing him.

Nat next went on to Rusk Institute for rehabilitation while Elliott was clever enough to quickly grow into the business. Nat eventually returned, though he walked with a cane, and his face never fully recovered from the paralysis either. Bob opened his own office in the Palace Building, and his little girl eventually recovered. I was among the many who visited him frequently, but I never made the switchover from Dunn to Fuller. I have no doubts that Bob would have doubled his efforts for me had I gone with him, yet I stood pat. Why? Some peculiar loyalty I guess. Or, was I just playing it safe and staying with the proven action. Bob and I remained good friends till the day he died. I remained with Elliott lo these many years, and we've been good for each other, but he never promised me anything other than club dates, and it's been just that ... club dates. He's a good businessman, but not a career builder. Nobody in the club date field ever was! Nat eventually passed away, and Elliott became the sole inheritor of a thriving business that would, in time, just like vaudeville, and the music halls before that, become doomed.

By doing the Carson Show I had touched the big time and I remained antsy for another shot at the brass ring. I had become friendly with a young agent at the William Morris Agency named Jerry Kellert. He was a refreshing departure

Elliot Gunty and Van. Broadway, NY.

from those pompous asses that dominated such agencies, and I appealed to him for help. He was wonderful. He placed me with Al Wilde and Morty Curtis, a couple of wily managers who were representing young Leslie Uggams. Jerry was very content with his position with William Morris, and asked nothing in return, only my friendship. Leslie was then in her early twenties and in her prime. I used to stop off in the Sugar Hill section of Harlem on my way to the Catskills, when she had been a little girl, and drive her and her momma up there whenever we performed together. Now, Wilde, Curtis, & Co. were happy to have me aboard. They got commissions only from whatever bookings they got me, and Elliott was content to do likewise, so there was no conflict whatsoever. Morty and Al immediately placed me into The Monticello Inn, in Framingham, MA. to open for Leslie, who had recently starred on Broadway in a musical called "Hallelujah Baby." We did very well together, and the club was not all that far away so that I was even able to come home several times during the engagement. From there we went into the world famous Copacabana, in New York. This time I was much better prepared in the publicity department. Al and Morty got me a high-powered PR man, and my advance notices in the newspapers were very well placed. Opening night, remembering the small fiasco Cutler and I had suffered at my Royal Box opening, I began to worry. "As the bartender said to the horse that walked up to the bar," Al quipped, "why the long face?" I told him I was concerned about what *Variety* might write. "Whaddya worried about?" Al replied, placing his hand on my shoulder to comfort me, "Your review is already in!"

The Copa was a major nightspot, but had nowhere the class that The Royal Box had. Yet it was still considered by many to be the premier nightclub in New York. If it was, I didn't sense it. There appeared to be an aloofness about the place, as though it was just a high powered money machine. Get 'em in, entertain them, and then get 'em out as quickly as possible so that the next customers can come in. The waiters, whose order of importance was signified by the color of their uniforms, ran the place like an army. The black jackets were the highest echelon, followed by the red jackets, and then the white jackets. The black jackets were the captains, answering only to the maitre D', who was the commander, and he answered only to the boss, who was never seen, but surely was around. Hecklers were not tolerated and were quickly ejected, which was greatly appreciated by the performers. However, occasionally groups of rather unsavory looking characters would occupy tables somewhere near the back of the club and would converse rather loudly, oblivious to what was going on onstage, and we were instructed that they were "very special people" who could do as they please. Business is business, so you do as you're told. There are reasons for everything.

I had sent letters, and made phone calls, to my many, many friends, and members of my family, and I drew heavily from them, and they reported that they were there because of me when they placed their reservations. I never even got so much as a "thank you" from management. It was a good lesson for me to learn. Leslie had the "S*T*A*R dressing room, with a color TV, and all the accoutrements, while I had to share a shabby dressing room with the musicians, with clothes strewn about all over the place. It was quite reminiscent of the "toilets" I used to work in, in my early days on the road, and it took a great deal of psyching myself before I went on, so that I could feel like I was somebody important that they had paid to see. The situation was not a morale booster by any means.

First show on our opening night I hit the floor, as the saying goes, "ready for bear." I gave it my best shot and was, much to my surprise, greeted with stony silence from beginning to end. I didn't know what hit me. I walked off stunned, and ready to cry, when Al, the "take charge" guy of the two, stopped me in my tracks n' said, "What a bum break. Did you see what you had out there?" I replied, "No! The spotlights were blinding me and I couldn't see out into the audience." "They were all Japanese exchange students," Al replied. They didn't understand or speak, a word of English!"

Appearing in a very famous club has its advantages though. My managers had no trouble getting me on the Merv Griffin TV Show, and I was even summoned to do the Ed Sullivan Show. I was back in the milieu that I loved and felt most comfortable in, and I felt eternally grateful to Jerry Kellert for having gotten me back into the business.

The Sullivan Show consisted of two performances on a Sunday. The first was in the afternoon, in front of a live audience at the Ed Sullivan Theater, but was not televised. It served a great purpose. It was actually like a full dress rehearsal, and also, all the kinks were ironed out during that time, so that the evening show, which was beamed from coast to coast, live, was near perfect. When the afternoon show was concluded, I was walking out of the stage door with Al when I heard someone call out to me. "Young man ..." It was a well dressed gentleman who was huffing and puffing as he struggled to catch up with me. We had just crossed 52nd St., and stopped to see who it was. "Young man, may I have a word with you?" We turned around and Al immediately recognized that it was Mark Leddy, Ed Sullivan's erstwhile personal manager. Mark was a healthy looking septuagenarian who had handled Sullivan practically throughout his entire illustrious career. He saw that Al and I were together, and they obviously knew each other. Al greeted him with a fond "Hello," and asked, "What's up? How've you been, Mark? Long time no see." "I'm fine," was the hasty reply, "I just want you to know that this young man is one of the best real comedians I have seen in a long, long time, and I felt that I just had to go after him and tell him how I felt." I was very flattered by his kind observation and thanked him. We continued to chat for awhile, and when we parted, he said to me, "Al knows where my office is, please feel free to drop in whenever you get a chance. I'd like to talk to you." As we continued on our way Al winked at me and remarked, "Good omen."

The show that evening, played beautifully and was truly a star studded extravaganza. I was in excellent company, sharing the bill with Sergio Franchi, Stiller and Meara, and The Three Stooges. My pal Ham Morgen was particularly attentive with the camera he was handling. It pays to have friends "in high places." Of course I had also done as I was advised beforehand, and made certain to stack the audience with as many members of my family as I could gather together, just to be sure of success.

I left the theater followed by my entourage, consisting of Shirley's parents, my mother and father, and, of course, Shirley, and whichever of the kids who had wanted to come.

Out in the street people were congratulating whatever performers they would recognize, and I too, was a willing recipient of their accolades. As we started to walk in the direction of where our cars were parked and people were still complimenting me, with many of them shaking my hand, a drunk staggered out of the crowd, grabbed me by the hand and shook it vigorously while he blubbered out, "My name is McGinty ... and I once licked Jack Dempsey." I was somewhat startled, then recognizing that he was harmlessly inebriated, I smiled at him and replied, "That's just great Mr. McGinty, but I really must be going now." He just kept pumping my hand, totally oblivious to the fact that I was in a hurry to leave, and that my whole family was waiting patiently for him to let go ... but he wouldn't. He just kept repeating, over and over, "I once licked Jack Dempsey."

Divine intervention made its welcomed entrance once more. Who should come walking by, but that hilarious old time comedy genius, Gene Baylos, who just happened to live in the neighborhood. Whenever I bump into that comical little man, he greets me by making funny faces, in an endeavor to break me up, before saying "Hello." "The very moment that he got through greeting me I said, "Gene, I want you to meet a friend of mine, this is Mr. McGinty." Gene automatically stuck his hand out. The drunk grabbed his hand, and we were scot free to go! When we were all a whole big block away we stopped and looked back, and there was the drunk, still holding on to Gene's hand for dear life, and Gene standing there with a puzzled look.

Five whole months had gone by and now it was the middle of August. Our youngest son David, tall, gangly, and ever so lovable, was on summer vacation from Oregon State University, and working as a boat boy on the lake at Kutsher's Hotel, in Monticello, NY. He and the other boat boy, doubled on the big rear spotlight for the nightly shows. That morning he had called us at our summer place nearby, and we all had a good laugh when he described what happened when he and his partner were working the spotlight while the famed old vaudevillian, and brilliant toastmaster, George Jessel, was performing the night before. Jessel, in his old age, had become obsessed with his personal patriotism, especially after having been appointed "America's Unofficial Ambassador to

Israel," and he was extremely, and ludicrously vehement about his feelings. He had announced, onstage, that he was going to recite a tribute to the "stars n' stripes," He stood there, with the flag nearby, and off to a side, and launched into his emotional spiel. The boys thought it only fitting that they should shine the spot on the flag, and followed their instincts. Jessel stopped the action and yelled out at the two well intentioned, hapless kids, "Don't shine the spot on the flag! ... Shine it on me ... you Communist bastards!" The boys were still laughing when they got up in the morning.

It was a warm, sunny Sunday, and I decided to take the short drive over to Kutsher's and visit with our "little boy." When I walked into the lobby of the hotel, I noticed on the bulletin board that Gene Baylos was scheduled to appear in their nightclub that evening. I found David, and during our visit I remarked, "I see that Gene Baylos is appearing here tonight. Have you seen him around?" "Yes," David replied, "he was just at the swimming pool area kibbitzing with the guests. Why don't you try to find him there?" I ambled over to the large, olympic sized pool, and, sure enough, there was Gene, with a bunch of people standing around him in their bathing suits, and laughing at everything he was saying. I excused myself and interrupted his performance. He was both surprised and happy to see me. I said, "Gene, I came here to offer you an apology. I last saw you standing and shaking hands with a drunk on 53rd and Broadway." He said, "You know, I just left him this morning!"

I dropped in to visit Mark Leddy, as he suggested. We became good friends. He had a long, productive life. I understand that he eventually retired to the west coast of Florida and passed away in Winterhaven at the age of 101. Mark asked if he could impose upon me to do some benefits at the Lambs. I never had any objections to performing for free, as long as I didn't have to give up any paying shows in order to do them. The Lambs is an old time theatrical social club that has its own building on W. 44th St., and the head honcho there at the time was the great Bert Wheeler, the survivor of the famous comedy team of Wheeler and Woolsey. The other theatrical club in our profession is The Friars, and they're located on E. 55th St. Each of these organizations has branches in California too, and they're both legendary meeting places that feature restaurants, health clubs, etc. Ours is a very democratic industry, with few exceptions, and considered to be non-sectarian. I don't really know how it came about, but the Lambs attract a bigger percentage of Gentiles, and the Friars have more Jews, and both exist extremely harmoniously. I did a number of successful turns for the Lambs, and also performed at a roast for marvelous Milton Berle, who was the Dean of the Friars at the time. At the Berle roast I was rudely awakened to the lack of grace that could be accorded to newcomers. I don't really know if it's attributable to jealousy or suspicion or what? Let's just call it fear of the unknown. Red Buttons, an enormously talented man whom I've always enjoyed and admired, was the "Roastmaster" at that affair. We didn't know each other at the time, and when it was my turn to perform, he introduced me very offhandedly, by saying, "Here's a new guy. I don't know much about what he does ... Van Harris!"

My club dates were what were supporting us, as always, and they were still abundant. I felt as though I was sitting on top of the world with so much to look forward to. We also never had to plan vacations because we had the Catskills in the summer, and any time we wanted to go away in the winter it was very easy to get booked to perform on a cruise ship, and the agents were already accustomed to the fact that I didn't accept any engagement on a cruise ship unless Shirley came along as part of the deal. We eventually worked all over the world on cruise ships The time, place, and the length of the engagement depended upon how comfortably our children were situated, and the older they got the easier it became. Our little "bambinos," and that pretty little "bambina" were always first and foremost on our minds and in our hearts.

I was coasting along, waiting to see what great gigs would develop next via the Messrs. Curtis and Wilde, and with the TV exposure I was getting, it was so much easier for Elliott to sell me on club dates. I was becoming a "known" personality. If a club date buyer would propose that an organization or a country club, should employ me, and if any of the groups were unfamiliar with my work and would innocently ask, "What does he do?" the answer was, "Turn on The Griffin Show on Tuesday afternoon," or, "You can catch him on The Ed Sullivan Show on the 25th." Things were really happening.

Alas the fates conspired to give me a jolt. Something that happened three thousand miles away, involving people I had no connection with however, would have a direct, and unexpected bearing upon my future. David Steinberg, the well-known comedian, wrote a piece of business for the Smothers Brothers to perform on their prime time Sunday night television show. The powers that be deemed it sacrilegious and offensive and were against their presenting it. They stood their ground, and the network stood its ground. In the end, the powerful Smothers Brothers show was taken off the air ... cancelled for good. The network started to search high and low for an immediate and more acceptable replacement, and the canny Al Wilde got there before anyone else did, and proposed The Leslie Uggams Show, which they bought lock, stock and barrel. Curtis and Wilde and Leslie left for the west coast and when I asked Al, "What about me?" he answered, "Don't worry, we'll write you into the show eventually."

They worked overtime to try to bolster the show with important guest stars, and even inserted a very talented, rotund Black comic-singer named Johnny Brown, as a regular. I had known Johnny from the old days when he had performed with Maurice and Gregory Hines, and their father, the drummer, in a couple of the Catskill lounges. On the occasions when Al and Morty would come to New York, I would speak to them on the phone, and Al would honestly confess to me that the show was floundering, not because of anything that Leslie was doing wrong, as she and the rest of the cast were all enormously gifted and contributed their all. They just weren't getting the ratings that a prime time Sunday night show should be getting, and they were all deeply involved in trying to piece together a winning formula. They even went as far as to incorporate some hilarious sketches about African-American domestic life, which, beside being funny, were carefully crafted so as not to cause any controversy. The result was a 13-week struggle that ended in being yanked off the air because "it contained material that was offensive to the Black populace." That was an absolute canard. The ratings were what did them in. It was not fair for anyone to have contrived such a terribly destructive excuse. They all came home with their tails between their legs, and very shortly afterward Al Wilde passed away in his sleep. The party had ended ... very ignominiously.

My young cousin Charlie, an affable giant of a man who was once a disc jockey in Florida and was now running a successful public relations firm on Long Island, for the paint industry, and was publishing a trade newspaper called "The Paint Bucket," asked me if I would permit him to try his hand, as a proven super salesman, to get me back on the Johnny Carson Show. He looked good, dressed well, and used the name, Bob Corey, which was the handle he had used during his radio days. He had a deep, mellifluous voice and was a real attention getter. I said, "Go to it Charlie, Morty Curtis is in mourning for his partner, and I don't wanna bother Jerry Kellert again. I think you've got what it takes. Let's give it a try."

Charlie went after that assignment with a flourish. He did all the right things. He made proper appointments and was always on time. He dressed magnificently (strangely, Jerry Cutler had proved that sartorial splendor was not exactly a requisite), and he showered the receptionists and secretaries with boxes of candy and flowers. They looked forward to his visits. He said to me one day, "I learned that the head gee up there, John Carsey, is a smoker and a gun nut, so when I finally had an audience with his majesty I presented him with a cigarette lighter shaped like a hand grenade. I think we're in." Charlie was so thrilled to see that his salesman approach was taking hold.

I knew John Carsey, who was Carson's right hand, and I had gotten along well with him in the past, and I wasn't surprised when Charlie told me that Carsey had chalked my name into a box on the booking blackboard for a future appearance on the show. In true show biz tradition, we waited, and waited, and waited some more. Charlie's phone calls were taken, and answered politely, but there was always some kind of an excuse given for the delay. After months of frustration Charlie threw his hands up and exclaimed, "I've been a salesman all my life. I've come up against the biggest, the best, and the toughest opposition you can imagine. I have never, ever been confounded like your farkakte business has done to me. I love you dearly, but I just cannot make myself sick because of your crazy profession ... I GIVE UP!"

Charlie had been a juvenile diabetic, and now that he was in his late forties, that dread disease was really taking its toll on him. If the public only knew what a destructive disease juvenile diabetes is. By the time he had reached his mid forties he had already lost an eye, his teeth, and both kidneys, and to look at this handsome giant of a man you'd never suspect that he was so decimated. His artificial teeth looked great; his dialysis treatments kept him alive and functioning; and the black patch he wore over his missing eye gave him an air of adventure. Now the surgeons were going to remove his leg. Despite it all he kept right on working and had a successful public relations business going full speed even after he was fitted with a prosthetic leg. He was a heavy man, and he even managed to walk proudly, without too much evidence of a limp, and maintained his infectious laugh and great sense of humor throughout. He facetiously referred to himself as "The Bionic Jew," and constantly reminded all who would listen, that he had already lived two years longer than his momma (my beloved, and tough as nails Aunt Yuspe) who had died of the very same illness at age 46.

Charlie was a "change of life baby" whose mother died when he was a little boy, and I was one of the big cousins who had helped to look after him. I can vividly recall his mother's funeral. I was assigned to distract him and took him for a long, long walk on busy, bustling Pitkin Avenue, in Brooklyn. "The Big Bopper," as we all referred to him, died at the age of 48, leaving behind a wife, an ex-wife, and a son and daughter. I delivered his eulogy at his funeral, which was one of the hardest things I ever had to do in my life. I could barely get through it. I was so choked up and blinded by tears. Funny, how I still looked after that little boy right up to the end. And he wanted so desperately to repay me ... and struck out!

It was becoming apparent, to me, that I was running out of options to somehow try to get back on television. I had seen how easy it was, and how comfortable I had felt in the big time, but suddenly I had exhausted my connections. I remembered how fond Sullivan's manager, Mark Leddy, had been of me, so I decided to give it a try, and see what he would have to say. Leddy's office was always open to me because of the relationship we had built up thanks to the benefits I had done for him at The Lambs. He was, however,

Mr. Sullivan's personal manager, and did not control the bookings on the show, that job was handled by Sullivan's son-in-law, Bob Precht, who was also the show's producer.

I went to see Mark Leddy in his office, and, as always, he was most gracious. After the usual banter about the business I put it to him straight and asked him, "Mr. Leddy, did you really mean what you said when you complimented me like that when we first met?" "Every word," was his reply, "I think you're one helluva comedian." "Then why is it I seem to be going nowhere?" and the answer he gave me is still indelibly inscribed in the back of my cerebellum, and I still wince when I think about it. He paused for a short moment to give my question some thought, and then said, "Some people are meant to dry up on the vine and die ... I guess you're one of them."

That was my wake up call. I wasn't about to feel sorry for myself. I knew what my capabilities were, and decided to concentrate on my club dates, which were, thankfully, still plentiful, and let the chips fall wherever they may. At the same time, I was keeping my eyes open for any and all opportunities that might come along. In addition, I went to those degrading "cattle calls" to audition for TV commercials, and even read for a few off-Broadway shows. The first commercial I attempted, I actually landed. They chose me right away. They told me that I would have to fly immediately to Tampa, FL to film it. That meant that I would have had to cancel a club date at the Concord Hotel in order to do so.. Feeling very impressed with the ease with which I had gotten the commercial, I figured that there would be many more such opportunities, so I opted for the Concord instead. I never did a commercial after that. I really blew it. I auditioned, and actually was accepted for a few more, but in each case, as is not unusual, the commercials, and not I, had been cancelled.

At the behest of a nightclub owner I knew who was an alumnus of NYU, I starred in a movie that was filmed at that great school by a grad student who was also a gifted director. The film was called, "The Palladium Routine," and I played the part of Lenny Bruce. It was a fascinating experience and took five long days. Unlike some of the others in the film, I had studied my part and knew all the lines when I appeared on the set, which was located in some large empty store on La

Guardia Place in SoHo. The director, like a number of young people his age, was not averse to experimenting with drugs, and his young female groupies were always in attendance during the long, grueling filming. The odor of marijuana, emanating from his harem, permeated the air a good deal of the time. It was no severe distraction though, and didn't interfere with the filming, but it sure taught me a great deal about the behavior of some of our college kids. The director would show up in the morning, uttering remarks like, "What a night I had. I don't remember if I was on uppers, or downers, or what?" It didn't seem to affect his ability though, as he proved to be extremely capable, and at the end of the filming he embraced me and complimented me for both my acting and my dedication to the role. He added, "This thing is so damn good that we're gonna enter it in a competition." My ego became so inflated that, that same night, when I performed at a fancy country club up in Rockland County, I came to work with an attitude like, "Hey, keep an eye on me folks. I may soon be leaving this small time stuff for greener pastures in the movies, or the theater." True to form however, because of someone's carelessness, the movie was filmed out of sync, and no amount of mechanical maneuvering was able to correct it. I became so disillusioned that I hastily receded into my protective womb, the club dates.

26 Cruises

Right around that time my agent was paying a lot of attention to the rapid proliferation of the cruise ship industry, and submitted me to the handful of bookers who controlled that busy, and well paying area. It had come a long way since the annual two week Caribbean stint that I used to do for the one controlling booking agent in the NY area. He lured his entertainers to what he called "the boats" by promising them a great winter vacation in warm climates, along with their mates. He paid a pittance, declaring that he wasn't being given much of a budget, (which we all suspected was an out and out lie), but we took the bait nevertheless, and I couldn't complain about the great fun we had. Of course, my club date manager, (first Nat, and later Elliott) still got his percentage, so after the tips, etc., were paid, we wound up with next to nothing. It all seemed worthwhile though, and we made everlasting friends from among the entertainers and the passengers. It was like being part of one big happy family at an elegant party. It was on those early cruises that we developed everlasting friendships. Bud Rosenthal, presently a Vice President with Viacom, signed on a cruise as a roving reporter and he would actually publish a gossipy newspaper describing the current doings of the cruise. To this very day, he remains one of my dearest friends. Jack and Jo Laflin celebrated their honeymoon on a cruise. Jack (a former sports announcer, and sports columnist, and a knocked out, crazy NY Football Giants fan) has since written a couple of novels. His first, about intrigue in Hawaii, is called, "Serpent In Paradise," and is a real page turner. Sid Thiel, an NBC TV newswriter, with a most impressive vocabulary, along with his comely wife Leah, also proved to be joyful additions to our ocean entourages. The intellectual stimulation provided by such tablemates surpassed our fondest expectations.

As the multi-million dollar cruise industry took on bigger and better proportions, more agents got into the act. The various cruise lines began to accumulate larger fleets, and whereas, in the beginning, most ships sailed out of the NY area (and the adjacent Port of Hoboken, NJ), Miami, Fort Lauderdale, Tampa, San Juan, and San Pedro CA became bustling seaports for cruise ships travelling all over the world, and for longer vacation periods. (The Florida ports had become the busiest of them all.) This meant loads of employment for entertainers of assorted stripes and colors, and many found permanent homes on the ships.

A whole new population of "cruise rats" was born. All sorts of acts, and even many who had difficulty getting steady work on land discovered a gold mine performing on the ships. The remuneration was quite generous, though you'd have to be very sagacious when it came to making your deal with the agents, some of whom were greedy beyond belief. I often found myself having to pay the cruise booking agent 15%, in addition to my manager who did me a favor by cutting his end down to 10%. Twenty-five percent constituted one helluva cut! When we would complain to the booker, "How come so much in commission?" he would invariably cover his ass by replying, "You don't know what I've got to pay off in kickbacks to my "connection" with the line." No one forced us to accept the deal, but the rationalization was that we were going to be working at sea for a good amount of time, without having to spend money for gas, hotels, food, or other expenses, so the high commissions were a small price to pay for the privilege of being able to sock away goodly amounts of money. Actually we were contributing to a scurrilous crime, but that's the nature of the actor, "anything to work and make money. So what can we do about it?"

The savvy acts were those who had enough chutzpah to befriend the cruise line's liaisons, and thereby get booked directly, bypassing the agents. The word "chutzpah" means "nerve," and it took some doing to tell the agent that had first put you on the ships to "Get lost! ... I don't need you anymore in order to work this line!" Perhaps such behavior is short sighted, as there will come a time in the future when you're going to have to come to that same person for other jobs on "terra firma." The mentality of the business, though, is that, if you're needed, if you're a request, or you're the only one available, for whatever kind of gig it is, then suddenly everyone, for the sake of convenience, suddenly comes down with a case of amnesia.

How does one know whether or not he is being taken advantage of? I accepted a well-paying, rather long engagement on a luxury cruise liner. I flew from NY to Bombay India to board the vessel. From there we sailed through the Middle East, into the Mediterranean waters, finally disembarking in Genoa, Italy, and flying back home. Shirley had to stay behind in order to attend to her aunt's funeral in Florida, and wind up her affairs, so we arranged for Shirley to catch up with me in Athens, Greece, once she got through with her ordeal. One of my favorite places in the whole wide world is Greece, along with its numerous quaint and beautiful islands, especially in the late spring. The Aegean is terribly romantic. Greece is for lovers.

The cruise booking agent made the arrangement with my manager, whereby my plane fare would be part of the deal, and Shirley's plane fare would come out of my salary. Before I made our agreement, having learned from my personal travel agent what a plane trip like that should cost, I remarked to the agent's "girl Friday," "Whew, her fare is gonna come to a lot of money." She replied, "Don't worry, it doesn't come out to as much as you think." I had learned, from past experience, that the cruise lines are accorded reduced fares for their employees, like the entertainers. When the great cruise was concluded, I picked up my check at the agent's office, in NY. I saw that Shirley's fare came to the huge amount that my travel agent told me it would be. When I protested to the lady, she remarked, "I'm sorry, but the cruise line was billed for the whole amount." That was an exorbitant amount of money, and who were we to believe? I complained to Elliott, and he said, "We can't go inquiring about that to the cruise company behind their booker's back. I'm afraid we're gonna just have to bite the bullet." We didn't want to antagonize anyone out of fear that it might jeopardize future bookings, so, I did the cowardly thing, and, against my better judgment, I just let the matter slide. I had no way of proving whether, or not, I had been taken advantage of, sad to say.

Another such situation arose on an ensuing cruise. This one involved our flying to Singapore and returning from Sydney, Australia. I had the same hinted assurance beforehand from the same lady in the agency, and was once again flabbergasted when she gave me the same lame excuse after they had deducted an even more exorbitant amount for Shirley's plane fare. How could we allow this to happen once more, and without double checking with the cruise line? Once again my manager advised, "If that's what they said it is, then, sorry to say, that must be the awful truth." This bothered me for months afterward, but without any proof of any underhandedness I had no recourse. The possibility that we may have been seriously over-billed was there, and I still think about whether or not we would have been able to have done some successful investigating, just to ease my mind. Very soon after that cruise, the line went out of business, and my suspicions, whether real, or imagined, had to be laid to rest. It's been quite a few years now, but the thought that there could have been some larceny involved still lingers, and yet, "thou shalt not falsely accuse" keeps croppin' up in the back of my head. As the Pennsylvania Dutch would say, "Ve grow too soon oldt ... und too late schmardt."

Performers don't work every night on a cruise ship. No matter how long the engagements are for, or how far away the ships travel, the line ingeniously works things out so that passengers generally vacation in ten days, or two-week increments. For example, passengers will fly to Hong Kong, tour those exotic ports in the South China Sea for that amount of time, then disembark in Singapore, where a new complement of passengers, flown in from the states, is already waiting to go back towards Hong Kong. During those two weeks, or ten days, whichever, the performers will appear on two or three different nights, and change their material during that time, so that nothing is repeated. The passengers are entertained royally by all the versatility displayed, and when they leave, the new passengers are treated to the same routines. This system enables the entertainers to stay aboard for long stretches of time, and also saves the cruise line the expense of having to constantly fly in new acts. Instead of revolving acts, we get revolving passengers.

The incomparable Jimmy Durante used to exclaim, "Everybody wants ta get inta da act!" meaning "Everybody wants to be a comedian." The novelty acts, like the magicians in particular, not content with dazzling the audiences with their mystifying tricks, figure that they would be a lot more effective if they would add humorous repartee to their performances. Where to get it? Simple! Steal it from the comedians! ... and boy ... do they ever! I would safely guess

Van and Shirley. Cairo, Egypt.

Public Latrines. Ephesus, Turkey.

that the biggest purloiners of comedy material on cruise ships are the magicians. The vocalists are not averse to stealing wit and whimsy to enhance their performances either. The pity is that so many of the offenders don't have the experience to extract a maximum of laughter from the jokes. Meanwhile, they selfishly succeed in emasculating the hapless comedians.

There was one magician who appeared on the same roster with me several times, and who was wanton when it came to plagiarism. An aging Englishman with an engaging, cheerful personality, he proved to be absolutely ruthless. I recognized every comedian's jokes in his performances, and the audiences, consisting of people from all parts of the country, were impressed. The magician had even gone as far as to have booklets published that contained jokes that he had pilfered from others, which he sold in the ship's sundry shop for about ten bucks apiece. Once as I was departing from one of our cruise tours, he remarked to me, "Hey, I liked that joke you told about the birth control pills. I'm going to use it in my act." That's real "chutzpah!" I figured that we'd never be working together again, and I shrugged it off. As luck would have it, we were booked together on another long cruise, and during one of my performances I told that joke. When I walked offstage he was waiting for me and blurted out, "Hey, you told my story. You can even find it in my latest book in the sundry shop." I was fit to be tied, and reminded him that he actually told me that he was going to steal it from me. "Oh yeah, now I remember," he replied, with no hint of remorse.

We all get excellent accommodations on the ships, with very few (sometimes downright insulting) exceptions. In the case of those exceptions it's up to the performer to threaten to quit, which I actually had to do once or twice. I feel sorriest for the musicians however, as, for some sadistic reasons, known only to cruise ship operators, nightclub owners, and resort hotel people, they are always treated shabbiest. They work harder than most, and they are least appreciated. I'm not referring to musical soloists who are booked as performers. I'm talking about the boys in the band. Generally they have to double up and even triple up in cabins located in undesirable areas of the ship, and they must also eat in the staff cafeterias along with the "lesser help." An enormously talented African-American pianist named Rogers Grant, whom I know from the resorts, and who is highly respected by, not only his fellow musicians, but by all the acts he accompanies, was booked on a "'round the world" tour on one of the ships I've performed on. He had to honor his long contract, but as he confided to me when he got home again, he'd never go back on a cruise ship. He said that they were all treated like second-class citizens. He referred to the ship as a "slave ship."

Yet cruising is, for the most part, a very elegant manner in which to vacation, and getting bigger and better all the time. The ship is a fantasy world filled with just about anything a vacationer could desire. The chosen ports all over the globe are fascinating and different, and the tours, though an added expense, are carefully planned and conveniently carried out. It's a wonderful, comfortable, and most educational way in which to see the world. Many everlasting friendships are engendered around the dining room tables. People who are strangers when they come aboard become like family members with the other strangers who were assigned to the same table, and before the cruise is over they get to know just about everything about each other.

There are cruise lines that attract younger, less sophisticated people who are out strictly for a good time. These are generally less expensive and the quality of food and entertainment is commensurate with the prices. But there too, the sheer beauty of the ports, the service aboard ship, the fact that they are out to sea, away from their troubles and having the time of their lives, generates deliriously satisfying vacationing. The introduction of gambling on the ships has made the adventure even more exciting. And, the amounts of food consumed border upon gluttony.

The seasoned voyagers are generally older, and moneyed, and cruise a great deal. Those who have been exposed to better entertainment, especially back home in the bigger cities, are more discriminating, and demanding, and not unwilling to pay for quality. Wealth and sophistication do not always go hand in hand though, so there's always a mix that does not entirely blend. Entertainment, of course, is still a matter of individual taste, and the people who are assigned to put their programs together, particularly if it's for a class ship, are confronted with a draconian feat. They do their utmost, and most of the time they succeed, but not always.

What started out with some fairly mediocre, but willing and hard working acts, has steadily been replaced by more gifted artists, and also some well-known movie, TV, and cabaret stars who are paid enormous sums. Some are even contracted just to mingle with the passengers, without having to perform. Some time during the cruise, they are interviewed by the Cruise Director, and that draws bigger crowds than the shows do. Everybody wants to tell the folks back home that "so-and-so" was aboard ship.

There are so many excellent singers, dancers, comedians, ventriloquists, jugglers, puppeteers, mimes, instrumentalists, classical music soloists, and assorted other entertainers aboard cruise ships, in addition to lecturers who dominate the daytime hours at sea. The cruise staff generally consists of friendly, accommodating, and yes, even talented, men and women, though there can be some self-aggrandizing, pompous asses mixed in among them. Some even border on the obnoxious. And, of course, there's always the imperious Captain, with his assortment of gold braid, and his ubiquitous crew of officers, good looking in their neat uniforms, and ever ready to accommodate the lonely ladies aboard. On better vessels they hire "hosts," gentlemen (some retired and some quite successful in various walks of life), who must be good ballroom dancers and willing to dance and converse with any and all ladies who are travelling alone. They are generally a homogeneous group, are well dressed, and truly epitomize the word "gentleman."

The biggest, and most successful entertainment attraction on the ship consists of an ensemble of fresh faced young boys and girls (generally there are eight or so, in the group) who put on dazzling musical extravaganzas about three nights out of every cruise. These are famous standard Broadway musicals that are expertly packaged in LA, Las Vegas, or Florida. The kids perform within a framework of pre-recorded background music, which is perfectly augmented by the ship's orchestra. The group sings and dances magnificently in the most glorious costumes, and brilliant settings.

Royal Caribbean Cruises came upon the scene with a flourish somewhere back in the seventies, if my memory serves me correctly, and their three great ships originated in the Port of Miami and sailed the Caribbean. I was among their earliest crop of entertainers, and Shirley and I spent parts of three whole years aboard, with full compliments of satisfied passengers. We worked when it was convenient for us and didn't interfere with our raising the kids, who were very independent and growing rapidly. Royal Caribbean had instituted a very successful system for the entertainers and passengers both. Our company of entertainers would leave Miami and sail down on one ship to Curacao in the Netherlands Antilles, performing and stopping at the beautiful Caribbean islands along the way. In Curacao we would meet another of their ships that had just pulled alongside, and we'd simply walk over and exchange entertainers. The passengers would be getting fresh entertainment, and we would be getting new audiences. Sometimes, we'd hop into a small, eight-passenger plane in Curacao, and we'd fly to San Juan, Puerto Rico and board a ship whose entertainers had flown down to Curacao to replace us. Then we would sail on to La Guaira, which is the port adjacent to Caracas, Venezuela, and when we were all done entertaining, we would cab into Caracas where we'd board a huge commercial Viasa airliner to take us back to Miami. There, the largest ship in their fleet, The Song Of Norway, would be awaiting us, with a full load of passengers, so that we could begin to make the round robin all over again.

We were enjoying La Guaira along with our friend, the violinist, Sascha Tormas, and a female companion, and we called ahead to the airline in Caracas to confirm our flight to Miami on the following morning. We were told that all was in order. It was teeming hot when our cab, loaded with all our luggage, pulled into the large, antiquated airport. The weather was getting hotter by the minute, and the airport was stuffy beyond belief. When we got to the ticket counter the attendant told us that they had not issued boarding passes for "las senoras," "But don't worry, just take the waiting airport bus out to the plane, and they'll be allowed to board." I inquired as to why that happened, and was answered with a very curt and convenient (for him) "No comprendo ... just go out to the plane." Sascha's friend, an experienced hand at these kinds of shenanigans, smelled a rat, and said, "I'm going back to the ship. I'll fly back from the next port," and she left. As it turned out, the wise lady knew what she was doing. When we arrived at the plane, (quite rung out from the rapidly escalating heat, and the surging crowd all around us) we climbed the stairs to enter, and Sascha and I were waived through. However Shirley was stopped. "Where is the senora's boarding pass?" the stewardess asked. "We were told that you would have it," I replied. "Sorry, we do not," she answered, "La senora will have to wait below. She cannot come aboard." The situation became more confused as Shirley stepped aside. Sascha and I went inside to see what was going on. Sascha sat down in his seat, and the seat next to him, which was mine, was empty, but Shirley's seat was occupied. "The dirty bastards," I thought to myself, "they've sold Shirley's seat to one of their own. If they wanna play games, I'll play games with them." Meanwhile the plane had rapidly filled up, and while it was standing on the ground, without any air conditioning in force as yet, things became very uncomfortable for everyone. Sascha looked at me quizzically, and shrugged his shoulders, as if to indicate, "Whadd'ya gonna do now?"

I ran to the door and yelled down to my confused wife, "Don't worry, Shirl, I won't leave without you!" I went back inside and was mortified when I saw that somebody had already been placed in my seat too. Sascha couldn't believe what was going on. I plunked myself down on the floor, in front of the pilot's cabin, and announced, in a loud, strong voice, "This plane is not leaving until la senora is allowed to come on!" I'm really very docile when it comes to standing up for myself, but these savages were messin' around with the love of my life. Besides, I'd never, ever, leave her all alone in this strange environment. Also, there was that other important underlying factor to consider ... Royal Caribbean's flagship was waiting for us in the Port of Miami, with over a thousand passengers aboard, waiting to set sail! The show must go on!

The flight attendants could not believe what was happening. The Spanish language was flying in all different directions. They summoned the captain, and he looked down upon this crazy "gringo" sitting on the floor in front of him in disbelief. I kept staring straight ahead, and managed to repeat what I had said earlier, several times. The captain realized that they were in a predicament, so he called the terminal, asking for help (in Spanish, of course). I was an A student in Spanish at Thomas Jefferson High School, but they were jabbering so fast that I couldn't comprehend everything that was being said. Meanwhile the grumbling from the uncomfortable passengers was increasing in volume. The one word I did make out easily, which sent a small shudder down my spine was "soldados," but I was determined to stand my ground.

Very soon a group of very young soldiers, all sporting rifles, appeared, and surrounded me, while the captain, and his crew were all deeply involved in conversation. Surprisingly, nobody laid a hand on me. What happened next was the solution to the problem, but it happened grudgingly. One of the stewardesses suggested that Shirley and I could sit in passenger seats for takeoff and landing only, in accordance with flight regulations. And, since there were a number of parents and grandparents aboard with small children, all that was required was for two of them to strap the babies onto their laps only for the takeoff and landing, while we occupied the children's seats. Then we would sit in the extra, pullout "jump seats" that are reserved for the flight attendants, which would all be perfectly legal. I had heard that we "ugly Americans" are not loved by our dear neighbors below the border, and it became very much in evidence that morning. Aside from the shabby treatment at the hands of the scurrilous ticket agents, it appeared as though the attendants were encountering a good deal of opposition in attempting to recruit two volunteers. I don't know if it was due to the heat and discomfort, or the fact that there were two kindly souls among them, but the deed was eventually accomplished, the soldados departed, and we took off, over an hour late.

During the flight, as we sat in those jump seats, which weren't at all uncomfortable, the flight attendants went out of their way to accommodate us. Smoking was permitted, and one of the male attendants approached me with two expensive looking cigars, and with a big grin on his face said, "Senor, look at what I've got for you." I replied, "Sorry to disappoint you, but I don't smoke." His smile quickly turned to a look of dejection, as he walked away apologizing, "Sorry senor."

Awhile later it was mealtime, and a stewardess handed us each a tray, saying, "Everybody else is eating chicken, but for you two I brought steak." I said, "I don't want to disappoint you, but we're vegetarians. Maybe you could find a salad, or some vegetables?" No matter how much they tried, they just couldn't make contact. They even brought us a bottle of champagne, thinking that it would really please us, and again were disappointed when I informed them that we don't drink. I'll bet they had a lot to say about us after everybody got off.

Meanwhile, at Miami airport, time was growing extremely critical. Shirley's clever aunt, Dorothy, who lived in Miami Beach, and with whom we had made up to rendezvous upon arrival, realized that there was some kind of a snafu, and that we'd have to get through customs very quickly if we were going to make it to the ship on time. She was there waiting for us all right, but she had, somehow, managed to explain our predicament to a the Customs Department, and actually had an inspector standing alongside of her when we arrived. He whisked the three of us through in a jiffy, and as we ran for the ship, with barely enough time to kiss and hug, Sascha was heard to remark, "Wow! ... Who was that wonderful woman?"

Needless to say, I was furious over the whole sordid affair, and emotionally, and physically rung out by it all. As we sailed south I composed a letter to Viasa chastising them for the manner in which we were treated. I minced no words and vividly explained everything that happened. I also pointed out that Royal Caribbean Cruises is an excellent Viasa customer, what with all the entertainers that make that Caracas to Miami flight just about weekly, and requested an explanation from them. I sent a copy of my letter to Viasa to the President of Royal Caribbean; another to Sascha's friend so that she could be apprised of what had happened, (in my letter I had also pointed out how they had forced her to change her travel plans); and I sent a copy to columnist and author, William F. Buckley, who had written a column in one of the NY newspapers just a short while back, complaining about an ill fated, abusive flight that he had taken on that very same

Viasa Airlines. I received no reply from anyone, except Mr. Buckley, who sent me a terse, hand written note saying, "Hah! Hah! Let me know if you hear from them."

Why on earth did I not receive a communique from Royal Caribbean regarding my letter to Viasa? After all, it was in the process of fulfilling our obligation to them that we had suffered such abuse. The simple answer is that they couldn't give a damn about us. We are treated well while in the process of working for them aboard ship, but the attitude of those in command, who are all foreigners, is that, "glorified help," or not, ... we are still considered "help," and not first class citizens, like the passengers.

An outstanding example of this occurred back in the late sixties or early seventies, when a Holland-America ship, The Princendam, caught fire and sank in Alaskan waters. Miraculously, there were no fatalities, and everyone aboard ship was evacuated to lifeboats. The very last lifeboat to be lowered, amid all the panic and bedlam, was for the entertainers. When the rescue vessels appeared on the scene, it took an heroic effort to lift the frightened passengers out of the small boats and into the welcome hands of the brave sailors. When it appeared as though each and every one had been taken aboard, someone pointed out that there was still one lifeboat unaccounted for. Despite the rapidly deteriorating visibility, somewhere off in the distance they were able to make out one lonely boat, furiously bobbing up and down, as it was being lashed unmercifully by the ever-menacing sea. It was the one with the entertainers. My friends, singer Richard Ianni, and magician Jack Mallon, who were part of that unfortunate group, later described, how (when it looked as though the rescue ships were getting ready to leave without them) they screamed at the top of their lungs, and cried hysterically until they were eventually discovered and taken into tow. To compound the incredible fright, after the incident had made worldwide news, and all the survivors had returned home, a TV station in NY asked Mr. Mallon to come in and be interviewed, and while he was on the air describing their hairy plight, his home was burglarized.

The very last time that I had performed on a Holland-America ship, a line that I had worked for many, many times, we were in Alaska. While at sea, I suddenly found myself unable to urinate. The doctor and nurses aboard were very attentive, and having done all they could to try to alleviate my condition, when the ship docked in Juneau they took me to the local hospital. There I was examined, and told that I was having some sort of prostate problem. They gave me some pills that they said would clear it up, if it had turned out to be only an infection. They also advised me that there were no urologists in all of Alaska, and that the nearest one was located in Seattle, WA. I then returned to the ship, hoping that the pills would do the trick.

Things only got worse, and I had to have a catheter inserted. I informed the Cruise Director of my plight, and told him to take his time in ordering a replacement, as I would perform until the right one was available. For the next two weeks I functioned with the aid of a catheter, and no one was any the wiser for it. Little did the audience suspect that while I was telling my jokes, singing, and doing my funny little shuffle, underneath my tuxedo pants was a catheter that was constantly filling up. We flew back home (after two weeks of discomfort that was getting more difficult each day) and I went right into the hospital where a successful T.U.R.P. (Trans Urethral Prostectomy) was performed. No one from Holland-America ever called to inquire about my health, and, strangely, I was never asked to work for them again. Such considerate people ...

The cruise ships have gotten a little more seaworthy since those early days. The ships are built larger, and move more swiftly, and the companies brag about something called "stabilizers" which are designed to make the ships negotiate rough seas more smoothly. Though Shirley and I consider ourselves to be seasoned veterans of the ocean by now, and proud of our "sea legs," under extreme conditions no amount of anything can ward off seasickness. When the stewards start to put out those "barf bags," you know that somethin's a'comin'. I have often joked, on land, "If you like to throw up and play Bingo, take a cruise."

At one time, many of the popular winter cruises sailed out of the New York harbors, which meant passing through the oft-times turbulent Cape Hatteras (which is off the coast of North Carolina), both going and returning. "Mal de mer" ruled the roost, but was almost always overcome by a genuinely good time. I would tell the story about the fabled humorist, Robert Benchley, who, on his first Caribbean cruise was so terribly affected by seasickness. The ship's doctor came to visit him in his cabin, as he lay there tossing and turning, and not knowing what to do with himself. The doctor chuckled, and assured him, "Don't worry Mr. Benchley, you're not going to die." At that point Benchley looked up at him and said, "Don't say that doctor. Thinking that I was going to die is the only thing that's been keeping me alive!"

It was on one of those early Caribbean cruises that we met Johnny Andrews. Every January, soon after the Christmas-to-New Years revelry had died down, the New York State Masons would charter a ship for two weeks. They all looked like very staid people when they came aboard in New York. The ladies appeared very prim, carrying their little hat boxes, while the men wore heavy coats over their conservative business suits. Once that ship got past the proverbial five-mile limit, all hell broke loose. The Empire State Masonic Order was filled with the most relaxed, fun loving ladies and gentlemen we ever had the pleasure of travelling with. They really had a knack for letting their hair down. This cruise was the agency's special baby and the music and entertainment were carefully selected. I was delighted to have been one of the chosen. We brought with us, in addition to the ship's orchestra, a jazz quartet headed up by Paul Gene, who played trumpet and sang, and featured Charlie Scardino on bass (his pianist wife, Dorothy, a dynamic recording artist, was also along), plus Sam Giuliano on accordion, and Alan Hanlon on guitar. That interesting combination of music makers played into the wee hours of the morning and had everybody dancing until they dropped from exhaustion. The man who was selected to play piano at the cocktail parties before dinner was Johnny Andrews, a fine jazz musician who, at one time played with a famous group that included Leonard Garment, who was also a jazz musician of note, and who later became President Nixon's lawyer. Johnny was an affable Irish-American, with a great gift of gab, who also emcee'd the shows. He had a marvelous resume that included having once been the steady weatherman on NBC Television, and he was employed extensively by various theatrical agencies to emcee some important club dates all over the country. In addition, he had a steady job at the well known Monkey Bar of the Elysee Hotel, a popular New York City watering hole located on W. 54th St., between Madison and Park, where he played piano and sang. He was so popular that management had put a stipulation into his contract that allowed him to take off for more important engagements any time he pleased.

During the Second World War, the tall, slim, freckle faced, sandy haired young man was a pilot who flew large transport planes in Europe. He was a real daredevil, having been reprimanded several times by his superiors for flying such large aircraft under bridges whenever he gauged that he could attempt such a hair-raising maneuver. Johnny had married a former Miss America contestant, with whom he had a son, but by the time we met him, he was already divorced. He had a magnetic personality without ever being overbearing, and he was a walking encyclopedia. He had many interesting facts and figures at his fingertips, and numerous fascinating stories to relate. We once sat around talking about our respective children and it was Johnny who came up with a quick tale about the late, great journalist, Bob Consodine. Consodine, when once asked if he had any children, replied, "Mrs. Consodine and I have four children. Two of them are adopted ... We've forgotten which two." Johnny was filled with such beautiful tales.

Johnny had worked, for the longest time, as the cocktail pianist at the famed Coconut Grove, in Boston, and had left there for a job in NY on the day before the historic fire. A great many people perished in that tragedy, including Buck Jones, the famous Hollywood Western star. Johnny's nephew, who was in the US Navy at the time, thought his uncle Johnny was still appearing there, and brought a date along to meet him on that fatal night. His nephew and the date, both perished in that horrible blaze. When Johnny heard the terrible news about the fire he had gone back as soon as it was quelled, and he gave us the grim details. Although the authorities had cordoned off the nightclub, he had no problems getting through. He described how just about everything had burned to the ground and how the remains of those crammed next to each other in the hallways and doorways, in their futile effort to escape, were painstakingly being evacuated, and crumbling as they were being lifted from the still-smoldering ashes.   "The scene at the bar was ghastly," he continued.   "It was ghoulish.   The charred remains of those who were there still sitting around the bar, and the third finger on the left hand of many of the ladies present was missing." It was as though we were all listening to a horrible ghost story as he told it to us while we all sat around one evening in one of the ship's lounges and listened incredulously.

27 Turns of Fate

There've been a lot of "Joe's" in my life, starting with my brother. Another "Joe" was one of my childhood friends whom I had lost touch with for many years. We'd had some interesting times together in our youth. Although he did not live in our neighborhood, he used to visit his cousin Ike, who was the smartest kid in our crowd. Joe was an only child, and the son of a very famous Jewish author and playwright. High intelligence was a family trait. In fact, the boys' uncle was also a world famous author who was eventually awarded the Nobel Prize for Literature. Joe lived in a fancy neighborhood in Manhattan, on Riverside Drive, and in summers he and his parents would move into their seaside residence in Seagate, which was the affluent area in Coney Island, Brooklyn, where the major stars of the then thriving Yiddish Theater also had their summer homes. He was basically a quiet boy and possessed an astute sense of humor, which rapidly ignited whenever he was in our midst. It was really a fun time when Joe came around.

His renowned uncle let the whole world know that his older brother (Joe's father) was his idol, and a great deal of the talent he had developed, he had learned from him. They were truly a family to be both respected and admired. Unfortunately they were all dealt a devastating blow when Joe's illustrious father died of a sudden heart attack while taking a shower one fateful morning. He couldn't have been any older than fifty at the time, or perhaps even younger. We saw Joe very soon after it happened. The shock was unbearable for Joe and his mother, both. The tragic turn of events was too much to bear, and he became very despondent and subdued. His visits to our part of the world became less and less frequent, and eventually he seemed to have disappeared entirely. We had heard from Ike that Joe had attended the Art Students League, a very prestigious school on W. 57th St. in NY, and had blossomed into an extremely talented artist, and that later he married his childhood sweetheart, June, a striking blonde Bohemian type, who herself was a very gifted lady, and that they eventually had three or four children. I knew nothing more ... until, that one evening, so many years later, when I received a surprise phone call from Joe.

It was as though we had never parted. "Van," ... It's me, your funny old pal, Joe, and I wonder if I can meet you and discuss something with you?" I was most pleasantly surprised. "Anytime you want, Joe, you sound so clandestine. I'd love to see you again. Obviously you know where I live 'cause you're callin' me here in Teaneck. Where are you, and what are you up to these days?" "June and I, and the children, live in Union City, which isn't too far away from you. How and where, do you propose that we get together?" "You workin'?" I asked. "I'm free lancing," he replied, which could have meant just about anything. "Well," I continued, "I've got a gig in NY tomorrow night. Are you free to go with me? I'll pick you up, and you can catch me at work and we can talk before, and afterward, and however long you'd like." "Tell you what," he said, "Gimme your address, and exact directions on how to get to you from Queen Anne Road, and I'll come to you, and we can go from there." "You got it," I said, and we ascertained all the details.

We were all neighborhood kids, so to speak, and Joe knew Shirley too, and it was a nice reunion when we got to see each other again. None of us had changed much. Perhaps Joe had lost a little more hair, but that was just about it. After I introduced the kids, and we all did a little kibbitzing, Joe and I got into my Cadillac and off the two of us drove to New York. I owned a Caddy in those years only because I did a lot of road driving, and needed a good, big, reliable car that I could depend on. I considered it to be one of the major tools of my trade.

We both got home late that night because we talked, and talked, and talked. There was so much to catch up on. My hair literally stood on end when he revealed to me all that he and June had gone through, and were still enduring. It was not a happy tale by any means.

Joe's thoughtful father had provided for his wife and child. Joe continued to live in New York with his mother, who eventually passed away. How much later he didn't say, and whether or not he was already married to June when that happened, I don't recall his telling me either. I do remember that his mother had had a wonderful relationship with his father, and was sitting on top of the world being married to one of the most outstanding celebrities in his glamorous and artistic field. His sudden, and totally unexpected demise was a crushing blow and the dear lady was never able to get over it. Joe had youth on his side, which provided him with the resiliency to adjust.

Joe, and June, and whichever of their little tots that they had at the time, moved to the Miami Beach area of Florida where he fatuously invested his entire inheritance in a hotel. The swindlers down there are as cunning, if not more so, as any of those that inhabit resort areas, and the desperate lout who became his partner took poor Joe for all he had. It was purely a case of a trusting, self-confident artist being financially decimated by a scheming, insensitive charlatan. There was nothing he could salvage there in the other guy's well-connected domain, so they cried a lot and packed up their car with all their belongings and their little papooses, and headed to the more familiar territory above the Mason Dixon line.

While they were driving through Alabama they realized that they had very little cash, and they passed a country carnival that featured a prize fight. On the billboard was written, "$100 WILL BE PRESENTED TO ANYONE WHO WILL STAY IN THE RING FOR ONE ROUND WITH THE CHAMP." Joe looked at June and said, "Here's a chance to make some money so we can feed the kids." June was taken aback. "Have you lost your mind? He's a professional. You don't even know how to fight. He'll kill you!" Joe wasn't even listening to her. He had started psyching himself the moment he read the sign. He was extremely myopic and had removed his glasses figuring that, without being able to fully see what was going on, he might just courageously manage to hang in there. He was furiously divesting himself of all negative thoughts. It was "straight ahead." He volunteered, much to the cheers of the assembled onlookers, and someone tied his boxing gloves on quickly, before he could change his mind. Nobody bothered to ask him if he wanted to remove any of his clothing, or what mortuary he would like to have his body shipped to. As the opponents got to the center of the ring to go through the senseless motion of listening to the so-called "referee's" instructions, Joe looked up into the bloodshot eyes of the

375

cauliflowered pug standing right next to him and silently pleaded, "Look pal, my wife and babies are watching. I've never done this before, but we need the hundred bucks very badly 'cause without it the kids are gonna starve. Please, please take it easy on me, will ya?" "Sure," the punchy pugilist assured him. "Gotcha!" The opening bell sounded and that was all that Joe could remember. The bum came out swinging like he was intent upon tearing Joe's head off and landed some terribly punishing blows. As June described it, the sadistic spectators roared with delight as each devastating haymaker was landed, and laughed uproariously as the poor guy in the shirt and pants which were rapidly turning crimson, attempted to run in every direction to avoid the senseless punishment. The promoters loved it, as it all looked so comical to them. Miraculously, when the bell sounded, signifying that the round had ended, Joe, who was down more times than up, was back up on his feet, but he had no idea where in the world he was at. They even gave Joe a tip, in addition," for having put on such a good show." Joe still doesn't remember how he managed to stay in that ring for as long as he did, which was an eternity. The people were still howling as the man in charge peeled the money into Joe's hand, which was shaking uncontrollably, and Joe wandered off in the direction of June's hysterical shrieking which was shrill enough to overcome the loud bells that were clinging in his head and fighting to escape through his ears. The only advantage to the whole affair, aside from the remuneration, was that, if Joe would ever become a celebrity in the future, and be asked to appear on any of those insipid TV and radio talk shows, he could rightfully claim, on his resume, that he was an ex-fighter.

They finally made it home, all the way to New Jersey, where they managed to settle into a tiny basement apartment in Union City. June kept saying, "I thank my lucky stars that the little ones fell asleep before you stepped into the ring with that animal. The sight of that horrible fiasco could have left a psychological scar upon them that could have lasted for the rest of their lives."

When they settled in back north, Joe had very little time to waste, and immediately went looking for a job, any job, as long as it would bring in some income. He was too proud to look to the family for help and tried it on his own. First thing he did was to answer an ad to work on an automobile assembly line somewhere near Elizabeth, NJ. He lasted only until the first paycheck, as the stupefying procedure of performing the same motion consistently, as the part he was assigned to, would quickly pass in front of him in a never ending procession, almost drove him out of his mind. To this very day he still cannot figure out how anyone can do that sort of work for a living.

Joe next took a Civil Service exam, and was educated enough to obtain a job with the US Postal Service. The pay was decent, and the government benefits were good, which, at least gave him the security of knowing that his family was covered for that all-important medical care, and that a pension had been established. Joe soon recognized that, as much as he needed to earn a living, the Postal Service was not for him.

With all his artistic ability, he was only able to scrape pennies together doing pastel portraits for people he was recommended to, and, he continued to go from one horrible job to another. The worst occupation he ever got involved in was working in a meat packing plant. That one didn't last very long. He told me how, very soon after he began working there, he stood in the huge refrigerator, bundled up against the cold, with the frozen carcasses swirling all around him, and looked down at his bleeding hands, as they grabbed each one that went by, and he just started to weep uncontrollably. "This is what it's all come down to? I can't bear it." He felt as though he didn't want to live any longer, but he had so many treasured reasons waiting at home for him to go on. It was right then and there that he decided that he was going to swallow his pride and appeal to his famous uncle.

Why had he been looking for me? Well, his uncle was writing all his brilliant works in his native Yiddish, in longhand, and on yellow legal pads, which required the use of a translator. Joe was ideal for the job, and it was only for personal reasons that he had not applied. His uncle was so prolific that he employed several translators, and, as I soon found out, he drove a very hard bargain when it came to compensation for this highly specialized and intricate work. Joe struck a deal with his niggardly relative, and that eventually provided him with enough income to move out of the three-room basement apartment that he and his brood were occupying in Union City, and actually move into a house in another section of the lovely city of Teaneck. Joe, with his superb sense of humor, had secretly entertained the thought of writing comedy material for anyone who would listen, and that's why he thought of me. It's been said that a great deal of humor is based upon tragedy, so who was better qualified than Joe?

It's a peculiar thing about writing for a comedian. We arranged for me to pay him a small amount each week, and that would go towards any piece of business that I would agree to buy from the many that he was submitting to me. We had an amiable understanding, and we enjoyed each other's company, and laughed a great deal, so it was fun. BUT, it's one thing to write humorous essays, and a totally other art to write things that are funny when spoken. Joe's stuff fell into the former category. I tried to put my own spin on some of his essays onstage, and perhaps if I really worked very diligently at it I might have made it work, but audiences are very impatient with stand up comedy, and your head tells you when you've reached the point of no return. If you're going to linger any longer with a routine that's slow getting off the ground you're gonna die. Such was the case with Joe's material, so after a good, fairly long try, we just threw in the towel and gave up the experiment.

There's an interesting addendum to this story: We saw Joe and June from time to time, though not a lot, even though they lived only a mile away. For one thing, it was difficult to visit with them because Joe had acquired a pet St. Bernard dog that he adored, and the lovable animal had no idea what a nuisance he was. He was unusually large, and playful, and extremely emotional. A visit to Joe would mean having to go home immediately afterward to change your clothes and shower. Upon seeing you, the beast would put his huge paws up on your shoulders, and slobber all over you. I still don't know if Joe, who was becoming more sardonic with each passing day, had adopted the animal out of love, or for protection, or, as I really suspect, for some kind of sadistic pleasure.

Meanwhile, some of his kids went to the same school with some of my kids, and they were fond of each other, were excellent students, and had a nice working relationship in a number of classes. One day Joe rang my doorbell and asked if I could grant him a favor. He needed $250 in a hurry and promised to repay me by the following weekend. That didn't present any problem, and I wrote him a check. Many weeks, and months, and years went by without my being repaid, and only once during all that time did I remind him that he owed me the money. His answer was, "I haven't forgotten. Believe me, when I have it I'll give it to you," ... and no more was ever said.

About ten years later, after we had all changed locations, his life took a very interesting turn. All the kids had become adults, and ours were already out of the house, and I assumed that so were theirs. We sold the house and moved into a condo in an adjacent city. We heard that they had moved away too, but we didn't know where. We also had heard that their daughter, our son Andy's classmate, had written a novel that was published, and we were so proud of her great accomplishment. We next heard a more surprising piece of news, June had written a sexy novel that had become a big hit, and she was working on another one. We didn't attempt to find them to congratulate them, as, somehow I got very busy, and Shirley and I were travelling around the world, while I was performing on cruise ships, but, needless to say, we were pleased as punch to learn about their successes.

One day, while I was in "The Big Apple" on business, Shirley received a surprising, and totally unexpected phone call at home. The male stranger on the phone inquired, "Is this the residence of Van Harris?" "Who wants to know?" she answered suspiciously. For many years some guy in the vicinity who had the same name as mine, had been running up debts from time to time, and I had been the innocent recipient of demands for payment of debts incurred by this scoundrel. In each case I received an almost instantaneous apology. The voice on the phone continued, "I represent Mr. Joseph _____, and I have been instructed to send Mr. Harris a check for $250." Shirley was startled. "You've got the right place. Kindly send it. By the way, how can we contact

Mr. _____?" and the terse reply was, "That was all I was instructed to tell you," and he hung up.

About six months later I had a club date in Long Beach, California, and we came into LA a day earlier so that we could visit our childhood friends from Brooklyn, Shirley and Jerry Hundert, who had become very successful in the optical business, and while we were at it, also see our beloved friends (my former agent and his lovely wife), Rabbi Jerry, and Jeff Cutler. We stayed over at the Hunderts and were planning what to do for breakfast when the phone rang. It was the esteemed rabbi with a message, "Joe and June are my congregants and I told them that you were in town, and they would like you to join them at their house for breakfast." I had heard that they had moved to LA but didn't know exactly where, and I asked Jerry for directions to their home. You can imagine my surprise when I was told that these two kids (who were living in that three-room basement flat in Union City when I had renewed our friendship) were now living in the exclusive Bel Air section of LA. They had bought Bing Crosby's house.

Needless to say it was both a joyous, emotional reunion that practically brought tears to the eyes of the Rt. Hon. Reverend Jerome Cutler, who stood by beaming. June greeted us in the same bohemian attire that she was noted for. The years hadn't changed her at all. Still big and blonde, with that same large smile, only looking far more relaxed than she had ever looked when they were living in Teaneck. Joe, still about the same, still a bit taciturn, and still cuttingly cynical, but with a constant edge of biting humor. There was a touch of Oscar Levant in my adventurous old friend. June showed us her study, where the desk was filled with pages being turned out for a forthcoming book, and Joe proudly walked us into his studio, with breathtaking originals crowding every available inch of space. "Joe, they're beautiful!" I exclaimed, I'll bet they're all sold" "Not a one," he proudly stated, "I'm keeping them all. I don't want anyone else to have my paintings." June smiled, a quizzical smile, and Shirley and I looked at each other. Same old Joe, only, even with their success, he was becoming more obstreperous. I kept thinking to myself, "Something seems to be missing," and then I realized what it was. Thankfully, they no longer had the St. Bernard.

While we dined on a traditional feast of bagels and lox and eggs and a whole assortment of goodies, the wondrous tale was told: June had written a novel and brought it to a publisher who was apparently impressed. He called her back two days later and said, "This is good. I can get it into a paperback edition, and I will give you the grand sum of $25,000. June was delighted, but also cautious. She said, "Thank you ... Let me think it over." ... and she hung up.

She gave the matter some serious consideration and then thought to herself, "If it was that easy, let me try a few more publishers." She presented her story to three publishing houses, two large and one small. Much to her surprise, the small one got back to her almost instantaneously, and the person in charge told her, "You're good! I can make you into a very wealthy woman. I'll give you $500,000." June handled it all very professionally. The deal was struck. The book became a success, and more books followed. She soon realized that she had an affinity for turning out such romantic tales, and her career blossomed. June had found her niche, and the family was poor no more. June had her work, for which she was paid handsomely, and Joe had his studio, in which he turned out a good number of marvelous originals, which, for reasons known only to himself, he refused to sell. I never did buy any of the routines he had attempted to create for me in those dark days, but I am delighted by the family's success, and remain puzzled by his eccentricity, though in mulling it all over in my mind, I should have expected it.

Sammy Glazer was one of my very best friends in High School. He was kind, considerate, thoughtful, outrageous, and really funny. We totally lost touch with each other after graduation, but many years later fate drew us together when we met in a restaurant, and discovered that we lived a couple of towns apart in New Jersey. Sam had a thriving upholstery shop on the main street in Hackensack, and had a sterling reputation in business for honesty, integrity, and excellent workmanship. We, along with our wives, would socialize considerably. We truly enjoyed each other's company. Sam and I were fused by one common bond. We were both diehard NY Giants fans, and we attended their games in good times and bad (and in those years, they were mostly the latter). It was through Sam that I met a short, quiet young man named Norman Thalheimer, who really "knocked 'em dead" in every artistic department when he attended the University of Syracuse, the college that prides itself in having turned out so many show biz celebrities.

One of the ladies who worked for Sam had a friend who was worried that her enormously gifted son Norman, a very recent college graduate, was vegetating. He had written and composed the music for a number of successful productions at school, and he was also a prolific artist, whose paintings adorned the walls. Since having returned home, he had been unable to obtain any gainful employment. Norman's mom had told her friend about her son's plight, and the friend, having heard so much about me through her boss, Sam, said, "I'll see if I can get Sam to prevail upon Mr. Harris to help him."

I met the kid in his home, and was so impressed by his versatility and his humility, that a daring thought struck me. Norman, after showing me around and pridefully displaying some truly dazzling artwork, sat down at his grand piano and played and sang a few of his compositions. I was impressed. "You're a very talented young man," I told him, "just what are you looking for?" "I've written a musical. It's complete, and it's great. I need to get someone interested in producing it." "That's quite a tall order," I replied, "What makes you think that it has any possibilities?" "Well, I've spent practically a lifetime putting the thing together. It's a classic, and would be a sure fire hit on Broadway." "What's it about?" I inquired further. "It's an original musical version of "Lysistrada." "Isn't that the famous Greek tragedy about the wives spurning their husbands' affections until they promise never to wage war ever again?" "You got it," he said, delighted that I had recognized the theme. I said, "Norman, your mother doesn't know anything about me. I'm just a variety act and have never made any forays into the Broadway theater scene, but I'm entertaining an idea as I sit here and talk to you. It's a wild, long shot, but I just may be able to pull it off. If I do, it might amaze you. Don't get your hopes up too high, but I just might surprise you. Put your entire presentation in order, and I'll get back to you as soon as I get any response to my plan, if I do, at all." We said our goodbyes, and as I was leaving, judging from the excitement that lit up in his eyes, I thought to myself, "I'm really gonna try. I would love to help this nice kid out."

In my very early years, growing up in Williamsburg, one of my very best friends was a neighbor and classmate named Murray Papirofsky. He had wonderful immigrant parents, poor, hard working, quiet and intelligent little people who were surprisingly well informed, and they were a delight to be with. I spent a good deal of time in their humble apartment on Boerum St., which was just up the street from our own cold water flat. Young as I was, they spoke to me like I was an adult, which I greatly appreciated. Murray was the kid who had read every book in the children's' section of the Bushwick Ave. library, and I ran him a close second, and we both enjoyed discussing what we had read with his interested parents and his two lovely sisters. They too, were very, very smart. They had an older brother named "Yussie," about whom they all spoke glowingly, and whom I had never met. He wasn't much older but apparently he was some sort of intellectual giant who was always away from the house involved in numerous projects. Just coincidentally, when my family moved into a heated flat in Brownsville, so did the Papirofskys. They moved about two blocks away, and although our folks were never close friends they did greet each other respectfully, and were delighted that we were all somehow together, especially the boys. Murray and I attended the same new elementary school and the same (John Marshall) junior high school. After we had both graduated from different high schools (I attended Thomas Jefferson and he went to Boys High), I never saw him again. His sisters, however, once attended a concert I appeared in at Brooklyn College many, many years later, and came backstage afterward to say hello. The strangest coincidence of all is that, when World War II had ended and I was a soldier working at the Separation Center at Fort Dix, Murray Papirofsky's army discharge papers passed through my hands.

Yussie Papirofsky, the "phantom brother," was in the US Navy during the war, and after he was discharged he became wholeheartedly interested in theater. I know nothing about how he formulated his career, but Yussie Papirofsky eventually became the most prominent impresario on all of Broadway, the legendary Joseph Papp!

I decided to write him a letter c/o The Public Theater, introducing myself and describing my entire history with his wonderful family, and asked if he would be good enough to lend an ear to my "protege," Norman Thalheimer, whom I also described in full. It didn't take very long at all, and I got a return letter telling me how much he enjoyed my revealing missive, and asking me to call his executive secretary, Ms. Merryfield (a lady he later married) to set up an appointment so that he could listen to what Norman had to offer. To say that I was thrilled is an understatement. When I told Norman about what had transpired I thought the little guy would faint from excitement.

We visited Mr. Papp, who was surprisingly youthful looking for his age, in his office at the Public Theater. He was most charming, gracious and courteous, and gave us all the time in the world. Norman sat down at the piano and delivered his original Greek musical with verve and panache, and all present seemed to be impressed. When he was all through, he was exhausted. The sweat was starting to run profusely from his forehead down onto his cheeks, and the serious youngster managed a weak smile when Mr. Papp applauded vigorously. Papp asked him to play a few of his original musical compositions, and when he was all through he asked us all to sit down while he ordered in some refreshments. As we sat around, relaxed and comfortable, he offered up his critique: "Norman," he began, "I've only been arrested once in my life, and that was when I presented a dramatic version of "Lysistrada" in San Francisco. The authorities deemed it obscene. They actually raided us and closed us down. I can't tell you how embarrassing it was, not to mention the damaging newspaper coverage. I swore that I would never do that show again, and here you are with a lovely new musical version, and I'm still haunted by visions of what had happened before. I'll be perfectly candid with you Norman, I wouldn't go near that property with a ten foot pole. If you've got any other show that you've written that you'd like me to listen to, I'd be happy to oblige. Just call me and we'll make an appointment. As for your original pieces, they sound good to me, but I'm not in that business. I suggest that, maybe through Mr. Harris here, you can arrange for some record producer to have a go at them." That was the end of our meeting. Norman was not at all shattered. The mere fact that a man of Joe Papp's magnitude heard him out was both comforting and exhilarating. In fact, it was downright inspiring. Returning home the kid was walkin' on air, and I was delighted to have been able to raise his hopes.

My next move was to call my pal, tall, elegant, classy Charlie Glenn, who was a vice president (in Marketing) at Paramount Pictures, in the Gulf and Western Building, across from the W. 59th St. entrance to Central Park. Charles was an Irishman from upstate Sydney, NY whose father had been a professional baseball player. Charles had been married to our friends, Dr. and Mrs. Maslow's daughter, Valerie, at one time. They had gotten divorced and now he was married again to another slender, lovely Jewish girl, and her name was Linda. Besides being my friend, Charles was one of my biggest fans. He laughed at everything I said. He used to attend the Variety Clubs International shows that I appeared at, and he was absolutely floored when I made a surprise appearance at his 50th birthday party at a posh Madison Ave. restaurant with many of the movie industry bigwigs in attendance.

It was no big deal for Charles, also an alumnus of Syracuse University, to arrange for me to bring Norman to the president of a recording company with a very popular label, in an endeavor to sell some of those songs he had worked on so diligently. As soon as we walked into the record producer's office, I got the feeling that this guy was all "window dressing" and was going through the motions as an accommodation. In an attempt to impress us, he spoke in expletives. I guessed that he was trying to show Norman that he was a youthful guy that's involved in an industry that caters to the "now generation." As polite as he tried to be, the vibes just weren't there. It ended with the same old bullshit that I'd gotten in my own profession for years. It's called "Catch 22." After he had heard Norman play and sing a few tunes at the piano, he dismissed him by saying, "Very good, young fella. Go out n' make some demos and send 'em to me." We politely thanked him for seeing us and couldn't wait to get outta there.

Norman never forgot how I tried for him, then and on ensuing other times, but, unfortunately, to no avail. He moved out to LA eventually, where he's made new friends, and he's still tryin' hard. He had one brief moment of glory when he was a contributing composer to a Broadway musical about Marilyn Monroe. Shirley and I were his guests in "house seats" at the Minskoff Theater when it opened. He had grandiose plans based upon the show being a hit. He was going to retire his then ailing father, and buy a big house for his parents. Alas, the show was a bomb, and he went back to LA, disappointed, but never defeated.

He was mercilessly attacked one night in the garage of his apartment complex. He had just come home from work in a comedy club he had been playing in, and some thug, or thugs, lay in waiting. Not only was his car stolen, (and later recovered, almost intact), but he was also beaten over the head with a tire iron. Fortunately my little pal miraculously recovered. My profound anger upon hearing about his devastating misfortune immediately brought me to tears and frustration. How could anyone do what they did to him? It's got to be some form of insanity. My little pal is okay now, physically, but he still looks over his shoulder a lot. Some time afterward I appeared at the famed Santa Monica Civic Auditorium, and picked Norman up at his new place and he was my guest for the evening at a funny show I did for Mickey Katz, Joel Grey's illustrious father. Another time I had Shirley with me and we picked up Norman, and also Charlie Glenn (who had, by then, moved to Hollywood) and they were my guests at a terrific variety show I had appeared in at the Wilshire Ebell Theater in Beverly Hills, that starred the hilarious comedian, Danny Thomas. I haven't seen Norman since, and I think of him often. I speak to his mother, who is now a widow, when I'm performing down in Florida, where she now lives. Each time I speak to her it's with the hope that talented little Norman has hit "pay dirt," and I'm still waiting.

Shirley and I had an extra day in the LA area around the time I performed at the Wilshire Ebell, and Charles invited us to visit him at Paramount studios that morning. We were very excited, and got the VIP treatment when we arrived. As we sat in his office, early in the morning, Charles suddenly said, "Van, y'know we do a lot of TV from the lot here too. Let's see if I can do anything for you. I'm gonna introduce you to the grand old man of casting at Paramount himself, Hoyt Bowers.

I couldn't believe what I was hearing. My charming friend picked up the phone and asked for Mr. Bowers. "Hoyt," he said, "I have a very dear friend of mine here visiting me. He's an excellent comedian and his name is Van Harris. I wonder if I could send him over to meet you? ... You'll see him right away? That's great, Hoyt. I sure appreciate it. I'm sending him right over." He hung up with a great big grin on his face and said, "Van, whadd'ya got to lose? He's waitin' for you. You can walk there. Here are the directions. Go see him. Maybe this'll be your lucky day. Shirley, how 'bout if you wait here with me? I promise not to be boring. In fact, if Van isn't back in time for lunch I'll take you to the commissary and let them all eat their hearts out when they see the pretty girl that I walked in with."

I was not anticipating anything in particular, so my attitude was perfect. I was relaxed and happy, and very anxious to meet the man whom Charles told me had been in that highly exalted capacity for eons, dating back to the early days, and who was loved and admired by all who knew him. I was ushered into his office, which was decorated very tastefully, and met a tall, well built older gentleman who appeared fit as a fiddle, energetic, and looking like a one time matinee idol. We hit it off immediately. In fact, the moment he saw me his eyes lit up and he said, "Van, this just might be your lucky day." He picked up the phone and spoke excitedly into it saying, "I think your "Herman" may have just walked into my office. He looks perfect for what you're looking for. Let me talk to him a little while and then I'll send him over," and he hung up. "What was that all about?" I asked. "Funny you should ask," he replied. "This is gonna sound strange to you, but listen to this. We're working on a spin-off of "Laverne and Shirley," and the central character, whom we're undecided about, and haven't cast, as yet, is a gym teacher named Herman. It's a quirk of fate that you should be visiting Charles today, because, from where I'm lookin' you are exactly what we've got in mind. Please, tell me about yourself. Where have you been, and what have you been doing?"

I knew that this couldn't have been some sort of "put-on," as this was a serious, intelligent man sitting across the desk from me. Why would he want to kid me or indulge me? I thanked my lucky stars for the fact that the timing had been so superb, and I immediately launched into an interesting, abbreviated verbal resume that, apparently, was quite effective. When I was all through, Mr. Bowers, who was impressed, continued on, "I'm sending you over to Tony Marshall, whom I just spoke to on the phone. Charm him like you've just done me, and who knows, this might just turn into a wonderful break for you." I couldn't believe what I was hearing, and, somehow, I felt very comfortable in the environment I was in. It felt as though I was born to be there. He gave me directions to Mr. Marshall's office, which was located in a nearby structure, and we shook hands warmly. As I turned around to leave, he patted me on the shoulder and smiled, as he said, "Go get 'em kid! Break a leg!"

Tony Marshall, a big, handsome man, and the father of both, Penny and Gary Marshall, was as friendly and imposing as Hoyt Bowers had been, and immediately put me at ease with his greeting. I surmised that he was an East Coast guy, like myself, and, in addition to his explaining what the premise of the show was going to be, we got into a little reminiscence about New York, that I was certain could have gone on a lot longer if there was more time, but there was business to take care of, and the charming man knew just when to wind things up. He got on the phone with someone and described me to a "T," and said, "I think you'll like this young man. His name is Van Harris, and he's a friend of Charlie Glenn. Hoyt and I both think he'd be right for the part of 'Herman.' I'm sending him right over to you. Be nice to him, and, for God's sake, don't forget who discovered him." It was all starting to sink in by then, and in my mind I was already going over how we're going to have to relocate the children, and, in time, sell or rent the house in New Jersey, etc. The nicest thought was being able to tell some parsimonious resort hotel owners that "I'm sorry, but I'm not available! Don't call me, ... I'll call you." I was brought out of my brief fantasy by Mr. Marshall's instructing me, "I'm sending you over to see a lady named Pat Harris. She's a real sharp gal, and she's from NY, and she's got the last word on this project. I hope it all works out. I'm looking forward to seeing a lot more of you."

Pat Harris, a nice looking, businesslike woman, just as Gary had described, and from NY, was what I would call "applied friendly." She filled me in on the show, and implied that, "her friend, Pat Morita" was the type she had in mind to play Herman. She was cordial enough, and we spoke about a number of things, but the name Pat Morita kept coming up. I surmised that her mind had already been made up, and I was wondering just how and when, she was going to reject me. Finally, she asked, "By the way Van, how old are you?" I wasn't fazed by the question. I wasn't old, and I wasn't very young, but if both Bowers and Marshall thought I appeared right for the role, why was she asking me that? I saw no reason to lie about anything and told her the truth. Before I even got through blurting out the numbers she snapped, "Oh, that's too old. I was looking for someone younger." I thought to myself, "I don't know Pat Morita," but remembered having seen him (if my memory serves me correctly) in one movie, which I think was "The Karate Kid!" and, he certainly looked older than I do. Anyway, Ms. Harris thanked me for seeing her and, in her own businesslike manner, apologized for not being able to offer me the part of Herman.

It was getting quite late and I saw no sense in going back to Mr. Bowers office, so I walked back to Charlie Glenn's headquarters, and all the way there, kept going over the day's events in my mind. Of course both Shirley and Charles were anxious to know all that had transpired, and I related everything, down to the most minute details. "And what did you tell her when she asked you how old you were?" Charles asked apprehensively. "I told her the truth," I answered. "No," he groaned, "ya never tell them the truth. You do what everyone else in this business does. Ya lop at least ten years off your age. Anyway, from what you're telling me, you certainly had an exciting day. I'm sure her mind had already been made up to hire Pat Morita. I'd say you made greater headway today than some guys do in a lifetime. I spoke to Hoyt Bowers. You evidently made quite an impression upon him. Meanwhile Shirley and I had a great lunch, and a lot of interesting people walked into the commissary." "Whadd'ya suggest I do next?" I asked. "Well, ya gotta hang around, maybe a couple of weeks, and look up calls in the trades, and elsewhere, and go out on them, and pray that you get lucky. If today was any indication ..." I said, "Charles, I love you for being such a good friend, but we've got a family waitin' back

28 Mr. Schitt

Soon after our return I received a call from Florence Maslow. We had purchased our house from that dear lady, and she and her equally lovable spouse, Dr. Harry Maslow, a long time Hackensack dentist, were, at that time, enjoying their retirement while residing in an elegant high rise in that same city while contemplating a move to Atlanta in order to live closer to their children and grandchildren. Florence, in her long ago youth, tall, slim, and dazzling, had been half of a popular ballroom dance team known worldwide as "Florence and Alvarez." They had even performed in motion pictures, and in one of those films she had also danced with Maurice Chevalier. She now belonged to that elite group of female show biz veterans, The Ziegfeld Girls, subscribed to *Variety*, and was up on everything that was still going on in the profession. Just coincidentally, she and Harry had seen me perform at a resort a short time before we had ever met. At the time that I had bid on the lovely English tudor house that I eventually had bought from them, they expressed a great deal of delight at meeting me like that. It marked the beginning of an everlasting friendship in which they had informed me that they considered themselves among my biggest fans. Florence developed a deep and abiding interest in my career. She was very much a part of that wonderful old time era when artistry was truly appreciated, and there were such individuals around who were known as "theatrical managers," and who were willing to stake their futures upon the success of their clients. She did not easily accept the callousness that had crept into our beloved industry. The lovely lady had been pampered throughout her professional career, in addition to her married life, and still believed in only goodness and light.

"Van," she hummed, "I just read in the *Times* that Maxine Marx is now the Talent Coordinator at Dancer and Fitzgerald. Why don't you call for an appointment and see if she can get you some TV commercials. She's Chico Marx's daughter. You know, I'm talkin' about the funny little guy from the Marx Brothers with the feathered little hat and the Italian accent. I knew her when she was a little girl and she was really nice.

Must be a married woman with children of her own by now. She's probably still nice. Why don't you go n'see her?"

I figured, "Why not?" "What've I got to lose?" I had auditioned for a few commercials again recently and was rejected. There were a few that I actually got, and they were cancelled. I heard that there was big money in those things, and the residuals could make them even more appealing. I thanked Florence for the tip and made the phone call. I was quite elated by how easy it was to get an appointment with Ms. Marx. Perhaps it was the mention of Florence's name that did it. Whatever the reason, we made up to meet and I was anxious and rarin' to go.

The receptionist at Dancer and Fitzgerald was most gracious and it didn't take long until I was ushered into Maxine Marx's office. Maxine turned out to be a young-ish, pretty, pert brunette with a winning smile and a welcome demeanor. She was immediately taken by the fact that I was a comedian by trade and launched into a long, whole dissertation on what it was like having been raised as the child of a comedy actor who was famous for the character he portrayed in the movies and was known the world over. As it turned out, she unashamedly continued to reveal a great deal of personal and somewhat embarrassing information, describing how he nearly drove her poor mother mad with his philandering, and how, as a result of it all, the entire family was affected adversely. The whole conversation caught me by surprise but I listened sympathetically for what appeared to become an eternity. The poor young lady, obviously gifted, or else she wouldn't have occupied such a highly exalted position with such a prestigious agency, was crying her heart out to me, a complete stranger. When she exhausted her conversation she matter of factly looked directly into my eyes and asked, "What brought you here today, Mr. Harris?" I couldn't believe my ears. "I ... I would like to audition for commercials," I stammered, surprised and deflated by her question. It was as though she had just come out of a trance. "Oh," she replied, "just leave your resume with our receptionist and we'll get back to you when something comes along." If ever I had undergone a sobering experience, that was it! I left there shaking my head and asking myself, "What the hell kind of a business is this anyway? How eccentric does it get?" "Screw this! This craziness is just too damn intangible. It's downright maddening! I give up!"

I went home smoldering over the time I had wasted up there, and, crushed by the fact that, with all my efforts, and even my shameful obsequiousness to some of the bullshit agents who send people out on commercial "cattle calls," it all just wasn't worth the effort. I decided right then and there to throw in the towel! I was giving up on those painful, unsettling quickie auditions and all the other bullshit that goes with trying out for commercials. Poor dear Florence would never understand what a real pain in the ass that phase of our business is. I'm cutting it out for good, ... but not without one last, perhaps foolish flourish.

While driving from a club date in the Catskills to a one nighter somewhere around Reading, PA, I passed through a rather bucolic little town called Kunkeltown, and it was at that moment, somehow inspired by the cute, catchy name of what had all the earmarks of a quiet country village, I devised a wild new resume in my mind. I gathered the fictitious material together, changed my name, and also put the irreverent new name on my composite photo, and this is the way it came out:

Andrew Hardy Schitt
better known as A. HARDY SCHITT

Actor   Singer   Dancer   5'10"   158 lbs.
Born: April 1, 1930   Birthplace: Kunkeltown, PA
Father: Dr. Oliver Cromwell Schitt   Obstetrician
Mother: Bessie Mae Verdie   Elementary School Teacher
One (older) brother   One (younger) sister
Graduate *cum laude* University of Chelm Warm Springs, WI

First acting role: "Puck" in "Midsummer Night's Dream"
(High School Production)

Professional roles:
    Biff   "Death Of A Salesman"   (St. Louis Playhouse)
    Stanley Kowalski   "Streetcar Named Desire"
(Topeka Kansas Summer Playhouse)
    Captain Wirz   "Andersonville Trial"
(Chicago National Company)
    Greenwald   "Caine Mutiny"   (San Francisco Art Playhouse)
    Emperor Hadrian   "Hadrian VII"   (Alameda, Ca. Players)
    Lenny   "Of Mice and Men"   (Atlanta Little Theater)

Prominent roles in:
    "The Iceman Cometh"   "Know I Can't Hear You"
    "Little Me"   "Petrified Forest"

Appeared in the following commercials:
    Randall Chevrolet (Moline IL)   Tooltown (Cincinnati OH)
    Fiesta Ford (Albuquerque, NM)   Garber's (Dallas, TX)
    Grassland (Atlanta, GA)   Noonan's (Portland, OR)
    Soapy Suds (Oklahoma City, OK)
    Klenger's Baby Products (Milwaukee, WI)

Appeared in the following films:
    Army training films
    NYU's Cinematography Experimental Theater

Married   three times   six children
Favorite sports: Tennis, swimming, fox hunting, bungee jumping
Hobbies: Reading and raising tarantulas

Agent: Mark Korman   212 JU6-6363

DON'T MAKE A MOVE UNTIL YOU'VE TAKEN A. HARDY SCHITT

There was absolutely no way that anyone could check on the veracity of the fictitious credits that I had amassed. I purposely chose Mark Korman because he's highly intelligent, and a good friend, and zany and gutsy enough to go along with the gag. Of course, I consulted with him first and he loved the idea. The composite, consisting of three different poses on one sheet, with the name "A. Hardy Schitt" emblazoned at the bottom, was very prominent and effective. You couldn't miss it.

I spent two whole days legging it all over Madison Ave., Third Ave., and wherever else the prominent advertising agencies were located, and personally dropped off a complete "package" in each one. Whoever accepted these resumes on behalf of the agencies didn't seem to notice the name at all. They all just gave me a polite "Thank you." It was like a damn form letter. I gave copies to my pal Charlie Glenn at Paramount Pictures and he howled, and made more copies, and passed them around to various departments, and they all had a good chuckle over it. I also gave copies to some of my friends who worked at smaller advertising agencies, and they too passed my resume around for laughs. As for the major agencies that I had dropped them off at, only one person out of the whole lot responded. That person was the famous, tough lady in charge of commercial casting at Grey Advertising. Her name was Rollie Bester, whom, I believe, has since passed on. She called Mark and growled at him, "What is this, some sort of a joke?" to which he replied, "If he hadn't contrived such a fluky resume, and outrageous name, do you think you would have even noticed him?" "Don't be a wise guy!" she yelled at him, and slammed the phone down.

29 Kathy

There are so many talented people in the world who remain forever anonymous because they don't have the knack for self-promotion, nor have they ever been fortunate enough to have had someone to do the selling for them. This has always been one of life's greatest injustices. One must shake his head in disbelief when he hears the expression that "the meek shall inherit the earth." From all that I've seen, heard, and learned, "the squeaky wheel gets the oil." Every now and then, thanks to some unexpected osmosis, someone miraculously manages to break through. I suppose that if we search real hard for an explanation we would, eventually, somehow, uncover one, but rather than rack our brains, we just accept the individual's success, and revel in his or her, glory. Such an unanticipated miracle, for however long it lasted, was Kathy.

She had been just another gifted young singer that I had appeared with on assorted club dates from time to time, when we first met. She had the pipes, and the looks, and was even capable of adding singing impressions to her performance whenever an audience required it. My personal opinion is that impressions serve as a very strong attention getter, and especially with simple people. That is not meant to demean the unique art of impersonation, which requires an inordinate amount of talent. Just ask anyone in the business, it's just a great, and generally foolproof way to arrest the onlookers. Kathy had all the tools that it took in order to be a "working act," and especially in that diverse, and taxing field that club dates represent.

Her road had not been an easy one. She arrived in the US from her native Ireland, a penniless, chubby, teenage orphan, with no particular trade, and almost immediately obtained work as a domestic for a kindly Jewish-American family. Her employers allowed her a great deal of latitude, and in noticing how beautifully she sang as she went about her household chores, encouraged her to try to develop her voice more fully as a possible future career. Kathy was both pleased and flattered, and one fine day she actually answered one of the numerous, and oft-times misleading, ads that appear in some of the show biz "trades" that appear on the newsstands.

It was a totally new experience for the naive "babe in the woods," and didn't turn out to be the sort of glamorous setting she had expected from the movies back home. She sat among a bunch of other eager hopefuls on assorted old folding chairs in a rather large, empty room, except for the worn looking upright piano, and its busy piano player. The man in command of the entire procedure was a young-ish, thin, self-styled impresario who offered his opinion after each singer did her, or his, two allotted songs. They all brought their own sheet music and each proceeded to instruct the accompanist on how they wanted the selections played. The harried, shirt-sleeved gentleman knew his business and played well. Kathy belted two excellent renditions, and when she was all through, waited for the auditioner's critique with baited breath. He was a serious looking "expert" who stuttered excitedly, and he looked at Kathy unemotionally and stammered, "Y-you're good k-kid. Y-you've got p-possibilities, b-but you're t-too f-fat." He then got a tighter grip on his speaking ability and advised her, "Come back after you've lost some weight!" abruptly turned his back on her, and went on to his next audition.

Kathy had a rather sweet disposition and accepted what he told her as a compliment, and thanked him. She left, undaunted, and determined to return, and with a newer, and more appealing figure. She had gotten a tiny taste, loved it, and was going to make more out of it.

With such heightened desire she really worked hard and honed herself into a rather good singer, and her diminutive figure cooperated splendidly with her concentrated weight reduction. Only her sizeable breasts were stubborn reducers, but that added a more attractive dimension to her appearance, and the man's eyes popped out of his head when she confidently strolled into the rehearsal hall for another audition some months later.

She and Tommy (the "mayvin" in charge), soon struck up a fast friendship, and he became her manager, chauffer, advisor, and full time confidante. He, eventually, also became her husband. She embarked on a new career, with her now ex-employers' blessings. Kathy and Tommy were soon seen everywhere together, ranging from club dates, to cruise ships, the then busy Catskills, and wherever else they could find an audience. Kathy, though still quite young, was rapidly gaining invaluable experience while becoming a "standard," the type that would generally never become world renowned, but could go on working forever. She was doing what she loved most, while also being paid to travel, and see the world, and with her devoted husband at her side. It was the realization of a dream, and she cherished every waking moment.

I would guess that about a dozen years of such prolonged personal appearances continued for Kathy until she hit the jackpot! Somehow, she managed to land a recording contract. In fact, it led to at least two, if not three LP's on well-known labels. Her albums consisted, almost entirely, of excellent popular standards, and her selections were backed by some of the most renowned orchestras in the business. The title of her most successful album was the title of a new hit song, and, although that beautiful ballad that became an almost instantaneous winner, was recorded by a few other artists, only Tony Bennett's rendition surpassed hers in sales. Kathy's peers and competitors, many of them still mired down in the club date field, and hoping against hope that they too, could enjoy her great fortune, were cheering for her all the way. She was a well-liked kid, a symbol, living proof that the pot o' gold at the end of the rainbow was still within reach. Kathy had now become a much sought after artist, and was appearing regularly on the all-important Las Vegas Strip, which, unfortunately, also proved to be her undoing.

The money was coming in steadily, and the old ennui that is so often indigenous to long, steady engagements, was rearing its ugly head. Her husband succumbed to the lure of the gambling tables and was throwing away huge amounts of her earnings. He was intoxicated by "their" success, and handled it abysmally. On the other hand, she was being romanced by a married suitor, the successful head of a large recording company, and he dazzled her with exciting promises that were never quite fulfilled. Eventually all came crashing down. She and Tommy were divorced; her lover stayed with his wife and kids; and she made a hasty retreat to the comfort of the cruise ships where she backed herself with a trio of jazz musicians, and they played the lounges for a number of years. Eventually she moved back to New York, where she became a "single" again, and worked wherever she could find employment. She would appear sporadically at the "Showboat," a fairly famous supper club located on the ground floor of the Empire State Building. They advertised their headliners generously, and whenever she appeared there, a lovely photo of her, with the emphasis on that ample cleavage, was prominently displayed in all the leading newspapers.

We would bump into each other on the occasional club dates that we were booked on together, and we would also meet socially from time to time when Shirley and I would attend parties at the gregarious singer, Judy Scott, and her trumpet player husband, Alan Jeffreys' apartment in midtown. Another fine singer, Josie O'Donnel, when she was married, ran an annual New Years Eve party in February (as most performers worked on New Years Eve and weren't available to socialize on that busy night, so Josie had the presence of mind to delay the festivities until a more propitious time), and Kathy was also among the revelers that gathered there. Josie (and Len, later to become her "ex") occupied a palatial estate in an exclusive section of Englewood, NJ, and what memorable parties they threw. Those were truly the halcyon days for most of us. Work was plentiful, and everyone was in a grand mood.

Our darling daughter, Madelaine, the youngest of our brood of four, and the only female, lived, with her husband, Mark, in an apartment on Riverside Drive, up in what's commonly referred to by the natives as "Zabar Country," (out of respect for that world famous food emporium located in the midst of that bustling New York City area). We dropped in on her one day, unexpectedly, just as she was leaving. Her arms were filled with loads of freshly prepared food in shopping bags, and the aroma was intoxicating. We asked her where she was going and volunteered to help her carry all her cumbersome packages down the long, five flights of stairs into the street. "I'm bringing dinner to Kathy," she replied. "Why," I inquired, rather surprised, "is she sick?" "Didn't you know?" she retorted, raising one eyebrow quizzically, a unique habit she had somehow inherited from her paternal grandfather. "Kathy has cancer!" "What?" we both exclaimed, "When did that happen, and how bad is it?" Maddy then proceeded to tell us all about Kathy having discovered a lump in her breast some time ago that her doctor had advised her to keep an eye on and schedule further examination. Somehow, because of her personal and artistic problems, she became dangerously deficient in following up, and the dread disease had metastasized. She was now a full-fledged cancer patient, with an added burden of no family, and not much money. "How long have you been doing things like this?" I asked Maddy. "As soon as I found out through Judy (Scott), who's the one that told me, and who's also been very attentive. Why don't you give Judy a call? You'll find out all the details from her."

A telephone call to Judy provided us with all the pertinent data, and I assured her that I would set up a "plan of attack" so that we'd all be able to help Kathy as much as we could. Judy agreed to cooperate to her utmost, which was most comforting. I next called Kathy and asked her if there was anything she needed. "I'm in good shape, Love," she answered in that charming accent, which she never lost. "Don't worry your little head off over me. I'll lick this damn thing yet!" I asked her if she was able to continue paying the rent for her apartment (somewhere in the W. 50's), and she replied, "So far, and the landlord has been very understanding when I'm a little late." I asked her about food, and comforts, and she said, "So far I'm not starvin', thanks to my good friends." I assured her that I would get to work on trying to arrange for her comforts, and would report to her periodically. I told her, "Don't worry, and I've recruited Judy as a partner, so you're in good hands." "That's why I call you 'Love,'" she giggled. "Thanks, and like I said, 'Don't worry so much.'"

First thing I did was type up a notice informing everyone within earshot that Kathy was desperately ill, and that we would appreciate whatever monies would be contributed by check to "The Kathy Foundation," and to have those checks sent, as soon as possible to either me, or Judy. I made copies of that notice, and Judy and I, separately, posted them backstage wherever we appeared. We also solicited money, in person, wherever we could. We next visited my beloved cousin (and idol), Arthur Cooperman, a highly respected lawyer who was then Chairman of the NY State Workmen's Compensation Board, up at Number Two World Trade Center, and solicited his expert advice as to how to go about setting up a fund for Kathy legally. We opened an account with the Manufacturer's Trust Company Bank, somewhere in the mid 70's, and we were on our way.

I called the biggest "yenta" (busybody) I know in all of show biz, comedian Joey Adams, the little guy with the biggest balls in the world, and told him what I was undertaking. He recommended that I contact "The Troupers," a show biz ladies organization that his equally famous wife Cindy was very active in, and relate the situation to her. From them I received a promise of so much money each month to be sent directly to Kathy to cover the cost of food and other staples. I am eternally grateful to that splendid group of ladies for its great munificence. The contributions that we had gotten as a result of my posters went for clothing, furniture, a new TV, along with important expenses like medical, etc.

Joey suggested that I contact Catholic Charities (since our patient was Catholic) to try to get them to spring for her rent. I thought it was a superb idea and contacted that good agency. The person in charge (I believe it was a priest) listened sympathetically, and regrettably informed me that they were fairly new in the business and didn't possess the funds for such an action. He apologized over and over and I told him that I appreciated his sincere concern, and that I was going to try to further pursue my quest through, hopefully, other agencies.

Joey told me, "Try Jewish Charities. Whadd'ya got to lose?" "The guy in charge is a man named Liebowitz and he's a Controller in the Accounting Dept. up at the William Morris Agency." I telephoned Mr. Liebowitz whose reaction sounded droll and unemotional. I prefaced my request by informing him that Kathy was not Jewish and that Catholic Charities begged off because they didn't have enough money in the till. "But she is a performer," I pointed out, "and she desperately needs help." His answer was, "Send me a letter explaining the whole situation and I'll see what we can do." I did as he said, and once my letter was received, this surprisingly kind gentleman made certain that her rent was paid for as long as she lived. What a guy!

In checking in with Kathy I was informed that, except for her physical "reminders," she was quite comfortable, and apparently not in need of anything but good health. "Oh, one more thing," she added, sounding like Peter Falk in "Columbo," "I would give anything in the world to hear from Frank Sinatra." "That's quite a request," I laughed, "I'm not important enough, but let me see what I can do."

My dear pal, Bud Rosenthal, one of the most erudite men I've ever known, was working as a V.P. in the Marketing Division up at Warner Bros., on W. 51st St. in NYC, and I'd visit with him from time to time. His boss at Warner's was a close friend of Mickey Rudin, who was Frank Sinatra's personal attorney. I told Bud all about Kathy's condition, and we decided to compose a letter to Mr. Sinatra requesting only that he would personally say a few kind words to the ailing singer whom he had met in Las Vegas. The letter was extremely well thought out and beautifully constructed. We asked for nothing more than a "hello," and Bud handed it to his employer, asking him to prevail upon Mr. Rudin to try to bring it to the attention of the world's best known singer. From what Bud later related to me, Rudin didn't appear too happy about the missive that did find its way to him, and mumbled something protective like, "Another one! ... Everybody wants somethin' from Frank!" "Well, at least we gave it a try," Bud shrugged, when I saw him again soon afterward, and we both wrote it off as a noble effort in a worthy cause ... all for naught.

About two weeks later Kathy called me very excitedly. "Guess what, Love? Jilly Rizzo paid me a surprise visit today and brought me a big, beautiful bouquet of flowers from Frank with a lovely "get well" message." Rizzo was a big, burly restaurateur, who was Sinatra's close friend and confidante. Kathy was walkin' on air. "Ol' Blue Eyes" came through once again...and for such a worthy cause.

In the interim, I had gone to California to appear in a truly exciting variety show at the Wilshire Ebell Theater in Beverly Hills. (This was the same trip where I met with all those Paramount executives who thought I might be perfect for the TV "Herman" role.) The star of the show was the exceptional comedian, Danny Thomas, and he paced up n' down nervously, terribly concerned about following yours truly and all the others who had preceded him onstage because we had all done so exceptionally well. Of course, in the end, true to form, he did sensationally. He provided a marvelous finish to what was an absolutely great show.

Before the show I was surprised by a visit in my dressing room by an excited gentleman whom I hadn't seen in quite awhile, and it took me a few moments to focus in on just who he was. The hasty patter and slight stutter refreshed my memory almost immediately. I couldn't say that I was unhappy to see him. After all, we had been friends, and he certainly had never done me any harm. In fact, I greeted him warmly, and said, "Tommy, how the hell are you? It's been such a long, long time." He hadn't aged much. He was still a fairly young man. He couldn't erase however, the evidence of pain that was so severely etched in his face. "I-I d-didn't know if you'd recognize me," he went on. "Of course I did, right away," I replied. "What's been going on in your life, and what brings you to LA?" I knew that he and Kathy had parted a long time ago. "I live out here and I'm doin' a few things here and there." Then his eyes welled up with tears and he sobbed into my shoulder (good thing I wasn't wearing a light colored suit), "Y'know, K-Kathy is in New York," and then he broke down and cried uncontrollably, "and she's s-sick. She's very s-sick ..." and here I could barely keep from crying myself, as he painfully cried out, "Kathy is d-dying!! ... and I don't even have the money to g-go to her funeral!" It was an awfully tough conversation to have just before having to go onstage to make people laugh. "Tommy," I put my arm around his shoulder and comforted him, "Kathy ain't dyin' so fast. She's a real tough little bird. And, if, God forbid, it happens, I promise you, I'll pay for your round trip flight to New York." He calmed down and quickly blurted out, "I'll pay you back as soon as I can." "No need to," I answered, and then I filled him in on all that had been going on, including the details of the fund that Judy and I had set up, and the help she was getting from other sources. I took down his address and phone number, and then I had to excuse myself because it was so close to showtime. "Tommy," I said, in parting, "Try to forget your troubles for the moment and enjoy the show. It's really good to see you again, and like they say in my neck o' the woods, let's see each other again, and only on happy occasions."

And so the saga continued with Kathy having her good days and her bad ones, but Judy and I, along with the others, made sure that she was as comfortable as possible. One day Kathy called to tell me that she hadn't received her rent money from Jewish Charities that month. I immediately called Mr. Liebowitz at the Morris Agency. In his usual unemotional manner, he replied, "What is she worried about? We've had a little bookkeeping snag. Tell her she'll be receiving it as soon as we straighten everything out."

Kathy took a turn for the worse on the following day and was taken by ambulance to Doctors' Hospital on York Ave. and put into I.C.U. Two days later I was called and informed that she had passed away quietly. They were awaiting funeral and burial instructions, and also asked me to please come by and pick up the few meager belongings that they were holding for her in a safety deposit box. The most valuable thing there was a small, inexpensive St. Christopher's medal on a thin necklace. The trinket was just like Kathy. It was small, inexpensive, and helpless. Kathy was thirty-nine years old. All that was left behind were some memories, and a few excellent albums that included one big hit. In that tragic short life she succeeded in accomplishing more than most singers do, and very soon thereafter, it all faded away. I decided that her passing was not going to go unnoticed. She was just too damn good to be forgotten. If nothing else, she was going to have a funeral that would be long remembered.

The first thing I did was call Liebowitz and tell him to stop the rent payments 'cause Kathy had died. There was a moment of silence on the other end of the phone and I could actually hear him crying. I thanked him for all his kindness and even made plans to take him to lunch so that we could meet face to face. After all, we only knew each other as voices on the telephone. Next I called Joey for advice about funeral arrangements and the dear man steered me right all the way. The Actors Fund paid for a sumptuous sendoff at the Walter B. Cooke Funeral Home on Third Ave., and a grave was being readied at the world famous Will Rogers Memorial Cemetery, in Valhalla, NY.

I then called Judy and asked her to invite all of Kathy's friends and admirers, which included some of the very best singers, musicians, theatrical agents, and assorted other performers. Shirley, and Maddy, and Judy, and Judy's husband Alan all rolled up their sleeves, and helped prepare a funeral that was fit for a queen. Kathy was treated in death as she deserved to be treated in life. There were splendid bouquets of flowers, of various sizes and shapes, as far as the eye could see. Each one could truly have been described as "magnificent." Perhaps the most outstanding of the lot was a huge, tastefully selected assortment, tied into one monumental display, and accompanied by a heartfelt, loving note, and that one was from Tony Bennett.

Every great "unknown" singer in the business was there, people considered by their peers, as "singer's singers." An outstanding example was Rosette Shaw, the great drummer, Buddy Rich's, half sister. She had been a virtual "unknown" in the US, having chosen to spend her prime years as one of the "Toasts of Paris" instead. They all flocked into the funeral home, so many of her fellow performers. All had come to say their last "goodbyes" to a fallen comrade. The eulogies were tasteful, plentiful, artistically beautiful. As a background to the many flattering accolades, we softly played Kathy's superb rendition of that great old standard, "You're Gonna Hear From Me," from her "It's The Good Life" album, and it reached a fitting, emotional crescendo immediately after the last words were spoken. At that point Tommy's uncontrollable sobbing could be heard above all the others.

As the funeral director approached the casket to have the pall bearers carry it to the hearse, Mimi Hines, who stood next to it, weeping and planting kisses upon it, refused to remove herself. With a wild, hypnotic look in her eyes, she stared at him and implored him, "Please, ... please, ... you must give me a little more time." The harried undertaker looked at me with an expression upon his face, as if to plead, "Please see what you can do. We need to get going." I gently convinced the grief stricken Ms. Hines to desist, and finally Kathy was borne away to her final resting place, to join all the other great talents that lie beneath the ground at the Will Rogers Memorial Cemetery.

30 Sylvia

On Thursday, January the 4th, exactly three days before the huge "Blizzard of '96" hit the eastern seaboard, our daughter Madelaine, a registered nurse specializing in pediatrics, left NJ for her new home in Las Vegas. She was to join her husband, Mark, a physicians' assistant, whose expertise was also in the pediatric area. Mark had obtained employment in that rapidly growing city because the climate and atmosphere there was more conducive to Max, the younger of their two teenage sons, who was suffering from juvenile rheumatoid arthritis. Max was very athletic (as was his big brother, Jason), but that dread disease had been wreaking havoc upon the poor kid, causing him no end of pain and consternation, and the outlook, for as long as he was to remain in the colder Northeast, was far from optimistic. The parents had made their decision, and at the risk of leaving their dear friends and family, and also removing two very popular teenage boys from their high school, where they both enjoyed great camaraderie and popularity, they felt that it was the only way to go. Mark was already there, and working. The furniture had all been shipped ahead, and the boys were left in the care of yours truly, their loving and devoted grandfather, until Maddy joined her husband in their new home. It was a most traumatic period for all, but they had to take the gamble, and where would be a better place to gamble than in Las Vegas.

Maddy had packed her late model Ford Explorer to the hilt, with whatever the movers had been unable to take, and she felt very secure and happy, having her darling mother along for the ride. They also had Maddy's two dogs in the van with them, "Chance," a very protective two-year-old male boxer-mix, and "Sylvia" an adorable, playful four month old golden retriever that had recently been spayed.

The ladies had chosen the longer, "southern route" for their arduous journey, in order to circumvent the dangerous weather conditions that are in existence on a cross country drive that time of the year. They even provided time to stop, for a day, at our youngest son, David's 60 acre farm and residence in the Blue Ridge Mountains of Virginia where they had a brief, and most enjoyable visit with the personable David, and his wife Janet, and their two teenage sons, Evan and Baikal. Maddy and Shirley were enjoying their trip, and each other's company, immensely. They were chatting and singing all the way, seemingly without a care in the world, and looking forward to a brighter future for all.

On the morning of January the 6th, while coming to the end of a bridge in Van Buren, Arkansas (a city with a population of about 13,000), they were very suddenly, and unexpectedly, jolted out of their merriment by an unforeseen "black ice" condition on the road, and their vehicle went completely out of control, plunging down an embankment, and turning over at least four or five times before coming to a dead stop. Maddy was trapped inside with the crushed sunroof lodged against her foot. Shirley managed to crawl out through the shattered windshield, escaping with some minor cuts and bruises. The frightened animals, in a state of shock, ran away. Several good samaritans had already approached the devastation in order to lend a hand in extricating the hysterical Madelaine. It was bitter cold out. There were sixty-two ice-related auto accidents in Van Buren that day.

The rescuers had to, literally, cut the car in half in order to get Maddy out, and she and Shirley were removed to a nearby hospital. All the while Maddy kept screaming, "My dogs! My dogs! Please somebody, find my dogs!" but they were nowhere in sight. X-rays revealed that Maddy's foot was very badly bruised, and several of her toes were broken. Shirley had several shards of glass removed, mostly from her hands. Maddy, who had spent ten years working as a veterinary technician before going on to become a nurse, was primarily concerned with the welfare of her beloved animals and kept pleading, over and over again, for someone to please find her dogs. The local animal control officers were very sympathetic and immediately set out in search of "Chance" and "Sylvia," and very soon thereafter the two-year-old male was recovered, nervous, and in a state of shock, but otherwise unhurt. The young female was nowhere to be found. Both dogs had been wearing collars with the name and phone number of a New York City veterinarian named Jay Moses on them. The ladies had escaped with their lives and were eternally grateful for that. All the local people were extremely kind and courteous, even supplying them with warm clothing and blankets, which made the terrible tragedy a little easier to tolerate. There was some comfort too, provided by our telephone conversations, but they still had a long way to go.

They stayed overnight at a local motel, and on the following morning, with Maddy on crutches provided by the hospital, they returned to the wreck in bitterly cold weather, packed whatever they could into cartons, and gave that which they had no room for (including food) to the local radio and TV people who had come to interview them. They also made a tearful plea on TV for "Sylvia's" return. That same night they left, with "Chance," on a plane, headed for Las Vegas. The airline wouldn't take "Chance" aboard unless he was properly crated, and they had to taxi all the way back to town, to find a pet store that would provide them with same. The store people socked it to them pretty good, but I suppose that they, perhaps, don't get many frantic calls for that size crate.

Before departing, Maddy placed a prominent ad in the regular pages of the Van Buren area newspaper, offering a substantial reward for the return of her adorable pup. Needless to say, we were all not too optimistic, but we certainly had our hopes up. She had to report for work, crutches and all, almost immediately upon her arrival in Las Vegas, and was deeply depressed. Her sons, back home in NJ were heartbroken, as was her husband, and, in fact, all of us. Meanwhile, back in Van Buren the animal control officers were diligently going about their endeavor to find poor little "Sylvia," but to no avail. There were a number of false alarms, and time was dragging on with no success.

A Home Economics schoolteacher in Van Buren named Beverly Ray, who owned seven dogs, one of which had just given birth to a litter of six more, now making her menagerie a total of thirteen in all, spotted Maddy's ad in the newspaper. She called her in Las Vegas and told her that she was enlisting herself and her entire class, to fan out all over the Van Buren area to hand out leaflets and place posters everywhere. She asked Maddy to send her a photo of herself and "Sylvia." She was very thorough, and she and her aides even covered truckstops, in the event that any passing truckers might have come across the hapless pup. She also added announcements over the school loudspeaker at basketball games. Soon afterwards, another teacher joined her along with her class, in this monumental effort, but all for naught. Ms. Ray kindly offered Maddy one of the new puppies, which, coincidentally, was a golden retriever, like "Sylvia," which she gracefully declined. While all this was going on, Mark, Maddy's husband, distressed by seeing her in so much emotional and physical pain, went to a kennel and brought back two little female twin golden pups. Maddy immediately dubbed them "Lucy" and "Ethel." It was the first time that Maddy had smiled since having come to Las Vegas.

About a week later, her sons, Jason and Max, finished their schooling in NJ and were put on a plane to Las Vegas by Maddy's dear friend Joy, who had once been her high school math teacher. I was involved in fulfilling an engagement in Fort Lauderdale, at that time, and was relieved that Joy had volunteered to help. There was a joyous and tearful reunion, but even that couldn't distract Maddy from her helplessness in trying to recover poor little "Sylvia."

Very early one morning, about two whole weeks after the mishap, while Maddy was at work on her new job in a hospital, and Shirley was preparing breakfast for the boys, and their father, who was about to leave for his daily routine at the clinic, the phone rang. It was Dr. Moses' wife, Jan, who was also a veterinarian. She was calling from New York City to tell them that a lady named Cathy Threadgill, who resided in Van Buren, Arkansas, had spotted a bedraggled looking, emaciated dog timidly shivering in the cold around a neighbor's porch, and took the poor little thing into her home. She read the dog's collar and immediately called the vet's phone number in New York that was listed on it. It became the catalyst for a glorious and exciting chain reaction. Miraculously, somehow, "Sylvia" had survived, in the wild, alone, for all that time. On the day she was lost, one of those highly qualified animal control officers had suggested that Maddy leave an article of her personal clothing near to where the accident occurred so that the dog might be attracted by her scent. Maddy recklessly threw down a practically new grey sweatshirt in the fervent hope that it would help. When "Sylvia" was eventually discovered, it was in an area within three blocks from where the car had rolled over, and she was carrying something in her mouth. It was a grey piece of cloth that was part of Maddy's sweatshirt.

"Sylvia" was immediately taken to an animal hospital where it was determined that she had pneumonia, and also some sort of foreign object lodged in her throat. She was placed in the care of an expert vet who took extremely good care of her and eventually brought her back to health. Meanwhile Ms. Threadgill called Maddy on the telephone and offered to drive the dog halfway to Las Vegas if Maddy would meet her. Maddy, unable to leave her job, explained that it would be more expedient if the dog was flown to Las Vegas, and, at the same time offered the wonderful lady the reward that she had posted in the newspaper. Ms. Treadgill passed on her offer and recommended that the money be donated to the Humane Society instead. The dog, and her story, dominated the local news for as long as she remained in the hospital. The front page of the *Press Argus-Courier* showed a photo of Ms. Threadgill and Dr. Mary Boone petting a rather content looking "Sylvia," and Maddy was interviewed, long distance. Ms. Ray, and Ms. Threadgill were frequent visitors to the hospital, and donations started to pour into the animal shelter. The veterinarian's bill came to $800, which was waived, and the entire incident turned into a windfall for the animal shelter. Over ten thousand dollars was raised in contributions, and a new section was eventually added, and appropriately named the "Sylvia Wing." Roger Caras, the famed animal authority, and President of the American Society for the Prevention of Cruelty to Animals, related the story on CBS Radio nationally.

"Sylvia" eventually returned to her family in Las Vegas, and there was great rejoicing. She now had a couple of new canine sisters, in addition to her devoted companion, "Chance." It was a reunion for the books, and one that will never be forgotten.

They all settled in rather conveniently, except that Maddy never quite recovered from the severe injury to her foot, which inhibited her working ability to a large degree and she was unable to continue working on a steady basis. The family did, however, manage to settle in to the best of their ability, and all appeared to be quite content, happily surrounded by their playful group of dogs. One year later however, the following announcement was sent out to all who might be interested:

> The Leinwand family regrets to inform you that the brief, happy life of our beloved golden retriever, Sylvia, ended on January 20th, 1997. She had been recently diagnosed as having lymphoma, blastocytoma, and lymphosarcoma, three dreaded forms of cancer, and it became necessary to have her put down in order to spare her the terrible pain and suffering that lay ahead.
>
> We are eternally grateful for having been blessed by her presence for however short a time it was. She was the love of our lives and we will miss her terribly.
>
> Poor, beautiful Sylvia, no longer with us. Gone ... at the ripe young age of a-year-and-a-half. She was truly a thing of beauty, a joy forever. The memory of her loveliness increases ... it shall never pass into nothingness. She will live in our hearts forever and ever.

31 Completing the Circuit

And so here I am, at an age, which to most, symbolizes that it's time to retire, whatever that means. I keep getting more and more of "When are you going to quit already?" from people who don't truly know me, and I'm offended by that question. I understand that it's well intentioned, coming from those who "paid their dues," collected their chips, and were now indulging themselves in whatever comforts they are able to afford. Many, if not most, feel that, for all of their lives they worked towards this hopefully rewarding moment, and those who are fortunate enough to be blessed with decent health, and the strength to carry on, desire to make the most out of what remains of their being. I admire them for whatever they have accomplished and pray that they can continue however they please. As for myself, I chuckle when asked that irritating question, and say, "Retire from what? Stop living? Walk out in the middle of the game?" As far as I know, my phone still rings. Agents keep calling all the time, asking if I'm available. I'm still a very desirable commodity. I'm a respected, working comedian, and I carry that badge with honor. "Have tux will travel (though in this day and age we rarely wear tuxedos anymore)." Nobody asks me how old I am. If I fill the bill, that's all they want, bless 'em, and I plan to continue performing, and updating my material, and endeavoring to appeal to assortments of audiences up until that ignominious moment when I'm no longer needed. If anyone is presumptuous enough to inquire about my age, I tell them that "I'm 39 ...plus tax."

I'm both confident and discriminating enough to work only where I want to work. Granted there are areas in our business that I wouldn't set foot in. There's a younger set out there that's doin' stuff that I fail to understand. I know it's a generational thing, but, as hard as I try, I somehow cannot fathom their humor. There are no longer any codes to govern good taste and respect, but as my concerned wife, and my well meaning friends keep pointing out to me, "You can't fight success." I suppose, in essence they're right, but I fear the price we will eventually have to pay for these so-called "successes" in future human behavior. There's a whole new society out there, more devoid of manners, polite language, and human decency and kindness, than I've ever encountered in my entire life, and I'm upset by it. I see some brilliantly talented performers among the unending stream of today's comedians, but I can honestly say that, in so many instances, I don't know what the audiences are laughing at, and it saddens me. A number of these youngsters represent terrible upbringing, or no upbringing at all. It's a case of foul-mouthed kids being "scouted" by other foul-mouthed kids who represent the agencies, TV shows, and the likes. And the filth spewed by some of the feminine gender is positively astonishing. I would hazard a guess that many of our "today" performers, successful or not, belong under a microscope instead of behind a mike. The biggest surprise is that they can be observed on TV by anyone, with no regard for the younger, impressionable viewers, and they go about dispensing their brand of poison unashamedly.

Just in everyday living I've come across lots of young people with college degrees and all, many of who are economically successful beyond our wildest dreams, and most of what they know is only the area they're employed in. They, for the most part, are so dismally uninformed. It's getting harder and harder to say something witty in the supermarket, or on an elevator, or while standing on line waiting to go into a movie theater, for fear that you will be misunderstood and looked upon as a fool. I must add however, that recently I broke 'em up when, one evening, in a crowded lobby of a movie complex, Shirley wandered off somewhere for a moment and I panicked when I lost sight of her just as the long line started to inch forward. I've always been able to locate her just about anywhere, by employing a shrill whistle that I've developed (among some of my other annoying and humor-provoking sounds), and so, desperately, I conjured up just one such loud blast. It caught everyone by surprise and they all turned around to stare at me. Seeing how startled they were by this unexpected attention getter (I once actually halted a mugging with that same trick), I broke out into a great big smile and innocently remarked, "In a moment either my wife will show up, or my dog will come a'runnin'!" The laughter was explosive ... I would have enjoyed it even more if they had applauded.

The club dates have virtually disappeared. Our young adults are not at all interested in fraternal organizations, so that once multitudinous area is virtually extinct. Only the old timers are left and a great percentage of them has moved to Florida. They reside in lovely condominiums down there, and most of those places have theaters, and that provides people like myself with some excellent, albeit seasonal, opportunities.

The once busy Catskills that boasted having close to four hundred venues in its heyday (hotels, spas, bungalow colonies, rooming houses, and a few isolated vaudeville-type theaters) now features perhaps a dozen such places at most. Gone are the glorious places like Grossinger's. which attracted some of the finest clientele in the world including the famous and near famous. Jenny Grossinger was a legendary hostess, and her able and generous progeny followed in her illustrious footsteps. Grossinger's was big, and sprawling, and featured just about everything that a vacationer would desire by way of cuisine, year 'round athletic facilities, and superb, top flight entertainment, and I was a delighted member of that elite retinue. All their employees, in every single department, were first class. Even their "talent coordinator" a refugee from Nazi Germany, named Jerry Weiss, who started out at Grossinger's in some sort of menial job, and graduated into that all-important position, was a surprisingly intelligent man who had a very keen eye for talent. He was also a very dedicated employee who had the good of the hotel first and foremost on his mind. He had no patience for tastelessness, and was able to make excellent choices in selecting the proper performances for such a class operation. Grossinger's was very fortunate to have such a fine, undemanding individual in charge of their theater and nightclub.

Paul's, in Swan Lake and Brickman's in South Fallsburg, catered primarily to a very young adult, mostly single crowd. Laurels Country Club, on Sackett Lake, run by a beautiful lady named Gladys Novack, was renowned as the best place for "single swingers" and the action ran all day and all night. There were so many other great hotels like Kutsher's, where Milt Kutsher took such pride in his great variety of vacation offerings, and particularly his diverse athletic facilities; plus

The Nevele; Fallsview; Stevensville; The Pines; The Granite; The Waldemere; Young's Gap; Brown's; White Roe; Klein's Hillside; The Raleigh; The Homowack (Native American for "Where the road bends") with its fabled, and gregarious owner, Irv Blickstein; The Flagler; both Ambassadors (one in Swan Lake and the other in Fallsburg); Tamarack; Sha-Wan-Ga Lodge (the very first hotel you came to as you drove up historic Route 17); Lebowitz's Pine View, with its emphasis on Jewish Orthodoxy; the very unique Chester's; the busy little Paramount; Zalkin's Birchwood Lodge; The Kenmore; Avon Lodge, where Sid Caesar headed up the social staff in his youth; and so many others too numerous to mention. The Concord was the giant that featured the very biggest stars in show business, and shared top billing with Grossinger's. Today just a tiny handful of those places remain.

My favorite resort hotel was on our show circuit but was not located in the Catskills. It stood at the edge of Long Island Sound, in Westbrook, Connecticut and catered to a very exclusive clientele. It was owned and operated by one of the most colorful and generous individuals in the whole wide world. His name was Bill Hahn, and that famous resort where stars appearing in Broadway shows would steal away to on the nights that their theaters were dark, was actually named after its colorful owner. Besides attracting such elegant, informed, and erudite vacationers, which made the sophisticated entertainer's job a delight, he would lavish so much attention upon the acts, which included special dinners and post show banquets for them that were the envy of all his guests. Bill was one magnificent individual. He emcee'd all the shows, and laid the law down to the audiences, "There will be no one coming, or going, while the show is on, so if the bathroom is your desire, then you'd better do it now!" He was tough, and they all loved him for it.

Of all the places mentioned, only a few owners would ever attend the shows that were being presented, and those who did, knew exactly what they wanted when they would reorder their prize performers from the theatrical agencies. The other hotel owners would be guided by reports from assorted individuals including bellhops, busboys, outspoken guests, and a few self styled "experts" on their social staffs, which left plenty of room for nepotism. Murray Posner of Brickman's was about the most astute owner of them all. He observed each and every show that played at Brickman's and, as a result, hand picked his acts, and also befriended them all to the extent that he would, at times, even offer up some very valid enhancement suggestions that actually worked. Murray, in addition to being a very successful entrepreneur, also held a law degree. He was a very articulate speaker who raised lots of money for charities, something that Bill Hahn excelled at doing too.

The hotel owners knew that they had a good deal of power in their hands, and most of them handled it quite well. There were occasional "boo-boos," that would cause heartbreak among some of the sensitive artists. One such instance that I recall very vividly happened at a lovely hotel called The Nemerson, in South Fallsburg, which was the only hotel up there that (to the best of my knowledge) featured a theater with a balcony. The Social Director there one summer was a young, handsome, dark haired baritone named Ralph Israel, who changed his name to Ralph Young. It was his job onstage to introduce the performers who came to the hotel via the circuit. It was a step down for that talented man who, prior to coming to The Nemerson, had a principal role in a Feuer and Martin Broadway musical called "Whoop Up." It was Ralph's misfortune that there was a rare, prolonged newspaper strike in New York when the show opened, and it resulted in such a paucity of publicity that it killed the show, forcing it to close very prematurely. There was no real TV coverage in those days to make up for the lack of print, so poor Ralph had to accept his fate, and in order to support his family he accepted the Social Director assignment that was available at The Nemerson.

Of course Ralph applied all his talent too, opening the shows with some robust melodic selections that were very well received. He was knocked off his feet when part way through the season, the uninformed Mr. Marcus, the owner, called him into his office one day and said, "Ralph, we have the professional singers coming here, so I would appreciate it if you wouldn't sing." That consummate insult was just too much to bear, and Ralph resigned, and very soon thereafter he left for Las Vegas where he accepted a job as a production singer in a revue at one of the hotels there. As the legend goes, it was during that time that he subsequently met a marvelous singer from Europe named Tony Sandler, and they began to put together an act that resulted in the world famous singing and recording team, Sandler and Young. The rest is history. They rose to great prominence and toured the world. Their personal appearances were received with great acclaim, and their recordings sold like hotcakes. I often wonder if Mr. Marcus ever realized what a great favor he did for Ralph Young?

The Pocono resorts, with all their mountainous beauty, and also a number of the lesser publicized Catskill areas where other assorted ethnic clientele were catered to with great enthusiasm and alacrity, did not, somehow, attract the higher level of sophisticated audiences that was indigenous to the Catskills. As a result, most of them did not present the same degree of entertainment that was so prevalent in the Grossingers, the Concords, and all those busy others. There were a few exceptions like the highly intellectual Tamiment, which was located in the heart of the Pocono Mountains, and The Unity House, which was right next door. Both of those large, excellent resort hotels had breathtaking landscapes, marvelous athletic facilities, and each also had an expansive and beautiful natural lake to compliment its beauty. Tamiment had an enormously talented and versatile social staff which presented original "book shows," and its entire entertainment program was directed by the brilliant Max Liebman, who later became famous as the director of TV's "Show of Shows," starring the gifted Sid Caesar. So many future Broadway, Hollywood, and TV stars began their ascent at Tamiment. Among them, throughout successive summer seasons, were such notables as Danny Kaye, Sid Caesar, Carole Burnett, Imogene Coco, Dick Shawn, Carl Reiner, Howard Morris, and a whole host of others. Among the comedy writers were Neil Simon, Woody Allen, Mel Brooks, and other such brilliant people who went on to fame and fortune. We all envied those vacationers who were fortunate enough to have been entertained by that array of unbelievable talent.

The Unity House, on the other hand, was owned and operated by the International Ladies Garment Workers Union, and was a haven for all the employees in that then thriving major, predominantly New York based, industry. They had a spacious, beautifully appointed theater with tufted leather seats, and presented the same assortment of entertainers that performed in the Catskills. The theater was under the aegis of a San Francisco show veteran named Bill Morlott, who also built and designed eye-catching background stage settings. They also had a marvelous sound system that featured a pre-set "Eisenhower board" that resembled a large, telephone switchboard, plug-ins and all. The clientele at Unity House consisted mostly of garment workers, all of different stripe and color, not particularly wise in the ways of entertainment, but they were such willing and enthusiastic audiences. Even though some of them were new immigrants, a great many from below the border who had difficulty understanding English, they cheered every act wildly. Morlott ran his theater with a very fine hand. He eventually retired to his native San Francisco, and lived into his nineties, no doubt basking in the glory of the great pleasure that he had presented to his people throughout those many, many years at Unity House. Both Tamiment and Unity House had extremely capable, good sized orchestras, led by fine conductors. Among them, Tony Sheldon, at Unity was my favorite. He was a gentle, dedicated musician who constantly strove for perfection. The obvious difference in presentation at these two hotels was, where Unity House had vaudeville type variety shows, Tamiment had all original "vest pocket" musicals that required long, hard rehearsals, but the end results at both these memorable places were ever so satisfying to all.

All the resorts, with the exception of Grossinger's, The Concord, and very few others were geared for summer vacationing only, but with the passage of time, changing vacation habits, and an upward economy, those that were able to survive the competition, and there were quite a few such stalwarts, went onto a year round basis. That altered the face of things in many ways, with the addition of ski lifts, ice skating rinks, and other winter attractions. It soon hastened the demise of the once popular winter resorts located in Lakewood, NJ

A number of religious resorts sprung up here and there in the Catskills, and, under the protection of the US

Constitution, they were tax-free, which caused a great strain on all the local towns. As a result, once thriving country towns like South Fallsburg, and Woodbourne, and Woodridge, were reduced to eyesores. The latter day vacationers, upon viewing them, found it hard to believe that they were once such glorious, colorful beehives of activity. Even the main streets of the two big cities, Liberty and Monticello, were reduced to rows of empty stores. It became hard to imagine that they were once the great county seats of the glorious Catskills of old.

We entertainers, in our heyday, even travelled upward, into those massive Adirondacks, where beautiful hotels like Green Mansions, and Scaroon Manor reigned supreme. It was at the beauteous Scaroon Manor that the legendary film "Marjorie Morningstar," based upon Herman Wouk's best selling novel, and starring Natalie Wood and Gene Kelly, was filmed. It was always such a great pleasure to perform there. There was also the popular Totem Lodge, located somewhere closer to Albany, the state capital, and a few other scattershot hotels off the beaten track, like Green Acres in Lake Huntington, Takanasee in Fleischmann's, and the luxurious Grand Hotel in High Mount, NY. They were all included on the entertainers' "wheel." Those were such glorious summers, and there was so much work around for all to partake in.

I would be remiss if I didn't give more attention to The Flagler Hotel in Fallsburg, which, long ago, was the most famous hotel up there. That was the hotel that Moss Hart wrote about in his fine memoir, "Act One." In it he described how he was the Social Director, working long, arduous hours in order to satisfy the guests, and the best that the hotel could offer him as housing, surprising as it may sound, was a chicken coop. He never forgot that supreme insult, and I don't think he ever forgave them. Having slept in like surroundings in my early years up there, when some pretty extreme parsimony ruled the roost among those early hotel owners, I can't say that I blamed him for pointing out this outrage. The Flagler, once upon a time, had the loveliest little nine hole golf course in all the mountains, and it was actually located on their property, but ran behind a local cemetery. It was also fortunate enough to have had one of the most dedicated golf pros in the profession. The hotel appeared to be way ahead of its time, yet it was destined to fall upon hard times. What now remains of that once proud resort, is a home for retarded people, and its past glory has been long forgotten. The original owners had eventually passed the hotel on to their nephew, a successful pharmacist who owned a chain of drugstores in New Jersey, and little by little he was forced to sell each, and every one, of his stores, in order to support the hotel, which had fallen into an unstoppable tailspin. He eventually applied for, and was granted a NY State Small Business loan, in order to keep up with his competition. Very soon thereafter he went out of business entirely, leaving some outstanding memories for those of us who lived through those exciting times.

That whole mountain scene has been reduced to just a handful of hotels, all gamely striving to survive. Many are living in the hope that, just as Atlantic City was rescued from oblivion by the introduction of gambling, that will also be their panacea. From time to time one notices fading signs tacked to walls, and in store windows, welcoming heretofore virtually unknown Native American tribes, hoping that they, and the legislators, can agree to set up casinos with the government's blessings, as was done in other parts of the country. The populace is greatly divided in its feelings about such a move, and so far, such a drastic transition still remains only a rumor.

The great nightclubs in many of our big cities, that we once knew and frequented, have virtually all disappeared and been supplanted by smaller, unattractive, and often untidy "comedy stores" that are enjoying great popularity among our young adults in their quest for entertainment. There are still country fairs, music fairs, and other "presentation setups" that will offer up whatever it takes to make satisfying profits from our large, hungry, hedonistic society. Theater, movies, and TV will continue to be the rage, and more power to them. They are still the best. There will always be places for entertainers to perform. Only he, or she, all of them, will have to find their own niche. I have been searching all my life, and am still doing so. We all live like that. I have no regrets. It has been one long marvelous roller coaster of a ride, and I am eternally grateful for having been granted such a wonderful opportunity. Most of all, I am thankful for all that this crazy, topsy-turvy, frustrating, rewarding, exhausting, and ever exhilarating profession has provided me with. It's been a great life.

I am of the opinion that, in order to fully succeed in any profession, one must dedicate one's self totally. It's got to be your number one endeavor and it's got to supersede everything else. All other considerations must come second. I've never met an extremely successful individual, in any walk of life, who can claim that he or she, was an ideal parent, or mate. As much as they try it's a virtually impossible task. It's impossible to give equal time to one's family and one's career. If I have failed to achieve the "stardom" that I once dreamed of, it's because I was never willing to compromise. Even if I possessed the enormous talent that it requires, in being perfectly true to myself, I've never applied the total dedication to my craft that it requires. I am the first to admire the exquisite talents of all the noted performers, whether it be in the field of acting, sports, and even politics, but I am saddened when I learn what fallible human beings they all are, and what dismal failures they are at home. They have to be driven, and in the course of their striving for success, they leave an awful lot of pain in their wake. Stardom requires a selfishness unlike anything else, and I have never, ever been willing to put that kind of a desire before the welfare of that beautiful family I've been blessed with. Of course, I'd love to accomplish even more in this field of endeavor that has provided me with so much, but never at the expense of my loved ones. If this is as far up the ladder as I am able to climb, then so be it. I've brought a lot of joy and laughter to so many. It has been a supreme privilege and a fantastic pleasure to have served.

My dearest, darling Shirley is a great lady. She's the love of my life. To me she will always be as young and beautiful as she was on the day I first saw her. I don't think it's the least bit strange that every time I look at her I am filled with the desire to hold her in my arms and remind her of how very much I love her. She has never done anything to make me feel otherwise. She is a strong, independent person, and also my partner. We have shared a lot together, and have always continued to be respectful and considerate of each other.

Our four children, Dan (the scientist, former college professor, and well known author of books on chemistry),

Andrew (the musician and entertainer), David (the soil conservation expert and landscaper), and Madelaine (whose service to all living things is unparalleled and who is more complex than the others), are all possessed of the very greatest qualities. They are honest, sincere, devoted, highly intelligent, interested, and inquisitive, and, above all, kind. From the day they became people, they never shirked responsibility. They get involved. They speak their minds, and they have wonderful taste and superb judgment. Dan put it all very succinctly when at the celebration of our fiftieth wedding anniversary, a party well attended by our chosen friends and family, he said, "Whatever we are, we can thank our mother and father for ...We have learned by example." Our seven grandsons are of the highest caliber, all great achievers, and each and every one someone to be proud of. They are consummate young citizens. They don't see race, creed, or color, only human beings, and we are proud as punch of all of those boys. They are both scholars and gentlemen, and their list of accomplishments is quite notable. I'd say we all did something right ... something very, very right.

Admiral Richard E. Byrd, in his book, "Alone," summed it all up for me when he wrote the following passage:

> *At the end only two things really matter to a man, regardless of who he is; and they are the affection and understanding of his family. Anything and everything else he creates is substantial; it is a ship given over to the mercy of the winds and tides of prejudice. But the family is an everlasting anchorage, a quiet harbor where a man's ship can be left to swing to the moorings of pride and loyalty...*

Hey, did I hear somebody say, "Thanks for the warning?"

Van's kids and grandkids at their house on Sacket Lake in 1982. From back to front, left to right: Dan, Sally, Andy, David (with Evan), Mark (with Jason), Janet, Maddy (with Max in the oven), Van (with Doug), Shirley (with David).